Pluralism, Transnationalism and Culture in Asian Law

The **ISEAS – Yusof Ishak Institute** (formerly Institute of Southeast Asian Studies) is an autonomous organization established in 1968. It is a regional centre dedicated to the study of socio-political, security, and economic trends and developments in Southeast Asia and its wider geostrategic and economic environment. The Institute's research programmes are grouped under Regional Economic Studies (RES), Regional Strategic and Political Studies (RSPS), and Regional Social and Cultural Studies (RSCS). The Institute is also home to the ASEAN Studies Centre (ASC), the Nalanda-Sriwijaya Centre (NSC), and the Singapore APEC Centre.

ISEAS Publishing, an established academic press, has issued more than 2,000 books and journals. It is the largest scholarly publisher of research about Southeast Asia from within the region. ISEAS Publishing works with many other academic and trade publishers and distributors to disseminate important research and analyses from and about Southeast Asia to the rest of the world.

Pluralism, Transnationalism and Culture in Asian Law

A BOOK IN HONOUR OF M.B. HOOKER

EDITED BY

GARY F. BELL

ISEAS YUSOF ISHAK INSTITUTE

First published in Singapore in 2017 by
ISEAS Publishing
30 Heng Mui Keng Terrace
Singapore 119614

E-mail: publish@iseas.edu.sg
Website: bookshop.iseas.edu.sg

The responsibility for facts and opinions in this publication rests exclusively with the authors and their interpretations do not necessarily reflect the views or the policy of the publisher or its supporters.

ISEAS Library Cataloguing-in-Publication Data

Pluralism, Transnationalism and Culture in Asian Law : A Book in Honour of M.B. Hooker / edited by Gary F. Bell.
1. Legal polycentricity—Asia.
2. 2. Transnationalism.
I. Bell, Gary F.
K236 P73   2017

ISBN 978-981-4762-71-7 (soft cover)
ISBN 978-981-4762-72-4 (e-book PDF)

Typeset by International Typesetters Pte Ltd
Printed in Singapore by Markono Print Media Pte Ltd

This book was made possible by a research grant by the National University of Singapore.

To M.B. Hooker,

whose scholarship and passion started it all.

Contents

Preface

This book stems from a symposium held at the Faculty of Law of the National University of Singapore on 27–28 September 2012 in honour of Professor M.B. Hooker. Professor Hooker was a pioneer in the field of legal pluralism. In fact, his scholarship laid the foundation of the field. His 1975 book *Legal Pluralism: An Introduction to Colonial and Neo-Colonial Laws* (1975) was seminal and opened this field of study. The man has been tremendously influential.

In the first chapter of this book, entitled *M.B. Hooker and Southeast Asian Law: Path-breaking Passions*, Veronica Taylor traces the career of M.B. Hooker and gives us a list of his publications. I will therefore refrain from doing this in this preface. I will however state my admiration for the man and scholar. Professor Hooker has been very influential on me (and so many others), yet I met him for the first time only at the symposium we held in 2012. Although by all accounts M.B. Hooker has been generous in his personal support for young scholars, in my case, due to distance, his influence was not personal but truly merely intellectual, which makes it clear that the man has been a leader in the field.

The chapters of this book are very diverse, reflecting the breadth of legal pluralism and of M.B. Hooker's scholarship, which covered legal pluralism, Islamic law, Malaysian and Indonesian law, *adat* law, etc. I will not here introduce each of the chapters — the table of contents should suffice to show the breadth of this collection. It is however an homage to M.B. Hooker that colleagues with such diverse interests readily volunteered for a symposium and book in his honour — it shows the breadth of his own scholarship and its influence. All the chapters relate to legal pluralism. All of them relate to Asia (which goes as far as Israel).

I wish to thank my colleagues Veronica Taylor of the Australian National University and Michael Dowdle of the National University of Singapore for assisting me in editing some of the chapters of this book.

On a sad note, we were very sorry to learn of the loss of two contributors between the symposium and the publication of this book. Professor H. Patrick Glenn, another giant in the field of comparative law, has passed away. His wife, Jane Glenn, also of McGill University, has kindly agreed to the publication of the final version of his chapter. Franz von Benda-Beckmann, who had co-written a chapter with his wife Keebet von Benda-Beckmann, also sadly passed away before the publication of this book. A great lost to all of us and to anthropology generally. We are grateful that Professor Keebet did the final editing on behalf of both of them.

I hope you will enjoy the book as much as I enjoyed working with this group of authors.

Gary F. Bell
National University of Singapore
28 August 2016

Acknowledgements

I would like to thank the National University of Singapore for the generous research grant that allowed us to hold a conference in 2012 from which this book stems. I would also like to thank the Faculty of Law of the National University of Singapore and its Centre for Asian Legal studies for their support.

I also would like to thank the *Asian Journal of Comparative Law*, a journal of the Asia Law Institute (ASLI), which authorized the reproduction of an article by Arif A. Jamal (Chapter 3). I would also like to thank the artists who authorized the reproduction of their work in Chapter 7.

But mainly all the authors of the different chapters would like to thank Professor M.B. Hooker for his leadership in the field of legal pluralism and for inspiring all of us.

About the Contributors

Associate Professor Gary F. Bell. After an undergraduate degree in theology (BTh) at the Université Laval (Quebec City), Gary F. Bell obtained degrees in both the common law (LLB) and the civil law (BCL) at McGill University in Montreal and an LLM at Columbia University in New York City. He was Editor-in-Chief of the *McGill Law Journal*, clerked for Justice Stevenson of the Supreme Court of Canada and taught at McGill University. He teaches in Comparative Law (Comparative Legal Traditions, International Commercial Arbitration, Indonesian Law). He does most of his research on Indonesian law and on the United Nations Convention on Contracts for the International Sale of Goods. He is the Director of the Asian Law Institute (ASLI).

The late Professor Franz von Benda-Beckmann was an honorary Professor at Leipzig University and at the Martin Luther University in Halle. He obtained his first law degree at the High Court in Schleswig, his PhD at the University of Kiel and his second law degree at the High Court of Hamburg. After working in Zürich for five years he worked at the University of Leiden, heading a small research institute dealing with law in the former Dutch colonies. In 1981 he was appointed Professor for Law and Rural Development in Developing Countries at Wageningen University. In summer 2000 he moved to Halle to establish and head the project group Legal Pluralism at the Max Planck Institute for Social Anthropology together with Keebet von Benda-Beckmann.

Professor Keebet von Benda-Beckmann is an honorary Professor at Leipzig University and at the Martin Luther University in Halle. She holds a law degree from the University of Amsterdam and obtained her PhD at the University of Nijmegen. She first was an assistant in sociology of law at the University of Zürich, then worked at the University of Leiden, and taught for a while in Wageningen. In 1982 she took a position in anthropology and sociology of law at Erasmus University Rotterdam, where she later received a personal professorship in the anthropology of law in 1998. In summer 2000 she moved to Halle to establish and head the project group Legal Pluralism at the Max Planck Institute for Social Anthropology together with Franz von Benda-Beckmann.

Dr Melissa Crouch is a Senior Lecturer at the Law Faculty, the University of New South Wales, Sydney. Her research contributes to the field of Asian Legal Studies, with a concentration on constitutional change, law and development, and law and religion. She is the editor of three major volumes on Myanmar: *Law, Society and Transition in Myanmar* (2014); *Islam and the State in Myanmar: Muslim-Buddhist Relations and the Politics of Belonging* (2016); and *The Business of Transition: Law, Development and Economics in Myanmar* (forthcoming 2017). She is the author of *Law and Religion in Indonesia: Conflict and the Courts in West Java* (2014). Melissa has contributed to numerous initiatives on constitutional and legal reform in Myanmar.

Dr Giora Eliraz is a Research Fellow, Harry S. Truman Institute for the Advancement of Peace, the Hebrew University of Jerusalem; Affiliate Instructor, Jackson School of International Studies, University of Washington, Seattle; Research Fellow, the Institute for Counter-Terrorism, the Interdisciplinary Center, Herzliya; and Member of a research group at the Minerva Humanities Center, Tel-Aviv University.

The late Professor H. Patrick Glenn was the Peter M. Laing Professor of Law, Faculty of Law, McGill University, a Member of the International Academy of Comparative Law and President of the American Society of Comparative Law. He taught and had research interests in the areas of comparative law, private international law, civil procedure and the legal professions. His book *Legal Traditions of the World* (2000) received the grand prize of the International Academy of Comparative Law. A fifth edition appeared in 2014. He has been Director of the Institute of Comparative Law and in that capacity worked on projects on the reform of the Russian Civil Code and judicial education in China. He was a member of the Royal Society of Canada and the International Academy of Comparative Law and has been a Bora Laskin National Fellow in Human Rights Law, a Killam Research Fellow, and a Visiting Fellow of All Souls College, Oxford. In 2006 H. Patrick Glenn received the Prix Léon-Gérin, a prestigious award bestowed by the Government of Québec, in recognition of his contribution to comparative law throughout his career. In 2010–11 he held the Henry G. Schermers Fellowship of the Hague Institute for the Internationalisation of Law.

Professor Andrew J. Harding is a leading scholar in the fields of Asian legal studies and comparative constitutional law. He commenced his academic career at the National University of Singapore (NUS) before moving to SOAS, University of London, where he became Head of the Law School. He joined NUS from the University of Victoria, BC, Canada, where he was Professor of Asia-Pacific Legal Relations and Director of the Centre for Asia-Pacific Initiatives. At NUS he has served as Director of the Centre for Asian Legal Studies and Director of the Asian Law Institute. Professor Harding has worked extensively on constitutional law in Southeast Asia and has contributed to scholarship in comparative law and law and development, having published fourteen books as author or editor. He is co-founding editor of Hart Publishing's book series Constitutional Systems of the World, a major resource for constitutional law in context, and has co-authored the book on Thailand in that series (2011) and authored that on Malaysia (2012). His most recent book is *Constitutionalism and Legal Change in Myanmar* (2017).

Virginia Matheson Hooker is Professor Emeritus and Fellow in the Dept of Political & Social Change, College of Asia and the Pacific, at The Australian National University. She retired as Professor of Indonesian and Malay in the Faculty of Asian Studies in January 2007. Her research focuses on Islam in Southeast Asia, literature and social change in Malaysia and Indonesia, Indonesian political culture and Islam-inspired art in Southeast Asia. Her *Voices of Islam in Southeast Asia* (2006), co-edited with Assoc. Professor Greg Fealy, is an award-winning sourcebook on contemporary Islam in Southeast Asia.

Dr Nadirsyah Hosen has been working as a Senior Lecturer at the Faculty of Law, Monash University since July 2015. Prior to this role Dr Hosen was an Associate Professor at the School of Law, University of Wollongong. He has a Bachelors degree (UIN Syarif Hidayatullah Jakarta), a Graduate Diploma in Islamic Studies, a Master of Arts with Honours (University of New England), as well as a Master of Laws in Comparative Law (Charles Darwin University). He completed his first PhD (Law) at the University of Wollongong and a second PhD (Islamic Law) at the National University of Singapore. Dr Hosen is internationally known for his expertise on sharia and Indonesian law.

Dr Arif A. Jamal is an Assistant Professor in the Faculty of Law, National University of Singapore (NUS). He has research interests in legal and political theory and comparative legal studies, in particular as these relate to the areas of law and religion and law in Muslim contexts. He is a co-editor of *Regulating Religion in Asia*: *Norms, Modes and Challenges* (forthcoming) and serves on the Executive Committee of the Centre for Asian Legal Studies at NUS and as an editor with the *Asian Journal of Comparative Law* (Cambridge University Press).

Professor Aharon Layish is Professor Emeritus of Asian and African Studies at Hebrew University of Jerusalem. He is known for his expertise in Islamic law and has conducted research in many areas, including on sharia and custom in a sedentary tribal society, the reinstatement of Islamic law in the Sudan by means of statutory codification and legislation, legal circulars and court decisions, and the Mahdi's legal methodology and its application in the Sudan (1881–85) as reflected in legal documents issued by the Mahdi.

Professor Ratno Lukito is a Professor at the Faculty of Syari'ah and Law at the State Islamic University Sunan Kalijaga Yogyakarta. His MA in Islamic studies was obtained from the Institute of Islamic Studies, McGill University, Montreal, Canada (1997), while his Doctor of Civil Law (DCL) was obtained from the Institute of Comparative Law, Faculty of Law, McGill University (2006). His thesis was on conflict and resolution among the three legal traditions of *adat*, Islamic law and civil law in Indonesia, under the supervision of the late Professor Patrick Glenn. He was a Postdoctoral fellow of KNAW-Van Vollenhoven Institute, Faculty of Law, Leiden University, the Netherlands (2009–11). He is currently a fellow of the American Institute for Indonesian Studies. He has authored twelve books and thirty-six articles, mostly on the topic of Islamic law and legal traditions in Indonesia. His book *Legal Pluralism in Indonesia: Bridging the Unbridgeable* was published in 2013. He has been working recently on a monograph entitled "Islamic Law and State in Indonesia: Confabulating the Sacredness".

Professor Veronica Taylor is a socio-legal scholar and Professor in the School of Regulation and Global Governance at the Australian National University and an ANU Public Policy Fellow. Her major contribution to socio-legal studies centres on rule of law assistance as a form of foreign policy and as an emergent field of professional practice. She examines (i) the rise of non-Western rule of law exporters, (ii) regulatory analysis of the rule of law industry and (iii) empirical study of the practice and professionalization of rule of law promotion and law and justice interventions.

1

M.B. Hooker and Southeast Asian Law: Path-breaking Passions

Veronica L. Taylor, with M.B. Hooker and Virginia Hooker

Few scholars become the intellectual architects of their field. Professor M.B. (Barry) Hooker is one of them: a truly original scholar who has forged a singular, path-breaking body of work on law and society in Southeast Asia. His scholarship has been foundational in the fields of legal pluralism, customary law (*adat*) in Southeast Asia — particularly Malaysia — and Islamic law (sharia) in Southeast Asia. Hooker has shaped the intellectual frameworks that govern the way that we think of legal pluralism and hybridity in Southeast Asia, but that also invite contestation, expansion and elaboration.

This essay invites Professor Hooker to reflect on his intellectual journey and the choices that propelled him from his early life in New Zealand to a career of research and teaching in Singapore, the United Kingdom and Australia. It proceeds as an edited interview with him, and with Professor Virginia Hooker, who is both his wife and research collaborator as well as a distinguished scholar in her own right.[1] The essay concludes with a full bibliography of M.B. Hooker's works to date, compiled by Virginia Hooker.

If you visit the library at the National University of Malaysia (UKM) you can ask to see the M.B. Hooker Collection. There, behind a screen, catalogued and air-conditioned, is the research and teaching library of more than 2,500 titles that Barry Hooker built over his scholarly lifetime. These are the books "on the history and philosophy and application of the legal systems in Southeast Asia" that "range by region from the Middle East through India, Burma and Indochina, to Malaysia and island Southeast Asia.... [works of] Islamic studies, philosophy, anthropology history, economics and law".[2] It includes substantial materials in the vernacular and the publications hunted by rare booksellers who supported Hooker's consuming passion. Virginia Hooker remembers, "Your library in your room in Kent was spectacular because you didn't have to go to any other library.... So when we moved [to Australia] you made that incredible decision to sell your entire library.... [Bookseller] John Randall insisted on selling it as the entire collection. Your papers, letters everything, the musical tapes, and so on. He spent a week cataloguing it, but it was a fantastic assemblage of material for the kind of work you did." She points out that academic fashions have changed, and so much of this material would now be read with a critical sensibility. Barry Hooker is characteristically unsentimental, "Look, if one person uses it, that's fine — that's a plus."

How does a country boy from New Zealand acquire and then release one of the world's great libraries of legal materials on Southeast Asia? It is a long way from Christchurch to the jungles of Malaysia and to academic appointments at the University of Singapore (later NUS), the University of Kent, and the Australian National University. But in retrospect, the logic of those pathways becomes clearer.

> We (New Zealanders) travelled a lot because we had to. I was offered a job in Singapore and at Monash, I think. I thought I would go to Singapore because it was different; I thought Melbourne would be like Christchurch, but bigger.
>
> I had straight degrees in law — an LLB and a Master's degree. [My master's thesis] was on Maoris — how Maoris' spirituality was really legal. I look at it now and I blush — it was appalling. My family knew a lot of Maoris; [I was brought up in] a semi-mixed

Maori community. But that did not mean anything.... [I worked on the thesis] by mainly reading — old Polynesian Society journals. I was working during the day in an insurance office. They got rid of me — it was mutual.

[This was at a time when legal academics in New Zealand] all did things like contracts and Section 55 of the *Evidence Act,* and did it apply to Magistrates or not? (That's if anyone was interested, and very few were). It was all pretty basic.

So to Christchurch, New Zealand in 1966 came the recruitment advertisement from the (then) University of Singapore.

Can you imagine? From the University of Singapore, saying "Assistant Lecturers Required". I mean, why the Christchurch press?... Who was on the end of sending that out?

There used to be a thing called the "circuit"; this is, of course, long gone now and people don't know what it was, but this was when Singapore was a colony and had only just become independent. From 1950 until the mid 1960s there was a circuit which went from the London School of Economics — usually unemployable socialist lawyers — then to either East or West Africa, Kenya, Nigeria, wherever, then to Bangkok on the way, then to Singapore. From Singapore they then went either to Adelaide or Queensland. These ... law teachers ... were appallingly bad, because everybody else was out in the newly formed legal profession making lots of money. So these people would go on the "circuit". I was on the end of those circuit days. I arrived as an assistant lecturer on a three-year contract.

What is now the Law Faculty at NUS was the old University when I was there ... it was the University of Singapore. It was nice. I left there in 1969. Forty years ago, my room was at the top storey at the very end, where the air-conditioning stopped. That was because I was the most recent and most junior appointment so I got the worst room with no air-conditioning and got the jobs that nobody else wanted to do. The lowest form of animal life. I was business manager of the *Malaya Law Review,* which was just banking cheques (I had a very nice Indian chap who did the books at the end of the year for me).

[Today, NUS is] a peaceful place, they've got infrastructure, money, libraries, the lot. They [have the potential to make] Singapore the centre of Asian law studies for all of Asia.

But in the 1960s the University of Singapore was not expecting much. The young M.B. Hooker was just another one of those "layabout whities". Their unwitting decision to have him teach *Introduction to Law* sparked his interest in legal pluralism. Virginia Hooker writes, "For Malaya and Singapore, newly independent nations with a long history of mixed foreign influence, colonial rule and multi-racial communities, the legal situation was complex. Very little was known about the development of the various legal systems, their application, or their inter-relationships. Descriptive articles by British colonial officers and European scholars were scattered in obscure journals."[3] And so came Hooker's first publication, *A Source Book of Adat, Chinese Law and the History of Common Law in the Malayan Peninsula*, "still the first source of reference for social scientists working on the area".[4] This established the model of Hooker's scholarly style — "able to visualize the larger framework, he presents the whole through its vital constituents. Each part is fully described and supported by indigenous data as well as scholarly commentary. There is constant reference to particular legal cases and judicial decisions, sources almost wholly neglected before his work."[5] What makes this mapping of sources so noteworthy is the unstinting effort to locate the best available information and to seek it from the best possible source:

> Islamic, Chinese, and Hindu law: you name it, it was all there. They were very clear that you had to teach legal history.... So I asked, "Where are the books?" and they gave me a magazine article dated 1938 — and this was in 1966. I had a great struggle, but one of the visitors at the Law Faculty then was Tun Suffian Hashim who was the Chief Justice of the Federal Court, the top court in Malaysia.[6] He was a very nice man and he asked me what I was doing and said that I should go out to Negeri Sembilan Malaya. He said, "I will fix it up for you, the State Secretary is an old friend of mine and you can go and do your research", which was a new thing.

What recommended the town and district of Kuala Pilah as a research site was that its population was predominantly Malay Minangkabau, a matrilineal ethnic group. It was thus a centre of matrilineal studies of Malaya, with Malay customary law and Islamic law coexisting and not in harmony.

When I said to the Professor in Singapore that I was going up to Malaya to do research, he said "What for?" I said, "Well, you've asked me to teach this" and he said "Yes, but it's in a book, isn't it?" and I said "Well, No, it's not actually". He asked me where I was going and I said a little town called Kuala Pilah: "Tun Suffian has got a friend there." He said, "Yes but why aren't you going to the Chief Minister?" We were not on the same wavelength.

The second stroke of luck was arriving in the Kuala Pilah District Office to find the District Officer, a nice man, who said "Yes, Yes Suffian said you were coming. I'm very busy", (this looking at his watch — he was actually going to play golf). I will hand you over to my Chief Clerk; This is Mr Ibrahim". He was a terrific man; he was in charge of all the land office records and he knew absolutely everything about land, taxation, transfers, transmission of title — you name it, he was it. [This was a legacy of] the old British colonial system, where a province or a position was divided into districts and each district was run by a District Officer who was land, taxation, crime, justice, police, town planning, the lot... He was God: he could arrest you, try you, hang you and then tax you, all within a week... His Chief Clerk was a very nice man and he took a liking to me, so he started telling me what to do, and explained how it worked. So I had it from the bottom up.

Although Hooker describes his Malay as "still pretty fractured and basic", it would have been remarkable at the time for a legal scholar from the Commonwealth to be in post-independence rural Malaya, trying to understand local legal culture through conversations in Malay. Hooker reflects,

I was lucky because Malaysia had been independent for less than 10 years and so there was a hangover of helpfulness or respect towards white people who knew some law and had some status. People were prepared to put themselves out for you and I was lucky to be on the end of that good feeling. Provided you were polite and interested and so on, you got along very well... So I was lucky, as I had one foot in the colonial period and one foot in the newly independent period — it really was a transition time.

From the vantage point of 2013, we would also say that Hooker was able to leverage his prestige: being white, educated, "from the

University" and introduced by the Chief Justice of the top court of the country:

> They knew all of this, they knew where my introduction came from … they knew I was trying to learn Malay, they knew I was sympathetic to religion and they knew I was not going to let anybody down or do the wrong thing.

How do you go about demonstrating that trustworthiness or that sympathy to new contacts in such an unfamiliar field?

> By being polite: good manners get you everywhere. Not shouting, ever… Politeness is everything and respect for status, respect for an older person and even for someone like, say, a Malay peasant woman of a certain age, who is a "nothing" person in terms of finance and power and so on, but you provide her the proper forms of respect, always. You never spoke down to, or were rude or uncouth to, poor people — ever. A lot of young people don't realise just how important it is.

Then, as now, this matters because whatever you say or do has an amplified effect; people often believe you to be more powerful than you actually are:

> There is a photo of me going into a court in Malaysia, to a district court, which is a low level state court. I took the trouble of putting on a white shirt and a tie and proper trousers; a lot of people were wearing shorts. A small thing like that makes a huge difference.

So we have a young researcher in the district office with access to all the records, with a very knowledgeable, helpful local professional. What was it that intrigued Hooker? How did he determine what would be fertile for research or inquiry?

> What happened was that everybody was very curious about what this fellow was doing, so the word got back to the head of the Land Office in Kuala Lumpur and they thought that they would get me to do a job for them. There was a huge program of land reform going on. What the Land Office wanted me to say was that matrilineal inheritance caused fragmentation of the States; this involved Muslims. So the Muslim side got onto this immediately: what they wanted me to say was that, Yes, that it caused fragmentation of the States and that it was also against religion. Then there was the third group, who

were the females — the women in the matrilineal area who owned the land — who wanted me to say that it was *not* against religion and it did *not* cause fragmentation. So I had three of them concentrating on me to give them the answer they wanted.

Well I went down and looked at the land titles and then I had to go out and physically measure the actual land; I was going around the paddy fields with a tape measure, starting at 5am in the morning, at first light, because by 11am it was far too hot, with too many leeches and mosquitos. It was really hard work. I did a pilot project. The conclusion I came to was that I couldn't say truthfully that any one of the three groups had a case. In some of the districts, at some time, there was fragmentation and at others there was not. They were all extremely angry with me — except the women who had clicked on very quickly that I wasn't going to go against them.

This was the basis of Hooker's 1972 book, *Adat Laws in Modern Malaya*, the realization that there was not "a" law: they were all mixed; even *adat* itself was a hybrid.

Adat was totally mixed — it was actually invented by some British in the 1920[s] and I invented bits myself, knowingly [as a kind of natural experiment]. In a strip village, a long village, that ran down the side of a road for about two miles, I said to top end "This is what they're doing at the bottom end" and I said to bottom end "this is what they're doing at top end". Five years later, ten years later, it had been totally incorporated and people believed it to be true. I am not particularly proud of this now. In fact it's a dishonest thing to do: I shouldn't have done it.

Hooker's understanding and renditions of local law, however, were also recognized and incorporated in more formal ways:

David Wong was a colleague of mine in Singapore, a very nice man David. He started life as a newspaper reporter on *Nan Yang Siang Pau* in Singapore and he knew all the newspaper people, including the older proprietors. We used to go out at night, David and I, and we would always end up at the newspaper offices at about 3am when they are just putting the paper to bed. So I got to know the proprietors and they would tell me hair-raising stories about who did this, and who did that, and what this Minister did — and they couldn't publish it. Then we got onto burial customs: somewhere there was a fight going on between two clans and two divisions in one clan about the proper ceremony for some very wealthy person who had died. Who was going to pay for it? It all came down to money and it wasn't a little money they were talking about, but hundreds of thousands of dollars, Singapore dollars, a huge amount at that time. I remembered most of this and I checked some of it later with David and then I just had a very short paragraph about it published somewhere, perhaps in one of the cases I was commenting on, about distributions of obligations — who has to pay, the reasons for it, how it works out in clan rules. It was picked up by a Judge who couldn't do a judgment [and became part of Malaysian case law]. I did the same thing in relation to a Muslim dispute — I set out my view of what Islamic law was, and it was picked up by Tun Saleh Abbas and appeared in a High Court judgment in Malaysia. He was a federal judge, their chief justice,[7] and it appears in his judgment as a statement of the law — it's actually what I said word for word, and he cites it and says this is where I got it from. I am much hated in some Muslim circles in Malaysia as a result.

A less well-known part of Hooker's work is his three-month sojourn in the jungles of the Malay Peninsula, living with a group called the Semai.

I was a great legal philosopher, as you are at age 25... [In the jungle] I discovered that all my theories were a load of rubbish. It became apparent in Week One that I was totally wasting my time. What all these books were saying — it's not like that at all. But then I stayed on because I had a tape recorder and some of them had beautiful singing voices and I spent days and days and days recording them singing. They loved it because they realised that they were being recorded and that it could be played back. So they could listen to themselves and they were thrilled to bits. People would come from miles, I mean several days' walk, to sing and then hear it played back. All of those tapes are now in MB Hooker collection at the National University of Malaysia (UKM), and I don't suppose anyone has ever listened to them.

This was the period that the aborigines (*orang asli*) of Malaya were becoming very famous in anthropological circles and in American sociology of family studies, because of their non-violent philosophies. But as Hooker points out, "That's not totally true, because there *was* violence."

But nobody else had lived with them except Bob Dentan, the American.[8] Dentan and Benjamin were trained as ethnographers: Dentan was from New York and Geoffrey Benjamin[9] was from Cambridge, and they were formally and professionally trained, but I had no idea what I was doing or going into. All I was doing at the end, actually, was recording music — it was gorgeous. These were the old big reels of tape and I used to write on the back of who had sung it and what date and so on, but I didn't know their names properly, so I used to put down my own descriptions of them (I hope nobody reads them).

So that little group of Dentan, Benjamin, and me, we were the trio that started aboriginal ethnography in Malaya in the modern post-war period, but my part was very tiny; it was basically Dentan and Benjamin who did this.[10] There was also Ivan Polunin, who was a doctor at the University of Singapore, he used to go out and doctor them as well.[11]

Virginia Hooker comments, "That work still stands, I mean it's still looked at as the baseline for studies in that field and the books are still being put together and being published in the US — not in Australia, as we have our own indigenous studies, but at the time it was really baseline stuff." Hooker continues,

I took a lot of photos there of course, I wasn't a very good photographer, but I had a whole lot of photos which I sent back to Singapore to get developed and then I would pick them up when I would go back. I went back once and they had disappeared. This was unheard of, I mean Kodak never, ever, lost anything. Now, it took me a while to work out that by the time I was taking those photographs, there was a man called Jim Thompson who probably was an American spy. He happened to be in northern Malaya and I was not far away, and he disappeared, never to be found. My photos were taken at about the same time as his disappearance. Kodak denied ever having received them, but a Malay clerk in Kodak, when I was complaining to him about this said "Yes" he had signed them in and they had disappeared. So Kodak no doubt stole them on the instructions of whatever spy agency was around there at the time. I'm not normally paranoid about spies — if they had asked me for them, they could have had them, but they stole them and I've always felt very bad about that.

So here is a young legal scholar doing highly original, innovative work, that in some cases records for the first time the complexity of competing legal and social norms at the local level in Singapore and Malaysia. What did Hooker's employer, the University of Singapore, think about their young faculty member at the time?

> They thought I was badly dressed, or at least the Vice Chancellor did. You see, it was a colonial university, which means it was an organ of the state: it was a government department. Their idea of a university at the time was that it's a place where you go to learn how to be [a] scientist, how to be a teacher, how to do this, how to do that. The strange thing about the old University of Singapore is that they were sensitive, newly independent, bureaucrats who didn't really know what they had. In the English department was Dennis Enright, who was a major minor poet; Paul Theroux; Norman Sherry who was the biographer of Conrad; Atkinson who was something else in Lit. It was one of the most outstanding departments in the whole of the Commonwealth, but they couldn't see it. There was also Willy Willits in the Art Museum, who was *the* authority on late Ming pottery. They had really talented people there and they couldn't cope — they saw them as disreputable, arrogant, or as nutcases... [As an instructor], you were supposed to behave like a bureaucrat.
>
> So in the end they said to me "Well you're very lucky to have a contract with us, what we're going to do now is, if you're very good and you behave yourself, we will give you another three year contract — but you have to behave yourself". At that time I had an offer of a job in England and another offer of a job at Australian National University, so I said thanks very much, but I'm off.

Hooker moved to the University of Kent in England, one of what were known as the "plate glass" universities; brand new institutions of the 1960s with generous funding. His was a joint appointment in Law and in Asian Studies. His opportunity to focus on Southeast Asia was partly serendipitous: the preeminent comparative law institution at the time was the School of Oriental and Asian Studies (SOAS) in London, and they had decided to focus on (funded) opportunities in the Middle East and Africa.

> Sheffield was stuck out at the end of east Yorkshire and was a very unfashionable place. So the government money ended up in Canterbury (at Kent): the Vice-Chancellor then said "Yes, we'll have it" and then he looked around and said, "We'd better find somebody".

I was picked up by Dennis Duncanson, who was an old [Malayan] civil servant and didn't have a clue about what he was doing.[12] So I got my job from him, as did Roger Kershaw and Jeremy Kemp and (later ANU Professor and Dean of Asian Studies) Tony Milner... I spent 18 months with no teaching: there were no classes, no courses, there was nothing, no students.

Dennis used to call these meetings: "We have to have a course" he would say, and look around. Then he would say "Barry what are you going to do?" I said, "I don't know, Dennis — I think I might do some Malay law, I know a bit about that." "Yes that's very good, we'll have Malay law". I am exaggerating, but not very much. Can you imagine now a new department setting up without a single course outline and syllabus? What saved us was a couple of my books had come out and somehow they had attracted the attention of Malay students in London who had come from Egypt.

The policy of the Malaysian Government then was that these *ash'aris*, as they called the Malay Muslim students studying abroad, were unreliable and needed to have some English language and English university training. I was known in Malaysia a bit by then at government level, so they were happy to send them to Kent. They wanted to do "the" PhD. So we started them off on MAs and MPhils (an MA by dissertation) and that worked very well. Some of them did very well and went back and the word spread and so we got a lot of Malaysian students, not just in Asian studies, but also in other subjects. So the Vice Chancellor was delighted.

It used to be called Kampong Kent; the students lived in a lovely seaside hotel called the Continental which had fallen into disrepair, and was much cheaper than accommodation in the cathedral town, Canterbury.

Some of the students were very able: one went back to Malaysia and became a chief minister; another became Dean of Law at the National University of Malaysia (UKM). The irony of this period was that few, if any, British students were being attracted to this new field.

The only "whities" who are really doing this sort of work at the time were Australians, actually, which makes sense. There were one or two English students, but in an amateurish way. The [serious students were mainly] Americans and Australians. The Americans who are now prominent in Southeast Asian studies came to see me in Canterbury because I was about 10 years ahead of them. I never actually taught them, but they visited Canterbury and had the advantages of language training and formal training, which I never had.

There were also a group of Indonesians left over from the 1960s, from Sukarno's time; they were communists and when '65 happened in Indonesia, the communists were slaughtered. This group had been in China on a friendship visit so they couldn't go back to Indonesia; they were exiled. There were two or three novelists; someone had introduced me to one of them and I met him in Amsterdam and was the sole person in England that they knew. So they would suddenly arrive at midnight at the house. It was a time when I didn't have any money at all, so they would sleep on the floor and their breakfast was toast with marmalade and a cup of tea. It was the best I could do, and they knew that. I was very lucky, because they were very fine people and very interesting — good people.

This became a very fruitful time for Hooker's new research.

In London there were libraries and [plentiful material on] Eastern European studies, which had a lot of central Asian material; there was absolutely no problem, I had open access to everything. There was no problem going back to Asia: we managed to get some money from the British Academy by convincing them that it was a good idea for the Academy to have a Southeast Asian division. We had fifteen hundred pounds for travel money annually, which was big money at the time.

I suddenly realised — and this is me looking back now (I don't know that I would have realised this at the time) — that there was all of this material which had to be put together about law in SE Asia, spanning Burma to Vietnam to China to the north and Malaya in the south. There was a place, there was a picture, there was a total Southeast Asian perspective and history which was quite special to that place, and I just wrote out what I thought, that's all.

What Hooker "thought" at the time became *The Personal Laws of Malaysia* (1976); *A Concise Legal History of South-East Asia* (1978); *Adat Law in Modern Indonesia* (1978); (with M.C. Hoadley) *An Introduction to Javanese Law* (1981); and the edited volumes *Malaysian Legal Essays* (1986) and *The Laws of South-East Asia* (1988). By his own admission, Hooker's opportunities to do serious work in the field were in Malaysia, with brief visits to Burma, Vietnam, the Philippines and Thailand. Then came the request from Sarawak in Malaysia to document their *adat* law.

> I had been in Sarawak, because I knew the Chief Justice of Sarawak, who I had met in Kuala Lumpur. He had seen the book on *adat*, he was interested in native law himself. So he said "Come and do native law"... Later on they wrote to England and said "Come", so business class airfare, state guest house, car and driver — it was very nice.

This begs the question why legal elites in Malaysia are writing to England to ask a New Zealander based at Kent to come and survey *adat* law in Sarawak. What was the state of legal education and research in Malaysia at the time?

> Nobody there was doing [fieldwork-based legal research]. There was no money. Their law faculties were strictly business orientated: you got a law degree to go into practice to make a lot of money, full stop. If you didn't do that, you would go into the civil service, and you get a pension and that's it. Hugh Hickling[13] used to tell the story of how he once asked a Dean of Law, somewhere in Malaya, "What's a law degree for?" and he was told "That's what you do". Hugh said "What about scholarship?" and this man said, "No, we don't do that". He was not joking, or telling a lie: he was telling the truth.

Hooker is perhaps best known for his serious corpus of work on Islamic Law in Southeast Asia. As he reflects, that interest dates from his earliest fieldwork, where the nature of local pluralism meant that "If you're doing *adat* you have to do *shari'a* [in the field], but the technical side came later, because I had to force myself to learn the technical stuff. I'm still learning it." That work ultimately became the edited volume *Islam in South-East Asia* (1983), *Islamic Law in South-East Asia* (1984) and *Undang-Undang Islam di Asia Tenggara* (The Islamic Laws of Southeast Asia; 1990). During the same period, the Faculty of Islam at the National University of Malaysia also requested help with the reform of their curriculum.

> They asked me in the 1980s when I was still at Kent, to go to the Faculty of Islam and look at their curriculum and then write a report. So I did that, I spent about six weeks there. It was lovely, I had a car and a driver and we had a great series of drives. They asked me to do this curriculum review, which I did. I wrote it all out and it disappeared. I handed it in — my mistake — to the Head of the Department. I should not have done that and it never appeared. I asked about it later and no one had ever seen it, presumably because they didn't like what they saw.

In 1980 Hooker met Virginia Matheson, who he would later marry. The setting was a slavery conference at ANU; historian Tony Reid wanted a panoramic survey of slavery in Southeast Asia, so had invited several notables from England, including Barry Hooker. Virginia recalls, "I gave a paper on slavery in the Malay texts, looking at what was said in indigenous primary sources. Barry gave a paper on slavery, the legal points in indigenous texts. At the final evening he came over to me and said we should put our papers together, because they were on the same topic." Barry Hooker remembers it slightly differently: "That's right, she ended up writing the whole thing, which is what I intended in the first place." They remained in touch, and in 1990 after his wife had died, Hooker moved to Australia and joined Virginia. After applying — and being turned down — for academic posts in Australia, Barry settled on a farm in rural New South Wales, to enjoy what he thought would be his retirement.

His old friend and colleague Tony Milner pointed out to a very young Asian law scholar at the Australian National University that a world authority on Southeast Asian law had just settled locally and might welcome a teaching opportunity. So against Hooker's strenuous protestations that he was fully retired with no intention of doing any more academic work, happy on the farm, busy with raising his prize-winning cattle, Taylor persuaded her Dean, Tom Campbell, to engage Barry Hooker and launch a course in Southeast Asian law in the Faculty of Law at ANU. In typically pragmatic fashion, Hooker says,

> I *was* very happy. I needed the money though. It wasn't much but it helped — it was the drought. I seemed to have gone through life having plenty of money and throwing it around and then having none at all. Don't do that; try to keep it even. So I was lucky you gave me a second run at it.

It proved to be an astonishing second run, almost a second lifetime of scholarly work, this time with a different focus. Key contributions from Hooker during this period include the edited volume *Law and the Chinese in Southeast* Asia (2002); *Indonesian Islam: Social Change through Contemporary Fatàwà* (2003); *Islam Mazhab Indonesia* (2003); and *Indonesian Syariah: Defining a National School of Islamic Law* (2008). Hooker explains it in this way:

It's Islamic stuff, it's *shari'a* stuff, but it's actually quite technical. Once you get into it, it becomes quite complex technically and it's impossible to go from A to B to C to Z and give a coherent story without dealing with the technicalities as you go along, otherwise you're not making sense to the reader. The problem is that there are very few readers at that level. So I am effectively writing for about ten people who will have, I hope, a PhD student or two themselves, so that will increase it to about 20 or 30 people. Think of Noel Coulson's *A History of Islamic Law* [Edinburgh University Press] which came out in 1964; the only people who read that are those who were very serious about understanding it and that book is still going — from 1964 to now. Because it's timeless and it's not going to attract any more than about 10 or 15 people a year: that's why it's there — that's its whole purpose. So that's the stuff I've been doing for Indonesia. It's there forever: people can say there is an error here, or a mistake, or that it should be this way, or whatever, and that's fine, but the basic stuff is there.

What prompted such an ambitious undertaking?

Once you start learning the technical aspect of this, you have to carry on doing it; you can't go back and you can't write something without having it absolutely, technically, correct. That's the short answer: you have to have it technically correct… There's a Southeast Asian version of *shari'a* which is Indonesian and Malay, which the people who do the technical stuff in northern Europe don't know and don't understand. So when they make all these big compilations in Amsterdam or London or New York about the technical side of *shari'a*, they totally ignore the Malay and Indonesian language versions of this, which are quite different and just as complex and as subtle and as complicated [as other versions of *shari'a* doctrinal writing]. But they don't know this because they don't know the languages.

This prompts the question of what we treat as authoritative texts; whether the texts in the vernacular — in Malaysia and Indonesia — are authoritative sources of Islamic law? In Hooker's view,

There are two sorts of authoritative texts, there's the Arabic one, of course, which is the authority. But then you've got the Malay and Indonesian versions of these in local languages, which are equally authoritative. This is something that the people in London and New York don't realise. They are stuck with the Arabic and they don't know the other. They are prepared to admit it for, say, India where there's Urdu texts, but that's a separate field. So what we've got, what I've actually invented for Southeast Asia is a *Southeast Asian* field [of sharia sources]. For the first time — it's out there; all they have to do is read it, but [Western scholars and those focussed on the Middle East] don't want to.

This corpus of work is read by those in Southeast Asia who want to better understand their own system and be able to point to something authoritative that is indigenous. Hooker's books have become set texts and have paved the way for a new wave of local scholarship within Southeast Asia on local and national sources of Islamic law. Here again, Hooker has played a generational bridging role:

> [The relatively recent wave of local *shari'a* scholarship is partly explained by the fact that] internal Indonesian traditions of Islamic scholarship were strong until the Dutch effectively killed them. For the 20th century they stayed like that; after Indonesian independence the place was a mess, the older generation [of Islamic scholars] had died off, it was in total shambles. They had no money, no training, nothing. It was a huge vacuum. That's when I stepped into that vacuum. Now that they are getting money, training, time, institutions, and facilities, they are now coming back to this field of work. So what I've done is to fill in a gap, bridge from what was before to now, and they can then take it forward. I've said, "This is what I think", and if they disagree that's fine, I don't care. At least it is something for them to start from, and they can now do it because there is money and time. But there wasn't before.
>
> There are people who are saying that I have made mistakes, which is fair enough. It is really too early to tell. What I have said to them is, "You are inventing the process of making [sharia] and there is in fact a local version of this, which you should be aware of, and proud of, and develop." That's given them the confidence; they didn't believe this before, but now they believe it. So I think that's my real achievement.

Hooker's most recent work extends this approach into new topic areas and geographies: Southeast Asian sharia, the Ahmadiyya and Muslim law in Singapore,[14] and another set of forthcoming essays, *Searching for Shari'a*, that focus on legal pluralism in the Philippines, particularly Mindanao. The latter is the fruit of two years of bibliographic work.

I asked Hooker about the intellectual influences that had shaped his approach to scholarship.

Masaji Chiba [was one]. He was a very nice old man; he put on a thing for me years ago in Tokyo in the early 80s. He made the Japanese scholarly community quite proud of what Japanese scholars had done in previous centuries, which was only now being realised. He brought that out. I think a lot of what he did was actually quite mistaken, but leaving that aside, you can't take away the tremendous boost to their own confidence that he gave them.

The other [Japanese scholar] I knew was [Yoneo] Ishii. He was a very good friend. He wrote in one of my books, *Laws of Southeast Asia*, about Thailand. A brilliant, nice man. I admire Ishii and another Japanese scholar who wrote on Cambodian Khmer.

[Of my contemporaries] Noel Coulson was a very good friend of mine. He was a technician, but a brilliant one, on [the] very difficult subject of succession in Muslim law. His book on succession is still the standard textbook.

It was great to meet the von Benda Beckmanns at NUS last year, and Andrew Harding I knew from years ago, Singapore days in fact.

The von Benda Beckmanns I hadn't met before; they were really nice [And of course sad to lose Franz immediately afterwards]. I had known their names for years and years, but we had never actually met. I was working in parallel with them; I had never actually been to Sumatra until much later than their period. It's huge and there is so much difference there and for Islam and Islamic studies it's really a terrific place. If you're in Indonesia, you must go to Sumatra. I didn't realise that for a long time; I was always in Java.

There are so many that I knew from the end of that colonial period: Hugh Hickling and [Roelof] Roolvink and all that lot and they all died not long after I started off. The great ones that I would look back to were the great colonial scholars, who were all dead by 1940 or 1950. [John] Jardine on Burma and the great works of Indo-Chinese French scholars who were active up until 1942. There was a whole group of them, and the Japanese killed them in 1942. So everybody I knew who had done significant things at that pre-war to post-war time, was just about dead or dying when I started. There was this huge gap, because there was all of that lot, and then there was me and nobody else. Then shortly afterwards it started up again. Looking back, I didn't realise it at the time.

> You see, I was in this middle period — the great colonial scholars were either inactive or dead when I was starting, and the younger local ones hadn't yet got underway. The younger American ones hadn't yet got underway either. So I was in this middle position, thrashing around, not really knowing what I was doing half the time, I felt quite confused.

Although Hooker claims to have had few direct intellectual influences, a significant part of his life has been spent with Southeast Asian historian Virginia Hooker (née Matheson), who is a distinguished historian of Southeast Asia. Hooker is quick to claim, "I disagree totally with whatever she says, mostly… [our debates] always end up with someone leaving the room." Perhaps so, but this has been a remarkably productive partnership. Hooker explains it this way: "There's two names but there's only one writer. I give the idea and Virginia works it out."

Virginia Hooker also sees their collaboration influencing Hooker's scholarly style: "I think that your style changed from when you did the first book on Indonesian Islam;… it's different from anything you have written before and I think that's because you always paid attention to local sources, but then you really started burrowing in…. I think it might [be] partly because of the way I worked." Hooker agrees: "Yes, this was basically about *fatwa*. In the introduction I looked at the surrounding history and non-legal stuff much more than I had before — Virginia said that I should do that. So yes, it's true [that my style changed]."

Hooker's work has been remarkable for both its concern with technical legal accuracy and the way that it has been infused with interdisciplinary insights from history and anthropology. In many ways it anticipates the growth in the socio-legal study of Southeast Asian law both within and outside the region that we now regard as commonplace. Generationally, his work predates contemporary concerns with, and understanding of, gender as a core element of understanding social and legal norms. Yet his work has always included significant treatment of women. He agrees, "They've always been there, right from the very beginning. But I don't go on about gender because I don't know the technical stuff about it."

After a lifetime of scholarly work, does Hooker have a favourite book or a favourite piece of work, something about which he could say, "I got it right, I'm thrilled that I pushed myself to do that"? He responds,

> I did used to think so, yes. But when I look at them now, they've all got flaws, or errors, or mistakes or could have been done better. So the answer really is "No".
>
> What I would really like to see is other, younger scholars doing better than me. That's really very good when they do it better and so they should — because they've had all the chances. They've got the formal training, the languages, the books, and all the stuff that I never had. They *should* be doing better, and that's why it's good when they are.
>
> I compare the young ones today with the giants that I knew in the past. Outside law, there was [J.G.] De Gasparis and Roolvink, for example. They had years of Arabic, really serious preparation.
>
> They [were committed to] the hard slog: I mean[,] to write the books that those men wrote, you had to sit there six days a week, 10 hours a day to do it at that level, and it shows. So younger scholars today, in my opinion, are nowhere near them, not even in the same paddock. Of course, that might just be me being old and crusty about this.

Hooker's pronouncements are often blunt, and his professional assessments uncomfortably accurate. Yet, in person he is immensely kind, with a real generosity of spirit towards younger colleagues. In "retirement" he remains relentlessly active, driven by new questions and possibilities but retaining a sharp, clear-eyed capacity to see himself, his host institutions and his research subjects and collaborators in all their complexity and imperfections. We are the beneficiaries of that uncompromising intellectual passion. After a lifetime of supervising Masters and PhD students from Malaysia, the United Kingdom, China and Australia, Hooker's message to younger colleagues remains the same: "You can't rely on being smart and clever and getting away with it. You've got to do better, and get on with [the serious scholarly work]."

MB Hooker: Publications 1967–Present

Books

1967

(ed. & comp.) *A Sourcebook of Adat, Chinese Law and the History of Common Law in the Malayan Peninsula.* Faculty of Law, University of Singapore. Malaya Law Review Monograph No. 1.

1970

(ed.) *Readings in Malay. Adat Laws.* Singapore: University of Singapore Press.

1972

Adat Laws in Modern Malaya. Kuala Lumpur: Oxford University Press. Reprinted 1976. Cited as authority in the High Court in *Hajjah Sitam* v *Hassan* [1973] 2 MLJ 110 at 111.

1975

Legal Pluralism: An Introduction to Colonial and Neo-Colonial Laws. Oxford: The Clarendon Press.

1976

The Personal Laws of Malaysia. Kuala Lumpur: Oxford University Press.

1978

A Concise Legal History of South-East Asia. Oxford: The Clarendon Press.

Adat Law in Modern Indonesia. Kuala Lumpur: Oxford University Press.

1981

An Introduction to Javanese Law (with M.C. Hoadley). Tucson: University of Arizona Press for the Association of Asian Studies. Monograph No. 37.

1983

(ed.) *Islam in South-East Asia.* Leiden: Brill. Reprinted 1988.

1984

Islamic Law in South-East Asia. Kuala Lumpur: Oxford University Press. Cited as authority in the Supreme Court of Malaysia, *Che Omar v Public Prosecutor* (1988) 2 MLJ 55 at 56.

1986

(ed.) *Malaysian Legal Essays.* Singapore: Malayan Law Journal Ltd.

(ed.) *The Laws of South-East Asia,* vol. 1, *The Pre-Modern Texts.* Singapore: Butterworths.

1988

(ed.) *The Laws of South-East Asia,* vol. 2, *European Laws.* Singapore: Butterworths.

1990

Undang-Undang Islam di Asia Tenggara. Kuala Lumpur: Dewan Bahasa dan Pustaka.

1996

Malaysia & the Original People: A Case Study of the Impact of Development on Indigenous Peoples (with R.K. Dentan et al.). Boston: Allyn & Bacon.

2002

(ed.) *Law and the Chinese in Southeast Asia*. Singapore: Institute of Southeast Asian Studies.

2003

Indonesian Islam: Social Change through Contemporary Fatàwà. Sydney: Allen & Unwin. Honolulu: University of Hawai'i Press.

Islam Mazhab Indonesia. Jakarta: Penerbit Teraju.

2008

Indonesian Syariah: Defining a National School of Islamic Law. Singapore: Institute of Southeast Asian Studies.

Papers

1967

"Semai House Construction in Ulu Slim, Perak". *Federation Museums Journal* 12: 27–34.

1968

"A Note on the Malayan Legal Digests". *JMBRAS* 41 (1): 157–70.

"Private International Law and Personal Laws". *Malaya Law Review* 10: 55–67.

"The Interaction of Legislation and Customary Law in a Malay State". *American Journal of Comparative Law* 16: 415–30.

"The Formal Statement of Chinese Law in Hong Kong". *Malaya Law Review* 10: 230–47.

1969

"The Relationship between the Adat and the State Constitutions of Negeri Sembilan". *JMBRAS* 42 (2): 155–72.

"The Relationship between Chinese Law and Common Law in Malaysia, Singapore and Hong Kong". *Journal of Asian Studies* 28: 723–42.

"The East India Company and the Crown 1773–1858". *Malaya Law Review* 11 (1): 1–37; also in *Grotian Society Papers*, edited by C.H. Alexandrowicz, 166–211.

1971

"Law, Religion and Bureaucracy in a Malay State". *American Journal of Comparative Law* 19: 264–86.

"The Early Adat Constitution of Negeri Sembilan (1773–1824)". *JMBRAS* 44 (1): 104–16.

"Hindu Law and English Law in Malaysia and Singapore". In *Contributions to Asian Studies*, edited by K. Ishwaran, 159–79. Leiden: Brill.

1973

"A Note on the Malaysian Petition Writer". *Journal of Asian Studies* 32 (4): 661–62.

"The Challenge of Malay Adat Law in the Realm of Comparative Law". *International and Comparative Law Quarterly* 22: 492–514.

1974

"Adat and Islam in Malaya". *Bijdragen tot de Taal-, Land en Volkenkunde* 130: 69–90. Reprinted in *Legal Essays in Memoriam B.A. Mallal*, edited by G.W. Bartholomew, 164–87. Singapore: Malaya Law Review.

1976

"The Trengganu Inscription in Malayan Legal History". *JMBRAS* 49 (2) 127–31. Reprinted in the JMBRAS *Centenary Volume* (1977): 350–55.

1978

"Toward a Legal History of South-East Asia". *JMBRAS* 51 (1): 110–21. (Lecture delivered to the Royal Asiatic Society in March 1977).

"India's Judiciary". *Asian Affairs* 10 (1): 112–13.

"The Indian-derived Law Texts of South-East Asia". *Journal of Asian Studies* 37 (2): 201–19.

1980

"The Administration of Native Law in Sabah". In *Cases on Native Customary Law in Sabah*, edited by H.H. Lee, xi–xxi. Kuching: Government Printer.

"An Outline History of the Administration of the Native Law in Sarawak". In *Cases on Native Law in Sarawak*, edited by H.H. Lee, xi–xxv. Kuching: Government Printer.

"Negri Sembilan: Adat, the Constitution and the Federal Court". *Malayan Law Journal*, cxc–cxciii.

1981

"The Hervey Malay Manuscript in the Welcome Institute Library" (with R.F. Ellen and A.C. Milner). *JMBRAS* 54 (1): 82–92.

1982

"Problems in Malay Law". *Malayan Law Journal*, xcvii–xcix.

1983

"The Translation of Islam into South-East Asia". In *Islam in South-East Asia*, edited by M.B. Hooker, 1–22. Leiden: Brill.

"Slavery in the Malay Texts" (with Virginia Matheson). In *Slavery, Bondage and Dependency in South-East Asia*, edited by A. Reid, 182–208. St. Lucia: University of Queensland Press.

Introduction to the Oxford University Press historical reprint of R. St. J. Braddell, *The Laws of the Straits Settlements*, pp. v–xi. Originally published 1911.

"Javanese Law" (with M.C. Hoadley). *ASAA Review* 6 (3): 136–38.

"Muhammadan Law and Islamic Law". In *Islam in South-East Asia*, edited by M.B. Hooker, 160–82. Leiden: Brill.

1984

"Asian Polities: States, Laws and the Ideologies of Modernisation". *Proceedings of the Thirty-First International Congress of Human Sciences in Asia and North Africa* 2: 723–24. Tokyo: Toho Gakkai.

Various entries in *Biographical Dictionary of the Common Law*, edited by A.W.B. Simpson. London: Butterworths.

1986

"The Law Texts of Java and Bali" (with M.C. Hoadley). In *The Laws of South-East Asia*, vol. 1, *The Pre-Modern Texts*, edited by M.B. Hooker, 241–346. Singapore: Butterworths.

"The Law Texts of Muslim South-East Asia". In *The Laws of South-East Asia*, vol. 1, *The Pre-Modern Texts*, edited by M.B. Hooker, 347–434. Singapore: Butterworths.

"The South-East Asian Law Texts: Materials and Definitions". In *The Laws of South-East Asia*, vol. 1, *The Pre-Modern Texts*, edited by M.B. Hooker, 1–22. Singapore: Butterworths.

"Islamic and Malaysian Law". In Hooker *Malaysian Legal Essays*, edited by M.B. Hooker, 1–14. Singapore: Malayan Law Journal.

"The Oriental Law Text". In *Malaysian Legal Essays*, edited by M.B. Hooker, 431–56. Singapore: Malayan Law Journal.

1988

"Adat". In *Encyclopaedia of Asian History*, vol. 2, edited by A.T. Embree, 414–17. New York: Scribner.

"The 'Europeanisation' of Siam's Law 1855–1908". In *The Laws of South-East Asia*, vol. 2, *European Laws*, edited by M.B. Hooker, 531–78. Singapore: Butterworths.

"English Law in Sumatra, Java, The Straits Settlements, Malay States, Sarawak, North Borneo and Brunei". In *The Laws of South-East Asia*, vol. 2, *European Laws*, edited by M.B. Hooker, 299–446. Singapore: Butterworths.

"Jawi Literature in Patani" (with Virginia Matheson). *Journal of the Royal Asiatic Society, Malaysian Branch* 61 (1): 1–86.

1989

Various contributions in *South-East Asia: Languages and Literatures*, edited by P. Herbert and A.C. Milner. Kiscadale Publications.

1990

"The 'Chinese Confucian' and the 'Chinese Buddhist' in British Burma 1881–1947". *Journal of South-East Asian Studies* 31 (2): 384–401.

1991

"The Orang Asli and the Laws of Malaysia". *Ilmu Masyarakat* 18: 51–79.

1993

"Fatàwà in Malaysia". *Arab Law Quarterly* 8: 93–105. (Coulson Memorial Lecture, University of London 1990.)

1994

"Rembau". *Encyclopaedia of Islam*, 2nd ed. Fasc. 137: 483.

1995

"Islam in South-East Asia". *Oxford Encyclopaedia of the Modern Islamic World* 2: 284–90. Oxford University Press.

1996

"Sharia". *Encyclopaedia of Islam*, 2nd ed. Fasc. 153: 326–28.

"Shahbandar". *Encyclopaedia of Islam*, 2nd ed. Fasc. 150: 194–95.

1997

"Islam and Medical Science: Evidence from Malaysian and Indonesian Fatàwà". *Studia Islamika* 4 (1): 1–33.

1999

"A Note on Native Land Tenure in Sarawak". *Borneo Research Bulletin* 30: 28–40.

"Chinese Customary Law in Contemporary Malaysia and Singapore". *Australian Journal of Asian Law* 1 (1): 34–54.

"Qadi Jurisdiction in Contemporary Malaysia and Singapore". In *Public Law in Contemporary Malaysia*, edited by M.A. Wu, 57–75. Kuala Lumpur: Longman.

"Thailand". *Encyclopaedia of Islam*, 2nd ed. Fasc. 169–70, p. 430.

"Islam and Medical Science: Evidence from Indonesian Fatàwà 1960–1995". In *Indonesia: Law and Society*, edited by Timothy Lindsey, 158–70. Sydney: Federation Press.

"The State and Syariah in Indonesia 1945–1995". In *Indonesia: Law and Society*, edited by Timothy Lindsey, pp. 94–110. Sydney: Federation Press.

2000

"Úlama" (South-East Asia). *Encyclopaedia of Islam*, 2nd ed., vol. 10: 807.

2001

"Wakaf" (South-East Asia), *Encyclopaedia of Islam*, 2nd ed., vol. 11: 97–99.

"Introduction" (with Virginia Hooker) to John Leyden's *Malay Annals*, 1–72. Royal Asiatic Society – Malaysian Branch. Reprint no. 20.

"Native Title in Malaysia". *Australian Journal of Asian Law* 3 (2): 198–212.

2002

"Native Title in Malaysia" (cont.). *Australian Journal of Asian Law* 4 (1) 92–105.

"The Syariah in Indonesia and Malaysia". *Reform* 80: 47–51, 73.

"Zerbadis". *Encyclopaedia of Islam*, vol. 10. Fasc. 187–88, pp. 492–93.

"Law and the Chinese Outside China". In *Law and the Chinese in Southeast Asia*, edited by M.B. Hooker, 1–31. Singapore: Institute of Southeast Asian Studies.

"English Law and the Invention of Chinese Personal Law". In *Law and the Chinese in Southeast Asia*, edited by M.B. Hooker, 95–130. Singapore: Institute of Southeast Asian Studies.

"Islamic Law in South-East Asia". *Australian Journal of Asian Law* 4 (3) 213–31.

"Public Faces of Syariah in Contemporary Indonesia" (with T.C. Lindsey). *Australian Journal of Asian Law* 4 (3) 259–94.

2003

"The State and Syariah in Indonesia". In *Sharia and Politics in Modern Indonesia*, edited by Salim and Azra, 33–47. Singapore: Institute of Southeast Asian Studies.

"Submission to Allah? The Kelantan Syariah Criminal Code 1993". In *Malaysia: Islam, Society and Politics*, edited by V. Hooker and N. Othman, 80–100. Singapore: Institute of Southeast Asian Studies.

"Mahkamah" (Singapore, Malaysia, Brunei). In *Encyclopaedia of Islam*, 2nd ed. *Supplement*, vol. 12: 566–69.

2004

"Perspectives on Syariah and the State". In *Islamic Perspectives on the New Millennium*, edited by Virginia Hooker and Amin Saikal, 199–220. Singapore: Institute of Southeast Asian Studies.

2006

"Syariah" (with Virginia Hooker). In *Voices of Islam in Southeast Asia*, edited by Greg Fealy and Virginia Hooker, 137–206. Singapore: Institute of South-East Asian Studies.

2007

"Sharia Revival in Aceh" (with Tim Lindsey). In *Islamic Law in Contemporary Indonesia*, edited by R. Michael Feener and Mark Cammack, 216–54. Cambridge, MA: Harvard University Press.

2009

"Bumiputera". *Encyclopaedia of Islam*, 3rd. ed. Part 4: 22.

"Faith & Knowledge: Nurcholish Madjid as Educator and Philosopher" (with V.G. Hooker). *RIMA* 43 (2): 1–12.

2011

"Construction of Individual Women as Iconic Representatives: Indonesia: Raden Adjeng Kartini" (with V.G. Hooker). *Encyclopedia of Women and Islamic Cultures*. Brill Online <http://www.brillonline.rl/subscriber/entry? Entry = ew_COM-0651>.

"Law: Modern Family Law, 1800–present: Southeast Asia". *Encyclopedia of Women and Islamic Cultures*. Brill Online <http://www.brillonline.rl/subscriber/entry? Entry = ew_COM-0704>.

2013

"Muslim law, Ahmadiyya and Islamic Doctrine in Singapore". *Australian Journal of Asian Law* 14 (1).

"Southeast Asian Shari'as". *Studia Islamika* 20 (2): 183.

Notes

1. Interview, Canberra, Australia, 28 July 2013.
2. Virginia Hooker (1991), "The Library of Professor MB Hooker", Catalogue, John Randall, London (unpublished), p. 1
3. Ibid.
4. Ibid.
5. Ibid.
6. Previously Chief Justice of Malaya; Lord President of the Malaysian Federal Court (1974–82), renamed the Supreme Court in 1985.
7. Lord President of the Federal Court from 1984, renamed the Supreme Court in 1985, when Malaysian appeals to the Privy Council were abolished.
8. <http://anthropology.buffalo.edu/people/emeritus/dentan/>.
9. <http://nanyang.academia.edu/GeoffreyBenjamin>.
10. Robert K. Dentan, Kirk Endicott, Alberto G. Gomes, and M.B. Hooker, *Malaysia & the Original People: A Case Study of the Impact of Development on Indigenous Peoples* (Boston: Allyn & Bacon, 1997).
11. <http://www.iseas.edu.sg/ISEAS/upload/files/Private%20Papers%20Ivan%20Polunin.pdf>.
12. Founder, Centre for South East Asian Studies, University of Kent, 1969 <http://www.tandfonline.com/doi/abs/10.1080/714041368?journalCode=raaf20#.UmkIjII1ijE>.
13. Colonial civil servant, legal scholar, Malaysian legislative drafter and later professor of Southeast Asian Law <http://en.wikipedia.org/wiki/Hugh_Hickling>.
14. M.B. Hooker, "Muslim law, Ahmadiyya and Islamic Doctrine in Singapore". *Australian Journal of Asian Law* 14, no. 1 (2013); M.B. Hooker, "Southeast Asian Shari'as", *Studia Islamika* 20, no. 2 (2013): 183.

References

Books

Dentan, Robert K., Kirk Endicott, Alberto G. Gomes, and M.B. Hooker. *Malaysia & the Original People: A Case Study of the Impact of Development on Indigenous Peoples*. Boston: Allyn & Bacon, 1997.

Periodicals

Hooker, M.B. "Muslim law, Ahmadiyya and Islamic Doctrine in Singapore". *Australian Journal of Asian Law* 14, no. 1 (2013).
———. "Southeast Asian Shari'as". *Studia Islamika* 20, no. 2 (2013): 183.

Other

Hooker, Virginia. "The Library of Professor MB Hooker". Catalogue. John Randall. London, 1991, p. 1 (unpublished).

2

Asian Thought and Legal Diversity

H. Patrick Glenn[1]

We owe much of our knowledge of legal diversity in Asia to the work of Barry Hooker, who appears early on to have appreciated its intrinsic interest and potentially global significance. His work in the field is, as the French say, *incontournable*; a nice combination of the unavoidable, the controlling and the greatly respected. These lines are offered in such a spirit of respect, but rather than attempting to emulate the master in richness of exposition, they take refuge in a larger and more abstract perspective, in attempting to situate Asian legal diversity in some broad currents of Asian thought, contrasted in some measure with the European thought which has contributed so greatly to contemporary concepts of states and state law in the world.

Classical European Forms of Logic

States and the law of states have developed in all cases as the result of the particular circumstances of each state, but there are common forms of thought which underlie, in some measure, all states. The most remarkable of these has been the dichotomy, first announced (apparently) by Plato and adopted in a massive manner subsequently by Western thinkers, legal and otherwise. Plato argued that in order to begin to understand the world, one should first divide it conceptually into two. He wrote that "it's not at all difficult to separate into two all of those things that come into being", and that we should "divide all cases of knowledge in this way".[2] This initial diaeresis or *divisio*, moreover, should be followed by others, each yielding more detailed forms of taxonomic division until a point was reached which satisfied the intellectual and practical needs of those effecting the divisions or separations. Platonists today are not thick on the ground, but this simple and crude idea has been the most wildly successful of his proposals, over millennia.[3] In civilian teaching it has been the foundation of the idea of a *summa divisio*, such as that between public and private law, or patrimonial and non-patrimonial rights, or contractual and extra-contractual liability.[4] Beyond legal taxonomy, there are still more fundamental legal dichotomies; those of law and morality, law and ethics, law and religion, law and culture, or law and custom — all impossible to avoid in contemporary legal reasoning.[5] These are but legal examples, moreover, of the pervasive grip of the dichotomy in Western thinking generally, which sets up an entire range of "hierarchical dualisms" such as those of mind/body, nature/nurture, reason/emotion, universalism/relativism, and on and on.[6] Those who complain of a "false dichotomy" in particular cases only confirm, moreover, the general acceptance of dichotomous reasoning.

Historically, dichotomous thinking would have been controlled in large measure by the conciliatory objectives of religious thought. There were "two swords" of the church and crown throughout much of Western legal and political history, but the two swords were not opposing or conflictual ones in principle. Dualities could thus be recognized if they existed, but they were brought together in what was meant to be a shared enterprise. For centuries the latent antagonism between religious and secular ways of thought was successfully bridged by the combined or collaborative effect of the two swords.[7] The really significant changes would have come about from the seventeenth century, also the time of emergence of the contemporary state, when Platonic forms of thought became resurgent and with them the idea that purely logical relations hold between eternal objects.[8] Bodin, now seen as the father of the concept of sovereignty, pronounced divisio in the sixteenth century to be the "universal rule of the sciences", and law was unquestionably seen as a "science juridique".[9] He proceeded by way of "separation and juxtaposition" and perceived the state as an "entity", though he was himself still concerned with human legal diversity. Hobbes in the seventeenth century advanced the binary cause still further and presented the radical, binary option of amoral anarchy *or* Leviathan. He was a "notorious dichotomiser" and had major, though unfulfilled, ambitions in the field of "Logike".[10]

Much was subsequently drawn from the basic principle of dichotomy, and notably in the structuring of contemporary states and defining the relations between them. These structures and relations can be defined with some ease in terms of so-called "laws of thought", which flow inexorably from the underlying principle of division, once it is accepted. The first so-called law of thought, in the Western world, is the law of identity, to the effect that a thing or concept is itself, and nothing other. In notational terms, the law of identity is expressed as "A is A". This appears to be tautological, and is meant to so appear, yet behind the apparent tautology is the unsubstantiated proposition that it is possible to radically separate A from all that which is not-A, a proposition which many Asian ways of thought find unsustainable. Plato's teaching having been accepted for centuries, however, the inevitable result of divisio was the notion of free standing and separated things, concepts or ideas.

Divisio and the law of identity, once accepted, the two remaining "laws of thought" then fell into place, creating the "classical" logic which has been known and accepted as such for the last century.[11] There is the "law of non-contradiction", notationally expressed as *not* (A and not-A), seen by many today as at the heart of "thinking like a lawyer" and prohibiting, as a logical *impossibility*, the coexistence of contradictory notions, arguments or norms. It is in itself an obstacle to any form of legal pluralism. The law of identity and the law of non-contradiction once accepted, however, the final law of thought, the law of the excluded middle, follows inexorably. Between a concept or proposition, and its negation, no middle ground is possible. Notationally, it is A *or* not-A. This excludes any possibility of conciliation of the contradictory, since it becomes logically impossible to find any middle ground whatsoever. Why is this so logically compelling? It follows from the terms of the original divisio. If A can be radically separated from not-A, the boundaries of not-A commence exactly where the boundaries of A cease. The two encompass the world and beyond, and not-A is galactic in character, devouring any possible middle ground. A world of As and not-As is a simple but ultimately brutal place.

"Classical" Western logic thus accompanied the national legal unification movements of the nineteenth and twentieth centuries. There was much going on at this time, but the influence of then-current notions of logic appears unquestionable. Kelsen in particular defined the national legal system in terms of its adherence to the law of non-contradiction.[12] The national codifications were intended to be instruments for the elimination of diversity within states, while codes themselves were elaborate efforts towards logical coherency, understood in the classical sense.[13] Inconsistent texts or sources could not persist, and choice between them was necessary. The national legal system thus was characterized by unity and non-contradiction, while at the international level it stood as an example of the law of identity, and the laws of non-contradiction and the excluded middle thus came into operation once again following the construction of the national/international dichotomy. Contemporary, national, private international law is generally hostile to the application of two laws (presumed to be contradictory), and choice is necessary between the law of the forum *or* the foreign law designated by a choice-of-law rule.[14] There is no perceived space between the two.

The colonial and post-colonial imposition of state structures over all the territory of the earth should (logically) be based on the type of logical thought which contributed to the contemporary state in the jurisdictions of its origin. Plato, however, has not been universally received, and in many if not most cases has been specifically rejected. This is, broadly speaking, the case throughout Asia, so the Asian state will be constructed according to a logic which is not necessarily, or not entirely, European in character. This different and more conciliatory logic appears to have a great deal to do with the legal diversity which prevails in much of Asia.

Asian Ways of Thought

It is possible to find a great deal of writing on logic in Asian thought, though the mass of writing is probably, and for specific reasons, less voluminous than in the case of Europe and the Western world in general. How can one understand the differences? It appears first necessary to approach logic in Asia in the most general terms possible, then to focus on the specific elements of logic which have been seen as so fundamental in the intellectual construction of Western legal systems.

Logic, recognizable as such in notions of *nyaya* or *niti* in India,[15] appears fundamentally different from the "classical" form of logic which emerged in Europe in the nineteenth and twentieth centuries. The dichotomy was known, whatever Plato's influence might have been,[16] but its significance has never become as great as in continental European thinking. This appears to be the case, and this is a very large generalization, because of the manner in which logic, in its various forms, has been understood in Asia. The largest and most general discussions of logic in Asia describe it not in terms of the relations between abstract and fundamental concepts, but rather as "epistemological" or even "psychologized" in character.[17] It would represent the study, not of validity derived from logical forms of argument, but of how inferences are actually made. It would give grammar a higher place than mathematics[18] and would constitute above all a means of generating new knowledge in specific fields.[19] In its Buddhist form it would seek to explain the relations between "a moving reality and the static constructions of thought".[20]

Because of this underlying epistemological position, a "pure" theory of logic would therefore never have developed, and the logic that did develop was that which appeared necessary in the search for reality. Logic would not have been studied as an independent subject[21] and mathematics never had the pride of place in logic as it did in the development of "classical" logic in the West.[22] The reasoning involved would be in principle a "field-variant",[23] and the notational form of logic developed in the West (A or not-A) is inherently suspect as it is too removed from the underlying reality. It would "grant implicitly the assumptions and presuppositions underlying it".[24]

Hindu and Buddhist thought would at least have recognized the possibility of a discipline of logical thought, though in field-variant forms. Greater opposition to purely formal notions of logic can be seen in both Islamic and Confucian thought. Islamic thinkers were certainly aware of Plato and Aristotle, contributing greatly to their diffusion in the West, but speculative philosophy or *kalam* could not prevail over the ways of thought more faithful to the primary sources of Islamic law. Law and the jurists, over the centuries, prevailed over any notion of an independent form of reasoning.[25] Confucianism does not display any such overt opposition to pure or classical forms of logic. It simply avoids it in the pursuit of moral judgment and the justifiable treatment of human affairs, as opposed to any abstract conceptualization of reality.[26] Law, if it is to be used, is characterized by a high level of casuistry; it is expressed in concepts which people know and recognize — "walnuts and mulberry leaves" rather than things and property. There is little room here for universal concepts and their relations.[27]

Given an epistemological bias or turn in underlying concepts of thought, the so-called laws of thought do not thrive in Asian thinking, legal or otherwise. They have certainly been known,[28] but the wider, epistemological bias excludes their dominance. Opposition to the law of identity is perhaps most explicit in Buddhist teaching, where it is said that "there are altogether no identical real things" since "[a] thing is not the same at different moments or in different places."[29] This would be so since "of Constancy and Identity there is no trace in the ever moving, ever changing reality".[30] Such scepticism towards a process of divisio and a law of identity has necessary consequences for the "laws" of non-contradiction and the excluded middle. For Buddhists the law of non-contradiction would be "nothing" but the fact that cognition is dichotomizing.[31] It cannot therefore stand as a necessity in understanding the world; only as a product of our own limited mental processes. The Buddhist position is one well worked out. Of the four possibilities of the Catuṣkoṭi (affirmation, negation, both affirmation and negation, and neither affirmation nor negation), the Buddha would accept none of them, not being interested in the formulation of logical truths.[32] The Jains would be even more explicitly and affirmatively opposed to the law of non-contradiction. They "flatly deny" it, and would see the concrete object as both a universal and a particular at the same time.[33] In the face of such negations, the law of the excluded middle can fare no better. The Jains again explicitly repudiate it, admitting either the possibility of multiple truth-values or that truth and falsity may be simultaneously applicable.[34] The Jainist position appears even more conciliatory than that of the Buddhists, whose "middle way" involves rejection of contradictory extremes, while the Jain position is compatible with both extremes and would involve an "attempted reconciliation between opposites".[35]

There are therefore multiple logics in Asian thought, and logical thinking implies a choice of logic. Most of the logics, however, are conciliatory, in that definitive choice of a single value among a stipulated two is not imposed. This has profound consequences for law and legal diversity, as will be seen in the next section. The conciliatory dimensions of Asian thought are enhanced, moreover, by explicit recognition of the need for "congenial" or "friendly" debate amongst proponents of different methods of thought. One should be "amicable" on such questions, and not "clever, disputative and quarrelsome".[36] These written views may flow from the oral, not written or notational, character of the historic debate over logic.[37] Whatever the reasons for the presence of such counsels of collaboration, they reinforce the conciliatory character of the logic deployed. The need for such conciliation has now made itself felt in the "new logics" emerging in Western logical thought. There are also indications of reception of these new logics in Western laws.

Contemporary or "New" Western Logics

The contemporary state is declining in importance in the circumstances of globalization.[38] As it declines so does its law, and regional and transnational forms of law are now growing in importance while there is increasing legal diversity within states, as immigrant populations continue to live by standards of their previous home, standards which may or may not be religious in character. The radical elimination of contrary laws through recognition of a single, state source becomes increasingly difficult to contemplate. Legal practice itself has become transnational in character, and lawyers are increasingly called upon to reconcile multiple and conflicting norms in their daily practice. In these circumstances, notions of binary division and single-value choice become increasingly problematical. There is recognition of this both on the part of lawyers and on the part of logicians who are concerned with the practical application of logic in law. While the legal developments in this regard are often submerged in intricate patterns of dispute resolution, the logical developments have become highly visible.

The most visible development in Western logic, which brings it much closer to Asian logics, is what has been described as a "multi-valued turn".[39] It is a turn away from classical or binary logic and towards recognition that the world is a more complex place than that contemplated by Plato's methodology of divisio and the so-called laws of thought.[40] The result has been an expansion of the field and a move to develop more flexible and extended forms of logical analysis, capable of capturing ordinary language reasoning. This would be necessary to ensure that "logic is to have teeth".[41] The multi-valued turn was preceded by devastating criticism of "classical logic" by Stephen Toulmin. Toulmin criticized classical logic precisely because of its pretention to be "topic neutral" or "field invariant"[42] and he used law and legal reasoning to show how ordinary language logic was vastly more subtle and complex than the classical laws of logic would allow. Logic therefore had to open up. It has done so principally by becoming multivalent, a form of new logic which would have "successfully challenged" classical logic.[43]

Multivalent logic appears intuitively relevant in a multi-valued world in which legal thought must be increasingly cosmopolitan in character. Its origins date from the early twentieth century, though there would be a "pre-history" dating from Aristotle.[44] The essential characteristic of multivalent logic is that it is "degree-theoretic" in replacing a binary option with one which tolerates degrees, usually expressed as degrees of truth (as in the ordinary language phrase "There is some truth in that").[45] This form of "paraconsistent" logic has obvious parallels with Buddhist notions of a "middle way" or Jainist reconciliation of extremes. Moreover, the emergence of the "new" logics means that choice of logic has become possible and that a new "logical pluralism" has developed in parallel with emerging forms of "legal pluralism".[46]

The newer forms of paraconsistent logics are already receiving approbation in Western jurisdictions. Kelsen thus acknowledged in his later writing the possibility of conflicting norms being both valid, though he held that such a contradiction could not be solved by logic and required the intervention of an act of will of legal authority or "customary non-observance".[47] In Belgium François Rigaux has written of the "illusion" of categorization by dichotomy and of the "perversity" of binary taxonomies,[48] while in Switzerland Andrea Büchler would have the debate on Islamic family law in Europe move "from dichotomies to discourse".[49] In Quebec Dominique Goubeau has described a North American abandonment of the dichotomy between "open" and "closed" adoptions, seeing rather "degrees of openness" in the relations between adoptees and biological parents.[50] In the common law world, Martin Krygier has criticized "pernicious" dichotomies, which "might just be aspects of complex phenomena which can manage to include them both".[51] Michael Taggart has decided that contemporary administrative law in New Zealand is no longer well served by the dichotomies that have prevailed in the past — appeal/review, merits/legality, process/substance, discretion/law, law/policy, fact/law — and that they should be replaced with a "sliding scale or rainbow" of possibilities of review, from correctness review at one end of the rainbow to non-justiciability at the other.[52] In construction of a law of peace or Lex Pacificatoria, Christine Bell has written of the need to straddle binary distinctions and to develop "constructive ambiguity".[53] Binary distinctions in the law of citizenship have been particularly criticized, and Neil Walker has expressed dissatisfaction with the "dichotomizing language of membership", arguing for denizenship as an "in-between concept, one that challenges the series of binary oppositions ... that reflect the political imaginary of the Westphalian system of states".[54] Perhaps most visibly and fully, Neil MacCormick towards the end of his career decided that legal reasoning was essentially defeasible[55] and that its forms of argumentation "cannot be properly conceived of in simply bivalent true-or-false terms".[56] The conclusion is based in part on the impossibility of avoidance of contradiction in legal systems, such that simple deduction from axiomatic, given premises is impossible in such cases.[57] The application of legal rules is therefore, in the language of the new logics, non-monotonic in character. Given a presumptively applicable rule, there is always the possibility of "invalidating intervention".[58]

Contemporary Europe, moreover, has been described as functioning according to a "logic of diversity" which entails both "vague, innocuous-looking framework legislation" and "political regulatory competition".[59] A logic of diversity is accompanied necessarily by a "shift away from binary conceptions of law".[60] European law has therefore been described by Miguel Maduro as "contrapunctual", and this would entail "integrating the claims of validity of both national and EU constitutional law".[61] This "both and" logic (A and not-A) is thus inherent in the institutional cosmopolitanism of the EU. It "allows the different legal orders to adjust to the claims of the others and so prevents conflict between these claims".[62] Nicholas Barber has stated explicitly that the law of non-contradiction is inapplicable in EU institutional relations, where one encounters "inconsistent" rules of recognition and there is no higher constitutional body to resolve the dispute through adjudication or legislation.[63] "Consistentizing" of the contradictions is therefore impossible, and the institutions must look beyond the contradictions to sustain their mutual relations. Europe is thus acknowledging the restrictive and inadequate character of "classical logic" in law. In so doing it is drawing closer to Asian ways of thought.

Conclusion

Legal diversity in Asia is profoundly rooted in millennia of conduct and belief. It is also rooted, however, in ways of thinking about diversity and ways of reconciling potential conflict. Asian ways of thought are now being replicated elsewhere in the world in situations of legal diversity. The logics are drawing together. Perhaps the most important counsel to be observed, however, is that the logical debate should be an amicable and not a divisive one.

Notes

1. The chapter is published posthumously with the kind permission of Professor Jane Glenn, wife of Professor Patrick Glenn.
2. Plato, *The Statesman*, 258e, 261b; and see *The Sophist*, 219a ("expertise falls pretty much into two types").
3. For its "taxonomic effectiveness" over centuries, see A. Errera, "The Role of Logic in the Legal Science of the Glossators and Commentators. Distinction, Dialectical Syllogism, and Apodictic Syllogism: An Investigation into the Epistemological Roots of Legal Science in the Late Middle Ages", in *A Treatise of Legal Philosophy and General Jurisprudence*,

vol. 7, *The Jurists' Philosophy of Law from Rome to the Seventeenth Century*, edited A. Padovani and P. Stein (Dordrecht: Springer, 2007), p. 91; for use by Aristotle, see Schiebinger, *Nature's Body* (Piscataway, NJ: Rutgers University Press, 2004), p. 43 (animals divided into blooded and bloodless, blooded into quadrupeds or non-quadrupeds, quadrupeds into mammals and reptiles).

4. For the distinctions in Roman law, see Eric Descheemaeker, "The Roman Division of Wrongs: A New Hypothesis", *Roman Legal Tradition* 5 (2009): 1 (obligations "vel ex contractu nascitur vel ex delicto"); Mario Talamanca, "Lo schema 'genus–species' nelle sistematiche dei giuristi romani", in *La filosofia greca e il diritto romano*, vol. 2, edited by Accademia Nazionale dei Lincei (Rome: Accademia nazionale dei Lincei, 1977), p. 1, generally for Greek influence and notably at p. 4 (genus-species reasoning paradigmatic example of divisory technique) and p. 22 (for dichotomous character); though for Roman law in spite of divisio being "un tissu de contradictions", see M. Villey, "Histoire de la logique juridique", *Annales de la Faculté de droit et des sciences économiques de Toulouse* 15 (1967): 74 (even a basket of crabs which devour themselves).

5. For the dilemma of any attempt to conflate law and ethics, and the absence of any appropriate vocabulary for doing so, see H. Patrick Glenn, "The Ethic of International Law", in *The Role of Ethics in International Law*, edited by Donald Earl Childress III (Cambridge: Cambridge University Press, 2011), pp. 246, 249 (dichotomy of law and ethics yielding no vocabulary adequate for their conflation); yet for reconceptualization of "law and ..." as "law as ...", and working towards "a new framework that does not depend on a binary, or a conjunction of two distinct fields imagined as outside of each other", see Catherine Fisk and Robert W. Gordon, "'Law As ...': Theory and Method in Legal History", *UC Irvine Law Review* 1 (2011): pp. 519, 524 ("imagined as the same domain").

6. Donna Haraway, *Simians, Cyborgs, and Women: The Reinvention of Nature* (New York: Routledge, 1991), p. 163.

7. For the "ambiguity" of the two swords doctrine as preventing formulation of a theory of sovereignty, see Brian Nelson, *The Making of the Modern State – A Theoretical Evolution* (New York: Palgrave MacMillan, 2006), p. 37.

8. Stephen Toulmin, *The Uses of Argument* (Cambridge: Cambridge University Press), p. 182 (on the "new thinkers" of the Enlightenment); and see Stephen Toulmin, *Cosmopolis* (Chicago: University of Chicago Press, 1990), p. 108 (for the "sharpness" of Descartian separations, seen "around 1700 as having indispensable merits"); and for the "essential duality" of modern

philosophy underlying modern notions of law, Villey, "Histoire de la logique juridique", p. 67 (two distinct worlds of Descartes [mind/body], Kant [being/phenomenon or existence/norm]); and for the first "modern" attempts of classical logic by Althusius (1563–1638), Otto Friedrich von Gierke, *The Development of Political Theory*, trans. B. Freyd (New York: Norton, 1939), p. 43 (though often the "required dichotomy" only set up by resort to arbitrary antitheses) or Grotius (1583–1645), Villey, "Histoire de la logique juridique", p. 68 (first major attempt at axiomatic system).

9. Mario Turchetti, "Jean Bodin", in *Stanford Encyclopedia of Philosophy*, edited by E. Zalta (2010), accessible online at http://plato.stanford.edu/entries/bodin, under section 2, "Bodin's methodology of History and Law" (recalling also that Plato had designated the principle of divisio as "divine").

10. Conal Condren, *"Natura naturans*: Natural Law and the Sovereign in the Writings of Thomas Hobbes", in *Natural Law and Civil Sovereignty*, edited by Ian Hunter and David Saunders (New York: Palgrave, 2002), p. 61 (also for dichotomous nature of debate *on* Hobbes).

11. For "classical" logic now taken largely as the "Frege-Peirce" logic developed in the late nineteenth and early twentieth century. Susan Haack, "On Logic in the Law: 'Something, but not All'", *Ratio Juris* 20 (2007): 1.

12. Hans Kelsen, *Pure Theory of Law*, trans. M. Knight (Gloucester, MA: Peter Smith, 1989), p. 206 ("the Principle of the Exclusion of Contradictions.... To say that a ought to be and at the same time ought not to be is just as meaningless as to say that a is and at the same time that it is not." In the case of contradictory norms, "only one of the two can be regarded as objectively valid"). For the later Kelsen, however, see the section below on Contemporary or "New" Western Logics.

13. For the so-called laws of non-contradiction, excluded middle as fundamental properties of French codification, see Denys de Béchillon, "L'imaginaire d'un Code", *Droits* 27 (1998): pp. 173, 182.

14. For a challenge to the idea, see H. Patrick Glenn, *La conciliation des lois – Cours général de droit international privé*, in *Collected Courses of the Hague Academy of International Law*, vol. 364 (Leiden, Boston: Brill Nijhoff, 2013).

15. Satis Chendra Vidyabhusana, *A History of Indian Logic – Ancient, Mediaeval and Modern Schools* (Delhi: Motilal Banarsidass, 1971), p. 40 (for Nyaya-sastra even as "second stage" of development of Indian logic), p. 240 (though Bhiksu-sutra or circa 100 CE only Pali work with explicit reference to it; translated into Chinese in the fourth century CE); and for "rational inquiry" into a large range of subjects by the fifth century BCE in India, Brendon S. Gillon, "Logic in Early Classical India – An Overview", in

Logic in Earliest Classical India, edited by Brendon S. Gillon (Delhi: Motilal Banarsidass, 2010), p. 6.

16. For the debate on Greek influence in India, see Vidyabhusana, *History of Indian Logic*, p. xv (only vague concept of Aristotelian syllogism by first century BCE), p. 511 (transmission however through Alexandria in Egypt up to 600 CE).

17. Bimal Krishna Matilal, *The Character of Logic in India*, edited by Jonardon Ganeri and Heeraman Tiwari (Albany: SUNY Press, 1998), p. 14; and see Th. Stcherbatsky, *Buddhist Logic* (New York: Dover 1962), p. 11 (epistemological in including sense perception, reliability and knowledge), p. 363 (not formal but epistemological).

18. Ibid.

19. Katherine Manchester Rogers, *Tibetan Logic* (Ithaca, NY: Snow Lion Publications, 2009), p 38 (not about propositions but about phenomena); and see Matilal, *Character of Logic in India*, p. 88 (as means of knowledge); Vijay Bharadwaja, *Form and Validity in Indian logic* (New Delhi: Indian Institute of Advanced Study, 1990), p. ix (concerned not with logic in the formal sense but with "justification of knowledge-claims ... what is and what is not to count as knowledge").

20. Stcherbatsky, *Buddhist Logic*, p. 2.

21. Krishna Kumar Dikshit, *Indian Logic: Its Problems as Treated by Its Schools* (Vaishali Bihar: Research Institute of Prakrit, Jainology and Ahimsa, 1975), p. i.

22. Surendra Sheodas Barlingay, *A Modern Introduction to Indian Logic* (Delhi: National Publishing House, 1965), p. 89.

23. Cf. S. Toulmin's description of "classical" Western logic as "field-invariant", Toulmin, *Uses of Argument*.

24. Bharadwaja, *Form and Validity*, p. ix ("No notation is conceptually innocent").

25. Majid Fakhry, *A History of Islamic Philosophy*, 2nd ed. (New York: Columbia University Press, 1983), notably pp. 203–4 (spirit of theological enquiry inspired by Greek philosophy "not completely snuffed out", jurists thereafter unable to continue "pure" form of early jurists and exegetes); Bernard G. Weiss, *The Spirit of Islamic Law* (Athens, GA: University of Georgia Press, 1998), pp. 25–30 (kalam eventually seen as "handmaiden to jurisprudence"; relying on aristotelian, deductive logic, though distinguishing between its own theological reflection and "falsafa", from Greek philosophia), pp. 67–68 (opposition even to analogical reasoning, since this would lead to more general rules and categories; Seyyed Hossein Nasr, *The Heart of Islam: Enduring Values for Humanity* (San Francisco: HarperSanFrancisco,

2004), p. 81 (teaching of kalam still prohibited in religious universities in Saudi Arabia); and for an extensive bibliography comparing Western and Islamic rationalities, John Makdisi, "Legal Logic and Equity in Islamic Law", *American Journal of Comparative Law* 33 (1985): 63, 67. For logic also being necessarily compatible with the Vedas in India, see Vidyabhusana, *History of Indian Logic*, pp. 38, 40–42.

26. Hu Shih, *The Development of the Logical Method in Ancient China*, 2nd ed. (New York: Paragon Book Reprint Corp., 1968), p. 4 (for "humanistic interpretation" of *wuh* or things as affairs, this having "determined the whole nature of scope of modern Chinese philosophy"), pp. 47–48 (Confucian preoccupation with "rectification of names" not for taxonomic purposes but moral ones).

27. H. Patrick Glenn, *Legal Traditions of the World*, 4th ed. (Oxford: Oxford University Press, 2010), pp. 334–35.

28. For Indian use of logical principles of non-contradiction, excluded middle from the second century BCE, see Gillon, *Logic in Earliest Classical India*, pp. 7–9 (though not an "extensive discussion" as in Aristotle).

29. Stcherbatsky, *Buddhist Logic*, p. 402.

30. Ibid., p. 419 ("Constancy and Identity are logical, they are in our head, not in the objective world.... The identical things are projected images") and p. 104 (for only unique thing the mathematical "point-instant" of change, since every relation or quality belonging to two realities at least); and see Rogers, *Tibetan Logic*, p. 28 (for "subtle impermanence" of reality, "momentary nature" of objects "forming, disintegrating, and reforming moment by moment"); and for recognition of moments of change as necessarily implying degrees of existence at the moment of change, see Graham Priest, *An Introduction to Non-Classical Logic* (Cambridge: Cambridge University Press, 2001), notably p. 126 for "truth-value gluts" of something being both true and false or in a momentary state of change.

31. Stcherbatsky, *Buddhist Logic*, p. 401.

32. Bharadwaja, *Forma and Validity in Indian Logic*, pp. 46, 55.

33. Stcherbatsky, *Buddhist Logic*, p. 415; and see Matilal, *Character of Logic in India*, p. 135 (affirmation of property of a thing necessarily implies non-existence of another property, the two being inextricable).

34. Barlingay, *Modern Introduction to Indian Logic*, pp. 197–98 (truth "may have infinite possibilities ... world is perhaps the totality of all the possibilities").

35. Matilal, *Character of Logic in India*, p. 129 ("*accepting* both with qualifications and also by reconciling them"); and for the Buddhist view that P and not-P "do not exhaust the whole universe", see Barlingay, *Modern Introduction*

to Indian Logic, pp. 79–80 ("As soon as we give up the two-valued logic ... the law of excluded middle ... will cease to operate").

36. Matilal, Character of Logic in India, p. 38 (on good vs. bad debate in Caraka (circa 100 CE); Vidyabhusana, History of Indian Logic, p. 27 ("should not be alarmed at suffering defeat ... nor ... rejoice in inflicting defeat").

37. Barlingay, Modern Introduction to Indian Logic, p. 189 (oral method also explaining lack of notational form in Indian debate).

38. Martin van Creveld, The Rise and Decline of the State (Cambridge: Cambridge University Press, 1999).

39. Dov M. Gabbay and John Wood (eds.), The Many Valued and Nonmonotonic Turn in Logic (Amsterdam: North Holland, 2007).

40. In the scientific world, for contemporary views which can be considered multivalent in biology, see Marc Ereshefsky, The Poverty of the Linean Hierarchy: A Philosophical Study of Biological Taxonomy (Cambridge: Cambridge University Press, 2001), p. 3 (for evolving lineages and no longer "static classes" or organisms), p. 15 (contrasting cluster analysis with genealogical descent), and p. 20 (later, empirical, Aristotle concluding that divisio "splits natural groups"); and in quantum physics, for the "underlying reality of protons" which "unseats classical logic" and allows reconciliation of "two seemingly contradictory ideas of what protons are", Frank Wilczek, The Lightness of Being: Mass, Ether and the Unification of Forces (New York: Basic Books, 2010), pp. 43, 54 ("we can eat our quarks and have them too").

41. Dominic Hyde, "Logics of Vagueness", in The Many Valued and Nonmonotonic Turn in Logic, edited by D. Gabbay and J. Woods, p. 296 ("restoration" of ordinary language, vagueness seen as "less superficial"); Dale Jacquette, "Introduction", in Philosophy of Logic, edited by Dale Jacquette (Amsterdam: Elsevier, 2007), p. 4 ("need to make logic more expressively adapted to specific areas of linguistic usage inadequately served by existing classical logics"); and see Susan Haack, Philosophy of Logics (Cambridge: Cambridge University Press, 1978), p. 163 ("logicians must take vagueness more seriously"); Scott Soames, "Vagueness and the Law", in The Routledge Companion to the Philosophy of Law, edited by A. Marmor (New York: Routledge, 2012), p. 95 (growing interest in vagueness in law and philosophy though separate inquiries to date); for philosophically informed enquiry in law, however, see Timothy A.O. Endicott, Vagueness in Law (Oxford: Oxford University Press, 2000) (vagueness a feature of law and not merely its language; rule of law not requiring, however, that content of law be determinate in all cases).

42. Toulmin, *Uses of Argument*, p. 7 ("Logic (we may say) is generalized jurisprudence"), p. 39 (asking "How far is a *general* logic possible?").

43. Katalin Bimbó, "Relevance Logics", in *Philosophy of Logic*, edited by D. Jacquette, p. 723 ("once the overpowering dominance of classical logic has been successfully challenged [and it has been] ...").

44. Siegfried Gottwald, "Many-Valued Logics", in *Philosophy of Logic*, edited by D. Jacquette, p. 680 (citing Lukasiewicz and Post in the 1920s), p. 681 ("prehistory" with Aristotle's future contingencies, notably sea battle which will or will not take place); Grzegorz Malinowski, "Many-valued Logic", in *The Many Valued and Nonmonotonic Turn in Logic*, edited by D. Gabbay and J. Woods, p. 14 (for future sea battle as root of many-valued logics); Haack, *Philosophy of Logics*, p. 204.

45. For "degree-theoretic", see Nicholas J.J. Smith, *Vagueness and Degrees of Truth* (Oxford: Oxford University Press, 2008), p. 10 (replacing binary values with "infinitely many degrees of truth"); and for the logic, Malinowski, *Many-Valued Logics*; Gabbay and Woods, *Many Valued Turn*; Priest, *An Introduction to Non-Classical Logic*, Ch. 7 ("Many-valued logic"), notably p. 126 for "truth-value gluts" of something being both true and false or in a momentary state of change. Multi-valued logic is often referred to as "*n*-valued" where *n* is the number of truth values a proposition may have. Sartor speaks of factors which are "scalable" as opposed to binary; Giovanni Sartor, *A Treatise of Legal Philosophy and General Jurisprudence*, vol. 5, *Legal Reasoning: A Cognitive Approach to the Law*, edited by E. Pattaro (Dordrecht: Springer, 2005), p. 182.

46. J.C. Beall and Greg Restall, *Logical Pluralism* (Oxford: Clarendon Press, 2006), p. 30 (and comes at little or no cost); and see Graham Priest, "Paraconsistency and Dialetheism", in *The Many Valued and Nonmonotonic Turn in Logic*, edited by D. Gabbay and J. Woods, p. 200 (determination of correct logic a "fallible and revisable business", need for historical perspective); Dale Jacquette, "Relation of Informal to Symbolic Logic", in *Philosophy of Logic*, edited by Dale Jacquette (Amsterdam: Elsevier, 2007), p. 132 ("whatever logical methods are best suited for my analytic purposes in trying to understand different types of logical problems").

47. Hans Kelsen, *Essays in Legal and Moral Philosophy*, selected by O. Weinberger, trans. P. Heath (Dordrecht: D. Reidel, 1973), p. 235 ("that two mutually conflicting norms should both be valid, is possible").

48. François Rigaux, *La loi des juges* (Paris: Editions Odile Jacob, 1997), pp. 69, 250–51.

49. Andrea Büchler, "Islamic Family Law in Europe: From Dichtomies to Discourse", *International Journal of Law in Context* 8 (2012): 196–97.

50. Dominique Goubeau, "'Open adoption' au Canada", in *Parents de sang: Parents adoptifs*, edited by Agnès Fine and Claire Neirinck (Paris: LGDJ, 2000), pp. 63, 65 (passive or active, anonymous or not).

51. Martin Krygier, "False Dichotomies, True Perplexities, and the Rule of Law", in *Human Rights with Modesty: The Problem of Universalism*, edited by András Sajó (Leiden: Martinus Nijhoff, 2004), p. 251, see also p. 253 ("they postulate contradictions between which one *must* chose", making choice the first task and excluding other and perhaps more appropriate options, "[l]ike refusing to choose").

52. Michael Taggart, "Administrative Law", *New Zealand Law Reports* 75 (2006): 75, 83.

53. Christine Bell, *On the Law of Peace: Peace Agreements and the Lex Pacificatoria* (Oxford: Oxford University Press, 2008), p. 166, and see p. 291 (law as "holding device"), p. 302 (embracing what would be otherwise an excluded middle).

54. Neil Walker, "Denizenship and the Deterritorialization in the EU", in *A Right to Inclusion and Exclusion?*, edited by Hans Lindahl (Oxford: Hart, 2009), pp. 261–62, 266 (binary oppositions of insider/outsider, national/international, territorial/extraterritorial, domestic/foreign, franchised/disenfranchised).

55. Neil MacCormick, *Rhetoric and the Rule of Law: A Theory of Legal Reasoning* (Oxford: Oxford University Press, 2009), p. 28 ("rule statements ... are always defeasible"), p. 33 (certainty in law is "at best, qualified and defeasible certainty"), p. 240 (validity of legal arrangements "presumptively sufficient").

56 Ibid., p. 77, and see also p. 54 ("strictly deductive inferences from axiomatic premises is indeed an idea at some remove from anything to be found in legal argumentation", legal deduction "embedded in a web of other practical arguments").

57. Ibid., pp. 53–54 ("Judicial decision-making includes the task of seeking to resolve contradictions as they emerge").

58. Ibid., p. 240 (resulting in "defeasance").

59. Jan Zielonka, *Europe as Empire: The Nature of the Enlarged European Union* (Oxford: Oxford University Press, 2006), p. 72 (and for increased diversity not yielding decision-making paralysis).

60. Nico Krisch, *Beyond Constitutionalism: The Pluralist Structure of Postnational Law* (Oxford: Oxford University Press, 2010), p. 305 ("a form of gradated authority").

61. Miguel Poiares Maduro, "Contrapunctual Law: Europe's Constitutional Pluralism in Action", in *Sovereignty in Transition*, edited by Neil Walker (Oxford: Hart, 2003), pp. 501, 524.

62. Ibid., p. 525.
63. Nicholas W. Barber , "Legal Pluralism and the European Union", *European Law Journal* 12 (2006): 306, notably p. 327 ("this inconsistency is sustainable if each side shows institutional restraint") and see pp. 309–10 (hope of establishing a system of deontic logic independent of particular systems of moral philosophy is too ambitious and "the principle of non-contradiction need not be present in every plausible normative order").

References

Books

Barlingay, Surendra Sheodas. *A Modern Introduction to Indian Logic*. Delhi: National Publishing House, 1965.

Beall, J.C. and Greg Restall. *Logical Pluralism*. Oxford: Clarendon Press, 2006.

Bell, Christine. *On the Law of Peace: Peace Agreements and the Lex Pacificatoria*. Oxford: Oxford University Press, 2008.

Bharadwaja, Vijay. *Form and Validity in Indian* logic. New Delhi: Indian Institute of Advanced Study, 1990.

Dikshit, Krishna Kumar. *Indian Logic: Its Problems as Treated by Its Schools*. Vaishali Bihar: Research Institute of Prakrit, Jainology and Ahimsa, 1975.

Endicott, Timothy A.O. *Vagueness in Law*. Oxford: Oxford University Press, 2000.

Ereshefsky, Marc. *The Poverty of the Linean Hierarchy: A Philosophical Study of Biological Taxonomy*. Cambridge: Cambridge University Press, 2001.

Fakhry, Majid. *A History of Islamic Philosophy*, 2nd ed. New York: Columbia University Press, 1983.

Gabbay, Dov M. and John Wood (eds). *The Many Valued and Nonmonotonic Turn in Logic*. Amsterdam: North Holland, 2007.

Glenn, H. Patrick. *Legal Traditions of the World*, 4th ed. Oxford: Oxford University Press, 2010.

———. *Collected Courses of the Hague Academy of International Law*, vol. 364, *La conciliation des lois – Cours général de droit international privé*. Leiden, Boston: Brill Nijhoff, 2013.

Haack, Susan. *Philosophy of Logics*. Cambridge: Cambridge University Press, 1978.

Haraway, Donna. *Simians, Cyborgs, and Women: The Reinvention of Nature*. New York: Routledge, 1991.

Hu Shih. *The Development of the Logical Method in Ancient China*, 2nd ed. New York: Paragon Book Reprint Corp., 1968.

Kelsen, Hans. *Essays in Legal and Moral Philosophy*, selected by O. Weinberger, trans. P. Heath. Dordrecht: D. Reidel, 1973.

———. *Pure Theory of Law*, trans. M. Knight. Gloucester, MA: Peter Smith, 1989.

Krisch, Nico. *Beyond Constitutionalism: The Pluralist Structure of Postnational Law*. Oxford: Oxford University Press, 2010.

MacCormick, Neil. *Rhetoric and the Rule of Law: A Theory of Legal Reasoning.* Oxford: Oxford University Press, 2009.

Matilal, Bimal Krishna. *The Character of Logic in* India, edited by Jonardon Ganeri and Heeraman Tiwari. Albany: SUNY Press, 1998.

Nelson, Brian. *The Making of the Modern State – A Theoretical Evolution*. New York: Palgrave MacMillan, 2006.

Plato. *The Statesman*.

———. *The Sophist*.

Priest, Graham. *An Introduction to Non-Classical Logic*. Cambridge: Cambridge University Press, 2001.

Rigaux, François. *La loi des juges*. Paris: Editions Odile Jacob, 1997.

Rogers, Katherine Manchester. *Tibetan Logic*. Ithaca, NY: Snow Lion, 2009.

Sartor, Giovanni. *A Treatise of Legal Philosophy and General Jurisprudence*, vol. 5, *Legal Reasoning: A Cognitive Approach to the Law*, edited by E. Pattaro. Dordrecht: Springer, 2005.

Schiebinger. *Nature's Body*. Piscataway, NJ: Rutgers University Press, 2004.

Smith, Nicholas J.J. *Vagueness and Degrees of Truth*. Oxford: Oxford University Press, 2008.

Stcherbatsky, Th. *Buddhist Logic*. New York: Dover 1962.

Toulmin, Stephen. *Cosmopolis*. Chicago: University of Chicago Press, 1990.

———. *The Uses of Argument*. Cambridge: Cambridge University Press.

Van Creveld, Martin. *The Rise and Decline of the State*. Cambridge: Cambridge University Press, 1999.

Vidyabhusana, Satis Chendra. *A History of Indian Logic – Ancient, Mediaeval and Modern Schools*. Delhi: Motilal Banarsidass, 1971.

Von Gierke, Otto Friedrich. *The Development of Political Theory*, trans. B. Freyd. New York: Norton, 1939.

Weiss, Bernard G. *The Spirit of Islamic Law*. Athens, GA: University of Georgia Press, 1998.

Wilczek, Frank. *The Lightness of Being: Mass, Ether and the Unification of Forces*. New York: Basic Books, 2010.

Zielonka, Jan. *Europe as Empire: The Nature of the Enlarged European Union*. Oxford: Oxford University Press, 2006.

Chapters

Bimbó, Katalin. "Relevance Logics". In *Philosophy of Logic*, edited by Dale Jacquette. Amsterdam: Elsevier, 2007.

Condren, Conal. "*Natura naturans*: Natural Law and the Sovereign in the Writings of Thomas Hobbes". In *Natural Law and Civil Sovereignty*, edited by Ian Hunter and David Saunders. New York: Palgrave, 2002.

Errera, A. "The Role of Logic in the Legal Science of the Glossators and Commentators. Distinction, Dialectical Syllogism, and Apodictic Syllogism: An Investigation into the Epistemological Roots of Legal Science in the Late Middle Ages". In *The Jurists' Philosophy of Law from Rome to the Seventeenth Century*, edited by A. Padovani and P. Stein, vol. 7 of *A Treatise of Legal Philosophy and General Jurisprudence*, edited by E. Pattaro. Dordrecht: Springer, 2007.

Gillon, Brendon S. "Logic in Early Classical India – An Overview". In *Logic in Earliest Classical India*, edited by Brendon S. Gillon. Delhi: Motilal Banarsidass, 2010.

Glenn, H. Patrick. "The Ethic of International Law". In *The Role of Ethics in International Law*, edited by Donald Earl Childress III. Cambridge: Cambridge University Press, 2011.

Gottwald, Siegfried. "Many-Valued Logics". In *Philosophy of Logic*, edited by Dale Jacquette. Amsterdam: Elsevier, 2007.

Goubeau, Dominique. "'Open adoption' au Canada". In *Parents de sang: Parents adoptifs*, edited by Agnès Fine and Claire Neirinck. Paris: LGDJ, 2000.

Hyde, Dominic. "Logics of Vagueness". In *The Many Valued and Nonmonotonic Turn in Logic*, edited by Dov M. Gabbay and John Wood. Amsterdam: North Holland, 2007.

Jacquette, Dale. "Introduction". In *Philosophy of Logic*, edited by Dale Jacquette. Amsterdam: Elsevier, 2007.

———. "Relation of Informal to Symbolic Logic". In *Philosophy of Logic*, edited by Dale Jacquette. Amsterdam: Elsevier, 2007.

Krygier, Martin. "False Dichotomies, True Perplexities, and the Rule of Law". In *Human Rights with Modesty: The Problem of Universalism*, edited by András Sajó. Leiden: Martinus Nijhoff, 2004.

Maduro, Miguel Poiares. "Contrapunctual Law: Europe's Constitutional Pluralism in Action". In *Sovereignty in Transition*, edited by Neil Walker. Oxford: Hart, 2003.

Malinowski, Grzegorz. "Many-valued Logic". In *The Many Valued and Nonmonotonic Turn in Logic*, edited by Dov M. Gabbay and John Wood. Amsterdam: North Holland, 2007.

Priest, Graham. "Paraconsistency and Dialetheism". In *The Many Valued and Nonmonotonic Turn in Logic*, edited by Dov M. Gabbay and John Wood. Amsterdam: North Holland, 2007.

Soames, Scott. "Vagueness and the Law". In *The Routledge Companion to the Philosophy of Law*, edited by A. Marmor. New York: Routledge, 2012.

Talamanca, Mario. "Lo schema 'genus–species' nelle sistematiche dei giuristi romani". In *La filosofia greca e il diritto romano*, vol. 2, edited by Accademia Nazionale dei Lincei. Rome: Accademia nazionale dei Lincei, 1977.

Turchetti, Mario. "Jean Bodin". In *Stanford Encyclopedia of Philosophy*, edited by E. Zalta, 2010 <http://plato.stanford.edu/entries/bodin>.

Villey, M. "Histoire de la logique juridique". In *La logique juridique*, edited by M. Villey et al., *Annales de la Faculté de droit et des sciences économiques de Toulouse* 15 (1967).

Walker, Neil. "Denizenship and the Deterritorialization in the EU". In *A Right to Inclusion and Exclusion?* edited by Hans Lindahl. Oxford: Hart, 2009.

Periodicals

Barber, Nicholas W. "Legal Pluralism and the European Union". *European Law Journal* 12 (2006): 306.

Büchler, Andrea. "Islamic Family Law in Europe: From Dichtomies to Discourse", *International Journal of Law in Context* 8 (2012): 196.

de Béchillon, Denys. "L'imaginaire d'un Code". *Droits* 27 (1998): 173.

Descheemaeker, Eric. "The Roman Division of Wrongs: A New Hypothesis". *Roman Legal Tradition* 5 (2009): 1.

Fisk, Catherine and Gordon, Robert W. "'Law As...': Theory and Method in Legal History". *UC Irvine Law Review* 1 (2011): 519.

Haack, Susan, "On Logic in the Law: 'Something, but not All'". *Ratio Juris* 20 (2007): 1.

Makdisi, John. "Legal Logic and Equity in Islamic Law". *American Journal of Comparative Law* 33 (1985): 63

Taggart, Michael. "Administrative Law". *New Zealand Law Reports* 75 (2006): 75.

3

Comparative Law, Anti-Essentialism and Intersectionality: Reflections from Southeast Asia in Search of an Elusive Balance

Arif A. Jamal[1]

My motivations for undertaking this essay were partly biographical. I was raised in Canada and undertook my initial legal training there. I then went to the United Kingdom for postgraduate studies and now work in Southeast Asia. By way of larger background, my family has roots in East Africa and before that in India. Through all of this geographical diversity runs the influence of the English common law; lawyers in all these jurisdictions would immediately recognize a reference to rotten snail-tainted ginger beer, and why that helps to answer the question "Who is my neighbour?", and also with the assertion that, in summertime, village cricket really *is* the delight of everyone. At the same time, these jurisdictions are very diverse. They are historically and culturally shaped by different forces and incorporate in their legal systems very different influences. Canada has a written criminal code, but this is different from the written penal code in India and Singapore, although those last two are so similar that debates about section 377A of the *Penal Code* in Singapore would immediately be comprehensible to an Indian lawyer. An Indian, Singaporean, Australian and Canadian lawyer may also share a reference to the case of *Liversidge v. Anderson*,[2] though it is interpreted differently in these jurisdictions. If your "tribe" is the Kikuyu or the Kalenjin, for example, your customary or indigenous law will have a greater place in the contemporary law of your country (Kenya) than if your tribe is the Haida or Cree in Canada. Muslim personal law is officially recognized in India through the regular courts, and in Singapore and Kenya through the Syariah and Kadi courts respectively; it has a rather lesser role in Canada and the United Kingdom. The list could go on.

In considering the jurisdictions with which I have personal connections, therefore, I am struck by the paradox of familiarity and similarity, on the one hand, and of opacity and difference on the other. Students at my university in Singapore, for example, have no problem in considering and receiving precedents from the United Kingdom or Canada or India, but they would hardly think of Cambodia or Thailand or Indonesia: jurisdictions that are geographically so much closer. When they travel to other common law environments on exchange, they know that they share a language — literal, legal and metaphorical — with their new classmates. Hence, there does seem to be something to what is shared, notwithstanding all the differences.

Clearly, the seeming paradox of similarity and diversity is not particular to legal regimes. In this essay I seek to explore it in the context of another environment where the effort has been made to look for commonality while having to encounter diversity: the case of feminist scholarship theorizing women's experience. More particularly, in this essay I attempt to see if there are any lessons that comparative law theory can learn from the perspectives of intersectionality and anti-essentialism that have been developed and explored in feminist scholarship. Intersectionality's major insight is that women participate in multiple identities simultaneously according to, for example, race, socio-economic position, educational background, sexual orientation, and so their identities are variously formed by all of these contexts. Anti-essentialism makes the point that there is not one, single, essential, sense of "womaness" that can be identified. The investigation will show how these perspectives have changed feminist scholarship in the same way that broader comparative studies changed the understanding of legal diversity and the contours of comparative law.

I will use the scholarship of M.B. Hooker, a leading scholar on Southeast Asia, as a case study of comparative law scholarship. In this respect I will argue that there is, perhaps, some methodological sharing that can take place between feminist theory and comparative law in terms of how to explain plurality and commonality. This essay will accept, however, that intersectionality and anti-essentialism have not been conclusive of how to address, and more importantly to make sense of, women's diversity. These challenges seem consistent and parallel with comparative law theory, which is still searching for its own narrative. I had hoped in conceiving of this essay that the insights from feminist jurisprudence could and would provide comparative law a means to deal with the paradox of familiarity and difference. What I have discovered, however, is that feminist jurisprudence perspectives also struggle — albeit in a different way — with what I think is the same issue. My conclusion, therefore, is that the intractability of this struggle and its implications may indeed be the important point, though some useful work can be achieved by adopting a framework of "contingent categorization", which I elaborate further below.

The Challenge

As others have noted, comparative law seems both more important and more confused than ever before. Catherine Valcke, for example, speaks about comparative law's malaise, noting:

> Much ink has been spilled on what is now commonly labelled the 'malaise' of comparative law. This malaise — perhaps the most serious crisis to strike the discipline since its inception — is not about quantity: the comparative law literature is voluminous by any standard. Rather, it relates to the fact that this literature has yet to congeal into a 'discipline' proper, that is, into 'a shared body of information and theory' with a designated set of tools and methodology, 'a scholarly tradition susceptible of transmission to succeeding generations', a 'shared foundation on which each can build'.[3]

In a like manner, Esin Örücü has written that:

> During the past decade we have witnessed increasing interest in all forms of comparative law, international law and transnational law. The character, quality and quantity of the work have increased and changed, but the basic problems have remained the same. There is no one definition of what comparative law and comparative method are.[4]

There is a lack of consensus, it seems, not only about what comparative law can do but also over what it might mean. Is this a problem? To some it may not be. One view may be that the enterprise of classification was always going to be a fool's errand and that what comparative studies have shown is that legal systems are sites of such great diversity and, to use Örücü's language, "mixing", such that they each must be taken on their own terms: "The new mixes are like cake mixes, where the outcome is not precisely known until the cake is fully cooked."[5] Of course, all the mixes are different — a little more sugar here, less vanilla there, and maybe a surprise sprinkling of cinnamon somewhere else — just as all legal systems will have their own peculiarities and, even if they draw or seem to draw from the same sources, they may do so in different and distinctive manners. One of the important contributions of comparative law, of which M.B. Hooker's scholarship[6] has been a major source for Southeast Asia, has been to expose and explicate the level and variety of this mixing. Hooker has been a salient expositor of the plurality of law in Southeast Asia both before and after the influence of European laws. He has argued that,"[t]he structure of the South-East Asian legal systems is pluralistic in nature"[7] and remarked that, in the pre-European period, "there was co-existence of legal ideas which occasionally resulted in a blend of principle; conflict was not inevitable".[8] Indeed, even though Hooker has noted that the impact of European laws has been a reformulation of much of the "indigenous" legal cultures of Southeast Asia, this did not lead to a straightforward replacement of the indigenous "old" for the European "new",[9] so even though much of the formal law in Southeast Asia has been reshaped by European influence (and is similar to these European models) it is not identical to that of Europe, retaining distinctive features of its historical and cultural contexts.

In other words, comparative law scholarship has made evident the legal pluralism — to use what has now become the term of art — that is present in the world beyond the paradigms of European legal systems which emphasized the "Common Law–Civil Law" duopoly.[10] This leads to our awareness that law is not static, that it moves and changes and that legal systems today are in flux. Irrespective of whether the future holds confluence or divergence for legal systems, one thing is certain: more and more systems will be mixed and mixing, be they in Europe, in Southeast Asia or in the Middle East. In line with these developments, the challenge for comparative research itself is to study this process of "mixedness" in order to facilitate an understanding of current and future patterns of legal development.[11]

This conclusion promotes an embrace of particularity and a move away from categorization.[12] Accordingly, we would assess any legal system (as any cake) on its own terms and merits; it should not matter that a system A has some of the same elements in its mix as system B, any more than we would judge two cakes the same way just because both recipes called for eggs. This approach has much to commend it. After all, using just my "biographical" systems as examples, it is clear that each legal regime can be understood properly only by a concerted study of its own rules, principles, context and history. One cannot fully understand Canada's legal system by studying Australia's legal system, notwithstanding their similarities, nor understand Australia's legal system by studying the legal system in the United Kingdom. Nonetheless, such an approach misses something that one can actually experience, namely a familiarity — not just with ginger beer and village cricket — but with methods of thinking about law and of organizing the legal landscape conceptually. Indeed, elevating difference risks giving due regard to similarity. This raises a challenge well articulated by Roger Cotterrell:

> Comparative law's central orientation today, I suggest, should be to balance the promotion of similarity in arrangements between legal systems, on the one hand, and the defence of differences in legal arrangements, styles, outlooks and ideas.[13]

Here Cotterrell is referring to legal systems more broadly than just my biographically inspired examples with their common law influence. Yet his point surely applies even more strongly where the similarities may be more marked. The key point, and the challenge, is to find that analytic and explanatory fine point of balance between observable differences and elements of similarity.

It is to this end that I turn to the insights of intersectionality and anti-essentialism scholarship in feminist legal discourse. While it may seem surprising to say this, I find that this material displays a commonality with comparative law work, inasmuch as both lines of scholarship have pointed out blind spots in the understanding of their subjects, which when exposed generate new, if still evolving, theoretical perspectives on their fields.

Intersectionality and Anti-Essentialism

Kimberlé Crenshaw is one of intersectionality's earliest, and now leading, scholars. Her locus of concern and case study is the experience of Black American women. In "Demarginalizing the Intersection of Race and Sex: A Black Feminist Critique of Antidiscrimination Doctrine, Feminist Theory and Antiracist Politics",[14] Crenshaw addresses the habit of thinking in single-axis categories of identity: if a black woman is discriminated against, can she clearly prove she was discriminated against because she is black, or because she is a woman? If her experience is different from that of black men, then she cannot easily prove the former. If her experience is different from that of white women, then she cannot easily prove the latter. And it does not help that feminists who try to isolate the experience of gender discrimination do so by removing race from the equation — which means the experience of gender discrimination is defined by the experiences of *white* women, and excludes the experiences of black women. The intersection is marginalized because it does not definitively belong to one or the other protected group. Crenshaw speaks about her project as follows:

> I will center Black women in this analysis in order to contrast the multidimensionality of Black women's experience with the single-axis analysis that distorts these experiences. Not only will this juxtaposition reveal how Black women are theoretically erased, it will also illustrate how this framework imports its own theoretical limitations that undermine efforts to broaden feminist and antiracist

analyses. With Black women as the starting point, it becomes more apparent how dominant conceptions of discrimination condition us to think about subordination as disadvantage occurring along a single categorical axis.[15]

To counter the domination and marginalization that comes from the single-axis perspective, Crenshaw argues that:

> [t]hese problems of exclusion cannot be solved simply by including Black women within an already established analytical structure. Because the intersectional experience is greater than the sum of racism and sexism, any analysis that does not take intersectionality into account cannot sufficiently address the particular manner in which Black women are subordinated.[16]

Intersectionality thus involves the idea that there can be multiple axes of identity and discrimination: it is less a fully fleshed out position than a reaction against what it sees as parochial perspectives, which foster discrimination. As Crenshaw puts it, intersectionality "is a provisional conceptualization, a prism refracted to bring into view dynamics that were constitutive of power but obscured by certain discursive logics at play in that context".[17] Anti-essentialism feminist scholarship has played a similar role: it has critiqued the idea that there are "essential" experiences of, for example, womanhood. The recognition of these differences is meant to empower marginalized subgroups, defined perhaps by race, colour, socio-economic position or sexual orientation, within the larger discourse of feminism. An example of this perspective comes from the work of Angela Harris. In looking at the work of white feminist scholars, Harris, who is herself a black woman, says:

> I argue that their work [viz., of white women scholars], though powerful and brilliant in many ways, relies on what I call gender essentialism — the notion that a unitary, 'essential' women's experience can be isolated and described independently of race, class, sexual orientation, and other realities of experience.

Moreover:

> [a] second and less obvious reason for my criticism of gender essentialism is that, in my view, contemporary legal theory needs less abstraction

and not simply a different sort of abstraction. To be fully subversive, the methodology of feminist legal theory should challenge not only law's content but its tendency to privilege the abstract and unitary voice, and this gender essentialism also fails to do.[18]

The subversive (and even destructive?) potential of anti-essentialism is noted also by Tariq Modood, who points out that:

> [i]t seems, then that anti-essentialism is inherently destructive. Each escape from its grasp (for example in the celebration of hybridities) proves to be illusory; while thoroughgoing embrace seems to leave us with no politics, no society, not even a coherent self.... What promised to be an emancipatory, progressive movement seems to make, with its 'deconstruction' of the units of collective agency (people, minorities, the oppressed and so on), all political mobilisation rest on mythic and dishonest unities.[19]

Harris resists these consequences, however, and is at pains to point out that she does not want her critique to result in a sort of "isolationary pluralism", from which nothing can be said about a larger group:

> I do not mean ... to suggest that either feminism or legal theory should adopt the voice of Funes the Memorious, for whom every experience is unique and no categories or generalizations exist at all. Even a jurisprudence based on multiple consciousness must categorise; without categorisation each individual is as isolated as Funes, and there can be no moral responsibility or social change. My suggestion is only that we make our categories explicitly tentative, relational, and unstable, and that to do so is all the more important in a discipline like law, where abstraction and 'frozen' categories are the norm. Avoiding gender essentialism need not mean that the Holocaust and a corncob are the same.[20]

Here I would like to re-invoke as a placeholder Cotterrell's challenge of balance, and how it may resonate with Harris' viewpoint (as I think it does). I will return to this point more fully below. Like Harris, Trina Grillo, another important feminist scholar, notes that essentialism may be useful in allowing us to speak about experiences which, while diverse, have commonality. Her caution is to remember the potential pitfalls that essentialist discourses entail. As she puts it: "[t]he question is whether essentialism, which is sometimes unavoidable, is explicit, is considered temporary and is contingent."[21] The point therefore is not to swear off generalization altogether, but rather to use the insights of intersectionality and anti-essentialism to act as checks on how we formulate our generalizations.[22]

There is much more scholarship that could be cited to explain the perspectives of intersectionality and anti-essentialism and the recognition of the challenges that they pose to generalization on the one hand, but also the potential value of generalizations that they acknowledge on the other. Engaging as these perspectives are, however, we are still left in a condition of malaise, in that we are no clearer about how to find a point of balance between diversity and generalization. Even if we are usefully informed and fully adopt the insight that any generalization must be seen as temporary and contingent, when do those conditions become so corrosive of generalizations that what we have said becomes irrelevant at best or even harmful? Ultimately, therefore, if we are being intellectually rigorous and extending these perspectives to their logical conclusions, are we not witness to an internal contradiction? That is, should we not admit that we really cannot say anything "general" (whether it be about women or the "common law") and so we collapse into isolated silos? Scholars who work with intersectionality and anti-essentialism literature are aware of these theoretical limitations; post-intersectionality discourse has tried to figure out how difference and diversity might be overcome so as to allow meaningful statements to be made about groups. Let me therefore turn, briefly, to explore some of these perspectives to see what insights they may offer.

One perspective that has been posited is to adopt a frame of "multidimensionality" that would recognize "the inherent complexity of systems of oppression ... and the social identity categories around which social power and disempowerment are distributed".[23] Multidimensionality posits that various forms of identity and oppression are inextricably linked and intertwined. Another perspective, coming out of literature addressing sexual orientation, is of "cosynthesis", which insists that identity categories are sometimes themselves constructed or synthesized out of, and rely upon, other categorical notions. Therefore, this mutually defining, synergistic, and complicit relationship between identity categories is a dynamic model of multiple subordinating gestures. It denies the priority of the deconstructive concerns of class over race, of race over gender, or of gender over sexual orientation, of anything over anything else.[24]

While initially tantalizing, both multidimensionality and cosynthesis are perspectives that seek to address cross-cutting and interlinked dimensions of oppression or subordination (depending on how one wants to describe it). Thus, like intersectionality, they focus on the interplay of marginalization that may arise by virtue of race/colour and sexual orientation, say, or gender and socio-economic position. In other words, they seem to re-emphasize the basic insights of intersectionality and the warnings of anti-essentialism, while providing a better basis for political solidarity and mobilization. That may be an important advance in practice but we are not, I think, conceptually closer to locating our balance point. Peter Kwan puts it well when he notes that:

> [i]ntersectionality tells us, for example, that the condition and subjectivity of and hence the legal treatment of Black women is not simply the sum of Blackness and femaleness, but it does not shed much light on what it is nevertheless. Narratives are often used to fill this gap. But narratives provide only the empirical data on which the theoretical work remains to be done.[25]

Southeast Asia: The Work of M.B. Hooker

I suggested that there may be some common intellectual ground in the literature on intersectionality and the pioneering scholarship of M.B. Hooker in illuminating what were previously blind spots in our understanding. The different bodies of work have highlighted that there is much more complexity and richness in the subjects of their study (the conditions of women, for example, or the legal systems of Southeast Asia) and have therefore challenged what had been the conventional understanding of scholarship before their insights. Furthermore, both bodies of literature force us to confront the theoretical challenge (with which it seems we are still struggling) of making sense of all the richness they have exposed.

Hooker noted that: "When we ask ourselves what it is to be compared, we very quickly find ourselves asking what we mean by the term 'law' in its comparative context. Its meaning cannot be limited to the lawyer's highly specialized use of the term."[26] In the introduction to his study of Southeast Asia, Hooker notes the several points of analysis of legal systems in the region; namely, written law, oral law, law in social institutions and indigenous adaptations.[27] He ends the introduction with the key insight of his study that is built on this framework of analysis: "The striking feature of modern South-East Asian law is legal pluralism.... Like most processes of change or development [the expression of this pluralism] is untidy and occasionally inconsistent with itself."[28] It hardly needs to be said that the development of the concept of legal pluralism and the understanding of its manifestations, which comparative law now takes for granted, is deeply indebted to Hooker's careful, detailed studies and reflection.

The "plurality consciousness"[29] that legal pluralism encourages in the comparative scholar helps us to see the remarkable variety beneath the formal unity of legal systems. In turn, and recalling the metaphor of the cake mix, this enables us to realize the capacity for similar "ingredients" to be combined in multitudinous ways. I suggest that the legal pluralism perspective has been able to do for our understanding of legal systems what anti-essentialism and, even more so, intersectionality, have done for their subjects of study — be it the experience of women or other groups. That is to say, legal pluralism has debunked straightforward narratives of legal development and demonstrated that analysis must proceed along multiple vectors which will almost certainly be differentially important in different systems. The reality of a legal system in Southeast Asia will not be defined by its "Southeast Asianness"[30] (nor would that of one in Africa or Europe be defined by its "Africanness" or "Europeanness", etc.) but rather by how written law, oral law, law in social institutions and indigenous adaptations are manifested. So, too, the experiences of black or Muslim women will not be definable by "blackness" or "Muslimness" or "femaleness" alone, but by and in the intersection of these aspects of their identity with class, race, socio-economic position and, one might add, their location in time and space. The challenge, therefore, is how to find and express similarity in this intersectional diversity.

Conclusion

In preparing to write this essay, I had hoped to square a circle. I wondered to what extent feminist theory's struggle with the challenge of plurality as a result of the perspectives of intersectionality and anti-essentialism might help to address comparative law's analogous challenge as a result of the understanding of legal pluralism. My first conclusion is that in neither context has the circle been squared. One might simply conclude with this and take some solace in that oft-quoted observation of Immanuel Kant: "Out of the crooked timber of humanity, no straight thing was ever made."[31] Surely, in saying this, Kant was cautioning us that to seek clear, straight order out of human experiences (whether in legal or social contexts) is impossible. I would, however, go further and propose two other potential lessons that this examination might have revealed. These still do not bring us close to squaring the circle, but they might help us in taking a step towards a point of balance along the lines Cotterrell suggests.

Anti-essentialism and intersectionality emphasize the plurality of women's experience. The studies of M.B. Hooker likewise point to the plurality within the legal systems of Southeast Asia. Just as women's experiences may be formed by the intersection of diverse identities, so too legal systems may develop out of the intersections of a variety of legal and social forces. Context matters and so does the impact of the context that, for want of a better term, we might call the "culture" within which the subject (the women; the legal system) exists. And so, while identities are formed by their cultures, cultures are not just endogenous, self-contained units. Rather, they draw in other imports. Hence, the impact of legal norms, procedures, categories or ideas developed in different contexts or from external religious, social or economic sources, will be relevant. For example, Muslim American women may have their experience defined by the fact that they are women, Muslims and Americans, even if their Muslim identity relates primarily to contexts outside of the United States (though of course over time the primacy of the external context might change as communities become more settled, so that "Muslim American" identity will be different and distinct from the identity of Muslims in the "home" countries). Equally, the intersections will keep the identities fluid. Culture is not static and its effects on the shaping of a legal system or on identities of a social group will constantly generate new combinations.

Secondly, within these processes, the narrative that we use about ourselves is important. In the case of the legal systems I mentioned in the opening of this essay, we can now relate their diversity to their varied cultural contexts. At the same time, however, there is what I call a "narrative of affinity" that is expressed — even if implicitly — in telling the "stories" of snails in ginger beer bottles and the like. Kwan, recall, thought that narratives were the empirical basis for theorizing. I would like to suggest that narratives that express affinity might bring us as close as we might hope to developing the balance between similarity and difference that Cotterrell mentioned. The narratives constitute a common set of references, normative concepts and analytical structures which are shared, *mutatis mutandis*, within a context, such as, for instance, the "Common law jurisdictions". In this sense a "narrative of affinity" resonates with sets of ideas that have been used to explain the construction of common references. One of these is the idea of interpretive communities developed originally in Stanley Fish's literary theory. Fish's key insight is that interpretation is shaped by cultural assumptions developed within communities about what a text means. Within comparative law scholarship, John Gillespie has employed Fish's idea in the context of understanding legal transfers in different parts of East and Southeast Asia. Gillespie says that "deep beliefs of an interpretive tradition or community form 'a lattice or web whose component parts are mutually constitutive' and determine what ideas, arguments and facts members find compelling".[32] Thus he claims that legal transfers may appear logical and desirable for those embedded in one interpretive community, but inappropriate and alien to members of a different interpretive community.[33]

Let us say we express "narratives of affinity" among a group (such as women) or in a legal tradition (say, the common law) but resist essentializing these categories by acknowledging that these narratives do not eliminate variety, since these broad groupings will continue to intersect with other aspects of identity shaped by their culture(s). We would be in a situation where there is, lurking within the consciousnesses of common law–trained lawyers, a sense that despite our different substantive rules of law, varied contexts, and national histories, there is something familiar that we share. The same may be true for what feminists see in women's experience: something shared despite — indeed, in spite of — diversity. Ugo Mattei has asserted that "[t]he pluralism of legal patterns should not become an excuse to avoid classification."[34] I am not suggesting full-blown classification here but rather a more modest endeavour at a narrative, one that still finds pattern, organization and meaning. Shared meaning between the narratives of common law systems can be as simple as the fact that the bulk of their imagined history is shared. The story of the first courts set up by the Norman rulers in Anglo-Saxon England is as much a part of the narrative of American law as it is of Indian law. These stories of ancient history may not be vitally important to comparative law in our contemporary world, but the idea of narratives nevertheless allows their presence to be felt in the grander scheme of things.

The idea of the common law as having a narrative of affinity suggests both that there are common sources which are taken as standard as well as a way of "reading" these sources — an interpretive matrix. Thus a paradigm of common law thinking is constructed by an interpretive community which cuts across geographical distances. Just as in science or literature, however, a narrative of affinity does not imply total uniformity; rather, its main import is the common set of references (snails in ginger beer, the delights of village cricket, carbolic smoke balls and so on) and techniques of understanding.

Does this give us enough? Narratives are not closed off. In fact, the very idea of narrative suggests a certain flexibility and openness to change and to (re)interpretation. At the same time, a narrative provides a certain type of conception in which we might locate ourselves. Tariq Modood has said that, "We do not have to be browbeaten by a dogmatic anti-essentialism into believing that historical continuities, cultural groups, coherent selves do or do not exist. Nothing is closed *a priori*; whether there is sameness/newness in the world."[35] So, if we do find that these narratives of affinity help us to explore normative or procedural or experiential commonality in the legal systems of Southeast Asia, or in the common law world, or in other contexts, then I believe we have found something as a basis to balance both sameness and difference. This point of balance will always be fluid and unstable but it is not meaningless.

In fact, because it is not meaningless it enables us to engage in what we might call "contingent categorization of legal systems". This categorization is contingent in two respects. First, membership of one group does not exclude simultaneous membership of other groups (common law and Islamic law; *adat* and civil law, for instance). This provides for the intersectionality of legal systems. Second, the border surrounding any one legal system is always in flux and subject to revision so that we get beyond a fixed identity for any one legal system. This incorporates an anti-essentialist understanding. Contingent categorization gives us a way forward because it allows us to make sense of commonalties as well as differences, which we can perceive even without looking too deeply. At the same time, contingent categorization speaks to the purpose of classification. That is to say, we seek to classify to know things about one case and to understand it relative to another case, to intelligently compare and contrast. Contingent categorization allows us to realize these ends, while always keeping us alert to the dynamics of the exercise in which we are engaged.

Notes

1. This chapter is reproduced with the kind permission of the *Asian Journal of Comparative Law* where it was first published: Arif A. Jamal, "Comparative Law, Anti-essentialism and Intersectionality: Reflections from Southeast Asia in Search of an Elusive Balance", *Asian Journal of Comparative Law* 9 (2014): 197–211.
2. [1942] AC 206.
3. Catherine Valcke, "Comparative Law as Comparative Jurisprudence – The Comparability of Legal Systems", *American Journal of Comparative Law* 52 (2004): 713.
4. Esin Örücü, "Developing Comparative Law", in *Comparative Law: A Handbook*, edited by Esin Örücü and David Nelken (London: Hart, 2007), p. 43.
5. Esin Örücü, "A General View of 'Legal Families' and of 'Mixing Systems'", in *Comparative Law: A Handbook*, edited by Esin Örücü and David Nelken (London: Hart, 2007), p. 178.
6. Classically in M.B. Hooker, *Legal Pluralism: An Introduction to Colonial and Neo-Colonial Laws* (Oxford: Oxford University Press, 1975); and see also his *A Concise Legal History of South-East Asia* (Oxford: Oxford University Press, 1978).
7. Hooker, *A Concise Legal History of South-East Asia*, p. 13.
8. Ibid., p. 9.

9. M.B. Hooker, *The Laws of South-East Asia* (Singapore: Butterworths, 1988), p. iv.

10. Örücü, "Developing Comparative Law", p. 181.

11. Ibid., p. 185.

12. In the case of Örücü's referred to in Note 5 above, her main target was the categorization coming from the "legal families" approach.

13. Roger Cotterrell, "Seeking Similarity, Appreciating Difference: Comparative Law and Communities", in *Comparative Law in the 21st Century*, edited by Andrew Harding and Esin Örücü (London: Kluwer Law International, 2002), p. 53.

14. Kimberlé Crenshaw, "Demarginalizing the Intersection of Race and Sex: A Black Feminist Critique of Antidiscrimination Doctrine, Feminist Theory and Antiracist Politics", *University of Chicago Legal Forum* (1989): 139.

15. Ibid., pp. 139–40.

16. Ibid.

17. Kimberlé Crenshaw, "Postscript", in *Framing Intersectionality: Debates on a Multi-Faceted Concept in Gender Studies*, edited by Helma Lutz, Maria Teresa Herrera Vivar, and Linda Supik (London: Ashgate, 2011), p. 231.

18. Angela P. Harris, "Race and Essentialism in Feminist Legal Theory", *Stanford Law Review* 42 (1989–90): 585.

19. Tariq Modood, "Antiessentialism, Multiculturalism and Religious Groups", *Journal of Political Philosophy* 6, no. 4 (1998): 381.

20. Harris, "Race and Essentialism", p. 586.

21. Trina Grillo, "Anti-Essentialism and Intersectionality: Tools to Dismantle the Master's House", *Berkeley Women's Law Journal* 10 (1995): 21.

22. See ibid., p. 30.

23. See Darren Lenard Hutchinson, "Identity Crisis: 'Intersectionality', 'Multidimensionality' and the Development of an Adequate Theory of Subordination", *Michigan Jouranl of Race and Law* 6 (2000–2001): 285.

24. Peter Kwan, "Complicity and Complexity: Cosynthesis and Praxis", *DePaul Law Review* 49 (1999): 688.

25. Ibid., p. 686.

26. Hooker, *Legal Pluralism*, p. 456.

27. Hooker, *A Concise Legal*, pp. 1–6.

28. Ibid., p. 14.

29. I draw this phrase from Werner Menski, *Comparative Law in a Global World: The Legal Systems of Asia and Africa*, 2nd ed. (Cambridge: Cambridge University Press, 2006).

30. Of course, Southeast Asia is itself a contentious category, but this is like other geographical groupings (South Asia, West Asia, the Indian Ocean etc.). See, on this, "Introduction", in *The Sociology of Southeast Asia:*

Transformations in a Developing Region, edited by Victor T. King (Copenhagen: NIAS Press, 2008).

31. Immanuel Kant, *Idea for a General History with a Cosmopolitan Purpose* (1784), Proposition 6.

32. John Gillespie, "Developing a Decentred Analysis of Legal Transfers", in *Examining Practice, Interrogating Theory: Comparative Legal Studies in Asia*, edited by Penelope Nicholson and Sarah Biddulph (Leiden: Martinus Nijhoff, 2008), p. 42. The internal quotation used by Gillespie comes from Stanley Fish, *The Trouble with Principle* (Cambridge: Harvard University Press, 1999), p. 280. I thank Sumithra G. Dhanarajan for bringing this material to my attention.

33. Ibid.

34. Ugo Mattei, "Three Patterns of Law: Taxonomy and Change in the World's Legal System", *American Journal of Comparative Law* 45 (1997): 15.

35. Tariq Modood, "Antiessentialism, Multiculturalism and Religious Groups", p. 382.

References

Court cases

Liversidge v. Anderson [1942] AC 206.

Books

Hooker, M.B. Hooker, M.B. *Legal Pluralism: An Introduction to Colonial and Neo-Colonial Laws.* Oxford: Oxford University Press, 1975.

———. *A Concise Legal History of South-East Asia.* Oxford: Oxford University Press, 1978.

Hooker, M.B. *The Laws of South-East Asia.* Singapore: Butterworths, 1988.

Kant, Immanuel. *Idea for a General History with a Cosmopolitan Purpose* (1784).

King, Victor T. *The Sociology of Southeast Asia: Transformations in a Developing Region.* Copenhagen: NIAS Press, 2008.

Fish, Stanley. *The Trouble with Principle.* Cambridge: Harvard University Press, 1999.

Menski, Werner. *Comparative Law in a Global World*: *The Legal Systems of Asia and Africa*, 2nd ed. Cambridge: Cambridge University Press, 2006.

Chapters

Cotterrell, Roger. "Seeking Similarity, Appreciating Difference: Comparative Law and Communities". In *Comparative Law in the 21st Century*, edited by Andrew Harding and Esin Örücü. London: Kluwer Law International, 2002.

Crenshaw, Kimberlé. "Postscript". In *Framing Intersectionality: Debates on a Multi-Faceted Concept in Gender Studies*, edited by Helma Lutz, Maria Teresa Herrera Vivar, and Linda Supik. London: Ashgate, 2011.

Gillespie, John. "Developing a Decentred Analysis of Legal Transfers". In *Examining Practice, Interrogating Theory: Comparative Legal Studies in Asia*, edited by Penelope Nicholson and Sarah Biddulph. Leiden: Nijhoff, 2008.

Örücü, Esin. "A General View of 'Legal Families' and of 'Mixing Systems'". In *Comparative Law: A Handbook*, edited by Esin Örücü and David Nelken. London: Hart, 2007.

———. "Developing Comparative Law". In *Comparative Law: A Handbook*, edited by Esin Örücü and David Nelken. London: Hart, 2007.

Periodicals

Crenshaw, Kimberlé. "Demarginalizing the Intersection of Race and Sex: A Black Feminist Critique of Antidiscrimination Doctrine, Feminist Theory and Antiracist Politics". *University of Chicago Legal Forum* (1989): 139.

Grillo, Trina. "Anti-Essentialism and Intersectionality: Tools to Dismantle the Master's House". *Berkeley Women's Law Journal* 10 (1995): 16.

Harris, Angela P. "Race and Essentialism in Feminist Legal Theory". *Stanford Law Review* 42 (1989–90): 581.

Hutchinson, Darren Lenard. "Identity Crisis: 'Intersectionality', 'Multidimensionality' and the Development of an Adequate Theory of Subordination". *Michigan Journal of Race & Law* 6 (2000–2001): 285.

Kwan, Peter. "Complicity and Complexity: Cosynthesis and Praxis". *DePaul Law Review* 49 (1999): 673.

Mattei, Ugo. "Three Patterns of Law: Taxonomy and Change in the World's Legal System". *American Journal of Comparative Law* 45 (1997): 5.

Modood, Tariq. "Antiessentialism, Multiculturalism and Religious Groups". *Journal of Political Philosophy* 6, no. 4 (1998): 378.

Valcke, Catherine. "Comparative Law as Comparative Jurisprudence – The Comparability of Legal Systems". *American Journal of Comparative Law* 52 (2004): 713.

4

Legal Pluralism and Legal Anthropology: Experiences from Indonesia

Franz von Benda-Beckmann* and
Keebet von Benda-Beckmann

When Barry Hooker's masterful study titled *Legal Pluralism: An Introduction to Colonial and Neo-colonial Laws* was first published in 1975, it fortunately became an instant classic. As he introduced his core ideas on legal pluralism that to this day guide his work, Hooker addressed a range of topics that were remarkably broad and far-reaching, certainly for the time, but even by today's measure. At a time when legal pluralism primarily connoted colonial or post-colonial situations, Hooker's study demonstrated the relevance of this emergent field beyond the historical parameters of coloniality; in effect, to include such histories as the voluntary adoption of Western laws in countries such as Turkey, Thailand, and Ethiopia. Similarly, at a time when the field lacked a comprehensive assessment of studies undertaken at the intersection of law and anthropology, Hooker was among the first to offer a thorough review of the colonial and post-colonial anthropological writings on law, which essentially made up the first chapter, "Legal Pluralism and the Ethnography of Law". Therein, he discusses the anthropological attempts to conceptualize law and the challenge of generating a comparative language devoid of ethnocentric assumptions, reiterating at the same time the importance of studying legal processes and court cases. The main failing of these anthropological studies of law and legal process, according to Hooker, was that they largely ignored the impact of colonial law (1975, p. 52). In confining themselves to a narrow study of a specific society (tribe, village) and its law, anthropologists rarely aspired to demonstrate the intimate link between the prevalent structures and the colonial legal administration. He notes in summary that "the important point for the student of plural laws is that both the legal ethnography of a particular society and the formal judicial machinery refer to one and the same people. The two fields of study, therefore, approach the same individuals from different standpoints" (1975, p. 53). At that time few anthropologists had proclaimed the importance of this overlooked connection, notably Bohannan (1965) and Moore (1970), who had shown a similar level of awareness as Hooker. No major critiques had yet emerged on the anthropologists' propensity to "edit out" the state, its law, and its administrative institutions from the analysis of "their" society (Moore 1978; Chanock 1985).

Our own academic work, published around the same time as Hooker's, centres on many concerns we share with him on legal pluralism. Franz von Benda-Beckmann published his doctoral thesis in law on "Legal Pluralism in Malawi" (in German) in 1970[1]. Legal pluralism, as it pertained to the domains of property, inheritance, and dispute management processes, was central to the research design we prepared for our anthropological research in West Sumatra in 1973 (F. von Benda-Beckmann 1979; K. von Benda-Beckmann 1984). Like Hooker, we were familiar with the writings of the Dutch *adat* (Indonesian custom or customary law) law scholars and could profit from their insights. By the time we returned from the field in 1975, Hooker's *Legal Pluralism* had just been published and it became a great source of inspiration to us. Our work in Africa, and later in West Sumatra, the Moluccas, Nepal, and the Netherlands necessitated that we adopt comparative analysis.

As legal anthropologists, however, our position in the broader context of legal studies is slightly different from Hooker's. He positioned himself squarely as a student of "jurisprudence", while we consider ourselves social scientists committed to active engagement with the complexities of normative and institutional orders, as well as their significance for and in social practices. Hooker was well aware of how (comparative) lawyers commonly deployed the "official record". Statutes, legal reports, or court decisions, as he put it, were,

> not sufficient to get a good grasp on the reality of plural legal orders, because the totality of the legal process is not contained in the official record. Sociological (especially ethnographic) data are therefore necessary as an addition and corrective to the official record in the description of plural legal systems. (Hooker 1975, p. 5).

We agree with that view. For us, this insight translated into a practice we have continued to uphold; namely, to include "the official record" as part of our ethnographic data and to subject it to the same social scientific analysis as other kinds of ethnographic material derived from observation, interviews, archival work, and the like.

In this chapter we revisit some points that were important to Hooker as early as 1975, but also in his later writings. Much has changed since 1975. The empirical and theoretical concerns of scholars in multiple fields have widened and deepened substantially. Scholarly explorations of the plurality of normative and institutional orders today rarely neglect the state organization, its law, and administration. In a trend noticeable over the past twenty years, transnational and international law and their so-called "glocalization" have taken centre stage in legal pluralism (Merry 1998, 2006; K. von Benda-Beckmann 1999). Despite these significant strides, not all of Hooker's critical concerns have to date been fully addressed. Two shall be discussed below. Firstly, infinite discussions, often stale, are still under way as to whether law should be conceptualized as being independent of the state, a question that directly concerns the underpinnings of legal pluralism. Hooker's conceptualization of "legal pluralism", as well as the contrast he draws between "servient" and "dominant" law, have met with much criticism — in our view, unjustly so: using flawed arguments and ultimately with no useful outcomes. The second point concerns the modes of entanglement and disentanglement of legal forms in relation to plural legal constellations. As one of the few scholars familiar with Ter Haar's 1929 article describing "the influence of western civilisation on the law of native civilizations", which addressed the issue of what we now would term "entanglement" for the Dutch Indies (Hooker 1975, pp. 258ff.), Hooker affirmed the significance of those entanglements for legal pluralism. We believe that such entanglements defy unequivocal qualification. We discuss below the problems related to an explosion of regulations promulgated at the local level (village and district) in the wake of reforms initiated in Indonesia after the fall of the Soeharto regime. These regulations add a new legal layer to Indonesia's complex legal pluralism in so far as they characteristically involve selective amalgamations of adat, Islamic and state legal forms, which coexist with older legal forms. We interpret this new layer of regulations differently. Rather than seeing it predominantly as symptomatic of the heightened role of Islam, we suggest this might also indicate the continued entanglement of adat, Islam and the state; a greater degree of autonomy accorded to villages; and their resultant repositioning vis-à-vis higher levels of state administration.

Perspectives on Legal Pluralism – Then and Now

How does a normative order attain its status as law? A line of thought that is dominant in legal theory and the sociology of law has restricted the label of law to normative conceptions generated or validated by state institutions. John Griffiths has criticized this position as "legal centralism". He has argued that "recognition" of other "non-legal" normative orders, such as customary or religious law, by the state organization validates the centralist ideology, in so far as the normative order can be assumed to have been validated *as law* by way of state legislation or court rulings (Griffiths 1986). Colonial and post-colonial state legal systems abound with fragments of other legal orders that have been made into law by virtue of state recognition. Hooker has described many examples of legal pluralism resulting from validation by state recognition, as did Franz von Benda-Beckmann (1970, 2007) for that matter, in his book on legal pluralism in Malawi. Hooker saw the relationship between the different legal orders as hierarchical, and distinguished the different legal orders as either "dominant" or "servient". His descriptions and analyses of plural legal orders have effectively turned around the distinction between dominant and servient legal orders, in which the law of the state, or municipal law, was characterized as "dominant" and the customary or religious laws as "servient" (Hooker 1975).

Hooker's conceptualization of legal pluralism has been criticized and branded "weak legal pluralism" (Griffiths 1986) or "relative legal pluralism" (Vanderlinden 1989). Vanderlinden (1989, p. 153) has asserted that a state legal system establishes such forms of legal pluralism "in order to conceal the inevitable failure of its totalitarian ideal" and as no more than "the acknowledgement by the state system of its incapacity to realize to the full its totalitarian ambition and a way to disguise what according to the first consideration should have been evident". Such construction was deemed normative-ideological because the existence of other normative or legal orders could not be fully captured in the selective recognition by the state. Griffiths (1986) has therefore called such legal pluralism a "myth". He contrasted this conceptualization of law to one that presumes the "reality" of plural normative orders, a form of pluralism in which normative orders were, or could be, "legal" irrespective of their recognition by the law of the state, which he called "strong" legal pluralism. He asserted that legal pluralism, as defined by the state legal system, could not provide a social scientific concept of legal pluralism.

We agree that state constructions of legal pluralism are normative, and often ideological, and that a social scientific definition of law should not be directly coupled with the political organization of the state. It is true that if legal pluralism were to be a mere construct of the state it could not serve its purpose as an analytical device. However, as a criticism directly aimed at Hooker's conceptualization of legal pluralism, such assertions as those of Griffiths and Vanderlinden are misconceived for several reasons. Hooker (1975) never claimed to present a social scientific concept of law in the first place, and even went so far as to proclaim that "this statement [the hierarchical relationship between dominant, municipal law and servient law] may be said to be a representation of reality, but of a *reality limited in nature and form by the characteristics of dominant systems*" (1975, pp. 45–45, our italics). In other words, he was aware of the limited scope of such representations and acknowledged the possible existence of other constellations of plural legal systems as representations of different realities.

More importantly, the very terms of the criticism pose a serious problem. The opposition of "weak legal pluralism" as mere "myth" with the presumed "reality" of "strong" legal pluralism is unfounded. Constructions and descriptions of the so-called "weak legal pluralism" are legal constructions of a hierarchy between normative orders. As such, they constitute a part of the "ought", or the normative dimension of plural legal constellations. They are "real" in the same way as any other element of law can be real, or as any other normative or ideological order is real. But, like any other normative rule or principle, such constructions do not reveal whether social practices are in conformity with these legal rules, or what the other consequences of such rules may be. Other legal or normative systems may coexist and inform social practices irrespective of the state legal regulations.

There is another reason why the opposition of strong and weak legal pluralism is problematic. It mistakenly implies that the "legalness" of a normative order can be presumed on the grounds of its mere existence. We suggest that it is not sufficient to prove the existence of an effective normative order to label it as law; the whole discussion makes sense only if the characteristic properties that render a normative order "legal" are specified. Further clarification is needed on what the core properties of "law", or those signifying the term "legal", are. Most advocates of a social scientific conception of legal pluralism view social carriers, legitimation, or effectiveness of normative orders as "variables" rather than as core properties of a legal order. But this requirement holds not just for the proponents of legal pluralism. We suggest that adherents of the law–state nexus are obliged to do the same. However, if one thing is clear, it is that even this sphere of scholarship has failed to put out a blueprint that garners general acceptance. In our publications we have outlined possible characteristics of a cognitive and normative conceptualization of what is "legal". We have argued that as empirical manifestations of these core elements tend to assume a variable form, the dimensions of the variation must become part of the conceptualization exercise.[2] The core properties, as we conceptualize them, while still underdetermined, gain greater specificity when viewed in concert with the dimensions of the variation, such as the degree of institutionalization, scientification, legitimation, or the mode of transmission. This offers a provisional litmus test that allows us on the one hand to decide whether norms can be labelled as law and, on the other, to provide a vastly more nuanced characterization of (variable) legal forms than the common conceptualization can offer.[3] Such a strategy seems more promising than cutting the discussion short by alleging that if law could be plural, "everything" would be law and important differences would be "melted down" (Merry 1988; Moore 2001).

This very abstract discussion still haunts contemporary discussions about legal pluralism in Indonesia. Scholars continue to contend whether adat, or rather parts of adat, can be conceived of as legal. It has been argued that the bodies of rules, institutions and procedures called adat in many polities within the Indonesian archipelago should not be referred to as "law", but rather as "custom". For instance, in the collected volume edited by Davidson and Henley (2007), adat is "custom" for Burns (2007), Li (2007) and Henley and Davidson (2007). Adat law is "customary law" for Davidson and Henley (2007), Fasseur (2007) and Acciaioli (2007). Adat is "culture" for Erb (2007) and Davidson and Henley (2007). Only Warren (2007), on Bali, and Biezeveld (2007), for Minangkabau (the dominant ethnic group of West Sumatra), speak of "adat" and "adat law". We have written an extensive critique of the assertion that adat law can be reduced to a colonial construct (F. and K. von Benda-Beckmann 2011). This approach is usually taken by those who privilege state law over what we call local law, and who assume that local law is mere custom, and by definition inferior to state law.[4]

Authors working within the framework of Islamic law, and its conditions for treating adat as legal, also tend to relegate Indonesian adat to the realm of custom.[5] The issue is more than merely a matter of words. The concept of custom suggests that people act according to their norms without reflection, simply because they are accustomed to doing so. This obfuscates the possibility that people may not always act in compliance with the norms, that norms may be contested rather than reinforced, or that norms are used strategically rather than out of sheer habit or in deference.

Criticism towards "weak legal pluralism" is only selectively directed against the centralist ideology of state law. This obscures the fact that folk, customary and religious legal systems may contain similar, equally centralist ideologies. Sharia (Islamic law) has its own conditionality clauses for the recognition of adat or *urf* (custom) as legal, as do some adat systems. Among the Minangkabau in West Sumatra, the question as to whether adat dominates Islam, or vice versa, has been a major political and legal issue for almost two centuries. Proponents of these systems, religious scholars and traditional leaders may also generate their own normative constructs of the relationship between different legal universes, be that in terms of conflict or harmony, political equivalence or subordination, or of dominant and servient laws. For example, the proverb "adat basandi syarat, syarat basandi adat", meaning "adat rests on the sharia and the sharia rests on adat", expressed the deep wish to see the two normative systems as fundamentally equal and compatible. Since the 1970s the proverb is mainly used in a changed form as "adat basandi syarat, syarat basandi kitabullah", or "adat rests on the sharia and the sharia rests on the Qur'an", which is an indication of a more unequal relationship in which Islam is considered higher in hierarchy. According to another saying, Minangkabau consists of "three intertwined threads", expressing the conviction that the Minangkabau identity hinges on three intertwined normative systems — adat, Islam and the state.[6] The important point is that within the same polity one may encounter a variety of normative constructs describing the interrelationships between existing normative orders. These relationships are established through state legislations and court rulings, not just by state agents but "in many rooms" (Galanter 1981). They may be different in the writings of legal scholars, legislative texts, court decisions, decision-making procedures and everyday practices upheld in villages. Individual persons or actor groups may clearly distinguish between the different legal orders and their choice may depend on the purpose or the situation at hand. Alternately, they may decide to accumulate validities by declaring more than one legal order to be valid, as often is the case in marriage. Or they may mix elements from different legal orders, not really caring whether or not such constructions are in line with any normative systemic requirements.

The Fascinating World of Legal Entanglements

A fascinating aspect of plural legal orders is the history of mutual influences, interactions and encounters of the different legal orders and their outcomes. A history of plural legal systems traces the development of the different orders — adat law, religious law and state law (and more recently international and transnational legal forms and actors). At the same time it is also a history of these encounters and of the resultant legal forms. In his discussion of post-independence legal developments in Indonesia, Hooker (1975, p. 284) emphasized that "one can no longer discuss law in terms such as adat and so on, but instead one must provide a framework within which these strands can be considered together". We could not agree more. Developing such a framework has been one of our primary aims in writing about legal pluralism in Indonesia and in general analytical publications. We would maintain, however, that the validity of this methodological imperative is not restricted merely to post-independence developments, as Hooker seems to suggest, but rather extends beyond the parameters of coloniality. Encounters between adat and Islam (or Hinduism or Christianity), their mutual influences, and hybrid legal forms prevailed long before colonization. Admittedly, the complexity increased considerably with the coming of the VOC, and later of the Dutch colonial state.

When tracing the emergence of such hybrid forms it is important to study the process and outcome, in the sense of Anthony Giddens' (1984) structuration theory. The plural legal conditions are a part of the context that, for instance, influences people to make donations, transfer a rice field, choose a marriage partner, or opt for a certain authority as a disputing forum — adat elders, religious scholars, civil, religious or administrative courts — as much as they are relevant for designing new institutions or for promulgating new regulations. In these processes the "language of interaction" (Lon Fuller 1969), or the medium of interaction, is contingent upon references to different legal forms. Often the parties mobilize the substantive legal forms of adat and Islamic inheritance law against each other, the judges ascertain "the facts" combining the procedural rules of evidence of the national legal system with adat principles of credibility, and the decision taken combines elements of adat and Islamic substantive and procedural law — all in one and the same process. The court may choose to formulate a legal rationale or justification for a decision using one legal order only, but it may also opt to combine elements of two or more legal orders.

One of the earliest combinations comprising elements of Dutch, Islamic and adat law that we came across in our own research were the testaments of Hasan Suleiman, the raja (prince or ruler) of *negeri* (city-state) Hila on Ambon. Between 1683 and 1707 he had made four testaments, in Dutch, at the office of the VOC factor in Fort Victoria, in the present town of Ambon. While it was believed that the testament had been prepared according to Islamic law (Dutch: *de Moorsche wetten*, the Moorish laws), in fact it had largely followed the Ambonese adat in a manner that would be invalid according to scriptural Islamic law.[7]

Such a hybrid form may represent a one-time event, without significant further consequences, but it may be followed by others. In other words, plural legal constellations evolve out of a series of decisions and legal acts rather than result from a single court decision or testament. In fact, systematic attempts of colonial governments to fit adat principles and institutions into the legal logic of the national law by reinterpreting or transforming them have had lasting effects. They generated a body of adat law that differed significantly from the adat law that was maintained within village settings. In the words of the Dutch adat law scholars, "lawyers' adat law" (Dutch: *adatjuristenrecht*) came to exist side by side with "adat folk law" (Dutch: *adatvolksrecht*), giving rise to a form of legal pluralism within the adat sphere.[8] Similarly, Islamic concepts and rules can take on local interpretations that differ in critical ways from the interpretation of official Islamic jurisprudence. And if the same concepts also were incorporated and transformed through government regulation, the result would be a threefold regulation. A striking example of this is found in the principles governing the payment, allocation, and distribution of *zakat fitrah* in the Moluccas of the 1980s (F. von Benda-Beckmann 1988).

Different legal elements come to be institutionalized in hybrid constellations, often by way of regulation or legislation, when inscribed into a single organization, such as the colonial *Priesterraden* (the contemporary religious courts), or the neo-traditional adat councils in Minangkabau. These new hybrid sets of rules defy a one-dimensional characterization as just "adat", "state" or "Islamic". How it is qualified depends on the characteristics the observer wants to emphasize. The Indonesian *Compilation of Islamic Law* of 1991 appears "Islamic" against the backdrop of state civil law or in comparison with adat law; but if contrasted with scholarly Islamic law and textbooks, it will appear as "state regulation" (see F. and K. von Benda-Beckmann 2009).

Hybridization, however, does not necessarily preclude the maintenance of so-called "pure" legal systems. In fact the two processes may go hand in hand. Hybrids may coexist with the pre-existing legal forms from which they are derived. One of the oldest examples illustrating the adoption of Islamic concepts to denote adat meanings in West Sumatra is the use of *warith, waris* (heirs), signifying members of a person's matrilineage. Another example is *hibah*, which exists in its scriptural Islamic meaning alongside its Minangkabau meaning indicating an adat type of donation. Adat versions of property transfer (*sando*) are expressed as *hibah* (*hibah laleh, pampeh*), where adat significations differ from Islamic law. In the village context, most people are unaware that their notion of hibah does not correspond to Islamic scriptural law, and they may claim that a donation is both an adat donation *and* a religious one. Persons well versed in Islamic law might make a sharp distinction between Islamic and adat donations. And when a dispute is brought to action, the court has instructions to enforce the rules for hibah, as defined in the *Compilation of Islamic Law*, which in turn differs from both adat and the sharia. In practice, courts customarily opt for the adat interpretation. The more general point is that a set of rules or concepts may in some contexts be attributed to one of these legal orders and applied as a distinct legal form carrying its own distinct legal substance and logic. In other contexts the same set of rules and concepts may be seen as belonging to multiple legal orders. That allows actors to pick and choose elements of each of the respective legal logics.

"Sharia Bylaws" or a New Layer of Legal Pluralism?

The boom in village and district regulations, including the so-called sharia bylaws issued in the context of decentralization and regional autonomy since 1998, has generated a host of hybrid regulations that have drawn much scholarly and political attention. These regulations have direct bearing on our discussion: on the one hand because they reveal some intricacies of the processes of entanglement, on the other because of the different ways in which such regulations are being interpreted. The chosen interpretive framework appears to have considerable social, legal and political implications.

Most of such sub-national regulations that are "reminiscent of shari'a law" (Buehler 2008, p. 66) and therefore are labelled "Sharia bylaws" are clustered in a handful of provinces, amongst them West Sumatra. Most observers, including ourselves, have analysed them to look into the reconfiguration of the relationship of civil society and the state (Buehler 2008, 2013; Sakai and Fauzia 2013). They have been interpreted as representing a heightened political role for Islam. But at least for West Sumatra this is only part of the story. Here the reconfiguration occurs in the context of three normative orders: that of the state, of Islam and of adat. As we shall argue, many of the bylaws cannot unequivocally be labelled as sharia regulations, but are also a sign of the rising political importance of adat.

The policies under the Soeharto regime effectively diminished the scope of adat to connote a shallow notion of culture. While adat's significance in matters of inheritance and property relations was kept alive, its currency in the public discourse no longer commanded the same influence and authority. Islam, though repressed, had provided the necessary idiom for criticizing the corrupt and authoritarian practices of the Soeharto regime. The greater freedom accorded to it in the wake of Soeharto's fall led to a simultaneous revitalization of democratic legal principles, of adat and of Islam. When people began to reclaim land that had been expropriated under Soeharto, adat became increasingly important because it could be mobilized to legitimize these claims. The same occurred in the public debates about village reorganization. That involved a return to a *nagari* (classic Minangkabau village) structure that had been initiated as part of the decentralization process when the *desa*-village organization, introduced in 1983, was abolished in exchange for the reinstallation of the previous (neo-)traditional Minangkabau organization of the nagari as the local government (F. and K. von Benda-Beckmann 2013).

The emphasis on adat in these policy fields was so overwhelming that some feared it would undermine Islam. In a countermove, as if to remind the population that "adat was based on the sharia, and the sharia was based on the Qur'an" (abbreviated as ABS-SBK), the movement calling for a return to the nagari paralleled a movement appealing for a return to the *surau* (the buildings of prayer and where religious and adat instructions were offered). It is remarkable that they chose the surau, and not the mosque, as the symbolic site, indicating that they strove not for Islamic values as such, but for a balance between religion and adat.

The same emphasis on the unbreakable connection of adat and Islam also characterizes many village and district regulations. As a consequence of decentralization, districts, municipalities and village governments were entitled to issue regulations. The scope of their jurisdiction, however, remained unclear for a long time, as no corresponding legislation had been passed for implementing the laws on fiscal and administrative autonomy. They included morality regulations; regulations stipulating dress codes for women (and some for men); a ban on "immoral" behaviour and "societal illnesses", such as gambling, drugs and alcohol, as well as pornography. The Hookers have collected a great number of such regulations and have classified them as religious or *"sharia* by-laws".[9] These have been interpreted as a sign of the increasing importance of Islam (Parsons and Mietzner 2009). Hooker (2008, pp. 243, 264ff.) goes a step further and sees district and municipality regulations on proper Islamic dress code as well as those against "societal illnesses" as evidence that Indonesia is moving towards, or even has achieved, a fifth, national Indonesian *mazhab* — school of Islamic law.[10] Irrespective of whether one shares this conclusion, both the advocates and opponents of a greater role for Islam agree that these regulations indicate the increasing influence of Islam on public life and the legal system.

In our view this conclusion is too simple, because it does not do full justice to the legal entanglements of, and within, these regulations. It dramatizes change and underestimates continuity. The number of regulations of public morality may have increased and references to Islam may have become more pronounced; however, with the exception of the prescription of Islamic attire for women and the prohibition in towns against women going out at night without a male chaperone, intrusive though these regulations may be, they do not differ greatly in content from the regulations on public morality of the 1980s. But at that time these earlier versions were considered adat regulations. More important for our discussion here is that the Minangkabau of West Sumatra do not see these rules as expressing merely religious principles, but almost always as embodying adat values and principles as well. All village regulations are made explicitly in the spirit of ABS-SBK, and adat and religious values are invoked as being one and the same.[11] "Un-Islamic" behaviour is also taken to be in breach of adat, and adat councils, or the adat village police that have recently been established in many villages, sanction violations of the rules of conduct bearing religious overtones.[12] Parsons and Mietzner (2009, p. 205) have highlighted the technical-legal reasons for making such combinations and argued that religious tenets could be integrated into official regulations more easily if combined with reference to the officially recognized adat. This is an interesting argument but perhaps too one-sided and focused on Islam. It works the other way round as well, in the sense that adat values are reasserted in conjunction with religious values that find general acceptance. Moreover, when sanctioning authority is assigned to the adat councils and adat police, there is more at stake than merely referring to Islam and adat as a means to gain public validity. The fact that adat institutions sanction the infringement of the regulations could equally be seen as evidence that adat was becoming more prominent in relation to Islam, or that adat and Islam were becoming increasingly entangled, without one dominating the other.

In Minangkabau the simultaneous reference to adat and Islam also has to do with long-term negotiations over the balance between state, adat and Islam and within ABS-SBK. Islamic principles have gained some traction but this has occurred mainly in the realm of rhetoric and symbolic politics. In our view the regulations are primarily an indication of local autonomy. In most cases, villages and districts exercise their new autonomy relatively independent of recognition by state law, often in outright contravention of state law. We would agree with Bush's observation (2010, p. 191) that these regulations have mainly been a tool in local politics for demonstrating regional autonomy vis-à-vis higher administrative levels and for reconfiguring the relations between adat, Islam and the state at the local level. Our own research findings support her claim, namely that their influence was on the wane now that the new relationships had achieved a greater degree of stability. Since 2003 the number of religious regulations, in fact, has declined (Bush 2010), and their official legal validity is increasingly criticized by women's organizations, legal scholars, judges, and religious authorities alike.

Yet another point eludes scholarly attention when too strong a focus is placed on an emerging fifth *mazhab*, rather than viewing the regulations in the context of legal pluralism. We suggest that regulations concerned with moral values and public order be viewed in the context of self-confident village governments exercising their autonomous right to issue local regulations. To a large extent these village regulations, ranging from dress codes to the regulation of lineage head installations, marriage, pledging of land and donations of property, merely clarify or modify what had already been regulated under sharia, or adat or the state law. These regulations generate new hybrids that often coexist with older versions. The morality regulations are symbolically important, in particular, as a statement of the relationship between adat and religion within the local context. But regulations pertaining to property relations are of far greater economic relevance. The adat restated in these regulations generally does not differ significantly from the rules and principles we found in the mid-1970s. And, as at that time, they make little reference to state law and simply ignore higher legislation. They are primarily concerned with organizing the relations of authority between state-regulated village government and adat leadership within the village, especially in the matter of control over village resources.

What makes these regulations particularly interesting, notwithstanding all their deficiencies and contradictions, is that they have added a new layer of legal forms and hybrids to the constellation of legal pluralism. They render the relevant legal orders entangled as a result, in ways that are as much informed by the internal concerns of the village as by developments in the wider political and legal settings in which the villages are embedded.

Notes

*Professor Franz von Benda-Beckmann passed away before the publication of this book.

1. An English translation was published in 2007.
2. See F. von Benda-Beckmann 1979, 1992, 1997, 2002; F. and K. von Benda-Beckmann 2006*a*. By contrast, J. Griffiths (1986) and Woodman (1989) use a functional attribute, namely social control, and reduce the conceptual

barriers between legal and non-legal norms to a continuum of more or less social control.

3. For more details, see F. and K. von Benda-Beckmann 2006*a*.
4. If one defines law strictly as rules "consistently enforced by a sovereign state", as Burns (2004, 2007) does, then adat, by definition, cannot be law; it can only be mere custom. Davidson and Henley (2007, p. 36) call the concept of adat law "a confusing myth". See also Jaspan 1965; Hadler 2008; Hooker 2008.
5. Hefner (2000, p. 33) speaks of "endogenous custom"; see also Bowen 2003.
6. See Abdullah 1966; F. and K. von Benda-Beckmann 2006*b*, 2009.
7. For details, see F. and K. von Benda-Beckmann 1987, F. von Benda-Beckmann 1994.
8. See F.D. Holleman 1938; K. von Benda-Beckmann 1984.
9. See the table in Hooker 2008, pp. 266–67. See also B. and V. Hooker 2006.
10. The debate about an Indonesian *mazhab* has a history that goes back to Hazairin's call for a *madhhab nasional* in the 1950s (Hazairin 1952). See also Keener (2002, p. 110) for a discussion of Hazairin's ideas.
11. Also see examples quoted by Hooker (2008, p. 270 and note 33).
12. Buehler (2008, p. 279) reports for South Sulawesi that this role is played by "a semi-official shari'a police, consisting of barely disguised petty criminals and hoodlums". Buehler (2008, p. 274) also reports that *zakat* in South Sulawesi constitutes a "predatory tax" to be used for political ends. We found no comparable findings for West Sumatra, where *zakat* collection was not extended beyond civil servants and did not nearly generate the same level of revenues.

References

Books and Monographs

Abdullah, Taufik. "Adat and Islam. An Examination of Conflict in Minangkabau". *Indonesia* 2 (1966): 1–24.

Benda-Beckmann, Franz von. *Rechtspluralismus in Malawi – Geschichtliche Entwicklung und heutige Problematik eines ehemals britischen Kolonialgebietes*. München: Weltforum Verlag, 1970. Subsequently translated as *Legal Pluralism in Malawi: Historical Development 1858–1970 and Emerging Issues*, Kachere Monographs no. 24. Zomba: Kachere Series, 2007.

———. *Property in Social Continuity: Continuity and Change in the Maintenance of Property Relationships through Time in Minangkabau, West Sumatra*. The Hague: Nijhoff, 1979.

Benda-Beckmann, Franz von and Keebet von Benda-Beckmann. *Political and Legal Transformations of an Indonesian Polity*. Cambridge: Cambridge University Press, 2013.

Benda-Beckmann, Keebet von. *The Broken Stairways to Consensus: Village Justice and State Courts in Minangkabau. Verhandelingen van het Koninklijk Instituut voor Taal-, Land- en Volkenkunde*, vol. 106. Dordrecht: Foris; Leiden: KITLV Press, 1984.

Bowen, John R. *Islam, Law and Equality in Indonesia: An Anthropology of Public Reasoning*. Cambridge: Cambridge University Press, 2003.

Burns, Peter J. *The Leiden Legacy: Concepts of Law in Indonesia. Verhandelingen van het Koninklijk Instituut voor Taal-, Land- en Volkenkunde*, no. 191. Leiden: KITLV Press, 2004.

Chanock, Martin. *Law, Custom and Social Order: The Colonial Experience in Malawi and Zambia*. Cambridge: Cambridge University Press, 1985.

Davidson, Jamie S. and David Henley, eds. *The Revival of Tradition in Indonesian Politics: The Deployment of Adat from Colonialism to Indigenism*. London: Routledge, 2007.

Giddens, Antony. *The Constitution of Society*. Oxford: Polity Press, 1984.

Hadler, Jeffrey. *Muslims and Matriarchs: Cultural Resilience in Indonesia through Jihad and Colonialism*. Ithaca, NY: Cornell University Press, 2008.

Hazairin. *Indonesia stau masjid*. Jakarta: Bintang Bulan, 1952.

Hefner, Robert W. *Civil Islam: Muslims and Democratization in Indonesia*, Princeton Studies in Muslim Politics. Princeton, NJ: Princeton University Press, 2000.

Hooker, M. Barry. *Legal Pluralism: An Introduction to Colonial and Neo-colonial Laws*. Oxford: Clarendon Press, 1975.

———. *Indonesian Syariah: Defining a National School of Islamic Law*. Singapore: Institute of Southeast Asian Studies, 2008.

Chapters

Acciaioli, Greg. "From Customary Law to Indigenous Sovereignty: Reconceptualizing Masyarakat Adat in Contemporary Indonesia". In *The Revival of Tradition in Indonesian Politics: The Deployment of adat from Colonialism to Indigenism*, edited by Jamie S. Davidson and David Henley, pp. 295–318. London: Routledge, 2007.

Benda-Beckmann, Franz von. "Islamic Law and Social Security in an Ambonese Village". In *Between Kinship and the State: Social Security and Law in Developing Countries*, edited by Franz von Benda-Beckmann, Keebet von Benda-Beckmann, Eric Casiño, Frank Hirtz, Gordon R. Woodman, and Hans F. Zacher, pp. 339–65. Foris: Dordrecht, 1988.

———. "Citizens, Strangers and Indigenous Peoples: Conceptual Politics and Legal Pluralism". In *Law and Anthropology: International Yearbook for Legal*

Anthropology, vol. 9, *Natural Resources, Environment and Legal Pluralism*, edited by Franz von Benda-Beckmann, Keebet von Benda-Beckmann, and André Hoekema, pp. 1–42. The Hague: Nijhoff, 1997.

Benda-Beckmann, Franz von and Keebet von Benda-Beckmann. "Beyond the Law-Religion Divide: Law and Religion in West Sumatra". In *Permutations of Order: Religion and Law as Contested Sovereignties*, edited by Thomas G. Kirsch and Bertram Turner, pp. 227–46. Farnham: Ashgate, 2009.

Benda-Beckmann, Keebet von. "Why Bother about Legal Pluralism? Analytical and Policy Questions". In *Papers of the XIth International Congress on "Folk Law and Legal Pluralism: Societies in Transformation". Hosted by the Institute of Ethnology and Anthropology, Russian Academy of Sciences, Moscow, Russia, August 18–22, 1997*, edited by Keebet von Benda-Beckmann and Harald Finkler, pp. 25–29. Ottawa: Department of Circumpolar Affairs, 1999.

Biezeveld, Renske. "The Many Roles of Adat in West Sumatra". In *The Revival of Tradition in Indonesian Politics. The Deployment of adat from Colonialism to Indigenism*, edited by Jamie S. Davidson and David Henley, pp. 203–23. London: Routledge, 2007.

Burns, Peter J. "Custom, That Is Before All Law". In *The Revival of Tradition in Indonesian Politics. The Deployment of adat from Colonialism to Indigenism*, edited by Jamie S. Davidson and David Henley, pp. 68–86. London: Routledge, 2007.

Bush, Robin. "Regional Sharia Regulations in Indonesia: Anomaly or Symptom?" In *Problems of Democratization in Indonesia*, edited by Edward Aspinall and Marcus Mietzner, pp. 174–91. Singapore: Institute of Southeast Asian Studies, 2010.

Erb, Maribeth. "Adat Revivalism in Western Flores". In *The Revival of Tradition in Indonesian Politics: The Deployment of Adat from Colonialism to Indigenism*, edited by Jamie S. Davidson and David Henley, pp. 247–74. London: Routledge, 2007.

Fasseur, Cees. "Colonial Dilemma: Van Vollenhoven and the Struggle between adat Law and Western Law in Indonesia". In *The Revival of Tradition in Indonesian Politics: The Deployment of Adat from Colonialism to Indigenism*, edited by Jamie S. Davidson and David Henley, pp. 50–67. London: Routledge, 2007.

Haar, Barend ter. "Western Influence on the Law for the Native Population". In *The Effect of Western Influences on Native Civilisations in the Malay Archipelago*, edited by Bernhard O. Schrieke, pp. 158–70. Weltevreden: K. Kolff & Co., 1929.

Hooker, M. Barry and Virginia Hooker. "Syaria". In *Voices of Islam in South-East Asia*, edited by Greg Fealy and Virginia Hooker, pp. 137–206. Singapore: Institute of Southeast Asian Studies, 2006.

Li, Tania M. "Adat in Central Sulawesi: Contemporary Deployments". In *The Revival of Tradition in Indonesian Politics: The Deployment of Adat from Colonialism to Indigenism*, edited by Jamie S. Davidson and David Henley, pp. 337–70. London: Routledge, 2007.

Moore, Sally F. "Law and Anthropology". In *Biennial Review of Anthropology*, edited by Bernard J. Siegel, pp. 259–93. Stanford: Stanford University Press, 1970.

——. "Archaic Law and Modern Times on the Zambezi: Some Thoughts on Max Gluckman's Interpretation of Barotse Law". In *Cross-examinations: Essays in Memory of Max Gluckman*, edited by Philip H. Gulliver, pp. 53–77. Leiden: Brill, 1978.

Warren, Carol. "Adat in Balinese Discourse and Practice: Locating Citizenship and the Commonweal". In *The Revival of Tradition in Indonesian Politics: The Deployment of Adat from Colonialism to Indigenism*, edited by Jamie S. Davidson and David Henley, pp. 170–202. London: Routledge, 2007.

Woodman, Gordon R. "How State Courts Create Customary Law in Ghana and Nigeria". In *Indigenous Law and the State*, edited by Bradford W. Morse and Gordon R. Woodman, pp. 181–220. Dordrecht: Foris 1987.

Periodicals

Benda-Beckmann, Franz von. "Changing Legal Pluralisms in Indonesia". *Yuridika* 8, no. 4 (1992): 1–23.

——. "Acts of Last Will in Indonesian Local Laws". In *Actes à Cause de Mort – Acts of Last Will. Transactions of the Jean Bodin Society*, no. 62, pt. 4, pp. 115–43. Bruxelles: De Boeck Université, 1994.

——. "The Case of Legal Pluralism". *Journal of Peace Studies* 9 (2002): 3–24.

Benda-Beckmann, Franz von and Keebet von Benda-Beckmann. "De Testamenten van Hasan Suleiman: Grondenrechtskwesties op Islamitisch Ambon". *Bijdragen tot de Taal-, Land- en Volkenkunde* 143 (1987): 237–66.

——."The Dynamics of Legal Pluralism". Special issue, *Journal of Legal Pluralism* 53/54 (2006a): 1–41.

——. "Changing One is Changing All: Dynamics in the adat–Islam–State Triangle". Special issue, *Journal of Legal Pluralism* 53/54 (2006b): 239–70.

——. "Myths and Stereotypes about adat Law in Indonesia: A Reassessment of Van Vollenhoven in the Light of Current Struggles over adat Law in Indonesia". *Bijdragen tot de Taal-, Land- en Volkenkunde* 167, no. 2/3 (2011): 167–95.

Bohannan, Paul. "The Different Realism of Law". In *The Ethnography of Law*, American Anthropologist (special publication), edited by Laura Nader, pp. 33–42. 1965.

Buehler, Michael. "The Rise of Shari'a By-Laws in Indonesian Districts: An Indication for Changing Patterns of Power Accumulation and Political Corruption". *Southeast Asia Research* 16, no. 2 (2008): 255–85.

———. Subnational Islamization through Secular Parties: Comparing Shari'a Politics in Two Indonesian Provinces. *Comparative Politics* 46, no. 1 (2013): 63–82.

Fuller, Lon. "Human Interaction and the Law". *American Journal of Jurisprudence* 14 (1969): 1–36.

Galanter, Marc. "Justice in Many Rooms: Courts, Private Ordering and Indigenous Law". *Journal of Legal Pluralism* 19 (1981): 1–47.

Griffiths, John. "What Is Legal Pluralism?" *Journal of Legal Pluralism* 24 (1986): 1–50.

Holleman, Frederik D. "Mr. B. ter Haar Bzn.'s rede 'Het adatprivaatrecht van Nederlandsch-Indië in wetenschap, practijk en onderwijs', besproken door Holleman". *Indisch Tijdschrift voor het Recht* 147 (1938): 428–40.

Jaspan, Mervyn A. "In Quest of New Law: The Perplexity of Legal Syncretism in Indonesia". *Comparative Studies in Society and History* 7 (1965): 225–66.

Keener, R. Michael. "Indonesian Movements for the Creation of a 'National Madhhab'". *Islamic Law and Society* 9, no. 1 (2002): 83–115.

Merry, Sally E. "Legal Pluralism". *Law & Society Review* 22 (1988): 869–96.

———. "Anthropology and International Law". *Annual Review of Anthropology* 35 (2006): 99–116.

Moore, Sally F. "Certainties Undone: Fifty Turbulent Years of Legal Anthropology, 1949–1999". *Journal of the Royal Anthropological Institute* 7 (2001): 95–116.

Parsons, Nicholas and Marcus Mietzner. "Sharia By-laws in Indonesia: A Legal and Political Analysis". *Australian Journal of Asian Law* 11 (2009): 190–217.

Sakai, Minako and Amelia Fauzi. "Islamic Orientations in Contemporary Indonesia: Islamism on the Rise?" *Asian Ethnicity* 15, no. 1 (2014): 41–61

Vanderlinden, Jacques. "Return to Legal Pluralism: Twenty Years Later". *Journal of Legal Pluralism* 28 (1989): 149–57.

5

Mapping the Relationship of Competing Legal Traditions in the Era of Transnationalism in Indonesia

Ratno Lukito

When there is plural normativity, competition occurs between different legal traditions. This seems the direct result of the plurality of norms itself, which leads to conflicts of law, especially on interpersonal matters among parties with different legal traditions. The current direction of legal pluralism studies seems to follow this trend, where the competition between different laws existing within national law occupies the central theme. The state factor is here understandably dominant since the study is preoccupied mainly with the state's role in the encounters and its efforts in the process of conflict resolution. Be that as it may, the approach used in this kind of study is always characteristically top-down, where the state, through its formal laws, is viewed as the main agent for the resolution of conflicts of laws. In our view, however, this method puts too much emphasis on the role of the state and neglects the real societal factors which lead people often to take active roles in the process of rapprochement between competing legal traditions. Using a top-down approach in the analysis of legal conflicts will therefore lead to the dire consequence of overlooking many actors and stakeholders involved in encounters between traditions.

In the context of present-day Indonesia, the situation of legal pluralism cannot be described as a static phenomenon where the competition between different legal traditions is understood as merely a domestic, single encounter between state law and non-state normative orderings. Especially in this new era where transnationalization overwhelms the nationalistic trend in the development of national law, the encroachment of international norms in the domestic sphere appears inescapable, with the result that the discussion of legal pluralism should not disregard the role and position of international law in the country's legal system. The discussion of competing legal traditions should therefore not only include those derived from domestic laws but also that of international law, as it is involved in the process of national law making.

This chapter will try to analyse the current phenomenon of the encounters among different legal traditions in Indonesia, particularly in the era of transnationalism. At a time when many international norms unavoidably take their roles in the building blocks of the national legal system, a viable approach of state legal pluralism will be proposed. And this is what this chapter tries to offer, i.e., understanding the competing legal traditions in the country not only from the perspective of a static and nationalistic point of reference but from one step ahead, offering an active point of reference beyond the frame of national law. Thus, beside discussing the patterns of the relationship between different domestic legal traditions that have been so far established in the framework of state legal pluralism in Indonesia, the main discussion will be on the process of domestication of international norms within the local context. Here the emerging practice of exploring international mechanisms in advocating migrant workers' rights will be discussed as an example to support the urgent need for developing a coherent approach in describing the new phase of legal pluralism.

Three Models of Relationship

I have argued elsewhere that in the framework of state legal pluralism in Indonesia, three models have characterized the relationship among the three great domestic traditions of *adat*, Islamic law and civil law.[1] The state has successfully played a dominant role in the encounter, reflected in its function as the main agent of resolution when conflict among the competing legal traditions arises. Using both legislative as well as judicative mechanisms, conflicts in interpersonal matters between people with different legal traditions have more often been resolved harmoniously, benefiting the postulate of national law that works hand in hand with the ideology of legal positivism. Here although the state's proclivity tends towards the collapse of interpersonal law (*intergentiel recht*),[2] the emergence of real cases involving people with different legal traditions have led legislators as well as judges to create legal panaceas effective for arriving at resolutions to the conflicts.[3] Depending on the cases in conflict, seen from the macro aspect of national law, the three models of the relationship, namely legal acculturation, legal assimilation and legal compartmentalization, appear to become the models conveying the relationship between official and unofficial laws. All have proven to work well in the country's legal history to build positive responses when interpersonal conflicts resulting from legal pluralism occur.

The three models have indeed worked to dictate the relationship of the three domestic legal traditions. The model to be used is here generally decided on the basis of the degree of the relationship between the state law and those non-state normative orderings; thus, it can be said that it all depends on the extent of the role that the state can play in such a relationship. The general principle seems to be that the state, with its national legal postulate, should represent the prime criteria for resolving the conflict. The centre would thus always be the state, which works as the sole agent of conflict resolution; and this is inescapable since those non-state normative orderings are basically considered based on their role in the process of national law making. It is therefore safe to assume that the closer the domestic legal traditions are to the principles of state law, the greater the tendency on the part of the state to respond positively to the role of non-state normative orderings in its project of creating a national law.

The scope of the relationship ranges from acculturation to assimilation and finally compartmentalization, depending on the degree of the conflict between the state and non-state legal values found in Islamic, adat or inherited Dutch civil laws.[4] In the acculturation model, the state creates a resolution by directly adopting a certain non-state normative ordering and incorporating it in the national legal system. This is done mainly based on the fact of the domination of the adopted legal values in society compared to others. Thus, the resolution is created by the state by way of choosing the most dominant legal tradition to be applied in the society despite the consequence of demeaning the others. In Indonesian legal history this can be seen in the state's experience when dealing with the problem of plural penal law traditions. The plurality of penal law since the early phases of the nation state in the penal teachings of adat, Islamic and Dutch civil traditions had created an enigma in the process of building a national criminal law system. The acculturation method could thus be viewed as the best choice to arrive at a resolution, i.e., by making the Dutch penal law (as emanated in the *Wetboek van Strafrecht*) as the tradition adopted as the national system of penal law.

Although this strategy betrays the substance of the pluralism itself, it is the best choice that can be made by the state in order to avoid the negative effects of a complicated penal plurality in society. Two reasons can be mentioned here. First, as the sole agent of lawmaking, the state was of the view that the Dutch penal law was so entrenched in society that to withdraw that tradition would be betraying the people's perception of justice. Second, the character of the Dutch penal law as a modern and secular penal tradition was believed to correspond to the fundamental premises of the national penal law. Put differently, the acculturation model was here seen by many jurists in the new country as the best method to resolve the conflict, as it could help the state uphold the ideals and values of the new national legal system being created. The state is understandably dominant in the process of resolving conflicts and possibly in using the language of power in this mechanism, characterized particularly by the acculturation of the Western (Dutch) tradition of punishment in the everyday lives of the Indonesian people.

Unlike legal acculturation, which relies more on the dominant role of the state in the whole process of the resolution, legal assimilation seeks to implement the more peaceful process of bridging different legal teachings. This mechanism was used for the first time when the country had an urgent need to create a uniform marriage law. In this case the state initiated a dialogue between different legal teachings and did not impose any values in the process of seeking a resolution.

What usually comes from this mechanism is the act of combining a number of existing substantive laws in society into a single national law. Thus, in contrast to the process of legal acculturation where a dominant legal teaching usually takes over in a whole new national law, in the process of assimilation a number of different legal teachings proven to be effective in the lives of the people work hand in hand to create a new law. Legal amalgamation is therefore the epitomic method here since the creation of national law is essentially made possible due to the state's ability to assimilate different legal values to become a single new law valid for the whole society. In Indonesia, the case of the new basic marriage law (Law No. 1 of 1974) is the best example. This law entrenched the plurality of marriage traditions in society, and any efforts to acculturate practices foreign to the people did not succeed. Assimilating those different legal teachings corresponded to the people's sense of justice, and the state adopted many articles in the marriage law based on its ability to assimilate (through legal transplants) those diverse marriage traditions. As a result we can now see in the marriage law a number of articles which were essentially derived from different teachings on marital relationship found in adat, Islamic or Dutch laws.

The third type of the strategy is found in what we call legal compartmentalization. In this method the state is found in its weakest position vis-à-vis certain non-state normative orderings. The state's strategy is to accept that a certain unofficial law plays such an important role in the lives of the majority of the people that the methods of acculturation or assimilation are not capable of resolving any conflict of laws. This seems valid in response to an unofficial law having national scope but only applicable for certain elements in the population. Islamic law is what is at issue here. As a religious law embraced by the majority, it is a valid example of a non-state normative ordering which is so much part of the life of the society that it acquires a "national law" character, despite the fact of Muslims comprising only one segment of the population. Legal compartmentalization of Islamic law here means that the teachings of the religious law, even if not secular law, are adopted into the system of national law and that law becomes state law. Compartmentalizing Islamic law is using state law in an effort to implement Islamic legal teachings so that Islamic law is implemented as state regulation, thus changing its informal, distinct character of unofficial law into the formal and official structure of state law, but making that law valid only for the Muslim population. Even though Islamic law has largely been nationalized as state law to include all the different Muslim schools of law, this Islamic law should nonetheless maintain its character as a system separate from other legal traditions.

This strategy seems to be taken as the key method in legal pluralism in the country, thus influencing the country's legal politics. Legal compartmentalization is here seen as the best avenue in facing the reality of the persistent efforts of many Muslim groups in the country to infuse Islamic legal teachings in the system of national law. What is called by many as the challenge of Islamization of law seems to happen mostly when many Islamic substantive laws are adopted by the state and accepted in the formal framework of the national legal system. The ideology of non-separation between state and religion arguably present in the country's constitution explains the difficulty of the state to resist some Muslims' struggle for legal Islamization, with the result that all efforts on the part of the state to reduce the implementation of Islamic law in the system of national law have been unsuccessful. Although national law is in principle secular in character, the acceptance of Islamic law in the national legal system is not viewed as betraying the secular nature of the law, since the Pancasila[5] and the 1945 Constitution as its *grundnorm* accept the element of sacredness in the secular national legal system.[6] Thus, accepting the religious law in the system of state law might even be seen as upholding legal pluralism, since compartmentalization is by any means amalgamating the sacred and the secular into one box of national law.

Legal compartmentalization seems to have worked well in Indonesia, especially since the collapse in 1998 of the New Order, to respond to the uninterrupted movement of legal Islamization which has been haunting the country since its early independence. Through this method the state has been able to create a legal panacea to arrive at resolutions of conflicts that may arise between the traditions of sacred and secular law. Although this method tends to weaken the bargaining position of the state law in its encounters with non-state normative orderings — illustrated in its proclivity to accept the whole substantive values of Islamic law — the state has been successful in its efforts to muffle the explosion of the socio-political bomb of Muslims' struggle to Islamize the state ideology. A number of acts and administrative regulations have therefore consecutively been promulgated using such a principle of legal compartmentalization to answer the need to implement Islamic legal teachings in everyday life. We can point to such important regulations as Law No. 7 of 1989 on Religious Judicature, Presidential Instruction No. 1 of 1991 on the Compilation of Islamic Law, Law No. 17 of 1999 on the Management of Islamic Pilgrimages, Law No. 38 of 1999 on the Reorganization of Islamic Alms-giving, and Law No. 41 of 2004 on Islamic Endowment as the best examples of such a legal compartmentalization.

Seen from the perspective of legal politics, the three models above have changed the pattern of the relationship among the different legal traditions in the country. Before the newly independent nation of Indonesia started its process of state building, the competition among the three legal traditions had been between the civil law tradition embedded in the state institution, on the one hand, and adat and Islamic law traditions, on the other. The colonial state had a proclivity to perpetuate the Dutch civil law tradition as the logical form of lawmaking, with the result that the civil law was more prevalent than the two other traditions. This kind of dichotomy also seemed to satisfy the political need of the new independent state to create a secular and individual legal system free from any influence of Islamic or adat normative values; and this could be fulfilled by way of adopting the Dutch civil tradition as the logical form for the country's lawmaking structure and judicial system. Accordingly, the ideology of national lawmaking accepted in the country was totally secular and state-centric, since the state was deemed the sole agent of legal creation, refuting the institution of religion and the adat community. From that moment, law was epistemologically a matter for the state — not God or the community — to decide.

The new political landscape of the country, particularly since the emergence of the post–New Order era (after 1998), seems to have influenced the relationships among the three competing legal traditions. This is what we can see from the recent phenomenon where the old dichotomy, explained above, has changed to a new relationship based on the similarity of non-state law with the state's official law. The principle at work seems to be that the higher the resemblance of the unofficial law with the official law, the more probable it is for the unofficial law to become state law. This is why we now see the civil law and Islamic law increasingly being adopted as state law, while adat law lies in another camp further away. With legal compartmentalization, the Islamic legal tradition adapts better to the new situation of the country's legal politics than its counterpart, the adat legal tradition.

The competition of the three domestic legal traditions in the country during the last four decades therefore seems to have resulted in an understanding of the relationship where the centre has always been the state law, weathering the changing pattern that might occur in the encounters between different legal teachings. Whatever the relationship, the centre of consideration should be the state law, while the others are in the periphery and to a great extent depend for their existences on their proximity to the state law. This is basically the main principle according to which a certain legal tradition that is part of the lives of the people can operate within domestic legal pluralism. As stated earlier, the state plays the key role in the practice of legal pluralism, particularly when conflicts between different substantive laws arise and are in need of immediate resolution. A question arises however when the new paradigm of competing legal relationships in the country involves not only domestic normative orderings but international ones as well. Can the state always be the main actor in the legal resolution process when conflicts between different legal traditions also involve foreign laws permeating the lives of the people? Put differently, should we maintain the top-down/state-centred approach in facing the reality of the new wave of transnationalism inasmuch as the presence of international norms cannot be ignored in the current relationship among different legal traditions? I now turn to this issue.

Domesticating International Law?

In line with a wider acceptance of human rights as a universal value in a borderless world, the view of international law as an institution inseparable from the regime of national law also gains momentum. This seems to have been influenced by the recognition of the principles of "rights talk"[7] in the current political discourse and by the rise of democratization in almost all the new emerging countries so that the use of international law in the process of building their domestic legal system seems inescapable.[8] Thus, it is believed that international law must play a role in strengthening democratic governance in countries where the national law is receptive to the modern values of human rights. From this perspective the principles of international law are not limited to international matters but are in fact made applicable to many domestic issues previously thought not to be within the purview of international law. The old positioning of international law as a foreign legal tradition opposed to state national law has hence lost its grip. This change can only be achieved by placing international norms not as normative orderings staying at a distance from domestic legal values but coming in the midst of different legal values existing in a society.

This new trend however does not yet reverberate in Indonesian law schools. This may be the result of a long pattern of legal studies in many law faculties which treat international law as a peripheral subject. The study of international law has developed very slowly since the start of modern legal studies in Indonesia as it is not a subject that is the main interest of many law students. This seems to have been the result of poor access to resources due to the limited capabilities in foreign languages, especially English, as well as limited books and reading materials provided in law libraries. Unfortunately this situation has been exacerbated by negative comments from a number of Indonesian international law experts who express their legal nationalism.[9] Many of them may still believe that international law is a product of foreign regimes, i.e., the West, having no concern for the domestic problems faced by the Indonesian people, and believe that the adoption of international law principles would have no positive effect on the advancement of national law.

This view of international legal studies has also led to the treatment of human rights as something unrelated to international norms.[10] Human rights are seen as a fully domestic issue inseparable from national law, the approach to which should involve only domestic stakeholders. This debate between universalists versus relativists on human rights still takes place in the circle of human rights activists as well as among scholars in the law faculties. Human rights studies from the perspective of international law are also not common yet in both mass organization circles and universities. This shows the scepticism of many jurists as well as activists towards the role that international law can play in handling domestic human rights cases. As a result, human rights advocates show a lack of enthusiasm for using international law arguments or exploring the existing international law mechanisms when faced with many cases breaching the principles of human rights. They treat the cases from the mere logic of national domestic law, not because of their ignorance of international law mechanisms but more as a result of their narrow perspective on the situation.

Viewing international law as something separate from the domestic agenda has thus led to a situation where the international law system is not seen as the building block, but more as the stumbling block, of national law. This might be the consequence of having embraced a perspective in which the state is the only agent of lawmaking as well as the medium through which the resolution of the conflicts is reached — a state-centred view of law which relies almost exclusively on legal positivism. This will certainly impede any efforts by institutions, whether inside or outside the country, to improve the discourse on international law within the national arena, as well as efforts to have international law positively affect the advancement of the country's legal system. Particularly in the era of transnationalism, where the influence of international norms is felt as irresistible, the continuation of such a negative attitude towards the role of international law in domestic matters will only hamper the development of a modern national law.

Nevertheless, and remarkably, a few Indonesian non-state organizations have started to use international law in solving domestic legal problems. An example is the Institute of Migrant Rights (IMR), based in Cianjur, West Java, which was established in 2007.[11] This non-state initiative uses international law to improve national domestic law. The institute tries to show the relevance of international law to national law for effectively solving many local legal problems. Although it has limited funding, this institution has been very active, in particular by publishing many works on international law and human rights law from an international perspectives. In practice, though its main concern remains migrant workers' rights, IMR shows how international law mechanisms can be explored to support the local need of advocating migrant workers' rights.[12] This could lead to a coherent theory with regard to the need to domesticate international norms in the local context. Migrant workers' rights therefore represents a practical example of how to use the international legal system to resolve local legal conflicts.

The issue of migrant workers is indeed a complex one; it cannot be understood as merely a domestic issue of national law or public policy, but involves legal conflicts between the laws of people living and working in different countries. In the case of Indonesia, this topic has been one of the most complicated issues for about two decades. Even though Indonesian migrant workers are a good source of foreign exchange for the country — which means a significant source of state income — the state itself is seen by many as having been unsuccessful in its responsibility to provide good management, security and legal services for those workers abroad.[13] This situation is often worsened by the bad practices of many Indonesian labour agents who abuse migrant workers for their own economic benefits, for example by sending incompetent workers to certain destinations illegally or even by engaging in human trafficking.

The Indonesian government faces many complicated problems related to the domestic management of the workers. Although the government has created a special institution to deal with Indonesian labourers working overseas (Badan Nasional Penempatan dan Perlindungan Tenaga Kerja Indonesia, or the National Agency for the Placement and Protection of the Indonesian Work Force, BNP2TKI)[14] and a specific law has also been promulgated on this issue,[15] many remain sceptical as several of the problems continue.

There are two levels of problem. First, at the level of governance, the coordination between the different institutions is weak and ineffective. The main role of the BNP2TKI, which was initially intended as a coordinating body among the different institutions and departments related to Indonesian migrant workers, has unfortunately been limited mainly to the placement of the workers in certain foreign countries. In some cases conflicts of interest have occurred among the different institutions, reflecting mismanagement. Second, at the level of society, most of the migrant workers cannot really see that the varied state institutions can provide an effective public service or legal security for them. Most of the time the workers do not receive legal protection, particularly when in conflict with their employers. It is therefore not surprising that newspapers are filled with cases of mistreatment or harassment of Indonesian workers in some host countries, while the state officials mostly keep silent or pretend the problems are out of their hands.

To make matters worse, it does not help that the state does not treat the problems as matters relating to international human rights law, even though the problems also relate to other countries' norms and rules, especially those of the countries hosting Indonesian workers. Such an attitude is reflected very clearly in the reluctance of the Indonesian government to ratify the International Convention on the Protection of the Rights of All Migrant Workers and Members of their Families (ICRMW) since its adoption by the United Nations General Assembly on 18 December 1990. That is why, although the problems of migrant workers have existed since the 1990s, it is only recently that the government has adopted the idea of correlating migrant workers' issues with international human rights law. Now Indonesia has finally ratified the ICRMW, on 31 May 2012, no less than twenty-two years after the first inception of the convention by the UN.[16] Better late than never — Indonesia is now included as one of forty-six state parties to the convention. This kind of late ratification in itself reflects a common attitude of some countries trapped with structural and political problems in facing issues of migrant workers, including their common managerial weaknesses in creating a healthy and effective system of regulation. Many of them prefer to focus on the perspective of alleviating unemployment, thus are often stuck in the logic of market demands rather than thinking comprehensively about the protection of workers.

Ratifying the ICRMW is certainly one of the best ways to handle the many problems of migrant workers. In a situation where domestic politics and legal systems are not sufficiently supportive of the interests of the workers, the best option is to allow access to best practices in the management of migrant workers through international human rights instruments and mechanisms. And this certainly illustrates the point reiterated above on the need to use international law as a tool to create a solution to local problems. Together with the ILO Migration for Employment Convention, 1949,[17] and ILO Migration Workers (Supplementary Provisions) Convention, 1975,[18] the ICRMW can be an excellent international instrument for achieving the right balance between business needs for migrant labour and the need to uphold the human rights of migrant workers. The three conventions can also become good instruments to balance the rights and interests of destination and origin countries.[19]

In Indonesia the ratification of the convention itself has many benefits, the most important of which are as follows: First, it helps create a sound system of national migration law which can regulate labour migration in conjunction with the regime of international law. Second, it may improve the practice of labour migration by following international standards and improving the management capability of all involved parties and institutions, both in the origin and destination countries. And third, it will improve the bargaining position of Indonesia so as to stand equal to other countries in the world of international labour migration.[20] This shows very clearly that the use of international law can also be expanded to deal with many local issues. In this case the use of international human rights instruments is not detrimental to the domestic issues of migrant workers. It is even very positive, since many of the objectives of the instruments are intentionally created to support the laws and rules existing at the local levels; the process of conflict resolution can thus be strengthened by the use of international mechanisms. In so doing, international law is not totally separated from national law. What we might need to do is adapt the two systems by way of domesticating many international instruments and mechanisms at the local level in such a way that divergence between the two different laws can be narrowed.

The Approach of Legal Pluralism

The idea of narrowing the gap between international law and the national law of the state is built on the need to extend the efficacy of international law in the domestic sphere. With the increase in transnational relationships in the world today, the influence of international norms is no longer confined to matters outside the jurisdiction of the nation state. The above example shows how impediments to the management of labour migration in Indonesia can be solved using the instruments of international human rights law.

Thus, when conflicts occur in the case of migrant workers involving parties with different legal norms, the solution may be offered through international mechanisms. Problems caused by weak management of the origin state may also be resolved using principles laid down in the conventions the state has ratified.

From the perspective of legal pluralism, the case of the migrant workers represents an encounter between different legal systems, not just the domestic laws of the state but the international legal system as well. This kind of encounter should thus employ a new approach, not the old style where the state law dominates the other laws. The old state-centred approach in solving conflict between different legal traditions should be abandoned, or at least the scope widened to allow for more varied agents. This will entail at least two possible theoretical consequences. First, the "state legal pluralism" theory would no longer be a perspective that limits legal encounters to those domestic legal traditions existing in the milieu of the nation state — international legal norms that benefit peoples' lives must be integrated into the domestic normative orderings. Second, because of the steady encroachment of international norms on the system of national law, the practice of legal pluralism is no longer one of "weak legal pluralism" but one of "deep legal pluralism" where competition between legal systems is more unstructured and unbound, freer from the domination of state law.

The difference between the two theories depends on the degree of state domination. We can assume that, as a general principle, when the domination of the state legal framework is strong, the possibility of using "state law pluralism" is higher, but when the position of non-state law is strengthened, the "state law pluralism" is weakened and the framework of "deep legal pluralism" gains momentum to dictate the relationship between different legal entities. In the new situation in Indonesia the principle seems to work very well, since the weak role played by state law will lead to a proclivity towards normative orderings found from non-state sources (in this case, international law) in the process of conflict resolution. The adoption of international norms to resolve local problems should therefore not be viewed as an impediment to the national legal system but more as an enrichment of the efficacy of the internal law itself. The ratification by Indonesia of the ICRMW signals the emergence of a new trend where the rigid boundaries separating international norms and the domestic legal system can be abandoned, paving the way for a more frequent application of international law in the domestic lives of citizens.

The increased receptiveness of the state towards international norms to solve domestic problems is in fact inseparable from new efforts to reconceptualize state sovereignty in the post-modern era. Thus, if the early 1900s was marked by a rigid conception of state sovereignty derived from the perspective of control over territory,[21] according to which the state was the sole actor in the lawmaking process and thus the only legitimate institution to deal with legal conflicts, the trend has led to a new understanding of state sovereignty as an obligation of the state to protect the citizen.[22] In other words, seeing "sovereignty" more from the perspective of an obligation than a right of the state. With respect to international law, this implies a state's obligation to uphold the rights of every person to have recourse to international law mechanisms, even when the problems they face have to do largely with domestic laws.

This view is in fact consistent with the principles advocated by the International Law Commission (ILC) on a state's responsibility for what is called "internationally wrongful acts". Article 12 of the document entitled *Draft Articles on Responsibility of States for Internationally Wrongful Acts* explains very clearly that "[t]here is a breach of an international obligation by a State when an act of that State is not in conformity with what is required of it by that obligation, regardless of its origin or character."[23] The transgression of certain international law principles could entail liability and the imposition of a penalty on the state concerned. The state should therefore comply with those international norms and instruments by making sure internal laws comply with them. And indeed in many cases international forums can provide an effective remedy for any breach by a state. On the issue of breaching international law, article 40 states:

1. This chapter applies to the international responsibility which is entailed by a serious breach by a State of an obligation arising under a peremptory norm of general international law.
2. A breach of such an obligation is serious if it involves a gross or systematic failure by the responsible State to fulfil the obligation.[24]

And article 41 explains that:

1. States shall cooperate to bring to an end through lawful means any serious breach within the meaning of article 40.
2. No State shall recognize as lawful a situation created by a serious breach within the meaning of article 40, nor render aid or assistance in maintaining that situation.
3. This article is without prejudice to the other consequences referred to in this part and to such further consequences that a breach to which this chapter applies may entail under international law.[25]

With respect to human rights, Indonesia has in fact tried to recognize the importance of the mechanism of international human rights law in the framework of national law. The promulgation of Law No. 39 of 1999 concerning Human Rights was a landmark of this positive attitude of the state. Article 7 of the law concerning human rights states that:

(1) Everyone has the right to use all effective national legal means and international forums against all violations of human rights guaranteed under Indonesian law, and under international law concerning human rights which has been ratified by Indonesia.
(2) Provisions set forth in international law concerning human rights ratified by the Republic of Indonesia, are recognized under this Act as legally binding in Indonesia.[26]

Thus it is the state's responsibility to use any means necessary to protect, promote, uphold and fulfil the human rights of every person in the country (article 8).[27] In theory, therefore, both the national law of Indonesia and international law can work together to create a harmonious situation where the two systems have basically the same objectives; namely, to secure order, establish a balance between conflicting interests, and maintain stability in society. The two laws should therefore uphold the principles of justice and provide protection to the people. This kind of rapprochement is in line with the new trend where international law is increasingly seen as concerned more with individuals than simply states. This is what we can understand from many international law scholars who explain the need to support the use of international law for the advancement of individuals rather than governments.[28]

Such a direction will certainly lead to the emergence of a new understanding of legal pluralism in Indonesia. The plurality of law should now be understood not only as a situation where more than one domestic legal tradition can live side by side but also as including international norms, thus increasing the plurality. This will certainly create a new map of pluralism, since the variations involve the introduction of foreign norms from beyond the state's jurisdiction. Competition between different laws will thus become more complicated.

The situation will entail a new approach to understanding legal pluralism and, more specifically, the competition between the different legal traditions. The new approach must be free from state domination in addressing conflicts. It needs to be a more bottom-up, non-state approach. This new approach to legal pluralism is consistent with the new perspective on legal studies in which law is not limited to state-centric law but rather it is seen as varied and dispersed in its character, thus expanding the possible centre of the lawmaking process. Such an understanding returns to the core of legal pluralism — plural normativity is not limited to those legal traditions existing in a given jurisdiction. There is no state monopoly on law, and principles of jurisprudence mean that any law must conform to a higher law.[29] With this principle, the practical legal criterion of validity or prevalence is no longer indicated solely by the rules of a given state jurisdiction, but rather by the efficacy of the legal norm to deliver fairness and justice.

The pluralistic laws of Indonesia should therefore not rely on mere domestic legal traditions for their legitimacy, but on their conformity with the common criterion of legal efficacy in delivering fairness and justice. Based on this criterion, although derived from international norms and values, international law may become one of the normative orderings accepted as part of the country's legal pluralism on the basis of their conformity with the "higher law". Therefore, in the era of transnationalism, in conjunction with the decreased use of the state-centred method, legal pluralism is no longer based on the degree of similarity to the values of the state's official law, but more upon conformity with the basic values of fairness, morality and justice valid for all existing normative orderings. This kind of perspective will enable different legal traditions to live side by side thanks to the common denominator that can be used to bridge the gap between them.

How can international law enter national legal pluralism without disrupting the existing relations between different legal traditions? The introduction of international law will certainly enrich the plurality of norms, yet it will also increase the degree of competition between the traditions. The question is, what can we anticipate for this more complicated scenario of legal pluralism where international norms come into play between different domestic laws? It is here that what Abdullahi An-Na'im wrote on cross-cultural approaches seems appropriate. With this approach a resolution of conflicts between legal traditions may be reached, not by annihilating or denigrating the others but by creating a space for dialogue among the different normative orderings.[30] Dialogue here is important because the cross-cultural approach necessitates "the existence of [an] internal struggle for cultural power within society".[31] The possibility of applying certain laws in the country should therefore depend on debate among the people themselves. In the case of international law, its application in society will depend on the active involvement of domestic agents of power, not on its imposition by any foreign agencies. As An-Na'im states:

> This internal struggle cannot and should not be settled by outsiders; but they may support one side or the other, provided they do so with sufficient sensitivity and due consideration for the legitimacy of the objectives and methods of the struggle within the framework of the particular culture.[32]

As in other processes of dialogue, it is unrealistic to expect the total acceptance or abolition of certain values impregnated in a particular legal tradition. The current relationship between legal traditions based on the language of domination may not be successful in reaching a just resolution. Old methods such as legal acculturation and compartmentalization may no longer be the best strategy, since acculturation entails the forced application of the Western penal tradition. It also means the total abolition of other penal law traditions. And the compartmentalization method creates an unhealthy legal segregation, with the dominant law interpreting the whole culture — in this case the uniform interpretation of Islamic law working for the whole Muslim community. In contrast, assimilation would be viewed as the best method of conflict resolution since it encourages internal cultural discourse and cross-cultural dialogue between different understandings of law in order to reach a resolution. And following An-Na'im, this should be done while keeping at least two considerations in mind: first, "it is necessary to safeguard the personal integrity and human identity of the individual";[33] and second, we should be aware of the dangers of cultural imperialism that may be involved in encounters between competing legal traditions. Any resolution resulting from such legal encounters should thus be coloured by fair and equal relationships, the result of which will not disrupt but strengthen the plurality itself, with the hope of building a prosperous legal system.

Conclusion

I have argued here that we cannot in today's Indonesia continue with the old state-centred approach to the relationship between different legal traditions. One can no longer understand legal pluralism merely as top-down, with the state's official law viewed as the main variable dominating the legal encounters between the traditions. Legal acculturation, assimilation and compartmentalization, as the three methods of relationship among the competing legal traditions of adat, Islamic and civil law, seem no longer sufficient, given the new trend in Indonesian law where international norms unavoidably influence the landscape of the country's legal pluralism.

In the current situation, where transnationalization becomes the common method of relationship between people with different legal traditions, the influence of international law in a national legal jurisdiction enriches legal pluralism — legal pluralism can no longer be limited to encounters between domestic legal traditions. The failure of the state to provide good management and legal safety for Indonesian migrant workers is a good lesson of how a narrow perspective on the issue, by treating it as unrelated to international human rights law, has dire consequences and may imply a breach of international law. This proves the inseparability of international law and the national legal system. The presence of international law in the national jurisdiction expands competition between existing normative orderings in society so as to create a new landscape of legal plurality.

This involves a new perspective on the problem of legal competition in the new milieu of legal pluralism. First, in the relationship between different legal traditions, bottom-up and non-state dimensions of law should be employed to understand deeply the character of the competition. This will entail the emergence of a broader scope in finding the resolution needed in cases of conflict. Second, building a rule according to a higher law should be a new orientation in the jurisprudence of legal pluralism in Indonesia. With this principle, all normative orderings existing in the lives of the people may be accepted on the basis of their conformity with the higher law, i.e., the universal principles of fairness, morality and justice, and not on their proximity with the character and logic of the official law. Third, related to the previous points, the new perspective of legal pluralism necessitates a new method. It is here that Abdullahi An-Na'im's cross-cultural approach in the standards of human rights law can be applied to understand the character of this new phase of legal pluralism. Enlightened by this approach, the method of conflict resolution between different legal traditions is reflected in its proclivity not to totally abolish or to accept a certain normative ordering, but rather to engage in a dialogue among those different traditions and allow an internal struggle in order to avoid a cultural imposition from without. Following this logic, legal assimilation seems to be a better alternative for the new pattern of legal pluralism compared to the old methods of legal acculturation or compartmentalization, but this assimilation should not be state driven.

Notes

1. See mainly in Ratno Lukito, *Legal Pluralism in Indonesia: Bridging the Unbridgeable* (New York: Routledge, 2013), esp. "Theoretical Reflections", pp 198–209.
2. *Intergentiel recht* is the Dutch term for interpersonal law used by the Dutch colonial government to manage conflicts of interpersonal matters that occurred in the Dutch East Indies. On the Dutch system of the

intergentiel recht, see R.D. Kollewijn, *Intergentiel Recht: Verzamelde Opstellen over Intergentiel Privaatrecht* (Bandung: 'S-Gravenhage, 1955). On the collapse of *intergentiel recht* in Indonesia, see Sudargo Gautama, *Hukum Antar Tata Hukum (Kumpulan Karangan)* (Bandung: Alumni, 1992), pp. 79–136.

3. Lukito, *Legal Pluralism*, pp. 137–97.

4. Lukito, *Legal Pluralism*, pp. 198–202.

5. Pancasila is the official philosophical foundation of the Indonesian state, comprising five principles: (1) Belief in the one and only God; (2) Just and civilized humanity; (3) The unity of Indonesia; (4) Democracy guided by the inner wisdom in the unanimity arising out of deliberations amongst representatives; and (5) Social justice for all of the people of Indonesia.

6. See Ratno Lukito, "Resisting the *Inbetweenness*: State Identity and the Current Islamization of Law in Indonesia", unpublished paper written as part of the postdoctoral research programme under the auspices of SPIN-KNAW, the Netherlands, 2009–11.

7. On the "rights talk", see in general Mary Ann Glendon, *Rights Talk: The Impoverishment of Political Discourse* (New York: The Free Press, 1991), esp. pp. 47–75.

8. Pranoto Iskandar, "Pemanfaatan Hukum Internasional dalam Tata-Kelola Migrasi Ketenagakerjaan di Indonesia: Sebuah Tinjauan Umum", in *Standar International Migrasi Ketenagakerjaan Berbasis HAM*, edited by Pranoto Iskandar (Cianjur: IMR Press, 2011), p. 5.

9. See what Professor Hikmahanto Juwana from the Faculty of Law, University of Indonesia, has said about international law as "the law of the jungle" (*Hukum Rimba*). I quoted this from Pranoto Iskandar, "Pemanfaatan Hukum International", p. 31. See also <http://hizbut-tahrir.or.id/2009/01/28/hikmahanto-juwana-phd-hukum-internasional-menjadi-hukum-rimba/>; <http://www.hukumonline.com/berita/baca/hol7797/hukum-internasional-tidak-berpihak-kepada-yang-lemah> (accessed 24 September 2015).

10. Pranoto Iskandar, "Pemanfaatan Hukum Internasional", pp. 32–33.

11. Interview with Pranoto Iskandar, Director of the Institute of Migrant Rights, Yogyakarta, 10 August 2012.

12. Interview with Pranoto Iskandar, Yogyakarta, 25 August 2012.

13. See Anita Rachman, "Indonesia's Unsung Heroes Remain Vulnerable in Foreign Lands", *Jakarta Globe*, 24 June 2012.

14. See their website at <http://bnp2tki.go.id/>.

15. Law No. 39 of 2004 on the Placement and Protection of Indonesian Workers Abroad. The Law can be accessed at <http://www.hukumonline.com>.

16. See Human Rights Watch, "Indonesia: Parliament Approves Migrant Workers Convention" <http://www.hrw.org/news/2012/04/12/indonesia-

parliament-approves-migrant-workers-convention> (accessed 27 August 2012).

17. Convention Concerning Migration for Employment (Revised 1949), adopted in Geneva, 32nd ILC session, 1 July 1949. Entered into force on 22 January 1952.

18. Convention Concerning Migrations in Abusive Conditions and the Promotion of Equality of Opportunity and Treatment of Migrant Workers, adopted in Geneva, 60th ILC session, 24 June 1975. Entered into force on 9 December 1978.

19. See UN Office of the High Commissioner for Human Rights (OHCHR), *Guide on Ratification. International Convention on the Protection of the Rights of All Migrant Workers and Members of Their Families*, April 2009 <http://www.refworld.org/docid/4a09710a2.html> (accessed 14 September 2015). The importance of those instruments is described as follows at pp. 6–7:

   (1) ...provide a comprehensive rights-based definition and legal basis for national policy and practice regarding international migrant workers and their family members.

   (2) ...provide common minimum norms for national legislation.

   (3) ...serve as tools to encourage States to establish or improve national legislation in harmony with international standards.

   (4) ...go well beyond providing a human rights framework and add up to a comprehensive agenda for national policy covering many major aspects of governing labour migration.

   (5) ...define a clear agenda for consultation and cooperation among States on labour migration policy formulation, exchange of information, providing information to migrants, orderly return and reintegration, etc.

   (6) ...provide explicit measures to prevent and eliminate the exploitation of migrant workers and members of their families, including an end to their unauthorised or clandestine movements and to irregular or undocumented situations.

   (7) ...reflect evolution of legal standards over the last half century that progressively extended recognition of certain basic rights to all migrant workers; further rights having been recognised specifically for authorised migrant workers and members of their families, notably equality of treatment with nationals of states of employment in a number of areas. The Conventions reflect the anticipation by its drafters that the increasing international mobility of workers requires explicit legal regulation to ensure the protection of workers

and their families not covered as citizens in their countries of employment, and that international cooperation and accountability among States need to be encouraged and focused by a common normative framework.

20. The International Steering Committee for the Campaign for the Ratification of the Migrant Rights Convention has also explained the twelve reasons to ratify the Convention, as follows:

1) To put in place the legal foundation essential for national migration policy to regulate labour migration and ensure social cohesion.

2) To uphold and strengthen the rule of law by ensuring that legal norms define the basis of labour migration policy, its implementation, and its supervision.

3) To contribute to ensuring that legal parameters define treatment of all persons on the territory of a country by setting the extent and limits of human rights of migrant workers and members of their families.

4) To signal that origin countries demand respect for the human rights of their nationals abroad and are accountable for the same standards as destination countries.

5) To reinforce the sovereign exercise of a State's prerogative to determine labour migration policy by affirming conformity with universal legal and ethical norms.

6) To obtain public support for and compliance with labour migration policy and practice by demonstrating legal soundness and conformity with internationally accepted principles of social justice and human rights.

7) To strengthen social cohesion by establishing that all persons must be treated with respect by virtue of legal recognition and protection of their rights.

8) To explicitly discourage the 'commodification' and consequent abuse of migrant workers by legally asserting their human rights.

9) To reduce irregular migration by eliminating incentives for labour exploitation, work in abusive conditions and unauthorised employment that fuel trafficking in persons and smuggling of migrants.

10) To facilitate the establishment of effective national policy by calling on advisory services as well as good practice examples provided by the relevant standards-based international organisations.

11) To obtain clear guidance for bilateral and multilateral cooperation for lawful, humane, and equitable labour migration.

12) To obtain international guidance on implementation of legal norms through the reporting obligations and periodic review by independent expert bodies.

(Guide on Ratification. International Convention on the Protection of the Rights of All Migrant Workers and Members of Their Families, p. 7.)

21. See A. Vali, *Servitudes of International Law: A Study of Rights in Foreign Territory* (London: P.S. King & Son, 1933), pp. 6–19.
22. See in general ICISS, *The Responsibility to Protect* (Ottawa: IDRC, 2001).
23. That is the text adopted by the International Law Commission at its fifty-third session, in 2001, and submitted to the United Nation's General Assembly as part of the commission's report covering the work of that session. *Draft Articles on Responsibility of States for Internationally Wrongful Acts*, in Report of the International Law Commission on the Work of its Fifty-third Session, UN GAOR 56th Sess., Supp. No. 10, at 43, U.N. Doc. A/56/10 (2001) .
24. Ibid.
25. Ibid.
26. *Undang-Undang Nomor 39 Tahun 1999 Tentang Hak Asasi Manusia* [Law no. 39 of 1999 on human rights]. The English text is taken from the Asian Human Rights Commission website. It can be seen at <http://indonesia.ahrchk.net/news/mainfile.php/hrlaw/19?alt=english> (accessed 4 September 2012).
27. Article 8 of the law: "The principal responsibility for protecting, promoting, upholding, and fulfilling human rights lies with the Government."
28. See for example in Philip Allot, *The Health of Nations: Society and Law beyond the State* (New York: Cambridge University Press, 2004), esp. Part Three.
29. The rule according to a higher law can be understood as requiring that a law may not be enforced by the government unless it conforms with certain universal principles of fairness, morality and justice, either in written or unwritten form. On the rule according to higher law, see M.N.S. Sellers, *Republican Legal Theory: The History, Constitution and Purposes of Law in a Free State* (Basingstoke: Palgrave Macmillan, 2003), pp. 26–31, 56–61.
30. Abdullahi Ahmed An-Na'im, "Toward a Cross-Cultural Approach to Defining International Standards of Human Rights: The Meaning of Cruel, Inhuman, or Degrading Treatment or Punishment", in Abdullahi Ahmed An-Na'im, *Human Rights in Cross-Cultural Perspectives: A Quest for Consensus* (Philadelphia: University of Pennsylvania Press, 1992), pp. 36–39.
31. Ibid., p. 37.
32. Ibid., p. 37.
33. Ibid., pp. 37–38.

References

Laws, Regulations, International Instruments

Convention Concerning Migration for Employment (Revised 1949), adopted in Geneva, 32nd ILC session on 1 July 1949, entered into force on 22 January 1952.

Convention Concerning Migrations in Abusive Conditions and the Promotion of Equality of Opportunity and Treatment of Migrant Workers, adopted in Geneva, 60th ILC session on 24 June 1975, entered into force on 9 December 1978.

Draft Articles on Responsibility of States for Internationally Wrongful Acts. In Report of the International Law Commission on the Work of its Fifty-third Session, UN GAOR 56th Sess., Supp. No. 10, at 43, U.N. Doc. A/56/10 (2001).

International Convention on the Protection of the Rights of All Migrant Workers and Members of their Families (ICRMW), adopted by General Assembly resolution 45/158 of 18 December 1990.

ILO Migration for Employment Convention, 1949.

ILO Migration Workers (Supplementary Provisions) Convention, 1975.

Law No. 1 of 1974 on Marriage.

Law No. 7 of 1989 on Religious Judicature.

Law No. 17 of 1999 on the Management of Islamic Pilgrimages.

Law No. 38 of 1999 on the Reorganization of Islamic Alms-giving.

Law No. 39 of 1999 concerning Human Rights.

Law No. 39 of 2004 on the Placement and Protection of Indonesian Workers Abroad.

Law No. 41 of 2004 on Islamic Endowment.

Presidential Instruction No. 1 of 1991 on the Compilation of Islamic Law.

Undang-Undang Nomor 39 Tahun 1999 Tentang Hak Asasi Manusia (Law No. 39 of 1999 on Human Rights). Indonesia.

Books

Allot, Philip. *The Health of Nations: Society and Law beyond the State*. New York: Cambridge University Press, 2004.

Gautama, Sudargo. *Hukum Antar Tata Hukum (Kumpulan Karangan)*. Bandung: Alumni, 1992.

Glendon, Mary Ann. *Rights Talk: The Impoverishment of Political Discourse*. New York: The Free Press, 1991.

ICISS. *The Responsibility to Protect*. Ottawa: IDRC, 2001.

Kollewijn, R.D. *Intergentiel Recht: Verzamelde Opstellen over Intergentiel Privaatrecht*. Bandung: 'S-Gravenhage, 1955.

Lukito, Ratno. *Legal Pluralism in Indonesia: Bridging the Unbridgeable*. New York: Routledge, 2013.

Sellers, M.N.S. *Republican Legal Theory: The History, Constitution and Purposes of Law in a Free State*. Basingstoke: Palgrave Macmillan, 2003.

Vali, A. *Servitudes of International Law: A Study of Rights in Foreign Territory*. London: P.S. King & Son, Ltd., 1933.

Chapters

An-Na'im, Abdullahi Ahmed. "Toward a Cross-Cultural Approach to Defining International Standards of Human Rights: The Meaning of Cruel, Inhuman, or Degrading Treatment or Punishment". In *Human Rights in Cross-Cultural Perspectives: A Quest for Consensus*, edited by Abdullahi Ahmed An-Na'im. Philadelphia: University of Pennsylvania Press, 1992.

Iskandar, Pranoto. "Pemanfaatan Hukum Internasional dalam Tata-Kelola Migrasi Ketenagakerjaan di Indonesia: Sebuah Tinjauan Umum". In *Standar International Migrasi Ketenagakerjaan Berbasis HAM*, edited by Pranoto Iskandar. Cianjur: IMR Press, 2011.

Newspapers

Rachman, Anita. "Indonesia's Unsung Heroes Remain Vulnerable in Foreign Lands". *Jakarta Globe*, 24 June 2012.

Online Citations

"Hikmahanto Juwono, PhD: Hukum Internasional Menjadi Hukum Rimba" <http://hizbut-tahrir.or.id/2009/01/28/hikmahanto-juwana-phd-hukum-internasional-menjadi-hukum-rimba/> (accessed 24 September 2015).

"Hukum Internasional Tidak Berpihak Kepada yang Lemah" <http://www.hukumonline.com/berita/baca/hol7797/hukum-internasional-tidak-berpihak-kepada-yang-lemah> (accessed 24 September 2015).

"Indonesia: Parliament Approves Migrant Workers Convention", Human Rights Watch <http://www.hrw.org/news/2012/04/12/indonesia-parliament-approves-migrant-workers-convention> (accessed 27 August 2012).

UN Office of the High Commissioner for Human Rights (OHCHR), *Guide on Ratification. International Convention on the Protection of the Rights of All Migrant Workers and Members of Their Families*, April 2009 <http://www.refworld.org/docid/4a09710a2.html> (accessed 14 September 2015).

6

Indonesia's Weak State Courts and Weak Law Fare Poorly in a Pluralist Commercial World

Gary F. Bell

The seminal work of M.B. Hooker on legal pluralism needs no introduction. As its title indicates, his book, *Legal Pluralism – An Introduction to Colonial and Neo-Colonial Laws,*[1] published in 1975, studied the forms of legal pluralism that are the result of Western colonialism. Hooker distinguished the plurality of sources of law within most legal systems from the legal pluralism of colonial and post-colonial systems which is characterized by the transplant of whole Western legal systems across cultural and religious boundaries. He wrote:

> LEGAL systems typically combine in themselves ideas, principles, rules, and procedures originating from a variety of sources. Both in the contemporary world and historically, the law manifests itself in a variety of forms and at a variety of levels. This fact has of course been known for a good many centuries and jurists have given it a considerable amount of study within their respective systems of law. The purpose of this book is not to repeat existing work on the diverse origins and legal ideas within civil law, common law, or

socialist law systems but to describe the systems of legal pluralism in the contemporary world which have resulted from the transfer of whole legal systems across cultural boundaries. This process began in the seventeenth century with the expansion of the civil law and common law systems outside Europe and reached its greatest extent in the nineteenth and twentieth centuries. The laws with which the 'Western' laws came into contact included the great ethical and religious systems as well as numberless varieties of unwritten laws. The result has been that large portions of the globe are subject to laws the principles of which are drawn from a number of widely differing cultures.[2]

M.B. Hooker pointed out what was in fact new about this form of legal pluralism: the prominence of the idea of the state as the source of law – in the Western concept of law, the state is the ultimate source of law and other laws can only apply if the state allows it. Hooker wrote:

> The form of political organization within which plural legal systems exist today is the nation-state. It is fundamental to the idea of the state that its institutions alone can be the source of law. Laws are valid only in so far as they are acknowledged in some way by the organs of the state. The law is defined, in other words, as a set of consistent principles, valid for and binding upon the whole population and emanating from a single source. The written, rational state system is the only one which is 'properly law'.[3]

Indeed legal pluralism is not a new phenomenon. What is new is the modern state's claim to a monopoly on law and, if one accepts this claim, that legal pluralism may exist only with state consent and only to the extent of such consent. Legal pluralism was to a large extent the norm, even in the West, until about two or three centuries ago; that is until the modern state, on a Westphalian nation-state model, started to claim a monopoly on law in Europe.[4] When the *Code Napoléon* was enacted in 1804, it was the first time that private law was singular (as opposed to plural) in France. Before that enactment, private law was governed by many different local, customary or religious laws, in a form of legal pluralism where the state played almost no role. Classical Roman law, in principle at least, was never imposed on non-Romans, who continued to enjoy the privilege of their own laws, the *ius gentium*. The West had no concepts of state monopoly on law and singularity of law within the state, until relatively recently, in fact until just about the same time as the West started colonizing most of the world. Therefore, indeed, legal pluralism in the colonies would have encountered the state's claim to a monopoly on law. To the extent that newly independent decolonized states continued that claim of a state monopoly on law (and pretty much all decolonized states adopted this Westphalian and Western concept of a nation-state claiming a monopoly on law), the concept of legal pluralism at the pleasure of the state and only to the extent authorized by it continued in post-colonial states. This is indeed what has happened in Indonesia for example — legal pluralism continued after independence under the Dutch model, with a few modifications of course, but without the state ever abandoning its claim of a monopoly on law.[5]

This led Hooker to speak of unequal laws within the plurality of laws — Western law was the dominant law (the law of the colonizer and, later, of the post-colonial state) and the other laws (Islamic law, *adat* etc.) were the servient law. According to Hooker, this relationship between the national legal system and the indigenous law has three main features:

> First, the national legal system is politically superior, to the extent of being able to abolish the indigenous system(s). Second, where there is a clash of obligation between systems then the rules of the national system will prevail and any allowance made for the indigenous system will be made on the premises and in the forms required by the national system. Third, in any description and analysis of indigenous systems the classifications used will be those of the national system. Indeed, we may speak of 'dominant' and 'servient' laws.

In looking at the phenomenon of legal pluralism within colonial and post-colonial states, M.B. Hooker therefore focused on the phenomenon of state-recognized legal pluralism — what has been the attitude of colonial states towards indigenous laws and their recognition; or, to ask the question differently, to what extent did the colonial state impose its Western law as opposed to allowing local law to survive in one form or another under the supervision of the state?

There is of course legal pluralism even when the state does not recognize other laws and does not enforce them.[6] When a Catholic abstains from eating meat on Fridays, he or she does this because of a legal obligation to refrain from meat found in canon 1251 of the 1983 *Code of Canon Law*[7] of the Latin Church of the Roman Catholic Church. This is law, but not a law that I think any state enforces (except maybe the Vatican on the menus of its refectories). Similarly, when a Muslim prays five times a day, he does so because of the requirements of Islamic law, even though that legal requirement is not enforced or formally recognized by the state in Indonesia, for example. Hooker did, in many other books and articles, study these other laws, whether religious or customary, even when not enforced or recognized by the state. But his original book on legal pluralism was about the interactions between colonial and post-colonial states and non-state laws, as well as the recognition (or not) of these local laws by the state.

This chapter will also focus on the relationship of the state with laws other than that state's law, but will take into account an important change that has occurred in our world and in the approach of most states to private international law since decolonization.

As far as world trade law and international commercial law are concerned, many things have changed in our world since decolonization. Decolonization has led to an increase in legal pluralism at the international level with the assent of most states. Let me briefly explain.

During colonial times, world trade took place within trading blocks — France traded with its colonies using its civil and commercial law, Britain traded with its colonies using its civil and commercial law, etc. The civil and commercial law was assumed to be the same throughout one's empire. This is the main way in which the common law and the civil law were imposed — as the singular civil and commercial law to be used in the colonies to facilitate trade with the "mother country",[8] which the French refer to as the *métropole* — a word I will use as I find motherhood to be an utterly inadequate description of any colonial relationship. Since the vast majority of world trade took place within an empire, there was little need for private international law (as it is called in the civil law) or for laws of conflicts (as it is called in the common law): within the empire it went without saying that the Western law of the métropole would apply.

After decolonization, with the opening up of world trade between parts of what used to be different empires, the common law and the civil law met. Whereas in the past what is now Indonesia used to trade with the Dutch using Dutch civil law, and Singapore with the British using English common law, now Singapore trades with Indonesia and there is no longer any presumption as to which law should apply to such trade and which courts or arbitral tribunals should have jurisdiction over commercial disputes which may arise. It should be added that, since decolonization, the civil law and the common law have also taken many different national forms — Indonesian civil law is now different from Dutch civil law and Singapore common law from English common law, and these countries have separate court systems with no common court at the apex.[9] Therefore, even when an Indonesian trades with a Dutch, the parties must choose between Indonesian and Dutch law, or maybe some other law, and choose between Indonesian and Dutch courts, or maybe other courts or arbitral institutions and tribunals.

This is repeated throughout the world and nowadays it is well accepted almost everywhere that traders have a very large degree of discretion in choosing the law that will govern their commercial transactions and the court or arbitral tribunal that will have jurisdiction over any commercial dispute. This is a relatively new post-colonial form of legal pluralism; one where national arbitration laws allow international parties to avoid national courts almost entirely and national rules of private international law allow the application of a law other then the substantive law of that state, and in some instances of any state (UNIDROIT Principles, *lex mercatoria*, Islamic law, Jewish law, etc.). Therefore there is more legal pluralism internationally as states relinquish, in part at least, the right to determine which law applies to international disputes and which courts or tribunals should hear such disputes. Most states no longer claim a complete monopoly on the determination of which law applies to international transactions and no longer claim that only that state's courts can hear disputes arising from such transactions — most states now recognize the parties' autonomy in choosing both governing law and jurisdiction.[10]

*   *   *

In this chapter I will first ask whether state law, in particular civil and commercial law of Dutch origin, and the Indonesian state courts are still dominant within Indonesia (Part I). After quickly concluding that of course they are still dominant within Indonesia, I will mention however that they are very weak compared to the civil and commercial laws, to the courts of other countries and to international arbitral tribunals. Therefore, in an international context where parties can choose the forum and the law (new commercial legal pluralism), Indonesian courts and law will often be avoided. I will show how the weakness of the courts leads to an increased use of arbitration with a seat outside Indonesia to solve commercial disputes (Part II) and how the weakness of Indonesian civil and commercial law (and I will here give only two concrete examples) leads to the avoidance of Indonesian law as the law governing international contracts (Part III).

I. Are State Law, in Particular Civil and Commercial Law, and State Courts Still Dominant in Indonesia Today?

There is no doubt that among the three main Indonesian sources of law — *adat* law, Islamic law and state law, including civil and commercial law of Dutch origin — state law remains the dominant law, and adat and Islamic law remain servient laws. I will not here make a full demonstration of this, especially since I can refer to M.B. Hooker's work generally and to his book on legal pluralism, but I will point to a few signs of the fact that indeed in Indonesia, even post-independence, law reform and the definition of what is law (recognition of servient laws) is dominated by state law.

At the time of independence, the Constitution provided that "all existing ... regulations remain applicable so long as there are no new ones adopted in accordance with this Constitution".[11] By saying that the old laws could be changed only by new ones adopted in accordance with the Constitution, clause II of the transitional provisions indirectly restated the dominance of state law, which alone could replace the laws in place at the time of independence — only state institutions can adopt laws and regulations, according to the Constitution. If the role and even the content of adat and Islamic law[12] were to be changed, it is clear that this would have to be through state law and regulation.

And this is how it happened. When in 1960 the *Basic Agrarian Law*[13] was adopted and purported to replace diverse local adat land laws with a uniform national legislation allegedly based on general adat principles, it was one instance of legislation by the state trying to replace what had been plural laws with one state law. The state was showing its dominance.

The adoption of legislation to allow Islamic Banking and Finance[14] is another example of how the state is still dominant over Islamic law in determining what that religious law can and cannot regulate in Indonesia. The same was true when Islamic law was given a greater role in the administration of the province of Aceh — this was made possible only by the adoption of special national legislation on the governance of Aceh.[15]

I realize that this is a very short exposé to support an important point — that state law and Western civil and commercial law are still dominant — but no one is in fact suggesting that state law is no longer the dominant law in Indonesia, and I therefore can assume that most would find this short demonstration sufficient.

There is also no doubt that state courts remain dominant and in fact have become the only available fora (as far as the state is concerned) to decide issues of adat law and Islamic law. The integration of the religious courts in the same state court hierarchy as all the other courts in Indonesia[16] completed the dominance of state courts over adat and Islamic law.[17] The Supreme Court now has jurisdiction over, and hears appeals from, the religious courts, and therefore the state court apparatus has the last word on all servient laws.

The real issue of this chapter however is not whether the state courts and the state law are dominant within Indonesia. This chapter looks at the international commercial legal pluralism that comes from the fact that commercial parties in international trade are now allowed to choose both law and forum. How will Indonesian courts and law fare in that context?[18]

II. How the Weakness of the Courts and their Application of the Arbitration Law Lead to a Choice of Arbitration outside Indonesia

The Weakness of Indonesian Courts Generally

This chapter will not demonstrate the weakness of Indonesian courts in any detail, and will assume that this is common knowledge. It is indeed common knowledge among scholars of Indonesian law and among Indonesians generally that most state courts in Indonesia (with the possible exception of the Constitutional Court[19]) are weak and problematic. This has been documented in detail elsewhere.[20] I have, for example, written elsewhere[21] about the ordinary courts:

> It is sad to report that there is widespread agreement in Indonesia that the court system and judiciary is in dire need of reform. Even though there are many good and honest judges throughout the country, the reputation of the courts is one where corruption is too common,[22] where competence and fairness are not always as high as they should be. Some even talk of the Supreme Court as a case of institutional collapse.[23] Not all the judges are to blame nor should the blame be entirely on the judges. After independence and before 1998, the judiciary was not entirely independent. For example, art 19 of *Law 19 of 1964 on Judicial Power* was used to grant the President power to intervene in the decision process of the courts. One should not be surprised that the judiciary comes out weakened from long non-democratic regimes which had little time or patience for the rule of law. It is normal that reform of the judiciary is now required in this new democratic era.
>
> The diagnosis is easy but the cure is not. There are about 7,000 judges with a staff of 27,000 throughout Indonesia.[24] One of the main difficulties is the lack of resources to provide decent salaries, working conditions and the infrastructure required to efficiently deliver justice. Some structural reforms have, however, been introduced recently through constitutional amendments and through legislation, both of which will go a long way toward improving the situation.

The situation remains far from ideal to this day. The courts have a reputation for corruption and incompetence. The district courts, high courts and Supreme Court that have jurisdiction in most (non-personal) civil matters and in most (non-Islamic) commercial matters do not have a good reputation, to say the least. They are best avoided, especially by foreign parties, and it is therefore not surprising that international traders usually avoid the Indonesian courts and choose to resolve their cases through arbitration whenever possible.

The Indonesian Arbitration Law

In order to avoid the courts, parties to commercial contracts include an arbitration clause in their contracts, taking away the jurisdiction of the Indonesian courts and granting jurisdiction to an arbitral tribunal. Under the Dutch, arbitration was governed by articles 615 to 651 of the colonial regulation on civil procedure applicable to Europeans, the *Reglement op de Burgerlijke Rechtsvordering*, known under its Dutch abbreviation as "Rv".[25] Arbitration was not provided for in the regulation on civil procedure applicable to non-Europeans, the *Herziene Indonesisch Reglement* (known as "HIR").[26] At the time of independence, the Rv was abandoned in favour of the HIR applicable to the local populations, and therefore it became unclear and uncertain how arbitration was regulated under Indonesian law, although it seems that, de facto, the articles of the old Rv continued to be applied by the courts even though they had been repealed.[27]

Under the Dutch (and under the Rv to the extent that it was applied de facto after independence) the law made no mention of international arbitration and the recognition and enforcement of foreign awards. The arbitration which the Rv contemplated seemed to have been strictly domestic and supervised by state courts (though in principle the courts would not have jurisdiction to decide any substantive issue).

The adoption of a new Arbitration Law in 1999[28] made it clear that foreign arbitration was also an option by allowing the recognition and enforcement of foreign awards in Indonesia.[29] That new legislation governs both domestic and international arbitration. Very importantly, it states at article 3 that "the District Court has no jurisdiction to try disputes between parties bound by an arbitration agreement".[30] Therefore the law clearly allows parties to an arbitration agreement to avoid a trial in the Indonesian courts.

There would be two options under the law: arbitration within Indonesia and arbitration outside Indonesia, since the Arbitration Law codifies the rules regarding the recognition and enforcement of foreign awards.[31]

Indonesian Courts' Interventions in Arbitrations Whether the Arbitral Seat is Inside or Outside Indonesia

It is well accepted throughout the world that by choosing arbitration, parties to an arbitration agreement choose to take away the jurisdiction of any national court over the substance of the dispute and choose to forgo any appeal to any national court of law on the substance of the dispute.[32] Even if arbitrators obviously misapply the governing law, the awards will stand and there will be no appeal. This is also accepted in Indonesia, at least in principle, in the Arbitration Law,[33] if not always in practice.

It is also accepted everywhere that, when the seat of the arbitration is within a certain country, the courts of that country will have a residual role in supervising the arbitral process and the validity of the award. Also, when a party seeks to enforce a foreign award (seat outside the country) in a given country, the courts of that country have a residual role: they could refuse enforcement if the foreign award is deficient in one of a very limited number of ways. By choosing the seat of an arbitration, one chooses the national court that will have a supervisory role over the process and the validity of awards. For example, if Indonesian parties choose Singapore as the seat of their arbitration, Singapore's arbitration law, not the Indonesian Arbitration law, will apply to all issues relating to the constitution of the tribunal, the validity of the arbitration agreement and the jurisdiction of the tribunal. In addition, it will be the Singapore courts, not the Indonesian courts, which will have jurisdiction over these matters. The Indonesian court could not intervene in an arbitration seated outside Indonesia.

The only role an Indonesian court may play with respect to a foreign-seated arbitration is, in principle, at the time of the recognition and enforcement of the award. If a party seeks to enforce in Indonesia an arbitral award issued by a tribunal seated in Singapore, an Indonesian court could refuse to recognize and enforce that award for a limited number of reasons (there should be no review of the substance of the case). For example, it could refuse to enforce an award that violates Indonesian public order.[34] But in principle it should be very difficult and rare for the courts in Indonesia to refuse enforcement.

Unfortunately, the courts in Indonesia do not have a good reputation when it comes to arbitration. They are known to intervene constantly, often doing so even if the seat is outside Indonesia and before any request for enforcement is filed. Schaefer and Mulyana wrote:[35]

> [The new Indonesian Arbitration Law of 1999] was enacted at the same time that Indonesia resurfaced as a prominent attraction in the context of international investment arbitration. In 1999, reports that Indonesian officials kidnapped the Republic of Indonesia's party appointed arbitrator to interrupt arbitration proceedings in The Hague spread throughout the world. This incident caused outrage (including within the Indonesian arbitration community) and further damaged Indonesia's already shattered reputation in international business and arbitration circles.[36] In the past, Indonesia's negative reputation stemmed from its poor record regarding the enforcement of foreign arbitral awards, despite the fact that it has ratified the United Nations Convention on the Recognition and Enforcement of Foreign Arbitral Awards of 1958 ('New York Convention').[37]

In the case of the so-called "kidnapping", the courts in Indonesia had issued an injunction against the arbitral tribunal proceeding with the arbitration. Although the above remarks concerned mainly international arbitrations, the situation is no different and may even be worse in domestic arbitrations: the courts in Indonesia are not arbitration friendly (to put it mildly) and constantly intervene to stop the arbitrations, more than would reasonably be expected in a jurisdiction that properly understood the need for the courts to avoid interfering in arbitration matters. The situation has somewhat improved lately, but unfortunately the reputation remains.

Consequences of the Weakness of the Courts – Choosing Arbitration Outside Indonesia

In a world where commercial parties have a choice as to jurisdiction and law, the weakness of the state courts in Indonesia will have quite a few consequences. The Indonesian courts may be dominant within Indonesia, but because of their weakness, commercial parties will often seek to exclude their jurisdiction by choosing arbitration. If the parties that would be most disadvantaged by frequent interventions by Indonesian courts have a choice, they would also seek to refer disputes to arbitration outside of Indonesia so as to reduce the chance of the Indonesian courts interfering in the arbitration process under the pretext of their supervisory role. It should be noted that choosing a seat outside of Indonesia also avoids the application of the Indonesian Arbitration Law to the supervision of the arbitration by foreign courts (foreign arbitration law will apply). Since the Indonesian Arbitration Law in many ways falls short of international practices and includes many oddities which may lead to surprises if not frustration,[38] most traders would prefer to avoid that law if they truly want the arbitration to be conducted according to widespread international practices.

It should be pointed out, however, that Indonesian courts cannot be avoided entirely if one needs to enforce an award in Indonesia (if the losing party has assets only in Indonesia, for example), but most traders who do not stand to gain by the Indonesian courts taking jurisdiction over their disputes will do their very best to avoid the Indonesian courts. Anecdotal evidence suggests that many important contracts binding an Indonesian party often have an arbitration clause that provides for arbitration outside Indonesia, and many disputes relating to Indonesia are indeed resolved by arbitration outside Indonesia.

All this to say that in this era of international commercial legal pluralism, the weakness of the Indonesian courts leads to their jurisdiction being increasingly reduced as parties chose other fora to resolve their disputes.

III. How the Weakness of Indonesian State Law Leads to the Choice of Other Laws in International Commerce

There are many ways in which state law is uncertain and weak in Indonesia. At the central government level, the legislation is often confusing, with different statutes contradicting one another and regulations that should complement statutes often contradicting them. There are often statutes that are to be implemented by regulations but the regulations are sometimes adopted only years later. The hierarchy of law is often confusing. There is even more uncertainty at the level of regional governments.[39]

My focus in this chapter however will only be on the state of civil and commercial law governed by the civil and commercial codes. Is Indonesian law in these fields as clear and developed as similar laws in other jurisdictions? If not, what is the effect of such weakness on the prospect of Indonesian law being chosen as the governing law of international trade contracts?

Weakness of Indonesian Civil and Commercial Law Generally

Unlike what happened in Japan, China and Thailand, where civil codes were adopted somewhat voluntarily as a way to "modernize" in order to avoid colonization, in Indonesia the civil and commercial codes were introduced as colonial legislation — the Indonesian civil code and commercial code are pieces of colonial legislation, almost entirely word-for-word copies of the equivalent Dutch codes. They were adopted in Dutch only. They were continued, in Dutch only, at the time of independence and were never reformed as codes or readopted in Indonesian. There are competing unofficial private translations in the Indonesian language of these codes, but none of them have been adopted by the legislator, and the codes are therefore still in force only in Dutch.

There has been a phenomenon of partial decodification after independence: some statutes adopted by the Indonesian state have replaced parts of the civil and commercial codes.[40] For example, the Basic Agrarian Law has replaced the part of the civil code concerned with immovable property (what common law lawyers call real property) and the new Company Law[41] has replaced the parts of the commercial code that dealt with company law. These new pieces of legislation, outside the code, are of course in Indonesian.

However, when it comes to international trade and commerce, the relevant parts of the civil and commercial codes have not been decodified and are still in force in Dutch only — this includes the parts of the civil code on contract law in general and on specific civil contracts (sale of goods, mandate, called agency in common law, etc.) as well as the parts of the commercial code on specific commercial contracts (commercial partnerships, negotiable instruments, etc.).

A common complaint one hears from some Indonesians and from some foreign lawyers (mainly the common law lawyers) is that these civil and commercial codes are very old and outdated, and are therefore not appropriate for modern commercial realities. Indeed the *Burgerlijk Wetboek* (the civil code, known in Indonesian as the *Kitab Undang-Undang Hukum Perdata*) is a statute proclaimed for Indonesia by the Dutch authority in 1847 (in force in 1948).[42] So is the *Wetboek van Koophandel* (the commercial code, known in Indonesian as the *Kitab Undang-Undang Hukum Dagang*).[43] One should note, however, that until 1992 the Netherlands used exactly the same codes as Indonesia. Even though the new Dutch civil code of 1992 codified the jurisprudence and doctrine and sometimes modified the law, it cannot be said that the old code (of 1838 in the case of the Netherlands) was unworkable and unclear before the new code was adopted in 1992. Similarly, the French civil code (1804) and some parts of the original commercial code (1807), which are for the most part word for word the same as the Indonesian codes, are still in force today in France,[44] and nobody is seriously suggesting that they are unworkable and inappropriate for modern commercial realities, even though indeed new drafts of reformed codes are presently under study in France.

The reason why these "old" codes in the Netherlands worked, and still work in France, is because the jurisprudence (court cases) and the doctrine (writing of law professors) have in fact updated and complemented the codes. When a provision of a code was ambiguous, the jurisprudence and doctrine would clarify the law. Sometimes the French and the Dutch would take different directions. For example, in the absence of provisions in the code for a general law of unjust enrichment in both France and the Netherlands, French jurisprudence and doctrine nevertheless created a recourse for unjustified enrichment (*enrichissement sans cause*) beyond the provisions of the code based on the *actio de in rem verso* of Roman law[45] — thus disproving the belief of some common law lawyers that judges do not make law in civil law. The Dutch courts refused to do the same, and it was only with the new code in 1992 that a general principle of unjustified enrichment was legislatively introduced in Dutch law.[46] Should Indonesia, which has the exact same codal provisions, follow the French example (unjust enrichment introduced by jurisprudence) or the Dutch example (courts refusing to introduce the recourse, forcing the legislator to update the law)? We just do not know. We do not have any indication of what the courts would do — no case law and no doctrine can tell us exactly what should happen if a case arose.

That is the problem — not that the law is old but that there is very little reliable Indonesian jurisprudence and doctrine interpreting and updating the law, and we are therefore left with no indication of how cases should be decided. Since independence, for all kinds of reasons, there has been very little published jurisprudence (cases) interpreting the codes, and understandably therefore there is very little doctrine commenting on jurisprudence and suggesting new interpretations. The doctrine and jurisprudence are insufficient to satisfy the needs for certainty of the business community. More recently, jurisprudence (in fact the full text of recent decisions) is being made available directly on the Internet, but without selection and classification, and it is therefore difficult to use as there is just too much, and the important cases are mixed up with the irrelevant, with very few tools available to distinguish the two (other than a general word search).

Typically, when trying to interpret specific provisions of the codes we are often left with one or two pre-independence cases and no reliable case from post-independence courts. Some of the doctrine (the writing of professors and scholars) relies on more recent Dutch precedents, which are of course not binding and need not be followed in Indonesia. In addition, whereas until recently one could use recent Dutch decisions interpreting provisions of the Dutch codes as possible interpretation of the Indonesian code (provided of course one could read Dutch, which is now very rare among Indonesian jurists), this is no longer the case as the Dutch since 1992 have a new civil code (which also includes commercial law and therefore replaces the commercial code as well). The new code is quite different from the Indonesian code, and Dutch cases interpreting the new code cannot be directly used as inspiration in interpreting the Indonesian codes.

I have elsewhere compared in detail the treatment of the doctrine of novation in civil law doctrine in both Indonesia and France and showed that unfortunately because of the lack of jurisprudence on the topic in Indonesia, the doctrine is skeletal and lacks certainty and clarity compared to the French doctrine on the very same articles of the code (the French and Indonesian articles on novation are almost identical).[47] The fact that the codes are still in Dutch does not help — young academics are not really interested in learning Dutch, and therefore specialize in other fields.

I will add two examples of what I mean by a lack of indigenous jurisprudence which leads to a skeletal doctrine.

An Example from Commercial Law: Promissory Notes

Promissory notes are very important instruments in international trade and, whether in civil or common law, there are very strict conditions for their validity as negotiable instruments. For a promissory note to be valid, for example, the promisor must make an unconditional promise to pay. If a condition is attached, then the note cannot be considered a promissory note, and is therefore not a negotiable instrument.

Article 174 of the Indonesian commercial code lists seven very specific requirements or conditions for a promissory note to be valid, including "an unconditional promise to pay a certain amount of money". The beginning of the first paragraph of the next article of the commercial code, article 175, states "a promissory note in which any of the matters mentioned in the preceding article is not contained, will not be valid as a promissory note". Articles 174 and 175 are word for word the same as the equivalent articles of the former Dutch commercial code and of the present-day French commercial code.[48]

One of the issues that arises of course is whether a purported promissory note which falls short of fulfilling all seven formal requirements, even though not valid as a promissory note, could still be valid as something else, short of being a negotiable instrument. After all, article 175 states that it will not be valid "as a promissory note", perhaps suggesting that it may be valid as something else.

In French law the answer to that question is extremely clear; there is plenty of jurisprudence to the effect that a purported promissory note which is invalid as a promissory note can be valid as something else, and the jurisprudence gives many concrete examples. The commercial publications of the *Code de commerce* have many annotations mentioning specific court cases where the courts have held that the purported promissory note can be enforced as a promise or a contract, or can be seen as a recognition of debts (*reconnaissance de dette*) or as a *commencement de preuve par écrit* (beginning of written evidence [of debt]). The doctrine can therefore summarize the jurisprudence and clearly state what the courts will do based on clear jurisprudence.[49]

There seem to be no Indonesian case on point nor is there much doctrine on point. There are a few books on negotiable instruments published by Indonesian scholars, and some do say that a note invalid as a promissory note may be otherwise valid, possibly for example as a simple promise to pay, which corresponds to the Dutch and French position.[50] But, unfortunately, the authors cannot point to clear examples in Indonesian jurisprudence, since there seems to be no case to that effect. The authors, understandably, rely on Dutch interpretations of a similar article — they cannot be blamed for the lack of Indonesian cases on the matter.

It is strange that in sixty-seven years since independence there seems to have not been a single reported case interpreting article 175 of the commercial code. This will seem incredible even to civil law jurists from other jurisdictions, who would know of many cases interpreting the equivalent of article 175 in their respective jurisdictions that would have led to unequivocal doctrine on this point. In a field as formalistic as promissory notes and negotiable instruments generally, this issue would be expected to have been resolved definitely and unequivocally through cases a long time ago. All this does not inspire foreign parties to agree to have their commercial contracts governed by Indonesian law.

An Example from Civil Law: From Good Faith to Abuse of Rights, or Not

The third paragraph of article 1338 of the Indonesian civil code, which is word for word the same as the third paragraph of article 1134 of the French civil code, states that agreements "must be performed in good faith". There is therefore a general obligation to act in good faith in contract law. However, the French, old Dutch and Indonesian civil codes make no mention of a prohibition against abuse of rights.

The French courts developed the concept of abuse of rights from the concept of good faith — under some circumstances, insisting on one's rights would be against good faith and therefore abusive. In one of its judgements the Canadian Supreme Court summarized the evolution of the concept of abuse of rights in French law through jurisprudence and doctrine. I could not summarize more succinctly the evolution of the jurisprudence and doctrine in France, and I therefore quote from the judgement:

> The French Civil Code did not contain any specific provision relating to the abuse of rights. However, courts soon began to apply the theory. Mazeaud and Tunc, op. cit., at No. 557, p. 647, discuss the famous decision of the Court of Colmar, May 2, 1855, D.P. 1856.2.9 (Doerr v. Keller), condemning a property owner to damages for building a false chimney with the sole purpose of [TRANSLATION] "removing almost all the daylight left in his neighbour's window". Marty and Raynaud, Droit civil: Les obligations (2nd ed. 1988), t. I, at No. 477, p. 538, comment:
>
>> [TRANSLATION] This line of authority has developed widely not only for the right of ownership but also with respect to many other rights, such as the right to bring an action or to defend an action at law and to use execution proceedings.
>
> The evolution and application of the abuse of rights doctrine grew quickly from the beginning of the 20th century. It then became an accepted recourse in French law. The extent of that acceptance was perhaps best summarized by J. Charmont, "L'abus du droit" (1902), 1 Rev. trim. dr. civ. 113, at p. 118:

[TRANSLATION] What we cannot help being struck by in considering this question of abuse of rights is the increasing importance it tends to have in lawyers' concerns — and the fact that it has had this position for only a short time. Ten or fifteen years ago it was barely mentioned: since then, cases of its use have multiplied; in strikes, labour unions, dismissal in contracts of employment, the right of criticism in newspapers....

That application of the doctrine by the courts translated eventually into legislation as regards dilatory proceedings, the unreasonable refusal by a landlord to rent his premises, and an express limitation on a husband's right to oppose the exercise of a separate profession by his wife since it had to be justified by the family's best interests (Mazeaud and Tunc, op. cit., at No. 558, pp. 648–49).

Consequently, by the early part of the 20th century, the doctrine of abuse of rights had acquired its "letters patent of nobility" in French law. This trend appears even stronger today. One need only note the words of the eminent French jurist, Gérard Cornu, in Droit civil (Introduction: Les personnes — Les biens) (4th ed. 1990), where he states, at No. 147, p. 57:

[TRANSLATION] The theory of abuse of rights, of Praetorian and doctrinal origin and expressly set out in legislation in various specific areas (such as a wrongful breach by an employer of a contract of employment), is now an integral part of French positive law.[51]

We therefore can see how, notwithstanding the silence of the code, the jurisprudence and doctrine created the concept of abuse of rights in French law. There are in fact numerous cases which delineate the doctrine and therefore prevent any abuse of the doctrine of abuse of rights. Notwithstanding the necessary generality of the theory of abuse of rights, through a study of these numerous cases we can predict quite accurately when the theory will apply and when it will not.

The Dutch courts however refused to create a similarly general theory of abuse of rights, rejecting the French approach, and it was only in 1992 that the new code introduced the concept of abuse of rights jointly with a reformulation of the obligation to act in good faith (now referred to as reasonableness and fairness) into Dutch law:

> Article 6:2:
> 1. An obligee and obligor must, as between themselves, act in accordance with the requirements of reasonableness and fairness.
> 2. A rule binding upon them by virtue of law, usage or a juridical act[52] does not apply to the extent that, in the given circumstances, this would be unacceptable according to standards of reasonableness and fairness.[53]

What is the position of the Indonesian courts? Do they follow the French or the Dutch approach in the absence of a mention of abuse of rights in the code?[54] We do have a few cases in Indonesia, but not that many. And I am afraid that they are not entirely clear. If there is a radical change of conditions (hyperinflation after the war, deflation of currency value, etc.), can the court amend the contract or, more precisely, not allow a party to insist on the enforcement of all that the contract entitles him to? When circumstances have radically changed, can the court modify the contract?

There are some cases where the courts refused to use the concept of abuse of rights, even when the termination of the contract was due to exceptional circumstances, such as World War II.[55] On the other hand, there was another case where someone bought a piece of land before World War II at a certain price, the payment of which became due after the war, that is, after the market value had gone up multiple times. The buyer was to re-sell immediately for an enormous profit, which may seem like an abuse of right. The court however refused directly to amend the contract price, speaking only of a vague obligation to share some of the profits — it is not clear what the consequences of the decision were.[56] On the other hand, in 1955 "the Supreme Court [of Indonesia] refused to allow land which had been pledged for Rp50 prior to World War II to be redeemed for the same price, and instead fashioned its own formula of redemption. The Court noted that the price of gold had increased 30 times during the intervening years. 'Justice' it said 'required that the risk of currency fluctuations be born equally by the parties.'"[57]

On the one hand, pre-Independence the Dutch courts have refused to reduce restrictive covenants of an abusive nature[58] (and Dutch law applied in Indonesia at the time), but on the other hand post-Independence courts seem less reluctant to intervene, sometimes even suspending the possibility of enforcing an obligation.[59] Indonesian courts are said to have taken a much more interventionist approach in some cases, particularly of late, going as far as reducing the interest rate of a penal clause without specific legislative authority.[60]

The leading authors seem to have concluded that there is now a great deal of discretion exercised by the courts to enforce good faith, although the concept of abuse of rights is not explicitly stated. For example, Professor Gautama wrote: "A contract must be performed by the parties 'in good faith'. To insure [*sic*] good faith, the judge in a civil suit has power to supervise the implementation of the contract, and to invoke *principles of reasonableness and justice* in doing so. In practice it means that a judge is free to deviate from the letter of the contract if such deviation is necessary to ensure good faith."[61] Similarly, Satrio concludes that "[i]t appears that several decisions in Indonesia indicate that the judge, based on equity (kepatutan) can change the basic rights and obligations of the contract without having to mention many reasons and that all that is necessary is the opinion of the court that the content of the contract is not fair."[62]

I am not sure however that the position is that clear in Indonesian law. First, the jurisprudence is not unanimous. Second, unlike the many French cases which detail the kind of circumstances where the exercise of a right would be abusive, there seems to be very little guidance in either the jurisprudence (very few cases with only skeletal reasoning) or the doctrine (far too general). Again, as Satrio put it: "the judge, based on equity (kepatutan) *can change the basic rights and obligations of the contract without having to mention many reasons and that all that is necessary is the opinion of the court that the content of the contract is not fair*".[63] This seems to grant excessive discretion to the judges without the kind of detailed guidance one could find in an elaborate jurisprudence and doctrine. Of course, the concepts of good faith and abuse of rights will always remain to a certain extent vague and general, but one would expect a bit more guidance by way of examples in the jurisprudence and the doctrine as to when the theory of abuse of rights can be invoked. This state of affairs leads to great uncertainty.

Avoiding Indonesian Law Whenever Possible

Given the great uncertainty of Indonesian civil and commercial law, which is due mainly to a lack of jurisprudence and therefore also a lack of doctrine (without jurisprudence, the doctrine cannot predict how the courts will decide or even criticize the court's decisions), parties often prefer to avoid Indonesian law altogether, unless of course the uncertainty created by that law could work to their own advantage.

There has even been an instance where an arbitral tribunal seems to have done its very best not to apply Indonesian law, even though Indonesian law was the governing law chosen by the parties. In the twin arbitration cases of *Patuha Power* and of *Himpurna California Energy*,[64] Indonesian law was the law governing the contract, except that the tribunal was not bound by strict rules of law if their application was "inconsistent with the spirit of this Contract and the underlying intent of the parties".[65] The tribunal was asked by the investors to grant damages for the loss of the full predicted profits, even though only part of the investment had in fact been made. For example, in one case the tribunal was asked for full damages of US$2.3 billion for lost profits on a partial investment of only US$315 million.[66] The tribunal stated that given the financial crisis and the fact that the termination was not an expropriation where the state of Indonesia would stand to profit from the investment, "to extract the full benefit ... with respect to investments *not yet made*, in a situation where that benefit will greatly exacerbate the already great losses of the cocontractant, strikes the Arbitral Tribunal as likely to constitute an abuse of right inconsistent with the duty of good faith which is fundamental to the Indonesian law of obligations".[67]

Yet, when confronted with debate between the parties as to what that theory of abuse of rights implied in Indonesian law, the tribunal decided not to rely on Indonesian law after all. It stated: "The Arbitral Tribunal does not find it necessary to rule on either of these objections because in this matter it will apply the doctrine of abuse of right as an element of overriding substantive law proper to the international arbitral process."[68] Interestingly, the tribunal did not say that it was ignoring Indonesian law because its application was "inconsistent with the spirit of this Contract and the underlying intent of the parties" as authorized under the contract. It simply ignored whatever Indonesian law had to say on the issue of abuse of rights and applied a rather new and also uncertain theory of abuse of rights as understood in international arbitration.

Another interesting point is that it seems that the parties had in fact only argued abuse of rights under Indonesian law and that the tribunal could not come to a decision based on Indonesian law — it was only after explaining the opposing positions of the parties and their experts on the theory of abuse of rights in Indonesian law that the tribunal stated that it would not decide the matter under Indonesian law, as if it was unable to determine what the Indonesian law actually was. Had Indonesian law been very clear on this issue, one wonders whether the tribunal would have dismissed it in such a cavalier way.

IV.   Conclusion

The weakness of Indonesian courts and therefore of Indonesian civil and commercial law (which needs jurisprudence for its development) are well known. In the current era of increased legal pluralism in international commercial law, this weakness of the law and courts leads commercial parties to exclude the jurisdiction of Indonesian courts and the application of Indonesian law. Even if the parties agree to apply Indonesian law, they are likely to choose arbitration outside Indonesia to solve their disputes. This becomes a vicious circle — the best cases with the best reasoning applying Indonesian civil and commercial law are nowadays decided by arbitration tribunals who hear such cases *in camera* and almost never publish their decisions, thus contributing to the lack of cases on Indonesian law.

One can only hope that quick actions are taken where they can be taken. The adoption of a version of the civil and commercial codes in the Indonesian language could be done quickly and at no great financial costs. This would allow Indonesian judges and jurists to deal with their own codes with more confidence and aplomb. It may lead to young academics taking a greater interest in this field of law (more doctrine) and would facilitate the work of judges (more and better jurisprudence). There are legal pitfalls when readopting a code in a different language (which provisions of the code are still in force, which translation to adopt, are we adopting a new law or continuing the old one?), but these, for the most part, can be avoided, and whatever problems this adoption of an Indonesian version may cause pales in comparison to the problems caused by having the civil and commercial law in a language which almost no judge or jurist understands.

In the long term, however, the reform of the courts is the only real solution to the problem. As long as the courts in civil and commercial matters, including arbitration matters, are not up to par with courts in other jurisdictions, Indonesia will lose out in the competitive world of international commercial legal pluralism. This is one reason why court reform should be a priority in Indonesia. It is not however the best of reasons — international traders are lucky in that they can avoid Indonesian courts and law. Ordinary Indonesian citizens are not so lucky, and therefore I can think of much better reasons why reform of the courts should be one of the highest priorities in Indonesia. One can only hope that ways and means, as well as political stamina, can be found to conduct such a reform in the next decade or two.

Notes

1. M.B. Hooker, *Legal Pluralism – An Introduction to Colonial and Neo-Colonial Laws* (Oxford: Clarendon Press, 1975).
2. Ibid., p. 1.
3. Ibid., p. 1.
4. Rod Macdonald once wrote: "[L]egal pluralism is really not novel. Until the seventeenth century in Europe the idea of a territorial State (later associated more with blood than with geography in the phrase "nation-state") claiming an exclusive capacity to regulate everyday activity would have been thought bizarre. Neither the Romans (with, inter alia, their conceptions of *jus civile* and *jus gentium*) nor the medieval kings of England (who tolerated both customary law of the realm and of localities,

and divergent manorial, ecclesiastical and mercantile legal systems) claimed a monopoly on law and normativity. What is more, even into the nineteenth century, the legal and political élites of England and France, for example, did not see law as singular. That is, only with codification on the continent and with the Judicature Acts in common law jurisdictions did the image of a single, State-managed legal system begin to emerge." Roderick A. Macdonald, "Metaphors of Multiplicity: Civil Society, Regimes and Legal Pluralism", *Arizona Journal of International and Comparative Law* 15 (1998): 74–75.

5. "The place of the indigenous laws is largely as determined in the colonial period". Hooker, *Legal Pluralism*, p. 2.

6. "[L]egal pluralism [does] not require state recognition. Defining legal pluralism as state-recognised legal pluralism would indeed be too limiting. It would seem to define legal pluralism to correspond to the form of pluralism practiced in colonial times and in some post-colonial states such as Singapore and Indonesia. It would seem to be a historical oddity, rather than a way for the future. More objectionably, it would validate the very idea that national state law is the only truly valid law and other legal traditions are subservient — the other laws would exist only to the extent that state law has authorised them and has chosen not to replace them yet. Defining legal pluralism by its state recognition would be recognising that ultimately there is no law but state law.

   Such a narrow definition would also fail to recognise the constant existence and the resurgence of other laws and norms, even in Western societies, that are not state law, whether these norms are recognised by the state or not. There is a post-modern revival of legal pluralism. [H.P.] Glenn talks of 'sustainable diversity in law' as the way of the future. Obviously this resurgence of legal pluralism should not suffer from a narrow and post-colonial definition." Gary F. Bell, "Multiculturalism in Law is Legal Pluralism – Lessons from Indonesia, Singapore and Canada", *Singapore Journal of Legal Studies* 315 (2006): 320–21.

7. "Can. 1251. Abstinence from meat, or from some other food as determined by the Episcopal Conference, is to be observed on all Fridays, unless a solemnity should fall on a Friday. Abstinence and fasting are to be observed on Ash Wednesday and Good Friday." *Codex Iuris Canonici*, 1983. The Latin text is the only official and authentic version. I here use the English translation prepared under the auspices of the Canon Law Society of America (Vatican: Libreria Editrice Vaticana, 1983), also available at <http://www.vatican.va/archive/ENG1104/_INDEX.HTM>.

8. One should add for completeness that the civil law has sometimes also been adopted without outright colonization, somewhat voluntarily. The

adoption of Western law was seen by some sovereign Asian States as necessary for "modernization" so as to better compete with the West and/or so as to avoid the extraterritorial application of Western law in some Asian countries. See for example the adoption of Western civil law in Japan, China and Thailand.

9. Singapore abandoned appeals to the Privy Council in 1994. See *Supreme Court of Judicature (Amendment) Act 1993* (No. 16 of 1993), the *Constitution of the Republic of Singapore (Amendment) Act 1993* (No. 17 of 1993) and the *Judicial Committee (Repeal) Act 1994 (No. 2 of 1994).*

10. It would be an exaggeration to say that all states have adopted a similarly friendly approach to choice of law and of jurisdiction in international commerce, but it is the case that the vast majority of states have done so. It should be mentioned, however, that even the states that are the most favourable to the parties' autonomy in choice of law and of jurisdiction will still reserve the right to intervene in a few instances, for example when public policy/public order is at stake.

11. Clause II of the Transitional Provisions of the original Constitution of 1945: "Segala ... peraturan yang ada masih langsung berlaku, selama belum diadakan yang baru menurut Undang-Undang Dasar ini." (Please note that I use the post-1972 spelling of the Indonesian language, even for documents produced before 1972.)

12. Of course, Islamic law is not state law and, therefore, in principle its substance cannot be changed by the state. This did not stop the state, however, from trying to influence the interpretation of Islamic law through the adoption of the *Compilation of Islamic Law (Kompilasi Humkum Islam)*, but as a Presidential Instruction (Instruksi Presiden), i.e., not as a law, regulation or decree. See *Presidential Instruction No. 1 of 1991.*

13. *Law No. 5 of 1960.* It is known in English as the Basic Agrarian Law, but its full Indonesian title is *Undang Undang No. 5 Tahun 1960 Tentang Peraturan Dasar Pokok-pokok Agraria.*

14. *Undang-Undang No. 21 Tahun 2008 Tentang Perbankan Syariah (Law 21 of 2008 Concerning Sharia [Islamic] Banking).*

15. See article 25 of *Undang-Undang No. 18 Tahun 2001 Tentang Otonomi Khusus Bagi Provinsi Daerah Istimewa Aceh Sebagai Provinsi Nanggroe Aceh Darussalam (Law No. 18 of 2001 on Special Autonomy for the Province of the Special Region of Aceh as the Province of Nanggroe Aceh Darussalam).*

16. With the exception of the Constitutional Court.

17. The Islamic courts were in any event already controlled by the Ministry of Religion, part of the state, even before they were submitted to the jurisdiction of the Supreme Court (Mahkamah Agung). See Gary F. Bell, "Indonesia: The Challenges of Legal Diversity and Law Reform", in *Law*

and Legal Institutions of Asia – Traditions, Adaptations and Innovations, edited by Ann Black and Gary F. Bell (Cambridge University Press, 2011).

18. It should be added that some domestic commercial disputes do go to domestic arbitration rather than to the courts in Indonesia, but surprisingly few considering the size of the country, perhaps in part because in such cases the Indonesian arbitration law gives the Indonesian courts a supervisory role over the arbitration.

19. However, the arrest of the Chief Justice of the Constitutional Court on charges of corruption and money laundering in 2013 and his conviction in June 2014 were a great disappointment for the public, which had high hopes for this young new court.

20. See, for example, A. Bedner, *Administrative Courts in Indonesia – A Socio-Legal Study* (Kluwer Law International, The Hague, 2001), p. xi; and S. Butt, "Surat Sakti: The Decline of Authority of Judicial Decisions in Indonesia", *Indonesia – Law and Society*, 2nd ed., edited by Tim Lindsey (Leichhardt, NSW: Federation Press: 2008), p. 346.

21. Bell, *Indonesia: The Challenges*, pp. 281–82.

22. E. McBride, "The Importance of Going Straight", *The Economist*, 9 December 2004 ("Members of the national parliament and the Supreme Court freely admit that their colleagues demand bribes to discharge their normal duties.")

23. S. Pompe, *The Indonesian Supreme Court: A Study of Institutional Collapse* (Ithaca: Cornell University Southeast Asia Program Publications, 2005).

24. S. Pompe, *Judicial Reforms in Indonesia: Transparency, Accountability and Fighting Corruption*, 2005 <http://unpan1.un.org/intradoc/groups/public/documents/un-dpadm/unpan043934.pdf>.

25. *Reglement op de Burgerlijke Rechtsvordering* (Code of Civil Procedure).

26. It should be noted that outside Java and Madura, a different regulation applied, which also did not provide for arbitration: the *Reglement tot Regeling van het Rechtswezen in de Gewesten Buiten Java en Madura* [Regulation for civil procedure for outside Java and Madura], known as *RBg*.

27. Jan K. Schaefer and Mulyana, "Indonesia's New Arbitration Law: Salient Features and Aberrations in the Application", *International Arbitration Law Review* 5, no. 2 (2002): 41.

28. *Law No. 30 of 1999 Concerning Arbitration and Alternative Dispute Resolution* (*Undang-Undang Nomor 30 Tahun 1999 Tentang Arbitrase Dan Alternatif Penyelesaian Sengketa*). Hereinafter, "the Arbitration Law".

29. Articles 65 and following of the *Arbitration Law* allow for the recognition and enforcement of foreign arbitral awards. In fact the enforcement of

foreign awards was possible even before 1999, through the New York Convention: "By way of Presidential Decree No. 34 of 1981 dated August 5, 1981 ('PD 34/1981'), the Republic of Indonesia ratified the United Nations Convention on the Recognition and Enforcement of Foreign Arbitral Awards of 1958 ('New York Convention'). However, the question of enforcement of foreign arbitral awards in Indonesia remained unclear until the promulgation of Supreme Court Regulation No. 1 of 1990 on Procedures for the Enforcement of Foreign Arbitral Awards dated March 1, 1990. Nevertheless even after this time the track record of enforcing foreign awards left a lot to be desired." Schaefer and Mulyana, "Indonesia's New Arbitration Law", p. 41. Note that article 34(1) of the *Arbitration Law* also mentions that disputes may be referred to national or international arbitration institutions, thus confirming the availability of international arbitration even for purely domestic commercial disputes (see article 66[b] of the *Arbitration Law*, which limits the recognition and enforcement of foreign awards to those that settle disputes "which, under the provision of Indonesian law, fall within the scope of commercial law").

30. "Pasal 3. Pengadilan Negeri tidak berwenang untuk mengadili sengketa para pihak yang telah terikat dalam perjanjian arbitrase". *Arbitration Law*.

31. Articles 65 to 69 of the *Arbitration Law*.

32. See for example article 5 of the *UNCITRAL Model Law on International Commercial Arbitration*.

33. Article 3 of the *Arbitration Law*. Even the old article 642 of the Rv provided: "Neither cassation nor re-examination of an arbitral award may be requested, even if the parties have so agreed in their agreement to arbitrate."

34. Article 66(c) of the *Arbitration Law*.

35. Jan K. Schaefer and Mulyana, "Indonesia's New Framework for International Arbitration: A Critical Assessment of the Law and Its Application by the Courts", *Mealey's International Arbitration Report* 17, no. 1 (2002).

36. Footnote 2 in the original quoted text: "See comments by J. Beechy, "International Commercial Arbitration: A Process under Review and Change", *Dispute Resolution Journal* 33 (2000): 32–34; P. Cornell and A. Handley, "Himpurna and Hub: International Arbitration in Developing Countries", *Mealey's International Arbitration Report* 15, no. 9 (2000): 39–47; M. Goldstein, "International Commercial Arbitration", *International Lawyer* 34, no. 2 (2000): 519–32; and V.V. Veeder, "The Natural Limits to the Truncated Tribunal: The German Case of the Soviet Eggs and the Dutch Abduction of the Indonesian Arbitrator", in *Law of International Business*

and Dispute Settlement in the 21st Century: Liber Amicorum Karl-Heinz Böckstiegel, edited by R. Briner et al. (Cologne: Heymanns, 2001), pp. 795–806.

37. Footnote 3 in the original quoted text: "See K. Mills, 'Enforcement of Arbitral Awards in Indonesia' in [2000] Int. A.L.R. 6 at p. 194."

38. For example, by law the arbitrator must be 35 years of age (art. 12[1][b]) and must have 15 years of experience and active mastery in the field (art. 12[1][e]) and the arbitration award must have a heading containing the words "Demi Keadilan Berdasarkan Ketuhanan Yang Maha Esa" (for the sake of Justice based on belief in the Almighty God) (art. 54[1][a]); it is the arbitrator or its representative, not one of the parties, who must file the award with the court to seek enforcement (art. 67 [1]) etc.

39. See Bell, "Indonesia: The Challenges of Legal Diversity", pp. 271–75.

40. The phenomenon of decodification is not unique to Indonesia and is quite frequent in civil law countries — consumer protection, company law and bankruptcy law are fields which have often been taken out of the codes and are now regulated by statutes.

41. The first company law to take that law out of the code was *Law No. 1 of 1995 on Limited Liability Companies (Undang-Undang No. 1 Tahun 1995 Tentang Perseroan Terbatas)*, which was later replaced by *Law No. 40 of 2007 on Limited Liability Companies (Undang-Undang No. 40 Tahun 2007 Tentang Perseroan Terbatas)*.

42. *S. 1947 No. 23.*

43. Also *S. 1947 No. 23.*

44. Although, on 1 October 2016, substantial amendments to the part of the French Civil Code on the law of contract came into force. See *Ordonnance n° 2016-131 du 10 février 2016 portant réforme du droit des contrats, du régime général et de la preuve des obligations.*

45. *Arrêt Boudier c. Patureau*, Cass., Ch. Req. 15 juin 1892, D.1892.596

46. Article 6:212 of the new Dutch civil code.

47. Gary F. Bell, "The Importance of Private Law Doctrine in Indonesia", in *Indonesia: Law and Society*, 2nd ed., edited by Tim Lindsey (Leichhardt, NSW: Federation Press, 2008), pp. 363–82.

48. These articles have been renumbered since the original French commercial code was first enacted, but their text has not changed. They used to be articles 183 and 184 in the original French *Code de commerce*, but are now found, word for word the same, in articles 512-1 and 512-2 of the new *Code de commerce*.

49. For example, one book lists the jurisprudence that decided that invalid promissory notes could be valid as something else: "Aux termes de l'article

L. 512-1, § II, du Code de commerce qui est à rapprocher de l'article L. 511-1, § II (V. *supra*, n° 18), le titre dans lequel une des énonciations indiquées à l'article L. 512-1 fait défaut ne vaut pas comme billet à ordre. Cette formule s'interprète comme la disposition correspondante relative à la lettre de change. Elle n'implique pas la nullité complète du titre. Celui-ci peut valoir comme billet au porteur ou comme reconnaissance de dette ou comme commencement de preuve d'un engagement du souscripteur envers le bénéficiaire (Paris, 5e ch., 30 sept. 1986 : D. 1987, somm. p. 70). Le billet à ordre dans lequel ne figure pas le nom du bénéficiaire vaut comme billet au porteur (Rennes, 1ʳᵉ ch. B, 14 déc. 2007, *Basle c/ Credit Mutuel de Rhan Reguinq: IurisData*, n° 357288. Sur le billet au porteur, v. infra, n° 170); Christian Galvada and Jean Stoufflet, *Instruments de paiement et de crédit – Effets de commerce, chèque, carte de paiement, transfert de fonds*, 7th ed. (Paris: Lexis-Nexis Litec, 2009).

50. See, for example, Abdulkadir Muhammad, S.H., Hukum dagang tentang surat-surat berharga (Bandung: Citra Aditya Bakti, 1998); H.M.N. Purwosutjipto, SH, Pengertian pokok hukum dagang Indonesia (Jakarta: Djambatan, 1978/85); and Emmy Pangaribuan Simanjuntak, SH, Hukum Dagang Surat-Surat Berharga – Wissel, Surat Sanggup/Aksep, Cheque, Kwitansi dan Promesse Atas Tunjuk (Yogyakarta: Seksi Fakultas Hukum, Universitas Gadjah Mada, 1974).

51. *Houle v. Canadian National Bank* [1990] 3 R.C.S. 122, (1990) 74 D.L.R. (4th) 577 [cited to D.L.R.] at 585–86, Justice L'Heureux-Dubé for the Court.

52. A contract is a juridical act.

53. Article 6:2 of the new Dutch civil code.

54. It should be mentioned that since 1 October 2016 the French code now makes explicit that good faith is required at the pre-contractual stage and in the formation of the contract. See articles 1104 and 1112 of the amended code.

55. For example, due to the Japanese occupation of Indonesia an insured ceased to pay the premiums on his life insurance and the company cancelled the policy. The widow alleged that the policy was cancelled against the requirements of good faith, given the circumstances (an abusive termination of sort). The court stated that if the policy was cancelled in bad faith, it could be revived, but held however that the cancellation was probably simply a permissible economic decision — the company could not afford to compensate the numerous deaths. *The Manufacturers Life Insurance Company v. Nelly Colthoff* in J. Satrio, S.H., *Hukum Perikatan, Perikatan Yang Lahir Dari Perjanjian – Buku II* (Bandung: Citra Aditya Bakti, 1995), pp. 166–69.

56. Case of the Mahkamah Agung, 28 May 1953, No 62aK/Sip/1952 under the name of "Jual-Beli Bersyarat", published in H.1953 – 2 & 3. Reported in part in Satrio, *Hukum Perikatan, Perikatan Yang Lahir Dari Perjanjian – Buku II*, pp. 170–72.

57. Sudargo Gautama, *Indonesian Business Law* (Bandung: Citra Aditya Bakti, 1995), p. 85.

58. 1936 Dutch case of *NV VN Rubbre Fabrieken* v. *Wilhemi* mentioned in Satrio, *Hukum Perikatan, Perikatan Yang Lahir Dari Perjanjian – Buku II*, pp. 181.

59. See "Sarong case" in Satrio, *Hukum Perikatan, Perikatan Yang Lahir Dari Perjanjian – Buku II*, pp. 189.

60. See the 1970 case on a penalty clause mentioned by Satrio, *Hukum Perikatan, Perikatan Yang Lahir Dari Perjanjian – Buku II*, pp. 230. In many other jurisdictions which followed the *Code Napoléon*, the legislator, faced with the refusal of the courts to intervene, had to amend the code to allow the court to modify an abusive penalty clause. See, for example, article 1152 of the French civil code as it was modified in 1975 and 1985. The Indonesian civil code (article 1249) was never amended to the same effect, which might explain why the courts seem to have taken the matter into their own hands. Please note that penalty clauses are legitimate in civil law, unlike the common law, which only allows for liquidated damages.

61. Gautama, *Indonesian Business Law*, p. 85.

62. My translation of Satrio, *Hukum Perikatan, Perikatan Yang Lahir Dari Perjanjian – Buku II*, p. 230.

63. My translation of Satrio, *Hukum Perikatan, Perikatan Yang Lahir Dari Perjanjian – Buku II*, p. 230.

64. "*Himpurna Cal. Energy Ltd. (Bermuda)* v. *PT. (Persero) Petusahaan Listruik* [sic] *Negara (Indonesia)*", *Mealey's International Arbitration Report* 14, A-1, A-53 (December 1999) (hereinafter *Himpurna Final Award*); "*Patuha Power Ltd. (Bermuda)* v. *PT. (Persero) Perusahaan Listruik* [sic] *Negara (Indonesia)*", *Mealey's International Arbitration Report* 14, B-1, B-44 (December 1999) (hereinafter *Patuha Final Award*). The facts of these twin awards are slightly different, but the story of the two cases is the same — electric plant projects terminated by the state-owned company due to the Asian financial crisis. The reasons given by the same tribunal in both cases are most of the time word-for-word identical, and I will therefore only cite the paragraph numbers in the Himpurna case.

65. Clause 8.3. of the relevant contract, quoted at paragraph 92 of the *Himpurna Final Award*.

66. Para 522, *Himpurna Final Award*.

67. Para 522, *Himpurna Final Award*.

68. Para 528, *Himpurna Final Award*.

References

Laws

Catholic Church

Codex Iuris Canonici, 1983 (Vatican: Libreria Editrice Vaticana, 1983) (translation under the auspices of the Canon Law Society of America).

Dutch East Indies

Burgerlijk Wetboek (the civil code, known in Indonesian as the *Kitab Undang-Undang Hukum Perdata*).

Herziene Indonesisch Reglement (known as "HIR") (*Revised Indonesian Regulation*).

Reglement tot Regeling van het Rechtswezen in de Gewesten Buiten Java en Madura (known as "RBg") (*Regulation for Civil Procedure for Outside Java and Madura*).

Reglement op de Burgerlijke Rechtsvordering (known as "Rv"). (Code of Civil Procedure).

Wetboek van Koophandel (the commercial code, known in Indonesian as the *Kitab Undang-Undang Hukum Dagang*).

Indonesia

Kompilasi Humkum Islam (Compilation of Islamic Law) officialized as *Instruksi Presiden No. 1/1991* (Presidential Instruction No. 1 of 1991).

Undang Undang Dasar 1945 (Constitution of 1945)

Undang-Undang No. 1 Tahun 1995 Tentang Perseroan Terbatas (Law No. 1 of 1995 on Limited Liability Companies).

Undang Undang No. 5 Tahun 1960 Tentang Peraturan Dasar Pokok-pokok Agraria (Law No. 5 of 1960 on the Basic Regulation of Agrarian Tenements, commonly called "Basic Agrarian Law").

Undang-Undang No. 18 Tahun 2001 Tentang Otonomi Khusus Bagi Provinsi Daerah Istimewa Aceh Sebagai Provinsi Nanggroe Aceh Darussalam (Law No. 18 of 2001 on Special Autonomy for the Province of the Special Region of Aceh as the Province of Nanggroe Aceh Darussalam).

Undang-Undang No. 21 Tahun 2008 Tentang Perbankan Syariah (Law 21 of 2008 Concerning Sharia [Islamic] Banking).

Undang-Undang Nomor 30 Tahun 1999 Tentang Arbitrase Dan Alternatif Penyelesaian Sengketa (Law No. 30 of 1999 Concerning Arbitration and Alternative Dispute Resolution).

Undang-Undang No. 40 Tahun 2007 Tentang Perseroan Terbatas (Law No. 40 of 2007 on Limited Liability Companies).

International

UNCITRAL Model Law on International Commercial Arbitration.

The Netherlands

New Dutch Civil Code.

Singapore

Constitution of the Republic of Singapore (Amendment) Act 1993 (No. 17 of 1993).
Judicial Committee (Repeal) Act 1994 (No. 2 of 1994).
Supreme Court of Judicature (Amendment) Act 1993 (No. 16 of 1993).

Court Cases and Arbitral Awards

Arbitral Awards

Himpurna Cal. Energy Ltd. (Bermuda) v. PT. (Persero) Petusahaan Listruik [sic]
Negara (Indonesia), 14 Mealey's Int'l Arb. Rep. A-1, A-53 (Dec. 1999).
Patuha Power Ltd. (Bermuda) v. PT. (Persero) Perusahaan Listruik [sic] *Negara*
(Indonesia), 14 Mealey's Int'l Arb. Rep. B-1, B-44 (Dec. 1999).

Canada

Houle v. Canadian National Bank [1990] 3 R.C.S. 122, (1990) 74 D.L.R. (4th) 577.

France

Arrêt Boudier c. Patureau, Cass., Ch. Req. 15 juin 1892, D.1892.596.
Paris, 5e ch., 30 sept. 1986 : D. 1987.
Rennes, 1re ch. B, 14 déc. 2007, *Basle c/ Credit Mutuel de Rhan Reguinq : IurisData,*
n° 357288.

Indonesia

Case of the Mahkamah Agung 28 May 1953 No 62aK/Sip/1952 under the
name of "Jual-Beli Bersyarat" published in H.1953 – 2 & 3, mentioned in
Satrio, S.H., *Hukum Perikatan -- Perikatan Yang Lahir Dari Perjanjian – Buku*
II (Bandung: Citra Aditya Bakti, 1995), pp. 170–72.
The Manufacturers Life Insurance Company v. Nelly Colthoff in J. Satrio, S.H.,
Hukum Perikatan -- Perikatan Yang Lahir Dari Perjanjian – Buku II (Bandung:
Citra Aditya Bakti, 1995), pp. 166–69.
"Sarong Case" in J. Satrio, S.H., *Hukum Perikatan -- Perikatan Yang Lahir Dari*
Perjanjian – Buku II (Bandung: Citra Aditya Bakti, 1995), p. 189

Netherlands

NV VN Rubbre Fabrieken v. Wilhemi in Satrio S.H., *Hukum Perikatan -- Perikatan*
Yang Lahir Dari Perjanjian – Buku II (Bandung: Citra Aditya Bakti, 1995),
p. 181.

Books

Abdulkadir Muhammad, S.H. *Hukum dagang tentang surat-surat berharga*. Bandung: Citra Aditya Bakti, 1998.

Bedner, A., *Administrative Courts in Indonesia – A Socio-Legal Study*. The Hague: Kluwer Law International, 2001.

Briner, R. et al., eds. *Law of International Business and Dispute Settlement in the 21st Century - Liber Amicorum Karl-Heinz Böckstiegel*. Cologne, Heymanns 2001.

Galvada, Christian and Jean Stoufflet. *Instruments de paiement et de crédit – Effets de commerce, chèque, carte de paiement, transfert de fonds*, 7th ed. Paris: Lexis-Nexis Litec, 2009.

Gautama, Sudargo. *Indonesian Business Law*. Bandung: Citra Aditya Bakti, 1995.

Hooker, M.B. *Legal Pluralism – An Introduction to Colonial and Neo-Colonial Laws*. Oxford: Clarendon Press, 1975.

Pompe, S. *The Indonesian Supreme Court: A Study of Institutional Collapse*. Ithaca: Cornell University Southeast Asia Program Publications, 2005.

Purwosutjipto, H.M.N., SH. *Pengertian pokok hukum dagang Indonesia*. Jakarta: Djambatan, 1978/1985.

Simanjuntak, Emmy Pangaribuan, SH. *Hukum Dagang Surat-Surat Berharga – Wissel, Surat Sanggup / Aksep, Cheque, Kwitansi dan Promesse Atas Tunjuk*. Yogyakarta: Seksi Fakultas Hukum, Universitas Gadjah Mada, 1974.

Chapters

Bell, Gary F. "The Importance of Private Law Doctrine in Indonesia". In *Indonesia: Law and Society*, 2nd ed., edited by Tim Lindsey. Leichhardt: Federation Press, 2008.

———. "Indonesia: The Challenges of Legal Diversity and Law Reform". In *Law and Legal Institutions of Asia – Traditions, Adaptations and Innovations*, edited by Ann Black and Gary F. Bell. Cambridge: Cambridge University Press, 2011.

Butt, S. "Surat Sakti: The Decline of Authority of Judicial Decisions in Indonesia". In *Indonesia – Law and Society*, 2nd ed., edited by Tim Lindsey. Leichhardt: Federation Press, 2008.

Periodicals

Bell, Gary F. "Multiculturalism in Law is Legal Pluralism: Lessons from Indonesia, Singapore and Canada". *Singapore Journal of Legal Studies* (2006): 315–30.

Macdonald, Roderick A. "Metaphors of Multiplicity: Civil Society, Regimes and Legal Pluralism". *Arizona Journal of International and Comparative Law*, no. 15 (1998): 69-92.

Schaefer, Jan K. and Mulyana. "Indonesia's New Arbitration Law: Salient Features and Aberrations in the Application". *International Arbitration Law Review*, 5, no. 2 (2002): 41-49.

————. "Indonesia's New Framework for International Arbitration: A Critical Assessment of the Law and Its Application by the Courts". *Mealey's International Arbitration Review* 17, no. 1 (2002): 39.

Newspapers
McBride, E. "The Importance of Going Straight". *The Economist*, 9 December 2004.

Online Citations
Pompe, S. *Judicial Reforms In Indonesia: Transparency, Accountability and Fighting Corruption*, 2005 <http://unpan1.un.org/intradoc/groups/public/documents/un-dpadm/unpan043934.pdf>.

7

When Laws Are Not Enough: Ethics, Aesthetics, and Intra-Religious Pluralism in Contemporary Indonesia[1]

Virginia Matheson Hooker

By the late 1960s it was clear that, in addition to many other challenges, the newly independent nations of Southeast Asia faced ongoing complexities resulting from the mix of legal systems they had inherited from their pre-modern and colonial pasts. M.B. Hooker experienced the situation at first hand when, as a young lecturer in law at the then University of Singapore, he observed the laws of Singapore, Malaysia, and Indonesia operating in a range of contexts, including religious courts, at local and national levels. In 1975, several years after leaving Southeast Asia, he published a study of legal pluralism, which he defined as "the situation in which two or more laws interact".[2] The aim of the study was "to describe the systems of legal pluralism in the contemporary world which have resulted from the transfer of whole legal systems across cultural boundaries", and he made it clear that what interested him was the action of law as an agent of social change.[3]

Twenty-five years after his study on legal pluralism was published, Professor Hooker began an extended analysis of a diverse range of fatwas[4] in modern Indonesia using materials that were very different from those used in his 1975 book. He was, however, still interested in the nature of pluralism, albeit pluralism within the framework of the same legal system — Islam in Indonesia — and expressed in the form of fatwas. He wrote, "It is important to stress that there is variation in principle and practice because multiplicity of principle and practice is the lifeblood of law and dogma".[5]

The point to make here is that Professor Hooker's research into legal pluralism began with analyses of differences among systems and later focussed on differences within the same system of laws (Islam). One of his primary interests remains the dialectic/dialogic relationship between the system and the society in which it is expressed. In the analysis of fatwas, he described in some detail the methods developed by a range of Indonesian religious scholars to apply Islamic law to problems confronting modern Indonesian Muslims. He argues that the fatwas are a means to knowing Indonesian Islam as it is understood and expressed at a particular time in its Indonesian context.[6]

This chapter takes up Professor Hooker's interest in differences within Islam and the relationship between legal systems and the society in which they are expressed. But whereas he used fatwas as the basis for his study, this chapter will shift focus to a little-studied form of Islamic piety, that is, art which is inspired by the Qur'an, or Islam-themed art. The artists do not draw on the formal sources of Islamic law which form the basis of fatwas, but they do base their work on a system of aesthetics and ethics which draws directly from the Qur'an, as will be described in Part I, below.

Introduction

Several recent studies of intra-religious pluralism among Indonesian Muslims have argued that diversity of opinion about religious issues within Islam is not necessarily divisive but can be a healthy outlet for differences among Muslim groups.[7] To quote Dr Nadirsyah Hosen, "pluralism in Islamic society cannot be avoided. In fact such diversity of views has been one of the characteristics of *fiqh* throughout its history."[8] So far, studies of intra-religious pluralism have focussed on the major socio-religious organizations representing Indonesian Muslims and the decisions of the Indonesian Council of Ulama (MUI).

The issues debated by those groups usually concern very practical points of law, such as methods for determining the beginning and ending of the fasting month. The experts involved are trained in Islamic jurisprudence (fiqh) and they interpret the finer points of that law using texts and methods developed over centuries of scholarship. This chapter aims to extend existing studies by focussing on Islam-themed art as a further example of expressions of intra-religious pluralism. This takes intra-religious pluralism beyond fiqh and the realm of jurists and into the area of ethics and aesthetics.

The chapter does this in three ways. First, when artists decide to use Qur'anic verses as the subject of visual representation, they make a series of choices about the interpretation of those verses.[9] The opportunity for individual Muslims to express their own interpretation of the Qur'an is usually reserved for exegetes (Muslims who have received training in the science of Qur'anic exegesis [tafsir]). Exegetes apply a strict series of rules to reach their interpretation, but even so there are differences among exegetes. Islamic scholarship recognizes this by acknowledging a series of reliable authorities that Muslims may use in their work to understand the meanings of Qur'anic verses.[10] While non-specialists, like the artists, might consult existing books of exegesis, they do not have to do so, nor do they consider themselves constrained by them. Rather, they choose a section of the Qur'an which speaks to their concerns and then express it visually, as described in Part II. The artist's choice of style of script for the verses, background images, colour, style, and even size of the painting, communicates to the viewer a particular understanding of the purpose of the Qur'anic verse. It is here that intra-religious pluralism is apparent, because it is rare for two artists to provide the same visual interpretation of the same verse. The diversity of interpretation which enables individual artists to respond to particular contexts (personal and social) in their visual depictions of Qur'anic verses keeps Revelation (the Qur'an) relevant to time and place, as is evident in the two paintings presented in Part II.

Second, and following on from the above, the artists' choice of Qur'anic verse is often in response to an issue in contemporary society, or an issue of particular concern to the Muslim community. Verses chosen might be Qur'anic guidance about disputation among

Muslims; petty corruption; lack of compassion for the suffering of others; greed; absorption with the material world; failure to acknowledge the omnipotence of Allah. These kinds of behaviours are not unlawful in the sense that they contravene specific state or religious laws, but they impact negatively on individuals and society. However, even if they are not specifically forbidden or discouraged by formal legislation, these negative behaviours and attitudes run counter to the values of the Qur'an. Japanese scholar, Toshihiko Izutsu, terms these Qur'anic values "ethico-religious concepts"[11] and the Indonesian artists refer to them as *etika* or ethics. Their argument for the philosophy of aesthetics and ethics is described in greater detail in Part I. The ethico-religious elements of this philosophy extend into an area not covered by fiqh or by secular law.

Third, although most theories of legal pluralism, including intra-religious pluralism, do not encompass ethics, the Japanese scholar of comparative law, Masaji Chiba, has formulated a theory of legal pluralism which is more broad in conception and recognizes that religious values can affect law.[12] Chiba suggests that in a context where different systems of law are applied to communities, any definition of "the law" must take into account three sets of dichotomies: "official law" and "unofficial law"; "indigenous" and "transplanted" law; and "legal rules" and "legal postulates". It is the third set of dichotomies which is directly relevant to understanding the significance of the Indonesian artists' efforts to formulate an aesthetic and ethical system to underpin Islam-themed works of art.

Chiba defines the "legal rules" in his schema as "the formalized verbal expressions of particular legal regulations to designate specified patterns of behaviour". He suggests that when a gap or "vacuum" exists in a system of law, it can be filled by "legal postulates", that is the principal values or ethics which underpin the primary system. Chiba explains further that these "postulates" are "the particular values and ideas and their systems specifically connected with a particular law to ideationally found, justify and orient, or else supplement, criticize and revise the existing legal rules".[13] Chiba notes that if "legal rules have become outdated or disappear", then the "legal postulates" which supported them can function independently.[14]

Chiba's theory recognizes that values and ideas which support legal rules and regulations can function independently from those rules and regulations, particularly if the rules are not being followed or applied. The possibility for independent functioning suggests an explanation for how non-specialists, such as artists, can draw on the ethical and moral elements of the Qur'an to address moral and ethical failures in society which the laws and regulations ignore. The artists have developed a philosophy of aesthetics in which the divine qualities of God (recorded in the Qur'an through references to the Compassionate, the Mighty, the Just, the Good, the Beautiful, and so on) are expressed visually through art.

The discussion which follows is divided into five sections:

I.   Beauty and Goodness: the context of Islam-themed art and the development of a philosophy of aesthetics and ethics;
II. Visual Islam: aesthetics in action;
III. Postulates and ethics;
IV. Postulates and aesthetics: the power of affect. Research on the relationship between the Qur'an, piety, aesthetics, and ethics has shown the importance of "affect", a concept which is particularly appropriate to Islam-inspired art;[15] and
V.   Conclusion: when laws are not enough.

I. Beauty and Goodness: Context and Philosophy

Visual art is a relatively new form of artistic expression in Indonesia and was only taught formally from the mid-1940s, developing its own national characteristics during the first decade of Independence. In the late 1950s and thereafter, Indonesian artists were awarded scholarships to study in Europe and the United States, experiences which inspired them and broadened their artistic vision. The artist A.D. Pirous, for example, first encountered examples of contemporary Western painting and classical Islamic art in galleries and museums in New York. He was moved to reflect on his own style and his Islamic heritage.[16] In the early 1970s he began creating works with obvious Islamic themes (often expressed through Arabic script and Qur'anic verses). He was not the first to do this, but he became one of the most active of a group of like-minded artists who staged exhibitions of their Islam-themed works.[17]

In the late 1980s, Pirous and several other prominent Indonesians persuaded President Soeharto to support a large-scale exhibition of Islam-inspired art to be held in 1991 at the national Istiqlal (Independence) mosque in Jakarta. In his preface to the exhibition catalogue, Pirous wrote that for the first time the exhibition brought together the concept of "modern Indonesian art inspired by Islam" with the great venue of the national Independence Mosque. He hoped that the exhibition with its diverse range of works would help the public understand the nature of modern Islam-inspired art.[18] Six and a half million visitors came to see the exhibition, which was held during the fasting month of Ramadan, 1991. Over eleven million visitors flocked to Festival Istiqlal II, which was held in Ramadan 1995, coinciding with the fiftieth year of Indonesia's independence.

In 1993, Pirous wrote an essay assessing the progress of Islam-inspired art in Indonesia.[19] He tried to draw out the reasons for the rapid development of Islam-inspired art and why it had received such strong support from both artists and the Muslim community. He described trends among Indonesian Muslims which indicated an increasing desire to manifest Islam in their social, artistic, and cultural lives as well as their more obvious religious lives. During the same period, Pirous noted, writers of prose and poetry included Islamic themes in their works and the prestigious national Qur'an Recitation Competition (MTQ) attracted increasing numbers of competitors.[20] Opportunities to learn Arabic calligraphy from master calligraphers became more accessible through the Institute of Qur'anic Calligraphy (LEMKA, Lembaga Kaligrafi al-Qur'an), founded in 1985 and led by the talented young calligrapher Didin Sirojuddin AR.

The growth of interest in these activities heightened Pirous's concern that Islam-inspired art in Indonesia lacked a system of aesthetics which could support its development. In his 1993 essay, he wrote that the desire to develop Islamic religious content in art was not supported by a special language to describe "visual Islam". He believed that one of the factors hampering the development of a philosophy of Islamic aesthetics in Indonesia was the response of some religious authorities who had issued fatwas which were often at odds with the creative, imaginative, and innovative nature of artistic creativity.[21]

But after considerable reflection about the responsibility of using the sacred words of the Qur'an, Pirous felt he could combine his artistic creativity with the ethical values of the Qur'an. He expressed it thus:

> ... Me what is my life all about? What is a good person? A good person is someone who is useful to others. If I give them something they want, I will be useful. And so I decided to be useful. This is the concept of *khairuqum an-fa'aqum linnas* – a person useful to others.... So I sacrificed myself, putting a limit on my free expression, but I came back to values that I could explore more frequently and more meaningfully in the Qur'an. I planted in the paintings concepts and philosophical values that would make them more enjoyable. *Aesthetic pleasure and ethical pleasure together* [sic].[22]

Didin Sirojuddin AR, the second artist whose work is described in this chapter, is known for his skills as a calligrapher. Like Pirous, he too was critical of those religious authorities who questioned the legality of using Qur'anic calligraphy in works of art. In response, Sirojuddin published an article defending the status of artistic expressions of Qur'anic calligraphy and used arguments from respected scholars of Islam to make his case.[23] Sirojuddin is also well known as a public speaker and in 2003 he was invited to speak at a Ramadan function in Bogor. [24] His topic was the role of Islamic art in social life, focussing on the relationship between beauty, goodness and Islamic art.

Sirojuddin began his talk by explaining that creating good art is an act of worship (*ibadah*). Art created in this way expresses beauty which feeds the desire to do good deeds in this world and the next. Quoting two verses from the Qur'an (Qur'an 50, Qaf, verse 6 and Qur'an 16, al-Nahl, verse 6), he explained how they show that Allah created beauty in nature to be a source of pleasure and enjoyment for humans. To ignore the beauty of Allah's creation, he explained, is like ignoring an aspect of Allah's greatness; to give expression to that beauty is bearing witness to His greatness. Sirojuddin quoted the twelfth-century theologian al-Ghazzali, one of the greatest scholars of Islam. The beauty of nature, wrote al-Ghazzali in his *Ihya Ulum al-Din* (revival of the religious sciences), stimulates reflection and contemplation. In a similar way, Sirojuddin argues, a beautiful work of Islam-based art can also inspire reflection, or *zikir* (being mindful of Allah through meditation).

Sirojuddin then describes the beauty of God's decrees and the beauty of His Qualities.[25] Drawing on two Hadiths,[26] that Allah is the most Beautiful and loves Beauty, and that Allah is the Most Good and loves Goodness, he presents a step-by-step explanation to argue that Beauty and Goodness are inseparable. Both, he says, are divine qualities, which, because they come from the Essence that is the One (God), are fused. Their inseparability means that beauty (art) is never expressed purely for its own sake, but always so that it inspires goodness and morality. Enjoying beauty for its own sake can lead to immorality. Thus, he emphasizes, in Islam aesthetics are linked with ethics and form the basis of the conception of Islamic art.

Both Pirous and Sirojuddin have reflected deeply about the meaning and purpose of Islam-inspired art. Their very different backgrounds, interests, and experience are reflected in the way they formulate their philosophies. There is a difference also in the style of argumentation. Sirojuddin, educated in one of Indonesia's leading Islamic religious colleges, takes his arguments from the Qur'an, Hadith, and the classical works of Islamic scholarship. Pirous rarely refers to these authorities when expressing his views. He uses self-questioning to analyse his personal motivation for using Qur'an-based themes in his works. So it is all the more striking that both artists broadly agree on the basic principles of Islam-inspired art: that there is an aesthetic in which beauty and goodness are inseparably linked to provide the ethical foundation which underpins artistic practice. In "good" art, viewers feel these qualities of beauty and goodness which can make them mindful of Allah and motivate them to follow His values in their lives. This is what both artists say they seek to achieve.

The Qur'an speaks to believers about the transcendence and omniscience of Allah and, as well, outlines the obligations of humans to Allah and to each other. This is expressed succinctly in the often-quoted Qur'anic verse, "And hold fast, all together, by the rope which God (stretches out for you)" (Qur'an Ali Imran 3: 103). Many Muslims describe this as the vertical tie which links human beings to God and the horizontal ties between fellow human beings. In other words, both personal piety and social action are essential expressions of Islam. The ethical propositions of the Qur'an should be manifest in the personal lives of Muslims, and the same values should be extended into social behaviour.

II. Visual Islam: Aesthetics in Action

Pirous and Sirojuddin have painted many Islam-inspired works.[27] Two of their paintings have been selected for discussion in this section because they depict the same Qur'anic verse. Although the two artists offer very different visual representations of the meaning of the verse, the ethical content of the painting is powerfully expressed. We begin with A.D. Pirous, an Acehnese who was born in 1933, several decades before Sirojuddin. Pirous was educated during the late 1950s at the secular, Western-oriented Faculty of Art and Design at the Bandung Institute of Technology.[28] His early works were not consciously inspired by Islam.[29] It was only after several years of postgraduate study in Rochester, New York, 1964–69, and the opportunity to view exhibitions of Islamic art in the United States, that he decided to work with Islam-based themes.[30] Pirous returned to Indonesia to pursue a very successful career as one of Indonesia's most famous artists and art scholars. He has curated and organized many major exhibitions as well as his own solo shows in Indonesia and abroad. In 1997 the Rockefeller Foundation appointed him a member of a curatorial team to mount a special exhibition of contemporary Islamic art at the forty-seventh Venice Biennale.[31]

This is how Pirous describes the relationship between the Qur'an, the source of his inspiration, and his art:

> The Holy Qur'an itself may not be changed, but to understand it, you must be free to interpret it. Each and every person may interpret it and glorify its essence, its message. So I take a verse and I try to animate it with my personal vision, with my personal understanding. Now why did I take that verse at that moment? And what is it that I want to say in such a personally meaningful way? If it all comes together and is read by someone else, that's what you call expressiveness, that's what you call spirituality. The meaningfulness might come from something I read, something I saw, something I dreamt about, or something I heard in a story and gets into the back of my head. And if it stirs me as an artist, I will want to put it onto my canvas. When I express it in visual language, that's when I use my aesthetic knowledge: composition, color, texture, line, rhythm, everything. I use all of that to make my dream real, so that it can be felt. So that I can tell a story. At last, the painting, its meaning, the Qur'anic verse, all of it becomes clear.[32]

Here, Pirous the artist is describing the "visual language" he creates to embody what was in his head; to make it "real" or tell a story inspired by the revealed words in a way that can be "felt". The painting shown below is one example of how he does this.

PLATE 1

A.D. Pirous, *Amanat kepada Sang Pemimpin: Tentang Mahligai Kefanaan, Tentang Awal Akhir Kehayatan: An Admonition to the Leader: Concerning the Transient Palace and the Beginning and End of Life*, 1995. 175 × 260 cm, marble paste, gold leaf, acrylic on canvas.[33] (Photography: Kenneth M. George).

This is a large, eye-catching work, with impressive use of gold leaf.[34] Pirous described the context and stimulus for his painting in response to a comment I had emailed him in which I had suggested that, although there are many expert commentaries and interpretations of the Qur'an (exegeses), individuals remain free to form their own understandings. This is his reply:

Indeed it is correct that the Qur'an is interpreted not translated by the experts. So there is a limited freedom for the exegetes, which later becomes the guide for Muslims. Certainly in the process of *ijtihad* [independent legal reasoning] the users from then on will give it a more contextual quality. This is what happened when I took Chapter Ali Imran, verses 26 and 27 to enrich the painting *An Admonition to the Leader*.

At that time there was a pressing situation which made me anxious and wanting to caution all parties to think again. Around 1995 the New Order government was very violent, many leaders in power went totally too far. It was as if power was something eternal and unending even though everything is transitory and every moment has an end as the Chapter Ali Imran verses 26 and 27 state. In the world of art certainly there is a freedom which is rather personal to express a message. It is as if there will be two identities which can become one, the identity through the language of visual expression (style) and the identity of conveying the message (content). Even if the content of the message is the same it will be expressed differently by a range of artists. [my translation][35]

The English translation of verses 26 and 27 from Chapter 3, Ali Imran, depicted in Pirous's painting reads as follows:

Say: "O God! / Lord of power (and rule),] / Thou givest power / To whom Thou pleasest, / And Thou strippest off power / From whom Thou pleasest: / Thou enduest with honour / Whom Thou pleasest, / And Thou bringest low / Whom Thou pleasest: / In Thy hand is all good. / Verily, over all things / Thou hast power.

Thou causest the night / to gain on the day, and Thou causest the day / to gain on the night; / Thou bringest the dead / out of the living; / and Thou givest sustenance / to whom Thou pleasest, / without measure.[36]

Pirous has explained his motivation for choosing this Qur'anic verse — the socio-political situation in Indonesia in 1995. The early 1990s saw unprecedented levels of corruption, collusion, and nepotism in President Soeharto's regime, including the behaviour of Soeharto's own children. This period also saw the Dili massacre by Indonesian troops in East Timor (1991), followed by increasing brutality. Open displays of abuse of power at the highest levels of the regime prompted Pirous to remind President Soeharto of the divine source and transitory nature of all power. The painting was exhibited at the second Festival Istiqlal

(1995), which was opened by the president and attended by New Order dignitaries as well as about eleven million other visitors. [37]

Pirous's choice of Qur'anic verses, and its Indonesian title,[38] clearly spell out the awesome, irresistible nature of transcendence. The verses issue warnings to humankind about Allah's omnipotence — over earthly power and who will hold it, over the cosmos, over life and death. It is a reminder that all existence is dependent on Allah's will. Mindful of Pirous's comments about fusion of style and message, how does Pirous convey this Qur'anic message to a contemporary audience?

The impact of the size and scale of the canvas reinforces the message of omnipotence. The double line of gold leaf dividing the canvas into equal halves or pages, and stretching from top to bottom, is perhaps a reference to the "rope of Allah", which according to the Qur'an links humans to Allah.[39] The canvas is covered with a variety of geometric shapes — rectangles of different dimensions, and triangles, some with softened apexes. A circle of red wax seems to unite the other shapes. The chunkiness of the forms, solid and tough, have been given textures of lines and fissures as if to indicate weathering and ageing. The central group of rounded triangles suggests various forms with iconic meanings in Islam — a mountain, a grave marker, a cave. A band of white, studded with star-like dots, perhaps represents the firmament, which Allah has divided into night from day. And below the firmament across the centre of the canvas, Pirous has copied the two Qur'anic verses as if they are on two pages of a book. They are presented in Arabic fashion, with the first verse copied on to the right-hand side and the second on the left-hand side of the central line. Viewers thus face two metre-high "pages" of a large book, which can also be "read" as a composition of rocks and pillars seeming to have existed since time immemorial. Humans may come and go, all subject to the cycle of birth and death, but the words and rocks will remain, testimony to the eternal nature of divine omnipotence. The title of the painting, "An Admonition to the Leader...", directs the viewer's attention to the contemporary relevance of the ethical message of the Qur'anic verse.

Master calligrapher K.H. Didin Sirojuddin AR was born in West Java in 1957 and educated at the famous Nahdlatul Ulama Islamic college, Pesantren Moderen Gontor, between 1969 and 1975. He studied Arabic calligraphy with two of Indonesia's most respected calligraphers, Professor H.M. Salim Fachry and K.H.M. Abdul Razzaq Muhili.[40] As their titles, K.H. (Kiai Haji) denote, these men were also noted religious scholars for whom calligraphy was an integral part of the deeper study of the Qur'an. They would have taught their students Qur'anic recitation (*'ilm al-qira'a*), exegesis (*tafsir*), theology (*kalam*), and the history of Islam. An education from these masters was training in the Islamic sciences as well as the art of arts, Arabic calligraphy.

During the early 1980s, Sirojuddin worked as a journalist, a teacher of calligraphy, and a lecturer at the State Islamic Institute Syarif Hidayatullah (now State Islamic University) in Jakarta. Since 1983 he has regularly served as one of the judges of the calligraphy sections of the national Qur'anic recitation competitions (MTQ), and in 1987 was winner of the ASEAN calligraphy competition held in Brunei.[41]

PLATE 2

Didin Sirojuddin AR, *Kuasa Sang Maharaja* [The power of the mighty ruler], 2001. 30 × 30 cm, mixed media. (Photography: Darren Boyd).

In this painting, Sirojuddin presents only the first (verse 26) of the two verses chosen by Pirous. The painting is 30 cm square, much smaller that Pirous's work. Sirojuddin painted it in 2001 and it was exhibited at two secular public venues in Jakarta.[42] Although the works of Pirous and Sirojuddin each depict the same Qur'anic verse, their styles are very different. There are just a few similarities. Both artists position the Qur'anic verse(s) in the centre of their works and each divides the canvas into upper, middle, and lower strata. Besides these features there is little else in common. Sirojuddin chooses a more legible form of Arabic script and sets the Qur'anic quote in a golden circle surrounded by a halo of pale light.

The lower circumference of the golden circle is penetrated by two lines of strong and arresting Arabic script. The first is thick letters which read "Allāhumma" (O God) and the second is a set of tubular letters, whose space is not filled with ink, reading "Mālik al-Mulk" (Lord of Power). Both sets of letters rest on pillars (or cubes) of intense black, which resemble the Kaaba in the Grand Mosque at Mecca. The border which runs across the upper part of the painting contains three fragments of text in Arabic calligraphy (of various styles), too fragmented to be understood. One piece of text in English is legible, although incomplete, and reads, "Arafah is the most important part..." and "...prophet said 'pilgrimage is Arafah'". These phrases clearly refer to one of the rites of the hajj.

Another border composed of textual fragments runs across the bottom of the painting and provides the foundation for three black (or one large?) cubic structure(s) which seem to rise out of the textual fragments of Arabic, Indonesian, and English. In the only fragment of text in English are phrases which refer, like those above, to rituals of the hajj. In the centre of this lower border is a clearly legible Indonesian translation of the Qur'anic verse written in Arabic in the golden circle. Indonesians who cannot read the Qur'an in Arabic can thus understand the verse.

Sirojuddin's painting, with its strong central focus on the Qur'anic verse stressing omnipotence, is linked to visual images of the hajj and textual fragments referring to hajj rituals. Many interpretations are possible. The hajj, one of the five "pillars" of Islam, is a ritual which brings together all Muslims, whatever their status, as equals. All the rituals of the hajj emphasize that humans are born and die equals in the sight of Allah and remain His servants throughout their lives. The Kaaba is the central pivot of the hajj, as well as marking the direction all Muslims face when they perform their daily prayers. These visual elements remind believers of their ritual obligations in Islam, of the omnipotence of Allah, and of the unity of their community.

Pirous has explained the socio-political context of his painting. Sirojuddin has not spoken about that aspect of his work, but it dates from 2001, that is, the early part of the post-Soeharto period of "Reformation". As well as being hit by the Asian financial crisis of 1997, Indonesia faced political turmoil, violent riots and killings in 1998, and inter-religious violence and killings in Eastern Indonesia. President Abdurrahman Wahid's time in office ended in July 2001. Against this background, Sirojuddin chose a particular verse from the Qur'an, supporting it with "trigger" images of rites of repentance and equality among all Muslims. The Kaaba and some of the rites of the hajj are also directly associated with Abraham/Ibrahim, the founder of the three monotheistic faiths — Judaism, Christianity and Islam. Some of those who viewed the painting when it was first shown in 2001 might well have seen in it a warning to those Indonesians engaged in inter-religious violence, especially in Eastern Indonesia, to remember the elements of faith that Islam and Christianity share.

Intra-religious Pluralism

The act of painting, creating "visual language", to use the words of Pirous, expresses the artist's interpretation of a subject. For artists inspired by Islam, the subject will often come from the Qur'an. As the two examples above show, even paintings that depict the same Qur'anic verses will express different aspects of the meanings of the verses, place them in different contexts, choose very different "visual languages", and convey different moods. The interpretation of revealed words and their painterly settings has further dimensions — as many as the viewers who "read" the visual language. But to engage with the painting the viewer has to stop, consider the images, and perhaps think and reflect on what they see. It is the aesthetics of the work which will make the initial link between painting and viewer. Something in the "visual language" has to connect with the viewer and stimulate them to pause and consider the work. Open-ended, plural interpretations are stimulated by the artists' use of aesthetics. Pirous, Sirojuddin and other artists inspired by Islam base their system of aesthetics on the divine qualities of Beauty and Goodness which they seek to reflect in their works.

During the fasting month of 2011, a large exhibition entitled "*Bayang*" (Shadows/Reflections) was held at the National Art Gallery in Jakarta. The organizers said they were seeking to invigorate Islamic art, and invited artists to respond to the theme with dynamic works.[43] Over three hundred works in a number of mediums (including new media, sculpture, installations and photography) covering a wide range of themes were on display. While most evaluations of the works were positive, one art critic blogged that, in general, the works lacked spiritual depth or relied on the inclusion of Qur'anic verses in the compositions to make them "Islamic". The critic praised one of the exhibits, an installation entitled *Last Journey* which included a set of sculptures, whose purpose seemed to be to remind viewers of the impermanence of this world. The blogger made it clear that he reserved his respect for those artists who tried to engage viewers in deeper levels of spiritual reflection.[44] For him, as for Pirous, Sirojuddin and others, the spiritual and ethical messages of works of art that claimed to be inspired by Islam are essential elements in their creation and reception.

III.   Postulates and Ethics

In Islam, Revelation is understood to be complete and perfect. In Islamic art this perfection is symbolized by the circle, complete and without beginning or end. Believers seek answers to Revelation in Revelation itself. The Qur'an, they claim, holds its own answers and is its own best commentary.[45]

We have suggested that Pirous and Sirojuddin stand as examples of Muslims whose professional, as well as personal, lives are inspired by the Qur'an. In Sirojuddin's words, "The Qur'an is the source of all inspiration and can become the hunting ground for endless creativity."[46] The unending nature of this inspiration, the endless possibilities for new insights, new levels of understanding are seen by believers as signs of Allah's power. They see multiplicity, diversity, plenitude, as evidence of Divine creativity. The plethora of diversity is also seen as proof of Allah's Oneness — a unity which encompasses all creation. Seen from this perspective, Revelation is not a closed system but, by its inimitable nature, is the most open.

Islam-inspired artists communicate or, as Pirous would say, develop their "visual language" through symbols and metaphors. In this way they exploit the full potential of the abstract to convey concepts, mood, and feeling. Mood and feeling offer a balance to the strict and often literalist argumentation of the jurists, and here we can identify another example of "pluralism" within Islam. As Masaji Chiba has suggested in his theory of legal pluralism, the "legal rules" and "legal postulates" in plural systems coexist and co-function, "as a rule, interactingly. However, in many cases they may fall into conflict, while in others either of them may cease to function or completely disappear. Such cases occur when either of them has lagged behind the other or the socio-cultural development of the society concerned." And to repeat the quotation from Chiba given above in the Introduction, "Among the various modes of relationship between the two [that is, between legal rules and legal postulates], particularly to be noticed is the independent function of legal postulates when the supported legal rules have become outdated or disappear." According to Chiba, when that happens, "legal postulates have the potential of reactivating outdated legal rules or even creating new legal rules to embody themselves."[47] We do not suggest that Pirous's and Sirojuddin's formulations of an Islam-inspired system of aesthetics and ethics aim in any way to create new legal rules. But based on their own descriptions, the aesthetic elements of many of their works are intended to encourage viewers to think more deeply about goodness, ethical behaviour and spirituality, all of which can also be described as in Chiba's terms as "legal postulates". The following quote from Pirous makes his position very clear: "I am trying through the language of beauty to give people something that will stir them to appreciate ethical values. By this I mean those ethical values that have a close connection with the values found in Qur'anic verse."[48]

Pirous states that he hopes the beauty of his paintings will "stir" viewers to become aware of ethical values. There is no criticism of lack of ethical awareness, no threats of punishment or suggestions of coercion. If we return to the summary of Chiba's thesis, made in the introduction above, and consider sharia as the "legal rules" of Islam and aesthetics and ethics among its "legal postulates", we see that the "legal postulates" suggested by the artists rest on basic principles in Islam — divine Beauty and divine Goodness.

In the contemporary Indonesian context, the "legal rules" of sharia-related regional legislation (*Peraturan Daerah Shari'at Islam*) focus largely on the negative qualities of immorality and "social ills".[49] These negative qualities are human qualities, not those of Allah. The "legal postulates" developed by the artists are, in their own words, based on reflections of divine qualities. The hope of the artists is that the beauty in the artworks might inspire self-motivated feelings of goodness. In this comparison of the legal rules of sharia and the legal postulates of aesthetics and ethics, the punitive and negative formulations of the legal rules (as expressed in regional regulations) are at odds with the inspirational nature of the positive qualities of Allah.

IV.   Postulates and Aesthetics: The Power of Affect

The memorized recitation of the Qur'an, the twin of Islam-inspired art,[50] suggests deeper ways of understanding relationships between Revelation, increasing piety, aesthetics and ethics. Reciting the Qur'an and creating art which is consciously inspired by the Qur'an are both activities which bring practitioners into direct contact with Revelation. Dr Anna Gade's study of intensive Qur'an memorization activities practised by thousands of Indonesians during the 1990s (the period which was also important in the public recognition of Islam-inspired art) is a complex analysis of direct engagement with the Qur'an through "modes of feeling". She argues that the positive feelings engendered by the intensive practice of direct experience of Revelation (through recitation) generate piety and ongoing religious commitment.[51] Dr Gade's identification of "the appreciation of beauty and enjoyable activities as the most effective means to 'motivate' (*memotivasikan*) people to deepen mainstream Muslim piety"[52] resonates with the terms Pirous and Sirojuddin use to describe the affect they hope their works have on mindful viewers.

Dr Gade describes how Revelation promises positive change to believers who engage directly with its message:

The Qur'an's statements about the dynamics of such affective engagement and especially about the impact of reading and hearing the Qur'an read show how the Qur'an claims an immediate, embodied encounter with its Message to be transformative of the enduring moral, ethical and social characteristics of a person.... The Qur'an makes numerous claims about its capacity to affect human experience in the present, to remake a person, reorienting him or her to moral sensitivity, social responsibility and an appropriate relationship to the Creator.[53]

Dr Gade develops the argument that "the inherent goodness of a practice may be accompanied by a natural desire among people to pursue 'goodness' in individual and collective experience".[54] Although viewers of spiritually charged, Islam-inspired art might also feel a sense of goodness as one of the emotions triggered by the painting, it is not quite the same as Gade's example. It is not the goodness of the practice which Pirous and Sirojuddin seem to describe as a motivation for their art, but rather the quality (not feeling) of Goodness which is one of Allah's attributes. In Islam this is a transcendent quality which humans cannot achieve or match in its perfection. But a recognition and acknowledgment of this very transcendence can arouse, or trigger, emotions of worship, gratitude, finiteness, and the desire to apply Qur'anic values in daily social life.

Dr Gade's research indicates that many Muslims believe that direct engagement with Revelation, through recitation of the Qur'an, has positive transformative effects. The artists whose works and writings have been analysed in this essay, together with art scholars and critics, similarly believe that Islam-inspired art also has the potential to awaken the ethical sensibilities of viewers. The two paintings presented above also show how Islam-inspired artists engage with contemporary social issues in direct and indirect ways.[55]

V. Conclusion: When Laws Are Not Enough

In his study of Indonesian fatwas, Professor Hooker included a discussion of "Islam as Object" in his Epilogue. He wrote, "The past 30 years or so have seen an Islamic resurgence; all this means is a renewed confidence in the face of secularism. Essential to this renewal is the realisation that Islam need not be defined or discussed in any terms other than its own."[56] Despite this, he continues, the need to develop a "canon" in response to the secular nation-state has meant that "from both the internal and external viewpoints Islam is subject to analysis in terms other than its own.... The mode of discussion is from outside Revelation; it is in contemporary theories of politics, social science, economics or any one of the philosophies of these."[57] The example of the philosophy of aesthetics and ethics developed by Indonesian artists and scholars suggests that their engagement with, and argumentation within, Revelation provides an exception to Professor Hooker's observation.

Applying Chiba's theory of legal pluralism to the art-based system of aesthetics and ethics proposed by the Indonesian artists has highlighted their positive and inspirational nature. Viewing artistic expressions of Revelation offers opportunities for diverse interpretations, that is, expressions of intra-religious pluralism. The artists have the hope that when viewers engage with their paintings, the combination of Qur'anic verses and images might stimulate their sense of ethical responsibility, for their social as well as their personal behaviour. The aesthetic presentation of the ethical component of the paintings suggests an added dimension to Chiba's definition of "legal postulates". It also suggests that at least some theories of legal pluralism can find material to support their positions in examples from "culture" in its broadest sense.

Notes

1. The author thanks Emeritus Professor A.D. Pirous and Dr Didin Sirojuddin AR for permission to reproduce their paintings and Professor Kenneth George for supplying the photograph of Pirous's work. The author is grateful to Professor M. Bambang Pranowo for his gift of a copy of Pirous's *Melukis itu Menulis* when she visited Bayt al-Qur'an in Jakarta in May 2003. Dr D. Sirojuddin generously provided copies of many of his writings to the author when she visited him several times in Jakarta and Sukabumi. Special thanks to Indonesian colleagues Ali Akbar, Yusuf Susilo Hartono, Hawe Setiawan, and Nadirsyah Hosen for ongoing help with references.

2. M.B. Hooker, *Legal Pluralism: An Introduction to Colonial and Neo-Colonial Laws* (Oxford: Clarendon Press, 1975), p. 6.

3. Ibid., p. vii; p. 5, "[A]ll the examples of legal pluralism described in this book involve the use of law as an agent or medium in changing social conduct."

4. The study was published as *Indonesian Islam: Social Change through Contemporary Fatawa* (Crows Nest: Allen & Unwin; Honolulu: University of Hawai'i Press, 2003). Hooker defines a *fatwa* as "a formal advice from an authority on a point of Islamic law or dogma. It is given in response to a question", ibid. p. viii.

5. Ibid., p. ix.

6. Ibid. See, in particular, "Epilogue", pp. 228ff.

7. Nadirsyah Hosen, "Hilal and Halal: How to Manage Islamic Pluralism in Indonesia", *Asian Journal of Comparative Law* 7, no. 1 (2012); and Mu'im Sirry, "Fatwas and Their Controversy: The Case of the Council of Indonesian Ulama (MUI)", *Journal of Southeast Asian Studies* 44, no. 1 (February 2013): 100–117.

8. Hosen, "Hilal and Halal", p. 17. Sirry goes further and suggests that "the critical engagement between Muslim progressives and liberals, as well as between radical and conservatives, serves to stabilise relations between groups by defining the position of each group in relationship to the others". Sirry, "Fatwas and Their Controversy", p. 117.

9. Not all Islam-themed works of art include verses from the Qur'an.

10. For a succinct explanation of the concept and form of Qur'anic exegesis, see Jane Dammen McAuliffe, *The Cambridge Companion to the Qur'an* (Cambridge: Cambridge University Press, 2006), pp. 181–210. For those exegeses which have been most influential in Indonesia, see Peter G. Riddell, *Islam and the Malay-Indonesian World: Transmissions and Responses* (London: Hurst, 2001), Chapter 12.

11. Toshihiko Izutsu, *Ethico-Religious Concepts in the Qur'an* (Canada: McGill-Queen's University Press, 2002).

12. Masaji Chiba, *Legal Pluralism: Towards a General Theory through Japanese Legal Culture* (Tokyo: Tokai University Press, 1989).

13 Ibid., p. 178.

14 Ibid., p. 178.

15. See Anna M. Gade, *Perfection Makes Practice: Learning, Emotion, and the Recited Qur'an in Indonesia* (Honolulu: University of Hawai'i Press, 2004).

16. See, further, Kenneth M. George, *Picturing Islam: Art and Ethics in a Muslim Lifeworld* (United Kingdom: Wiley-Blackwell, 2010), p. 43.

17. For examples, see Machmud Buchari and Sanento Yuliman, *A.D. Pirous* (Bandung: Galeri Decenta, 1985).

18. *Katalog Seni Rupa Modern*, edited by Setiawan Sabana et al. (Bandung: Badan Pelaksana Festival Istiqlal, 1991), p. 1.

19. A.D. Pirous, "Seni Bernafaskan Islam di Indonesia: Kajian Khusus Seni Rupa Masa Kini Dalam Perspektif Seniman Muslim" [Islam-inspired art in Indonesia: a special study of contemporary art from the perspective of Muslim artists], in *Melukis itu Menulis* [Painting is writing], edited by Dudy Wiyancoko (Bandung: Penerbit ITB, 2003), pp. 102–23.

20. Pirous included further examples of increased Islamization, such as: the appearance of Islamic hospitals in most of Indonesia's large cities; Arabic language lessons on government television stations; increasing numbers of Islam-oriented schools and colleges; new mosque-building programmes; and increasing numbers of young people choosing to wear contemporary, designer-styled Islamic fashion clothes, including the Islamic styles of head covering for both men and women. See Pirous, "Seni Bernafaskan Islam di Indonesia", pp. 116–18.

21. Ibid., pp. 120–21.

22. Translation by Kenneth George, *Picturing Islam*, p. 61.

23. Although originally published in 1985, the article was reprinted in 2008 in a widely read Jakarta arts magazine because the use of Qur'anic calligraphy in art was still being debated. See D. Sirajuddin [sic] AR, "Dicari: Fatwa untuk Kaligrafi: Jawaban untuk Syaiful Adnan" [Wanted: a fatwa on calligraphy: an answer for Syaiful Adnan], *Majalah Seni Rupa Visual Arts* 5, no. 27 (October–November 2008): 108–10.

24. The text of the talk appears in a privately published collection of Sirojuddin's writings. The details are: "Orasi Ilmiah Mutiara Ramadhan 1424H, Peranan Seni Islam dalam Fenomena Kehidupan Sosial" [Ramadhan 1424 Anno Hijra Mutiara Oration, the role of Islamic art in social life], in *Nuansa Kaligrafi Islam: Kumpulan tulisan sekitar ide-ide pengembangan seni kaligrafi Islam di Indonesia* [Islamic calligraphy: collected writings about the development of Islamic calligraphy in Indonesia], by D. Sirojuddin AR (Studio Lemka: Ciputat, Jakarta Selatan 15412, 2005), pp. 287–92.

25. The Qualities (*sifa*) of Allah are the abstract qualities which lie behind His Names. The Names themselves are the epithets applied to Him as descriptives in the Qur'an. See H.A.R. Gibb and J.H. Kramers, eds., *Shorter Encyclopaedia of Islam* (The Netherlands: Brill, third impression, 1991), p. 545.

26. The origin of and reference for both these well-known Hadiths is not given.

27. The majority of Pirous's works since the early 1970s are obviously inspired by Islam, but he has also painted works with other themes. All of Sirojuddin's works are clearly Islam-themed.

28. Where he was taught formalism and abstract art. See Kenneth M. George, "Art and Identity Politics: Nation, Religion, Ethnicity, Elsewhere", in *Asian and Pacific Cosmopolitans: Self and Subject in Motion*, edited by Kathryn Robinson (Basingstoke: Palgrave Macmillan, 2007), p. 39; and Astri Wright, *Soul, Spirit, and Mountain: Preoccupations of Contemporary Indonesian Painters* (Kuala Lumpur: Oxford University Press, 1994), pp. 71–72.

29. See Wright, *Soul, Spirit, and Mountain*, p. 72 for Pirous's own description of his earlier works.

30. For further details, see George, *Picturing Islam*, pp. 47ff . Pirous was also aware that the greatly admired abstract painter Ahmad Sadali drew inspiration for his works from the Qur'an. See George, *Picturing Islam*, p. 51.

31. Ibid., p. 108.

32. Ibid., p. 85. Translated by Kenneth George.

33. Description provided in George, *Picturing Islam*, colour plate 18, following p. 46.

34. George, *Picturing Islam*, p. 104.

35. "Memang benar isi Al Quran itu ditafsirkan, bukan diterjemahkan oleh para ahlinya. Karena itu ada kebebasan terbatas para penafsir, yang kemudian menjadi pegangan oleh umat, yang tentunya dalan proses ijtihad para pemakai seterusnya ada pula penyesuaian yang sifatnya lebih kontekstual terhadapnya. Demikianlah yang terjadi ketika saat saya mengambil Surah Ali Imran 26 dan 27 itu, untuk memperkaya lukisan Amanat kepada Sang Pemimpin. Ada situasi yang mendesak saat itu yang membuat saya gelisah dan ingin menyatakan pendapat untuk memperingatkan semua fihak untuk merenung kembali. Sekitar 1995 dimasa pemerintahan Orde Baru, keras sekali nuansa lupa diri yang berlebihan bagi banyak pemimpin yang berkuasa, seakan2 kekuasan itu suatu yang abadi, tiada berkesudahan, padahal itu semua adalah yang fana, sementara, setiap saat dapat berakhir, sesuai seperti yang diujarkan dalam ayat 26 dan 27 Ali Imran itu. Dalam dunia seni rupa memang ada kebebasan yang agak pribadi untuk dapat mengungkapkan pesannya, sehingga seakan akan ada dua identitas yang dapat menyatu, antara identitas bahasa pengucapan visualnya (style), dengan identitas penyampaian messagenya (content), walaupun isi messagenya sama tetapi oleh para seniman seakan diucapkannya berbeda." A.D. Pirous, personal email to Virginia Hooker, sent from Indonesia, 13 June 2013.

36. 'Allama Abdullah Yusuf 'Ali, *The Holy Qur'an: Arabic Text, English Translation & Commentary* (1934; repr., Elmhurst, NY: Tahrike Tarsik Qur'an, 2008), p. 129.

37. See George, *Picturing Islam*, pp. 77–78, 104.
38. Even if viewers could not read and understand the lines of Arabic script, all Indonesian speakers could understand the meaning of the title.
39. Qur'an 3, Al-i-Imran, verse 103.
40. Salim Fachry was chosen by Sukarno, soon after he became president of the newly independent Republic of Indonesia, to prepare the official, large scale, handwritten copy of the Qur'an for the new nation state. It is now known as the "Qur'an Pusaka" (Heirloom Qur'an) and symbolizes the role of Islam in the new nation. Abdul Razzaq Muhili was also highly regarded, and in 1961 published the first Indonesian text book on Arabic calligraphy, entitled *Tulisan Indah* (Beautiful Writing). See further "Dinamika Perkembangan Seni Kaligrafi" [The development of Indonesian calligraphy], 1 February 2011 <http://lemkaonline.blogspot.com/> (accessed 22 May 2013).
41. Sirojuddin has judged calligraphy competitions in the Middle East, Pakistan, and Turkey as well as throughout Southeast Asia. He has exhibited his calligraphy and his calligraphic paintings in many exhibitions and is well known in Indonesia for his dedication to spreading a love for calligraphy, especially through the courses he and his colleagues teach at LEMKA.
42. At Hotel Grand Melia in 2003 and Menara Kebon Sirih in 2005. The paintings were a gift to M.B. Hooker from the artist in 2007. A more detailed description and analysis of this set of paintings appears in Virginia Hooker, "Lines of Meaning: Three Calligraphic Paintings by Didin Sirojuddin", *Suhuf: Jurnal Kajian Al-Qur'an dan Kebudayaan* 4, no. 2 (2011): 315–39.
43. Virginia Hooker, "Reflections of the Soul", *Inside Indonesia* 112 (April–June 2013) <http://www.insideindonesia.org/feature-editions/reflections-of-the-soul> (accessed 9 April 2013).
44. Ibid.
45. There are numerous verses in the Qur'an which support this statement. See, for example, Qur'an 29, Al-'Ankabut, verses 47–49 and verse 51; Qur'an 7, al-A'raf, verse 2 and verse 203.
46 See Sirojuddin, *Nuansa*, p. 12. "Alquran adalah sumber segala inspirasi dan dapat dijadikan ajang perburuan kreasi yang tiada habis-habisnya."
47. Chiba, *Legal* Pluralism, p. 178.
48. Translated by George, *Picturing Islam*, p. 95
49. For more on the phenomenon of regional regulations claiming to be inspired by sharia, see Robin Bush, "Regional Sharia Regulations in Indonesia: Anomaly or Symptom?", in *Expressing Islam: Religious Life and Politics in Indonesia*, edited by Greg Fealy and Sally White (Singapore: Institute of Southeast Asian Studes, 2008), pp. 174–91.

50. They are twins in the sense that there is overlap in approach to ethics and aesthetics as well as a shared organizational link — Islam-inspired arts which incorporate calligraphy grew national roots and gained in authority by being held in conjunction with the national Qur'an recitation competition (MTQ) events from 1979 onwards.
51. Gade, *Perfection Makes Practice*. See particularly pp. 48–59.
52. Ibid., p. 17
53. Ibid., p. 38–39.
54. Ibid., p. 276.
55. Sirojuddin also creates calligraphic paintings for reproduction as calendars and chooses a significant social issue (for example, corruption or education) as the theme for each year.
56. M.B. Hooker, *Indonesian Islam*, p. 234.
57. Ibid., p. 234.

References

Books

'Ali, 'Allama Abdullah Yusuf. *The Holy Qur'an: Arabic Text, English Translation & Commentary*. 1934. Reprint, Elmhurst, NY: Tahrike Tarsik Qur'an Inc., August 2008.

Buchari, Machmud and Sanento Yuliman. *A.D. Pirous*. Bandung: Galeri Decenta, 1985.

Chiba, Masaji. *Legal Pluralism: Towards a General Theory through Japanese Legal Culture*. Tokyo: Tokai University Press, 1989.

Gade, Anna M. *Perfection Makes Practice: Learning, Emotion, and the Recited Qur'an in Indonesia*. Honolulu: University of Hawai'i Press, 2004.

George, Kenneth M. *Picturing Islam: Art and Ethics in a Muslim Lifeworld*. Wiley-Blackwell, 2010.

Gibb, H.A.R. and J.H. Kramers, eds. *Shorter Encyclopaedia of Islam*. The Netherlands: Brill, 1991.

Hooker, M.B. *Legal Pluralism: An Introduction to Colonial and Neo-Colonial Laws*. Oxford: Clarendon Press, 1975.

———. *Indonesian Islam: Social Change through Contemporary Fatawa*. Crows Nest: Allen & Unwin; Honolulu: University of Hawai'i Press, 2003.

Izutsu, Toshihiko. *Ethico-Religious Concepts in the Qur'an*. Canada: McGill-Queen's University Press, 2002.

McAuliffe, Jane Dammen. *The Cambridge Companion to the Qur'an*. Cambridge: Cambridge University Press, 2006.

Riddell, Peter G. *Islam and the Malay-Indonesian World: Transmissions and Responses*. London: Hurst, 2001.

Sabana, Setiawan et al., eds. *Katalog Seni Rupa Modern*. Bandung: Badan Pelaksana Festival Istiqlal, 1991.

Wright, Astri. *Soul, Spirit, and Mountain: Preoccupations of Contemporary Indonesian Painters*. Kuala Lumpur: Oxford University Press, 1994.

Chapters

Bush, Robin. "Regional Sharia Regulations in Indonesia: Anomaly or Symptom?" In *Expressing Islam: Religious Life and Politics in Indonesia*, edited by Greg Fealy and Sally White. Singapore: Institute of Southeast Asian Studies, 2008.

George, Kenneth M. "Art and Identity Politics: Nation, Religion, Ethnicity, Elsewhere". In *Asian and Pacific Cosmopolitans: Self and Subject in Motion*, edited by Kathryn Robinson. Basingstoke: Palgrave Macmillan, 2007.

Pirous, A.D. "Seni Bernafaskan Islam di Indonesia: Kajian Khusus Seni Rupa Masa Kini Dalam Perspektif Seniman Muslim". [Islam-inspired art in Indonesia: a special study of contemporary art from the perspective of Muslim artists]. In *Melukis itu Menulis* [Painting is writing], edited by Dudy Wiyancoko. Bandung:Penerbit ITB, 2003.

Periodicals

Hooker, Virginia. "Reflections of the Soul". *Inside Indonesia* 112 (April–June 2013) <http://www,insideindonesia.org/feature-editions/reflections-of-the-soul>: 1–4.

———. "Lines of Meaning: Three Calligraphic Paintings by Didin Sirojuddin". *Suhuf: Jurnal Kajian Al-Qur'an dan Kebudayaan* 4, no. 2 (2011): 315–39.

Hosen, Nadirsyah. "Hilal and Halal: How to Manage Islamic Pluralism in Indonesia". *Asian Journal of Comparative Law* 7, no. 1 (2012): 1–18.

Sirajuddin [sic] D. AR. "Dicari: Fatwa untuk Kaligrafi: Jawaban untuk Syaiful Adnan" [Wanted: a fatwa on calligraphy: an answer for Syaiful Adnan]. *Majalah Seni Rupa Visual Arts* 5, no. 27 (October–November 2008): 108–10.

Mu'im Sirry. "Fatwas and their Controversy: The Case of the Council of Indonesian Ulama (MUI)". *Journal of Southeast Asian Studies* 44, no. 1 (February 2013): 100–117.

Online Citations

"Dinamika Perkembangan Seni Kaligrafi" [The development of Indonesian calligraphy], 1 February 2011 <http://lemkaonline.blogspot.com/> (accessed 22 May 2013).

Other

Sirojuddin, D. AR. "Orasi Ilmiah Mutiara Ramadhan 1424H, Peranan Seni Islam dalam Fenomena Kehidupan Sosial" [Ramadhan 1424 Anno Hijra Mutiara oration, The role of Islamic art in social life]. In *Nuansa Kaligrafi Islam: Kumpulan tulisan sekitar ide-ide pengembangan seni kaligrafi Islam di Indonesia* [Islamic calligraphy: collected writings about the development of Islamic calligraphy in Indonesia]. Studio Lemka: South Tangerang, 2005.

8

Legal Pluralism and the Constitutional Position of East Malaysia's Indigenous Peoples: The View from the Longhouse

Andrew Harding

Malaysian Constitutionalism and the Indigenous Peoples

With increasing awareness of, and concern about, the legal position of indigenous peoples across the world, there is naturally increasing attention to the ways in which this position is affected by constitutional provisions. These days the concern also embraces the fact that indigenous peoples have their own legal traditions, or forms of "chthonic law" as Patrick Glenn has it.[1] John Borrows, for example, in his book *Canada's Indigenous Constitution*, argues for the inclusion of indigenous law within the recognized legal traditions of Canada, and for this law to be taken seriously on its own terms, as well as protected by the Constitution. Hooker, in his extensive work on the indigenous peoples of East Malaysia (Sabah and Sarawak), was concerned with the *adat* of these states' indigenous people. His work explores the nature and the detail of this law as it has been enforced in the courts in Sabah and Sarawak as an aspect of official or formal legal pluralism.

The intention in this chapter is not to explore this further or to distil anything of relevance to legal pluralism directly from Hooker's work; it is rather to explore the extent to which it is possible to assert that this pluralism has been constitutionalized — in other words, to inquire into its constitutional status within the Malaysian federation. However, in building on Hooker's extraordinary foundation of knowledge and understanding of adat, we should not ignore, as an aspect of legal pluralism, the relevance here also of how constitutionalism frames, recognizes, embraces or responds not just to the laws but also to the protection of the *rights and interests*, of indigenous people. The issue of recognition as such of adat, or what in relation to East Malaysia is known as "native law", is relatively unproblematical, due to the prevailing legal pluralism in the legal systems of Sabah and Sarawak. The issue is therefore how far this recognition of legal pluralism is constitutionalized, and how far federalism, which was designed (in relation to Sabah and Sarawak under the Malaysia Agreement of 1963) to protect the rights of the indigenous people, has succeeded in doing so. For this reason the chapter is directed only towards Sabah and Sarawak, and not towards the indigenous peoples of West or Peninsular Malaysia, whose laws are not protected and whose status is not congruent with their East Malaysian equivalent groups, giving rise to a somewhat different set of issues.[2] Due to considerations of space, and also because the relevant issues have been extensively covered elsewhere, notably by Hooker himself,[3] I refer only briefly, later in the chapter, to the complex issue of native customary land rights.

The chapter is thus an attempt to take for analysis a particular slice of Malaysian constitutionalism or constitutional identity[4] — the slice that deals with the indigenous peoples of Sabah and Sarawak. Does this slice of constitutionalism, I ask, actually protect indigenous people and recognize their law? Hooker's work is obviously seminal for anyone attempting such a task. It is at once encouraging, because he has done so much one can rely on or build on, but at the same time daunting because he shows one how much there is to learn about this subject. Hooker's work, as far as is directly relevant here, is concerned principally with the nature, content and context of adat.

He does not in general discuss constitutional issues. Nonetheless his work is of great indirect relevance to an enterprise such as this, which looks at the issue of indigenous law from a constitutional perspective. In this chapter I do not attempt a comprehensive analysis, but examine just three related issues: the gradual constitutionalization of native law, as I call it, during the colonial period; the *Ningkan* case in 1960s Sarawak, as a test of federalism's impact on the rights and interests of Sarawak's indigenous peoples; and the application of human rights to the indigenous people over the last fifteen years since the creation of the National Human Rights Commission, Suhakam.[5]

Legal Pluralism in Malaysia

Malaysia was referred to by T.N. Harper as having "the classic pluralistic society".[6] Since independence in 1957 it has struggled with the problem of accommodating the contradictory interests of the majority Malay/Muslim community, the Chinese, and other groups amongst the 179 officially recognized ethnicities. The "natives"[7] of Sabah and Sarawak comprise a large number of tribal people indigenous to those two Borneo states, including the Iban, Murut, Kadazan, Kenyah, Penan, and many other groups.[8] The Iban constitute around 31 per cent of Sarawak's population, while the Kadazan are the largest group in Sabah at 17 per cent.[9] Taken altogether, the indigenous peoples at around 2.2 million constitute about half of the population of these two states. In general these native groups live in longhouses and owe their subsistence to cash crops or the produce of the sea and the jungle, but development has introduced other forms of employment in the logging, oil, gas and palm oil industries. But the considerable economic development has largely left behind the native communities; indeed development in the form of logging, construction and new dams often threatens their land and their traditional way of life.

Ethnicity and religion inform almost every issue arising in the public domain in Malaysia. Principally the problem of ethnic and religious diversity has been dealt with via the *bumiputera* (lit. "sons of the soil") preference policy,[10] which is expressed in a multitude of laws, regulations and policies; and by the recognition of Islamic law as a separate system of law.[11] These institutions form the basis of Malaysian legal pluralism, and many of its governing principles are in turn derived from the so-called social contract embodied in the 1957 Constitution.[12] This social contract did not, however, engage indigenous peoples, who are mainly located in the East Malaysian states of Sabah and Sarawak and comprise most of the 179 officially recognized ethnic groups but are also a minority of the total population. On the contrary, the social contract was an agreement between the leaders of the Malay, Chinese and "Indian" communities, an elite project that excluded the indigenous perspective. This is of course partly due to the fact that the social contract was made between the political leaderships of Malaya, and the East Malaysian States of Sabah and Sarawak only became relevant to that agreement a few years later — in 1962–63 when the federation took its present shape, and again in 1969–71 when the indigenous people of Sabah and Sarawak were included within the ranks of the bumiputera, and in this respect were treated differently from the *orang asli*, the indigenous peoples of West Malaysia.

Thus from 1971 the indigenous peoples of East Malaysia came to enjoy the special position already accorded the majority Malay/Muslim people of Malaysia and recognized in the form of special quotas for trade licences, positions in the public service, and in other areas.[13] The remaking of Malaysia's social contract in 1971 also resulted in political parties representing the interests of Sabah and Sarawak's indigenous people being absorbed into the ruling Barisan Nasional (BN) coalition, which since before independence in 1957 had comprised principally parties representing only the Malay, Chinese and Indian communities.

Given that the incorporation of the indigenous people within Malaysia depended on assurances that their rights would be guaranteed; that "Malaysia" (the federation of Sabah and Sarawak with the Federation of Malaya) celebrated its 50th birthday in 2013; that Hooker places the beginning of Sarawak's modern legal system at 1863, 150 years earlier; and that we celebrate Hooker's work; this is perhaps an opportune moment to consider these issues. Indeed, revisiting the terms of federation and consulting the interests of the indigenous people has never gone out of fashion, and is currently a point of controversy in the context of, for example, indigenous land claims and the nature of federalism. The events surrounding the Sulu Sultanate's claim to Sabah and the

Lahad Datu incident,[14] not to mention concerns over citizenship in Sabah[15] and corruption allegations in Sarawak,[16] have kept alive interest in the federal angle on these issues.

Legal History

In the spirit of Hooker's work, and drawing on it, we should start with history. I take as the historical starting point the first attempts to "constitutionalize" the indigenous people and their law; by which I mean the attempts to put into writing the idea that the indigenous people should be protected on a continuing, legal basis, and their adat recognized as official, not unofficial, law. To some extent it also involves actually committing to writing their traditional adat.

Here Hooker's contribution to Lee Hun Hoe's casebook of indigenous adat in Sarawak[17] is very instructive, balancing judiciously on the one hand factual information about the law and the institutions and, on the other hand, astute and pithy insights. What one notices here is that legal pluralism is not precisely treated as a theory which Hooker applies to the facts; rather, legal pluralism is a preoccupation that arises naturally from consideration of the facts. It is, as it were, the medium in which Hooker's thoughts swim; and it is consciousness of this medium that gives rise to the analysis he undertakes.

One very interesting example of this is the way he draws attention to (the first white) Rajah James Brooke's (1803–68) fascinating statement of judicial method,[18] which draws a sharp distinction between the rule of law as conceived by an assumed but invisible English reader and the social and psychological realities of Sarawak. For example, a leading question should, according to Brooke, be allowed because, "here, for the purposes of justice, it is indispensable; for the people, being ruled by fear, and apprehensive of consequences often falter before the face of the accused, and their testimony has to be wrung from them". Brooke instigated the rule of law in many respects, however, by, for example, fixing the revenue at a proper rate "so that everyone may know certainly how much he has to contribute yearly to support the government" (Hooker 1980). Here we can see the very beginnings of constitutional government. But even the equal contributions, for the indigenous people, are settled in terms of rice, sago, and cash, taking into account their economy and their culture. One wonders whether the contributions actually collected were in fact equal, as between the indigenous people of the jungle and the urban Chinese, for example.

Equality then did not mean that there was equal citizenship in which the attributes of different groups were simply ignored by the state. The European view, famously set out by Clermont-Tonnerre during the French Revolution where he said, "Everything must be refused to the Jews as a nation and everything must be accorded to the Jews as individuals",[19] clearly had, and has, no application in Sarawak, or indeed, if one follows Hooker's line of thinking, in Southeast Asia generally — even today.[20] In fact, Hooker observes, it was "apparent from the Orders [the Rajah's Order Books, which began in 1863, the point at which Sarawak's legal system begins, according to Hooker] that the Rajahs were concerned to establish a *distinct system of law* for each racial and religious group" (my emphasis). It was a particular concern to protect the indigenous people against "their oppressors crafty and bold" (one assumes he meant the Chinese). Here indeed is the beginning of the constitutionalization of adat.

Pervasive legal pluralism was in fact the main social condition that spurred legal change and a move towards legal formality during the latter part of the nineteenth century and the earlier part of the twentieth. An example is the Marriage Order of 1871, which deals with marriage between people of different religion or of no religion. Principally the issue here was the children of these marriages, who were under the 1871 Order legitimized, custody going to the mother. The facility of registration of marriages was provided to clarify these inter-ethnic marriages. Conversion of indigenous people to Islam or Christianity complicated further the nature of legal pluralism. Largely, where potential conflicts of law were not in question, the indigenous people were left with their own adat, in which disputes were "administered" (Hooker's word) by the Resident: in other words it was amicable settlement in the shadow, as it were, of adat, that was prevalent and required, rather than strict *application* of adat in the juridical and judicial sense.[21]

Eventually the Laws of Sarawak Order 1928 introduced the common law, but "only so far as it is applicable having regard to native customs". Indeed the Native Courts Ordinance 1940 introduced Native

Courts with the express function of applying indigenous law to indigenous people. In 1941 a Constitution Ordinance was brought into effect, ending Sarawak's absolute monarchy, which had prevailed for a century, and of course had applied even before James Brooke was handed the title of Rajah by the Sultan of Brunei in 1842. Constitutionalism, confirmed after the Japanese Occupation with the Constitution Ordinance 1946, went along with the judicialization of adat. This judicialization goes much further in recognizing legal pluralism than the mere modification of the common law in its application to various communities in the Straits Settlements, which was honoured more in the breach than the observance.[22] Even now, Sarawak, a legal pluralist's seventh heaven, can fairly claim to recognize the different forms of customary law in plenitude greater than almost anywhere in Asia. Chinese customary law, for example, not just indigenous forms of adat, is recognized officially, even though it is not so recognized in either China or Taiwan.[23]

Legal pluralism involves modification and adaptation as well as recognition. Hooker draws attention, for example, to the need to modify common law principles in relation to guardianship: the Guardianship of Infants Ordinance 1953 "while introducing principles drawn from English statute, contains special provisions as to native infants", taking the form of a power to use native assessors in reaching their decisions. The 1946 Ordinance, commencing a theme which was to become familiar in Malaysia, defined "native" as "a race declared to be indigenous to Sarawak". Here the need to protect natives is recognized by applying special laws and giving the government the power to declare who is a native. Unfortunately, in the contemporary situation in East Malaysia, especially in Sabah, this power is considered to have been abused by the designation of comparative, or even very recent, newcomers as "indigenous" citizens, capable of affecting an election result.[24]

Finally, the Native Courts Ordinance and the Native Customary Laws Ordinance of 1955 settled the shape of the institutions applying adat to the indigenous people.[25] Essentially, what the latter statute does is to schedule lists of fines for different groups as punishment for different wrongs. It also provides for "authorized versions" of native law and the recording of decisions. As Hooker insightfully concludes, this made native adat a distinct part of an English-derived legal system, based on formal precedent, as opposed to the fact-based decisions of the Residents under the Rajahs. Legal pluralism did not preclude, then, the modernization of indigenous law. It is trite that the writing down of customary law renders it no longer customary. In Borrows' words, writing about Canada, it becomes "romanticised, essentialised, and fossilised in an inflexible framework".[26] It becomes, let us say, *lex scripta* as opposed to the *lex tradita* we associate with customary law. This process was virtually completed in Sarawak when Iban customary law was codified in the Iban Customary Law 1993, which has the force of a statute. This presents a dilemma: if adat is not written down it may die out; but if it is written down its nature is irrevocably altered. Sarawak, at least, has provided its own solution to this dilemma.

Sabah presents a similar yet slightly different story. As North Borneo it was under company rule (the North Borneo Company) from 1881 until 1941. However, a similar policy of protecting native custom applied. An earlier attempt was made, by G.C. Wooley in the 1930s, to write down the variants of adat,[27] although in practice, as Phelan reports, these versions are not binding but are at best persuasive.[28] Native Courts were introduced in North Borneo in 1953. Hooker, in his book *Native Law in Sabah and Sarawak*,[29] has given us a splendid account of the content of adat in both Sabah and Sarawak. He notes that the legislation on adat in Sabah contains much more substantive law than other similar examples. Given the codification attempts in Sarawak, one wonders if this is as true as it was when Hooker wrote. Clearly, however, this is an aspect of the constitutionalization of indigenous law in which the writing down of adat has been a first and perhaps necessary step towards constitutional entrenchment. With regard to the tragic choice referred to above between the reification and survival of adat, on the one hand, and on the other hand keeping its traditional nature but perhaps losing it altogether, Hooker is firm in believing that law has to keep pace with society, and this applies to adat as much as to any other kind of law.[30]

My conclusion here is that indigenous legal traditions have in fact been in a continuous process of constitutionalization over the last 150 years. As we will see, this process is by no means completed.

The Context of Federalism

Since my intention is to discuss the indigenous people and their law in a constitutional context, we will proceed to look at the politics of constitutional government post-1963 insofar as it affects them.

Tunku Abdul Rahman's (Malaya/Malaysia's first prime minister, 1955–71) grand design for decolonization, which was in the main consonant with British policy too, was to incorporate the remaining Southeast Asian territories under British control in the early 1960s — namely, Singapore, Sabah, Sarawak and Brunei — into a larger federation spanning Malaya and Borneo. The only realistic other options for the Borneo territories were to become independent separately; form their own federation; or join Sukarno's increasingly unstable and hostile Indonesia. The Communist insurgency determined this issue for the majority of people in these territories.

At the same time there was, of course, some unease in Sabah and Sarawak about the possibly deleterious effects of joining the federation. Prominent in this respect was the perceived need to protect the special position and interests of the indigenous people who formed about half of the population in these two states. The Malaysia Consultative Committee, a Committee of the Commonwealth Parliamentary Association, consisting of representatives of the governments of Britain, Malaya, Sabah and Sarawak, supported the federation of Sabah and Sarawak with Malaya and Singapore in its Memorandum of February 1962. Brunei took part only as an observer, and ultimately declined to join Malaysia, partly because of disagreement about the exploitation of Brunei's oil revenues, and partly over issues relating to the precedence of the Sultan of Brunei in the proposed federal scheme. The Cobbold Commission, consisting of representatives of the British and Malayan governments, visited Sabah and Sarawak in 1962 and reported that the majority supported federation with Malaya, provided due regard was had to the special position of Sabah and Sarawak; the ethnic implications; the physical distances involved; and these territories' political immaturity compared to Malaya and Singapore. The legislative assemblies of both territories voted in favour of federation subject to appropriate safeguards. An Inter-Governmental Committee was then set up, comprising representatives from the same four governments, to thrash out constitutional safeguards for Sabah and Sarawak, reporting in February 1963.[31] The Malaysia Agreement was eventually signed on 9 July 1963 by all the governments concerned, and Malaysia came into being on 16 September 1963. This was effected not by a new federal constitution but simply by the admission of new states to the existing but renamed federation under article 1 of the Constitution, and by numerous amendments to the Constitution giving effect to the negotiated settlement that was embodied in the Malaysia Agreement. It is to be noted that a deliberate decision was taken not to engage in debate about a *new* constitution: the rights and interests of the indigenous people were therefore not specifically addressed in terms of the entire constitutional scheme, but dealt with by grafting relevant provisions relating to these rights and interests on to a constitution embodying a social contract to which they had not been party.[32]

A principal point of concern in Sabah and Sarawak was of course, as explained above, the protection of the special position and interests of its numerous indigenous ethnic groups under the new governance arrangements. Another major issue was the possible effect of migration from *"semananjung"* (Peninsular Malaya) and Singapore on land, commerce, and the employment and professional opportunities of Sabahans and Sarawakians faced with competition from more qualified people from Malaya and Singapore. In this latter connection a draft bill on immigration was appended to the Malaysia Agreement and promptly passed into law as the Immigration Act 1963 a few days before Malaysia came into being. However, there was concern about other issues too: financial arrangements and development; the national language; religion; the legal system; representation in the Federal Parliament; and of course how these states would be protected from future constitutional changes affecting any of these issues. Malay was the national language; Islam was the religion of the federation; and the existing legal systems in Sabah and Sarawak, as we have seen, recognized "native law". All of these issues potentially divided East from West Malaysia. Between them, Sabah and Sarawak have about sixty per cent of Malaysia's land but only about a fifth of its population. These states saw their problem as essentially the need for protection against more powerful neighbours. The Cobbold Commission had stressed the need for a sense of equality and partnership in the new federal scheme. According to Lord Cobbold, it was to be a "partnership", not a "takeover". But as we will see, the reality that emerged all too soon after 1963 was otherwise.

As a result of this process of negotiation, Sabah and Sarawak were placed in a position that was not available to the states that had formed the Federation of Malaya in 1948, precisely in that they were able to *negotiate* their part in the federal scheme. These states were both resource-rich and underdeveloped. Accordingly, they were given the benefit of special grants and other fiscal privileges.[33] Quite apart from the central issues of finance and immigration powers, Sabah and Sarawak have substantially more powers than the other states. The federal parliament's powers to legislate for land (always a critical issue, but especially so in East Malaysia) and local government, for example, do not apply to Sabah and Sarawak; this allows these states exclusive legislative control over these two matters. Crucially, the governments of Sabah and Sarawak also have special powers to veto constitutional amendments affecting their states, and in this respect they have a considerable advantage over the other states, who have no such powers. Under Article 161E(2), no amendment shall be made to the Federal Constitution without the concurrence of the government of Sabah or Sarawak, as the case may be (oddly, though, the concurrence of the State Legislative Assembly is not required), if the amendment is such as to affect the operation of the Constitution with regard to: Malaysian citizenship and the equal treatment of persons born or resident in the state; the Constitution and jurisdiction of the High Court of Sabah and Sarawak, and the appointment, removal and suspension of its judges; the state's legislative and executive powers and financial arrangements between the federation and the state; religion and language in the state, and the *special treatment of natives of the state*; and the quota of MPs allocated to the state in proportion to the total number of MPs. To a large extent this was an attempt to reassure doubters that the status quo would be maintained so far as was possible under a federal arrangement. This included the existing special privileges of the indigenous people.

The reference to the judiciary is an unusual one. The object here was to preserve the separate nature of the High Court and the legal profession serving it. This was designed to guarantee the judicial enforcement of the law in Sabah and Sarawak, bearing in mind that essentially each of these states had, as we have seen, its own legal history, statute laws, legal system, and legal profession; and to protect its legal profession from being swamped by lawyers from

Malaya seeking to practise before the courts in the state. Part of this justification is the fact that the indigenous people have, as we have seen, their own customary laws which are enforced through the official legal system. Indeed article 76(2) of the Federal Constitution restricts federal legislative power where exercised in pursuit of international law with regard to "any matters of native law or custom in the States of Sabah and Sarawak". The judiciary in the two states has remained largely unaffected by turbulent developments regarding the judiciary in Peninsular Malaysia;[34] however, the joining of the three separate legal systems at the federal level via the umbilical cord of appeals to the (federal) Court of Appeal and the Federal Court mitigates the significance of legal-system autonomy to some extent. It is still possible for a lawyer from Peninsular Malaysia to be admitted to practise in Sabah or Sarawak by the court on an ad hoc basis, but this is without prejudice to the need to obtain an entry permit from the immigration authorities, which are under state, not federal, control.[35]

Apart from institutional factors (the legal complex was clearly protecting its monopoly at the ground floor), an obvious justification for the special position of the judicial system is the fact that native law represents a substantial part of the legal systems of Sabah and Sarawak, and is not a legal subject necessarily known to the Malaysian judiciary as a whole. Nonetheless, the three legal systems (Malaya, Sabah, Sarawak) are, as we have seen, joined at the top, and if one reflects that Malayan judges could be the final authority on the laws of Sabah or Sarawak, then the "different law" justification for judicial separation seems to slip between one's fingers. If native law is really to be specially protected, then, as with the sharia courts, the final authority should be judges familiar with the legal tradition in question.

I do not argue here that the existence of a separate legal system should be a constitutional guarantee; rather, that native law is worthy of being taken seriously — how one does that is of course a separate issue. If the need to protect the legal profession was paramount, as I think it was thought to be at the time, one could ask why other professions were not to be similarly protected. A simple if cynical answer might be that lawyers are involved in constitution-making, whereas architects, surgeons and accountants are generally not. One could also ask, even more relevantly, whether indigenous people were actually represented in such professions at all. In the early 1960s it seems there were no indigenous lawyers at all in Sarawak, for example.[36]

Indigenous Politics and the Curious Case of Stephen Kalong Ningkan

The native peoples constitute a narrow majority in both Sabah and Sarawak, and from the beginning of federation in 1963 there have been political parties representing their interests.[37] Further, the politics of these two states impact on the ethnic balance and, therefore, on the politics of the entire country.[38] For these reasons the autonomy of these two states is critical for them, for Malaysia as a whole, and of course for the indigenous peoples whose interests are supposed to be protected primarily by the constitutional provisions discussed above.

The importance of constitutional protection of these two states' powers within the federation is illustrated by the severe early test of autonomy to which this structure was put very soon after Malaysia came into being in 1963 — the Ningkan episode. It was an episode with particular implications for the protection of the interests of the indigenous people.

By 1966 tensions had developed between the federal and Sarawak governments. The ruling party in Sarawak, the Sarawak National Party (SNAP), had been founded in 1961 to protect the interests of the indigenous peoples of Sarawak; it was a member of the Alliance, which ruled at the federal level. The chief minister of Sarawak, Stephen Kalong Ningkan, a Dayak leader and one of the founders of SNAP, pursued an independent policy which irritated federal leaders. Constitutional chicanery followed as the federal government undermined Ningkan's position behind the scenes. A letter, signed by 21 of the 42 members of the Council Negri, the state legislature, was sent to the Yang di-Pertua Negeri (governor) saying that the signatories no longer had any confidence in Ningkan as chief minister. On the basis of this letter, the Yang di-Pertua Negeri asked for Ningkan's resignation, and when this was not forthcoming, Ningkan having asked that "the matter be put to the constitutional test" (that is, in a confidence vote in the Assembly), he dismissed Ningkan by publishing a declaration in the Gazette that he had ceased to hold office, and appointed another member of the Council Negri as chief minister. There had been no motion of no confidence, and Ningkan refused to accept his dismissal, commencing proceedings in the High Court for declarations that he was still the chief minister.

The issue was whether the power to dismiss the chief minister could be implied into the State Constitution, and if so, whether it had been properly exercised. Article 7(1) of the State Constitution, in line with Westminster-style conventions, said: "If the Chief Minister ceases to command the confidence of a majority of the members of the Council Negri, then, unless at his request the [Yang di-Pertua Negeri] dissolves the Council Negri, the Chief Minister shall tender the resignation of the members of the Supreme Council [State Cabinet]." The High Court held that even if there was a power to dismiss the chief minister, the term "confidence" implied a vote in the legislature, not a letter, even leaving aside the ambiguous mathematics of the case.[39] The dismissal was therefore unlawful and Ningkan resumed office. This decision is at odds with the decision in the recent case concerning a similar situation in the State of Perak.[40]

The response from the federal government was to proclaim, on the grounds of a threat to the security of Sarawak, an emergency, under which the Federal and State Constitutions were temporarily amended by the Emergency (Federal Constitution and Constitution of Sarawak) Act 1966, so as to give the Yang di-Pertua Negeri power to dismiss the chief minister, and also power to summon the legislature without receiving advice to that effect. However, there was no real security threat; the real reason, at least excuse, for the proclamation being the existence of a constitutional crisis which offered no immediate resolution in favour of the federal government's interests. The Council Negri was duly summoned. Ningkan lost the vote on the ensuing no-confidence motion, and was dismissed from office.

This was not quite the end of the story. Ningkan challenged the emergency proclamation in the courts, alleging, plausibly, a fraud on the Constitution, and took his case eventually to the Privy Council, but without success.

The problem with this episode from the perspective of Sabah and Sarawak and its indigenous peoples is that it means there are essentially — in the final analysis — no legal or even, probably, political limitations, on the power of the federation to interfere with the state constitution, state government or the division of state and federal powers. Even emergency powers may be invoked: the Privy Council gave a broad interpretation to this concept that would embrace a perceived constitutional breakdown at the state level. The only restriction on the federal power here is the need to obtain the consent of the state government, as is indicated above, to constitutional amendments affecting the state. This can be circumvented by invoking emergency powers, as we have seen with the Ningkan case. This only applies to the duration of an emergency, but given that an emergency can be of extended duration and there is no judicial review of its continuance, emergency powers operate as a very serious threat to the autonomy of Sabah and Sarawak and therefore to these states' ability to protect their indigenous peoples — a threat which it seems was not foreseen when the federal bargain was concluded in 1963.

In some cases methods even more hidden than in the Ningkan episode have been used to interfere with the state governments in Sabah and Sarawak. Sabah, indeed, provides another good example. Following the February 1994 state elections in Sabah, Parti Bersatu Sabah (PBS), under a Kadazan leader, Datuk Joseph Pairin Kitingan, was returned with 25 of the 48 seats in the State Legislative Assembly — the BN under Tan Sri Haji Sakaran Dandai taking 23 seats. After a rather unseemly delay, during which he remained in his car, parked outside the Istana (governor's residence) for two days, Pairin was appointed chief minister and shortly afterwards his cabinet also received their appointments. Immediately on Pairin's resumption of office, moves began to unseat him. He soon learned of the defection of three PBS assemblymen, which turned his majority of the elected members into a minority. Attempting to forestall what seemed inevitable, he requested that same day a further dissolution of the assembly. This was refused by the Yang di-Pertua Negeri. He then learned of a petition to the Yang di-Pertua Negeri, signed by 30 members of the assembly, saying they had no confidence in him and demanding his resignation. Less than one month after taking office, Pairin resigned, without (as in Ningkan's case) there having been any motion of no confidence in the assembly. By this time he commanded only 21 votes in the assembly, as against 27 for the BN. Sakaran was then appointed chief minister.[41]

Unfortunately, paying assembly members to switch parties has happened on many occasions and the courts have struck down anti-hopping laws designed to prevent this occurring on the ground that they contravene freedom of association under article 10 of the Constitution.[42] Although such episodes are not exclusive to Sabah and Sarawak, three leading instances of manipulation of state government have occurred in these states, which are supposed to have special protection under the Constitution. In each case an indigenous leader with an approach independent from that of the Malay-controlled federal government in Kuala Lumpur was ousted. The federal opposition, too, has tried to manipulate state politics in its favour. Following the 2008 election a plot was hatched under which a number of Sarawak MPs would defect to the opposition and a government of national unity would be formed. The plot failed when information reached the prime minister, and forty East Malaysian MPs were sent to Taiwan by a backbenchers' club "to study agriculture".[43]

Although the federation has not actually sought to alter the formal balancing of legislative powers in its favour, the underlying reality of federal politics means there are limits to states' political autonomy, even where they receive what looks like special constitutional protection. Of particular concern here is that the use of emergency powers can, as discussed above, sidestep the consent of the state government, which is the main guarantee against abuse of the power of constitutional amendment.

Added to this, or even symptomatic of the lack of real autonomy despite special protection, is the problem of citizenship referred to earlier. In recent years the very large numbers of illegal migrants into Sarawak and even more into Sabah have undermined the state governments' power to control immigration. Often these illegal migrants are given citizenship, diluting the control that "genuine" Sarawakians and Sabahans (that is, an inbuilt majority of indigenous people) have over their affairs. The implications for indigenous people, still fragile groups in these two states even though in a majority, are clear, given that the migrants are mainly Indonesians and Filipinos.

Let me conclude this section with my main point. It is that if indigenous people, the majority in Sabah and Sarawak, are to receive the protection and promotion of their interests that nobody denies they need, then it is fundamental as an aspect of democratic, constitutional government that these states should have their own government in a federal system that reserves to them substantial powers.

The Context of Human Rights

In Malaysia the word "indigenous" is an ambiguous one. The Malays themselves lay claim to indigenous status, as is implied in the common use in everyday contexts of the word *bumiputera*. Under Malaysian constitutional law, bumiputera are entitled to certain special privileges amounting to a constitutionally entrenched affirmative action programme. The communities entitled to this status are defined in the Constitution since 1971 as Malays and natives of Sabah and Sarawak.[44]

The Constitution and the law have been thoroughly tested by the problem of vulnerable indigenous communities being threatened by development. Indigenous rights have in fact been strongly advocated by the Malaysian Human Rights Commission ("Suhakam") in recent years and have become an area of significant activity both for Suhakam and in the courts. Currently there are more than a hundred native land claims in the courts in Sarawak alone. In recent years, in Sabah and Sarawak, the focus of complaints to Suhakam has been mainly on land issues, especially encroachments on indigenous land.[45]

Indigenous people as a whole "suffer disproportionately from preventable diseases, have higher infant and maternal mortality rates, are poorly provided with basic services and utilities, and have lower levels of education ... the great majority ... continue to suffer widespread and persistent poverty, high rates of illiteracy, and limited access to medical care".[46]

These days there are many support groups and advocates for indigenous people. There is a concerted attempt to insist on their fundamental rights by litigation. The Malaysian courts have not, on the whole, however, been supportive of public interest litigation,[47] and have not in general adopted broad interpretations of fundamental rights provisions or advanced the interests of vulnerable groups. In the present instance it took several years of patience and extremely hard, unremunerated legal work and factual research by a number of lawyers and NGO advocates to get indigenous customary land rights legally recognized. In *Director-General of Environmental Quality v Kajing Tubek*, for example, in 1997, the Court of Appeal even cast doubt on whether representatives of ten thousand natives of Sarawak had standing to challenge the environmental impact assessment for a dam that would flood their traditional lands and deprive them of livelihood.[48]

The decisive breakthrough came in 1997 when fifty-two *orang asli*, whose land rights were affected by development in the West Malaysian state of Johor, succeeded in a representative action against the Government of Johor in securing the recognition of their land rights in terms that were unequivocal. In this case, *Adong bin Kuwau v Government of Johor*,[49] the Court of Appeal referred to a line of similar cases in different jurisdictions culminating in well-known Australian and Canadian cases.[50] They rejected the notion that indigenous peoples had no rights except those granted by the subsequent conqueror or discoverer, and affirmed the notion that their land rights, in the form of usufructuary rights (rights to harvest the produce of the land), remained in force at common law except where clearly and specifically extinguished by legislative or executive action. A broad interpretation was given to the constitutional right to property (article 13) and to adequate compensation for its deprivation, as applied to indigenous land rights.

As one would expect, a similar line of decisions became apparent in East Malaysia. In Sarawak, native customary land rights, under the Sarawak Land Code 1957,[51] had been frozen as of 1 January 1958, with some limited opportunities for creating such rights after that date. In *Nor Anak Nyawai v Borneo Pulp Plantation Sdn Bhd* in 2000,[52] an impressive judgment in the High Court of Sarawak adopted the same reasoning as in *Adong*, following the Australian and Canadian cases as well as *Adong* itself in establishing the legal nature of the customary land rights in Sarawak. Furthering a tendency to look also at international norms, the judge referred to the Draft Declaration on the Human Rights of Indigenous People. This decision offered further encouragement to customary land claims, and the *Adong* case was then affirmed and extended in the High Court of Malaya and the Court of Appeal in 2005 in the apex case of *Government of Selangor v Sagong Tasi*,[53] and in another striking case in October 2013.[54]

This case related to the Temuan people, who had occupied land for generations, part of which had been gazetted as aboriginal land under the Aboriginal Peoples' Act 1954. Part of this land was compulsorily acquired for the construction of the main highway between Kuala

Lumpur and the new Kuala Lumpur International Airport. The Temuan were "evicted rather unceremoniously and left to fend for themselves and their families".[55] They sued the Selangor state government for statutory compensation and trespass. Whereas the *Adong* case had asserted that the orang asli had usufructuary rights over their designated land, *Sagong Tasi* went much further. It decided that the orang asli have not just usufructuary rights but "customary community title" at common law, and that their property is constitutionally protected. The Land Acquisition Act 1960, which provided only a power to grant compensation, was modified in its application to accord with article 13 of the Constitution, which states that "no person shall be deprived of property save in accordance with law" and that "no law shall provide for compulsory acquisition or use of property without adequate compensation". The Court of Appeal affirmed *Adong* in deciding that the state authorities owe a fiduciary duty to the orang asli: "a duty to protect the welfare of the aborigines including their land rights, and not to act in a manner inconsistent with those rights, and further to provide remedies where an infringement occurs". It held also that their rights extended to land which had erroneously not been gazetted by the defendant state government. For good measure the court awarded the plaintiffs full costs and exemplary damages, reflecting the brutal manner in which they had been treated.[56]

Again the same principles have been extended to the indigenous peoples of Sabah and Sarawak in *Madeli Salleh v Superintendent of Lands and Surveys, Miri Division*.[57] In a 2011 case, *Andawan bin Ansapi v Public Prosecutor*,[58] six natives were convicted of criminal trespass when they cultivated rice paddy in a forest reserve. The High Court overturned the conviction on the basis that they were exercising customary land rights that pre-existed the reservation and that the exercise of their customary rights was guaranteed by the right to life under article 5(1).

Since the *Sagong Tasi* case, courts, especially in Sabah and Sarawak, have been flooded with native land claims.[59] But these developments take the human rights of indigenous peoples beyond land rights, and even beyond the right to life, as there are undoubtedly many other issues to be addressed. What the cases have done, apart from establish indigenous land rights, is to establish indigenous rights more generally as a matter of concern rather than resistance.

In 2010 Suhakam established its first National Inquiry Committee, which investigated the land rights of indigenous peoples.[60] Suhakam has also established offices in Sabah and Sarawak to provide access to its services for indigenous peoples, and has mounted initiatives for their education and towards the recognition of their customary law. In 2010 it also investigated and referred to the police allegations of long-term sexual abuse of Penan women and girls by timber workers in Sarawak.[61] All this tends towards establishing the rights of the indigenous people in a way that is envisaged both by notable judgments from other Commonwealth countries and by international instruments. As the judge in a recent Sarawak case said,

> Finally, given that natives are the original inhabitants of the country it might be questioned whether it is entirely correct to treat claims for NCR by looking at them only from the standpoint of ownership of the lands. Rather such claims should be looked [at] differently, namely, that the natives are part of the land as are the trees, mountains, hills, animals, fishes and rivers.... The fruits on the wild trees, the fishes in the river, the wild boars and other animals on the land are their food for survival.[62]

Conclusion

Despite the exclusion of indigenous people from the constitution-making process and the social contract that formed its foundation, the 1957 Constitution attempted to safeguard their rights and interests in many respects that are relevant. It does attempt to give substantial power to Sabah and Sarawak, and a prime reason for this is the need to protect indigenous peoples. It also acknowledges special treatment for indigenous people in terms of land and the special status of their customary law.

The verdict has to be a mixed one.

The constitutionalization of native customary law has seen a continuous process since the days of the first white rajah. This can be seen as a matter of legal formality; although it could be argued that the significance of this constitutional entrenchment of native customary law is undermined by the socio-economic processes of development and the indigenous peoples' ability to maintain their legal traditions in practice. Some progress has also been made in the context of human rights, both with regard to land rights and the socio-economic issues addressed by Suhakam. The real difficulty seems to be that the political system is reluctant to embrace these issues in any meaningful respect. In particular the ability of Sabah and Sarawak to deal with them as a policy issue in the context of, for example, immigration, health and education, exercising the autonomy that is their due under the Constitution, is limited in spite of the supposed, and in some respects real, special status of these states within the federal structure. Until these states are able to demand the fulfilment of the Constitution's intention, the rights and interests of indigenous peoples will it seems remain a matter of ambiguity.

A Note on Hooker's Contribution to the Study of the Adat of Malaysia's Indigenous People

Hooker's work in this field falls into three categories. First, there is work that places the indigenous people and their laws within a broader conceptual framework which we can (no, *must*) call legal pluralism — the concept most people associate indelibly with Hooker's work. These works are principally:

1. 1975. *Legal Pluralism: An Introduction to Colonial and Neo-Colonial Laws*. Oxford: The Clarendon Press.
2. 1978. *A Concise Legal History of South-East Asia*. Oxford: The Clarendon Press.
3. 1986. (ed.) *The Laws of South-East Asia*, vol. 1, *The Pre-Modern Texts*. Singapore: Butterworths; and *vol. 2, European Laws*.

Secondly we have general works on Malaysia which deal with this theme:

1. 1976. *The Personal Laws of Malaysia*. Kuala Lumpur: Oxford University Press.
2. 1986. (with R.K. Dentan et al.) *Malaysia & the Original People: A Case Study of the Impact of Development on Indigenous Peoples*. Boston: Allyn & Bacon.

Thirdly we have work specifically on the indigenous peoples, their law and their legal issues.

1. 1980. "An Outline History of the Administration of the Native Law in Sarawak". In *Cases on Native Law in Sarawak*, edited by Lee Hun Hoe, xi–xxv. Kuching (Malaysia): Government Printer.
2. 1980. "Native Law in Sabah and Sarawak". *Malayan Law Journal*.
3. 1991. "The Orang Asli and the Laws of Malaysia". *Ilmu Masyarakat* 18: 51–79.
4. 1999. "A Note on Native Land Tenure in Sarawak". *Borneo Research Bulletin* 30: 28–40.
5. 2001. "Native Title in Malaysia". *Australian Journal of Asian Law* 3, no. 2: 198–212.
6. 2002. "Native Title in Malaysia" continued. *Australian Journal of Asian Law* 4, no. 1: 92–105.

Hooker has contributed enormously to this area of study over four different decades — and it must be noted that this is essentially still a small footnote in the context of his scholarly contribution overall.

Notes

1. H. Patrick Glenn, *Legal Traditions of the World: Sustainable Diversity in Law* (Oxford: Oxford University Press, 2010), chap. 3.
2. Cheah Wui Ling, "*Sagong Tasi* and *Orang Asli* Land Rights in Malaysia: Victory, Milestone or False Start", *Law, Social Justice and Global Development Journal* 2 (2004) <www.go.warwick.ac.uk/elj/lgd/2004_2/cheah>.
3. M.B. Hooker, *A Concise Legal History of South-East Asia* (Oxford: Oxford University Press, 1978), p. 13; M.B. Hooker, *Law and the Chinese in Southeast Asia* (Singapore: Institute of Southeast Asian Studies, 2002).
4. Gary J. Jacobsohn, *Constitutional Identity* (Cambridge, Harvard University Press, 2010).
5. Amanda Whiting, "Situating Suhakam: Human Rights Debates and Malaysia's National Human Rights Commission", *Stanford Journal of International Law* 39 no. 1 (2003): 59; Amanda Whiting, "In the Shadow of Developmentalism: The Human Rights Commission of Malaysia at the Intersection of State and Civil Society Priorities", in *Human Rights and*

Development: Law, Policy and Governance, edited by C. Raj Kumar and D.K. Srivastava (Hong Kong: LexisNexis, 2006).

6. T.N. Harper, *The End of Empire and the Making of Malaya* (Cambridge: Cambridge University Press, 2001), p. 2.

7. This is the term employed in the Constitution, in statutes, and in Malaysian scholarship. In the body of the chapter, I prefer to use the term "indigenous peoples" to refer to the natives of Sabah and Sarawak, and so do not include the *orang asli* of West Malaysia.

8. Article 161A(6)(a) of the Federal Constitution defines a "native of Sarawak" as a person who is a citizen and either belongs to one of the races specified in clause 7 as indigenous to the state or of mixed blood deriving exclusively from those races. Clause 7 lists the following races to be treated as "native" and indigenous to Sarawak: "Bukitans, Bisayahs, Dusuns, Sea Dayaks, Land Dayaks, Kadayans, Kelabits, Kayans, Kenyahs (including Sabups and Sipengs), Kajangs (including Sekapans, Kejamans, Lahanans, Punans, Tanjongs and Kanowits), Lugats, Linsums, Malays, Melanos, Muruts, Penans, Sians, Tagals, Tabuns and Ukits."

9. "Malaysia", in *World Directory of Minorities and Indigenous Peoples* <http://minorityrights.org/country/malaysia/> (accessed 5 March 2016).

10. Andrew J. Harding, *The Malaysian Constitution: A Contextual Analysis* (Oxford: Hart, 2012), chap. 2.

11. Ibid., chap. 8.

12. Ibid., chap. 2.

13. Federal Constitution, Art. 153, as amended by the Constitution (Amendment) Act 1971.

14. This incident involved a group of two hundred armed men from the Philippines taking over a village in Sabah, asserting a claim to the state by the Sultan of Sulu. See, further, "The Lahad Datu Standoff: Telling the Story – Bob Teoh and Chiara Zambrano", *Malaysian Insider*, 13 September 2013 <http://www.themalaysianinsider.com/sideviews/article/the-lahad-datu-standoff-telling-the-story-bob-teoh-and-chiara-zambrano> (accessed 5 March 2016).

15. '"Parliament: Granting of Citizenship in Sabah Suspended Pending RCI Outcome", *The Star Online*, 2 July 2013 <http://www.thestar.com.my/news/nation/2013/07/02/sabah-rci-granting-of-citizenship-sabah-suspended/> (accessed 5 March 2016).

16. "Inside Malaysia's Shadow State", in *Global Witness Report*, 9 March 2013 <http://www.globalwitness.org/insideshadowstate/> (accessed 5 March 2016).

17. M.B. Hooker, "An Outline History of the Administration of the Native Law in Sarawak", in *Cases on Native Law in Sarawak*, edited by Lee Hun Hoe (Kuching [Malaysia]: Government Printer, 1980), pp. xi–xxv.

18. Ibid., p. xiii.

19. Lynn Hunt, ed., *The French Revolution and Human Rights: A Brief Documentary History*, translated by Lynn Hunt (New York: St. Martin's, 1996), p. 88.

20. Hooker, *A Concise Legal History of South-East*, p. 13.

21. Hooker, "An Outline History", p. xxi.

22. Andrew B.L. Phang, *The Development of Singapore Law: Historical and Socio-Legal Perspectives* (Singapore: Butterworths, 1991), chaps. 1 and 2.

23. Yet again, Hooker leads the way. See Hooker, *Law and the Chinese in Southeast Asia*.

24. "Anger in Sabah over ICs for Votes", *Straits Times*, 9 February 2013.

25. Section 2 of the Native Courts Ordinance, 1992 (Ord. No. 9/92), defines customary law as "the custom or body of customs to which the law of Sarawak gives effect". The Sarawak Native Customs Council Ordinance 1977 (Majlis Adat Istiadat Sarawak Ordinance, Number 5 of 1977), defines "*adat*" as "native customs or body of native customs to which lawful effect has not been given". These definitions seem to raise more issues than they determine.

26. John Borrows, *Canada's Indigenous Constitution* (Toronto: University of Toronto Press, 2010), p. 8.

27. Danny T.K. Wong, "Woolley and the Codification of Native Customs in Sabah", *New Zealand Journal of Asian Studies* 11, no. 1 (2009): 87–105. Wong reports that "Woolley contributed a total of 12 articles to the *Journal of the Malayan Branch of the Royal Asiatic Society*. They included 'Keris Measurements' (Vol. 16, Part 2, 1938), 'Origin of the Malay Keris' (Vol. 16, Part 2, 1938), 'Malay Cannon' (Vol. 20, Part 2, 1947) and five on the Muruts."

28. Peter R. Phelan, *The Traditional Legal System of Sabah* (Yayasan Sabah: Pusat Kajian Borneo [Centre for Borneo Studies], 2003), pp. 10ff. Phelan's work is clearly inspired by Hooker, as the style, approach, and attention to detail profess.

29. M.B. Hooker, *Native Law in Sabah and Sarawak* (Singapore: Malayan Law Journal, 1980).

30. Hooker, "An Outline History", p. xxiv.

31. Tan Tai Yong, *Creating 'Greater Malaysia': Decolonisation and the Politics of Merger* (Singapore: Institute of Southeast Asian Studies, 2008), chap. 6.

32. See, especially, Federal Constitution of Malaysia, Part XIIA.

33. For the details of this, see Federal Constitution of Malaysia, Schedule 10; and Harding, *The Malaysian Constitution*, chap. 5.

34. Ibid., chap. 7. The judiciary and legal professions of Sabah and Sarawak were not involved, given the distances involved and the fact that the legal professions are not represented by the Malaysian Bar Council but have their own associations.

35. Federal Constitution of Malaysia, art. 161E.

36. Research by the author and Dr Lynette Chua is being conducted on the legal profession of Sarawak. A review of registered lawyers in the archives in Kuching in June 2012 did not reveal any having native names until the 1970s; the statement in the text requires confirmation.

37. R.S. Milne, "Political Parties in Sarawak and Sabah", *Journal of South East Asian History* 6, no. 2, (1965): 104–17.

38. This can be seen very clearly in the general election of 2013, in which in forming the Dewan Rakyat, or House of Representatives, a large BN majority in East Malaysia effectively trumped an opposition majority in West Malaysia, handing the government to the BN. See "Sabah, Sarawak, Remain BN Bastions", *Malaysian Times*, 9 May 2013 <http://www. themalaysiantimes.com.my/sabah-sarawak-remain-bn-bastions/> (accessed 5 March 2016).

39. *Stephen Kalong Ningkan v Government of Malaysia* [1968] 2 MLJ 238.

40. *Datuk Nizar Jamaluddin v Datuk Seri Zambry Abdul Kadir* [2010] 2 MLJ 285. For an extensive critique and discussion of the Perak crisis, see Audrey Quay, ed. *Perak: A State of Crisis: Rants, Reviews and Reflections on the Overthrow of Democracy and the Rule of Law in Malaysia* (Petaling Jaya: LoyarBurok, 2010); and Harding, *The Malaysian Constitution*, chap. 4.

41. See, further, Andrew J. Harding, "When is a Resignation not a Resignation? A Crisis of Confidence in Sabah", *Round Table* 84, no. 335 (1995): 353–59; see also Andrew J. Harding, "Turbulence in the Land below the Wind: Sabah's Constitutional Crisis of 1985–6", *Journal of Commonwealth & Comparative Politics* 29, no. 1 (1991): 86–101.

42. *Dewan Undangan Negeri Kelantan v Nordin Salleh* [1992] 1 MLJ 697.

43. Sean Young, "Malaysia Lawmakers Fly to Taiwan amid Uncertainty", *USA Today*, 8 September 2008 <http://usatoday30.usatoday.com/news/ world/2008-09-08-2207496898_x.htm> (accessed 5 March 2016).

44. Federal Constitution of Malaysia, art. 153(1).

45. Human Rights Commission of Malaysia (SUHAKAM), *Annual Report 2010* (Kuala Lumpur: Human Rights Commission of Malaysia, 2011), p. 3.

46. S. Robert Aiken and Colin H. Leigh, "Seeking Redress in the Courts: Indigenous Land Rights and Judicial Decisions in Malaysia", *Modern Asian Studies* 45, no. 4 (2011): 830.

47. See, for example, *Government of Malaysia v Lim Kit Siang* [1988] 2 MLJ 12; Tey Tsun Hang, "Public Interest Litigation in Malaysia: Executive Control and Careful Negotiation of the Frontiers of Judicial Review", in *Public Interest Litigation in Asia*, edited by Po Jen Yap and Holning Lau (London: Routledge, 2011).

48. [1997] 3 MLJ 23; see Gurdial Singh Nijar, "The Bakun Dam Case: A Critique", *Malaysian Law Journal*, no. 3 (1997): ccxxix–xxlii.

49. [1997] 1 MLJ 418, affirmed by the Court of Appeal in [1998] 2 MLJ 158; see M.B. Hooker, "'Native Title' in Malaysia: Adong's Case', *Australian Journal of Asian Law* 3, no. 2 (2001): 198–212.

50. Especially *Mabo v State of Queensland* [1992] 66 ALJR 408; *Calder v A-G of British Columbia* [1973] 34 DLR (3d) 145.

51. Laws of Sarawak, c.81, ss.2,5. For Sabah, see the decision in *Sipadan Dive Centre Sdn Bhd v State Government of Sabah* [2010] 1 LNS 1218; and Amity A. Doolittle, *Property and Politics in Sabah, Malaysia: A Century of Native Struggles over Land Rights, 1881–1996* (Seattle: University of Washington Press, 2005).

52. [2001] 6 MLJ 241. An appeal succeeded on the facts but the Court of Appeal affirmed the law as stated in the High Court. See [2005] 3 CLJ 555.

53. [2002] 2 MLJ 591; [2005] 5 MLJ 289.

54. Ng Ai Fern, "Court of Appeal Returns NCR Land to Ibans, Affirms Native Customary Rights", *FZ.com*, 10 October 2013 <http://www.fz.com/content/appeals-court-overturns-high-court-decision-returns-ncr-land-ibans> (accessed 5 March 2016). This latest case affirms the state's fiduciary duty towards the indigenous people, and that quarrying licences cannot be granted over native land without their consent.

55. Ibid.

56. M.B. Hooker, "Native Title in Malaysia Continued—*Nor's Case*", *Australian Journal of Asian Law* 4, no. 1 (2002): 92–105.

57. *Madeli Salleh v Superintendent of Lands and Surveys, Miri Division* [2008] 2 MLJ 677.

58. Suit No KK-41-128-2010, High Court, Kota Kinabalu.

59. See Bian Baru, "Native Customary Rights (NCR) over Land in Sarawak", in *Pengayau*, 9 February 2011 <https://pengayau.wordpress.com/2011/02/09/native-customary-rights-ncr-over-land-in-sarawakmalaysia/> (accessed 5 March 2016). See also Aiken and Leigh, " Seeking Redress in the Courts", p. 867.

60. See Ramy Bulan and Amuy Locklear, *Legal Perspectives on Native Customary Land Rights in Sarawak* (Kuala Lumpur: Human Rights Commission of Malaysia, 2009).

61. Joseph Tawie, "Prioritise Issue of Penan Rape", *Free Malaysia Today*, 30 September 2011 <http://www.freemalaysiatoday.com/category/nation/2011/09/30/prioritise-issue-of-penan-rape/> (accessed 5 March 2016).
62. *Agi Anak Bungkong v Ladang Sawit Bintulu Sdn Bhd* [2010] 1 LNS 114.

References

Laws, Regulations, Cases

Kuwau v Government of Johor [1997] 1 MLJ 418, affirmed [1998] 2 MLJ 158.

Agi Anak Bungkong v Ladang Sawit Bintulu Sdn Bhd (2010) 1 LNS 114.

Andawan bin Ansapi v Public Prosecutor, Suit No KK-41-128-2010, High Court, Kota Kinabalu.

Calder v A-G of British Columbia (1973) 34 DLR (3d) 145.

Constitution (Amendment) Act 1971. Act A30 (10 March 1971).

Datuk Nizar Jamaluddin v Datuk Seri Zambry Abdul Kadir [2010] 2 MLJ 285.

Dewan Undangan Negeri Kelantan v Nordin Salleh [1992] 1 MLJ 697.

Director-General of Environmental Quality v Kajing Tubek [1997] 3 MLJ 23.

Federal Constitution of Malaysia.

Government of Malaysia v Lim Kit Siang [1988] 2 MLJ 12.

Government of Selangor v Sagong Tasi [2002] 2 MLJ 591, affirmed on appeal [2005] 5 MLJ 289.

Mabo v State of Queensland (1992) 66 ALJR 408.

Madeli Salleh v Superintendent of Lands and Surveys, Miri Division [2008] 2 MLJ 677.

Native Courts Ordinance 1992 [Ord. No. 9/92].

Nor Anak Nyawai v Borneo Pulp Plantation Sdn Bhd [2001] 6 MLJ 241, overturned on appeal [2005] 3 CLJ 555.

Sarawak Land Code 1957. Laws of Sarawak, c.81, ss.2, 5.

Sarawak Native Customs Council Ordinance [Majlis Adat Istiadat Sarawak Ordinance]. Ord. no. 5 of 1977.

Sipadan Dive Centre Sdn Bhd v State Government of Sabah [2010] 1 LNS 1218.

Stephen Kalong Ningkan v Government of Malaysia [1968] 2 MLJ 238.

Books

Borrows, John. *Canada's Indigenous Constitution*. Toronto: University of Toronto Press, 2010.

Bulan, Ramy, and Amuy Locklear. *Legal Perspectives on Native Customary Land Rights in Sarawak*. Kuala Lumpur: Human Rights Commission of Malaysia (SUHAKAM), 2009.

Doolittle, Amity A. *Property and Politics in Sabah, Malaysia: A Century of Native Struggles over Land Rights, 1881–1996*. Seattle: University of Washington Press, 2005.

Glenn, H. Patrick. *Legal Traditions of the World: Sustainable Diversity in Law*, 4th ed. Oxford: Oxford University Press, 2010.

Harding, Andrew J. *The Malaysian Constitution: A Contextual Analysis*. Oxford: Hart, 2012.

Harper, T.N. *The End of Empire and the Making of Malaya*. Cambridge: Cambridge University Press, 2001.

Hooker, M.B. *A Concise Legal History of South-East Asia*. Oxford: Oxford University Press, 1978.

———. *Native Law in Sabah and Sarawak*. Singapore: Malayan Law Journal, 1980.

———. *Law and the Chinese in South East Asia*. Singapore: Institute of Southeast Asia Studies, 2002.

Human Rights Commission of Malaysia (SUHAKAM). *Annual Report 2010*. Kuala Lumpur: Human Rights Commission of Malaysia, 2010.

Hunt, Lynn, ed. *The French Revolution and Human Rights: A Brief Documentary History*, translated by Lynn Hunt. New York: St. Martin's, 1996.

Jacobsohn, Gary J. *Constitutional Identity*. Cambridge, MA: Harvard University Press, 2010.

Phang, Andrew B.L. *The Development of Singapore Law: Historical and Socio-Legal Perspectives*. Singapore: Butterworths, 1991.

Phelan, Peter R. *The Traditional Legal System of Sabah*. Yayasan Sabah: Pusat Kajian Borneo (Centre for Borneo Studies), 2003.

Quay, Audrey, ed. *Perak: A State of Crisis: Rants, Reviews and Reflections on the Overthrow of Democracy and the Rule of Law in Malaysia*. Petaling Jaya: LoyarBurok, 2010.

Tan Tai Yong. *Creating 'Greater Malaysia': Decolonisation and the Politics of Merger*. Singapore: Institute of Southeast Asian Studies, 2008.

Chapters

Hooker, M.B. "An Outline History of the Administration of the Native Law in Sarawak". In *Cases on Native Law in Sarawak*, edited by Lee Hun Hoe. Kuching: Government Printer, 1980.

Tey Tsun Hang. "Public Interest Litigation in Malaysia: Executive Control and Careful Negotiation of the Frontiers of Judicial Review". In *Public Interest Litigation in Asia*, edited by Po Jen Yap and Holning Lau. London: Routledge, 2011.

Whiting, Amanda. "In the Shadow of Developmentalism: The Human Rights Commission of Malaysia at the Intersection of State and Civil Society Priorities". In *Human Rights and Development: Law, Policy and Governance*, edited by C. Raj Kumar and D.K. Srivastava. Hong Kong: LexisNexis, 2006.

Periodicals

Aiken, S. Robert, and Colin H. Leigh. "Seeking Redress in the Courts: Indigenous Land Rights and Judicial Decisions in Malaysia". *Modern Asian Studies* 45, no. 4 (2011): 825–75.

Cheah, Wui Ling. "Sagong Tasi and Orang Asli Land Rights in Malaysia: Victory, Milestone or False Start". *Law, Social Justice and Global Development Journal* 2 (2004).

Harding, Andrew J. "Turbulence in the Land below the Wind: Sabah's Constitutional Crisis of 1985–6". *Journal of Commonwealth & Comparative Politics* 29, no. 1 (1991): 86–101.

———. "When is a Resignation Not a Resignation? A Crisis of Confidence in Sabah". *Round Table* 84, no. 335 (1995): 353–59.

Hooker, M.B. "'Native Title' in Malaysia: Adong's Case". *Australian Journal of Asian Law* 3, no. 2 (2001): 198–212.

———. "Native Title in Malaysia Continued — Nor's Case". *Australian Journal of Asian Law* 4, no. 1 (2002): 92–105.

Milne, R.S. "Political Parties in Sarawak and Sabah". *Journal of South East Asian History* 6, no. 2 (1965): 104–17.

Nijar, Gurdial Singh. "The Bakun Dam Case: A Critique". *Malaysian Law Journal* [1997], no. 3 (1997): ccxxix–xxlii.

Whiting, Amanda. "Situating Suhakam: Human Rights Debates and Malaysia's National Human Rights Commission". *Stanford Journal of International Law*, 39, no. 1 (2003): 59ff.

Wong, Danny T.K. "Woolley and the Codification of Native Customs in Sabah". *New Zealand Journal of Asian Studies* 11, no. 1 (2009): 87–105.

Newspapers

"Anger in Sabah over ICs-for-Votes". *Straits Times*, 9 February 2013.

"The Lahad Datu Standoff: Telling the Story – Bob Teoh and Chiara Zambrano". *Malaysian Insider* (online), 13 September 2013 <http://www.themalaysianinsider.com/sideviews/article/the-lahad-datu-standoff-telling-the-story-bob-teoh-and-chiara-zambrano> (accessed 5 March 2016).

Ng Ai Fern. "Court of Appeal Returns NCR Land to Ibans, Affirms Native Customary Rights". *FZ.com*, 10 October 2013 < http://www.fz.com/content/appeals-court-overturns-high-court-decision-returns-ncr-land-ibans> (accessed 5 March 2016).

"Parliament: Granting of Citizenship in Sabah Suspended Pending RCI Outcome". *The Star Online*, 2 July 2013 <http://www.thestar.com.my/news/nation/2013/07/02/sabah-rci-granting-of-citizenship-sabah-suspended/> (accessed 5 March 2016).

"Sabah, Sarawak, Remain BN Bastions". *Malaysian Times* (online), 9 May 2013 <http://www.themalaysiantimes.com.my/sabah-sarawak-remain-bn-bastions/> (accessed 5 March 2016).

Tawie, Joseph. "Prioritise Issue of Penan Rape". *Free Malaysia Today*, 30 September 2011 <http://www.freemalaysiatoday.com/category/nation/2011/09/30/prioritise-issue-of-penan-rape/> (accessed 5 March 2016).

Young, Sean. "Malaysia Lawmakers Fly to Taiwan amid Uncertainty". *USA Today* (online), 8 September 2008 <http://usatoday30.usatoday.com/news/world/2008-09-08-2207496898_x.htm> (accessed 5 March 2016).

Online Citations

Bian, Baru. "Native Customary Rights (NCR) over Land in Sarawak". *Pengayau*, 9 February 2011 <https://pengayau.wordpress.com/2011/02/09/native-customary-rights-ncr-over-land-in-sarawakmalaysia/> (accessed 5 March 2016).

"Inside Malaysia's Shadow State". *Global Witness Report*, 9 March 2013 <http://www.globalwitness.org/insideshadowstate/> (accessed 5 March 2016).

"Malaysia". *World Directory of Minorities and Indigenous Peoples* <http://minorityrights.org/country/malaysia/> (accessed 5 March 2016).

9

Sharia, State and Legal Pluralism in Indonesia: How *Law* Can You Go?

Nadirsyah Hosen

M.B. Hooker has produced at least two important books on Islamic law in Indonesia: *Indonesian Islam: Social Change through Contemporary Fatawa* (2003) and *Indonesian Syariah: Defining a National School of Islamic Law* (2008). The two books demonstrate how Islam and sharia in Indonesia are understood and practised in a different way compared with the Middle East and other regions. Hooker offers his critical reviews of the method and application of fatwas, along with his evaluation of many different public faces of sharia from tertiary curricula, the Friday sermon in mosques, and a bureaucratic form of conducting the hajj, to the debates on public morality. Hooker's books show how elusive is the meaning of sharia in contemporary Indonesia.

My chapter considers some of Hooker's findings and focuses on how the issue of sharia is placed in the context of Indonesian law reform. As Hooker observed, until the early 1990s, "the status of Syariah in the Indonesian legal system was much as the Dutch had left it".[1] But things changed after the Soeharto era. The topic of sharia and pluralism in Indonesia is a complex arrangement of legal and public reasoning, moral practice, and political authority. There is understandable anxiety about the role of religion in public life, and Indonesian society's attempts to inculcate the values of respect, tolerance and pluralism. The main question is: Does legal pluralism still have a place in Indonesian Islam? My chapter examines the Indonesian experience as a vehicle to answer these questions. Among other things, I argue that Indonesia should be seen as a laboratory for legal pluralism, where state law coexists with sharia in legal postulates, official and unofficial laws.

Law Reform

The issue here is the unfinished discussion on religion, state and pluralism after the Soeharto era: how a state should, at the same time, accommodate and restrict the emergence of sharia into public life? If a state law was proposed and inspired by a particular rule from a particular religion, through public reasoning, would this situation damage the principle of state neutrality? Law and religion are entwined in the constitutional foundations of nations. The constitutional protection of freedom of religion is a necessity. In a religiously pluralistic world, granting the guarantee is also in the state's best interest. However, in so doing, the constitutional state faces the paradox of tolerance.[2] It grants a protected sphere to individuals and organizations that may not be inclined to reward the protection by being tolerant themselves with competing religions or with the state. Andras Sajo warns that strong religion is a threat to both secularism and the constitution in that it pushes the secular legal system to reach a compromise and concessions. For instance, the supporters of a strong religion would take the idea of pluralism to the extreme by putting one religion's rule over other normative systems.[3]

An-Na'im argues that the coercive enforcement of sharia by the state betrays the Qur'an's insistence on voluntary acceptance of Islam. Just as the state should be secure from the misuse of religious authority, sharia should be free from the control of the state. State policies or legislation must be based on civic reasons, accessible to citizens of all religions. He maintains the very idea of an "Islamic state" is based on European ideas of state and law, and not sharia or the Islamic tradition.[4] The fear that democracy in the lands where Islam becomes or is the religion of a majority would produce Islamic theocracy is very real. In 1992 the Islamic Salvation Front (Front Islamique du Salut; FIS) won the majority in Algeria, in 2006 Hamas won the elections for the Palestinian Legislative Council, and in 2012 the Muslim Brotherhood won the elections in Egypt.

However, Indonesia's experience is somewhat different from that of "Islamic democracies" in the Muslim world. The democratic transition began in 1998 when Soeharto resigned from his thirty-two-year presidency, following the economic crisis which hit Indonesia in mid-1997, mass demonstrations, student demands for reform, along with international pressure. There have been some significant achievements in Indonesian law reform following the Soeharto era, such as the eradication of the power of the minister for information to issue or withdraw a press publication business licence (SIUPP); the adoption of a multi-party system; the peaceful transfer of power in the last two general elections; the adoption of Indonesia's first comprehensive human rights law; the establishment of the Anti-Corruption Commission (KPK), and the amendments to the 1945 Constitution.

Soeharto's resignation provided an opportunity for meaningful social, economic, political and legal reforms. In terms of economic reform, during the Habibie period the Indonesian government was required to sign no less than sixteen letters of intent (LoI) with the International Monetary Fund (IMF), drawing up its agreement to act in accordance with several reform programmes. Some of the agreements required the cancellation of huge industrial projects and trading cartels at the heart of the Soeharto regime. In these areas, the IMF played an active role in "helping" the Indonesian government draft the required bills. In terms of political and legal reform from the perspective of the student movements, the call for "clean and good governance which is accountable, constitutional, transparent, democratic, just, and free from corruption, collusion and nepotism"[5] was central to the struggle for democratic transition.

Reform of the 1945 Constitution has been one of the most important aspects of the transition to democracy in Indonesia. The amendments have altered the basis of the political game. Among other changes, the amendments have established the democratic principles of the separation of power and of checks and balances, and have also substantially revised the constitutional framework for executive–legislative relations. These amendments have fundamentally altered the rules of how the state relates to its citizens; how the three branches of government deal with one another; how civilians and the military interact; and how the national, provincial, district and village authorities relate to one another.[6]

The developments of the Arab Spring raised interest in whether Indonesia's emergence as the third-largest democracy could show the way for reform movements elsewhere in the Muslim world.[7] Indonesia remains the only country in Southeast Asia to be rated "Free" in Freedom House's annual survey of political rights and civil liberties. The question is, where and how do we put the role of sharia in this process of economic, political and legal reform?

Sharia and State Law

Soeharto's departure created the opportunity for several Muslim groups and political parties to propose the accommodation of sharia into state law. From the perspective of democracy, this process is important, since it accommodates different and conflicting views. Under Soeharto, debate was forbidden, since his government was afraid of its disruptive potential. The moment for free dialogue and debate, through proper legal mechanisms, came after President Soeharto's resignation.

Despite the fact that the 1945 Indonesian Constitution does not refer to Islam, there are some laws which regulate Muslim affairs, such as the laws on religious courts, zakat (alms), *waqf* (religious endowment), and hajj (pilgrimage). By contrast, other religions do not have such special regulations. A recent example is Law No. 18 of 2001, which granted Aceh special autonomy and included authority for Aceh to establish a system of sharia as an adjunct to, not a replacement for, national civil and criminal law. Before taking effect the law required the provincial legislature to approve local regulations (*qanun*) incorporating sharia precepts into the legal code. In practical terms the Ministry of Religious Affairs has become a Muslim institution; no non-Muslim has ever been appointed to head the ministry.

The state requires official religions to comply with Ministry of Religious Affairs and other ministerial directives, such as the Regulation on Building Houses of Worship (Joint-Ministerial Decree No. 1 of 1969),

the Guidelines for the Propagation of Religion (Ministerial Decision
No. 70 of 1978), Overseas Aid to Religious Institutions in Indonesia
(Ministerial Decision No. 20 of 1978), and Proselytising Guidelines
(No. 77 of 1978). All these regulations are supposedly aimed at
supporting and protecting Muslim affairs. Many members of minority
faiths complain of unequal treatment regarding the building of houses
of worship. It is more difficult for non-Muslims to acquire a building
licence than for Muslims.[8]

The Indonesian constitution does not specifically identify Islam
as a source of law, but religious courts have been established to deal
mainly with family law matters and economic sharia. At the same
time, however, as the religious courts are part of the court system,
not separated from the Supreme Court, all decisions of the religious
courts must be based on Indonesian law, not on the text of the Qur'an
or the Hadith. A law that is inspired by an Islamic text is not
considered and treated as sharia, as it has been formulated, made and
passed through a number of parliamentary procedures. It is a state
law. By the same token, while individuals make choices and decisions
as part of social interaction founded ostensibly on secular political
and legal principles, those decisions could be in fact grounded in
religious values.[9]

Prior to 1989, the decision of a religious court needed the fiat of a
district court. However, with Law No. 7 of 1989, the status of religious
courts became equal to those of other courts (state courts, military
courts and administrative courts). Law No. 7 of 1989 defines "Religious
Justice" as the justice system for adherents of Islam. Religious courts
only service the Muslim community, since only they observe Islamic
law. However, the authority of religious courts is limited to specific
areas: marriage, divorce, inheritance, waqf, *hibah* (gifts), and economic
sharia (Law No. 3 of 2006).

A plurality within legal pluralism was highlighted in cases
pertaining to economic sharia. On the one hand, Law No. 3 of 2006
authorizes the religious court to deal with economic sharia disputes.
However, on the other hand, it is clearly mentioned in section 55 of
Law No. 21 of 2008 that:

(1) Settlement of Islamic banking disputes is carried out by a court
in the Religious Court.

(2) In the case that the parties have already agreed to the settlement of disputes other than that considered in paragraph (1), the settlement of dispute shall be carried out according to the akad (contract) content.

(3) Settlement of disputes as considered in paragraph (2) may not be contrary to the Syariah principle.

Section 55(1) above clearly stipulates the competence of the religious court in the settlement of Islamic banking disputes. However, paragraph 2 of this section provides the option for disputing parties to choose another forum besides the religious court to settle their dispute. The meaning of "the settlement of dispute shall be carried according to the akad content" is defined in the elucidation of section 55(2) as: (a) *Musyawarah* (consensus by deliberation), (b) banking mediation, (c) through the National Syariah Arbitration Body (BASYARNAS) or other arbitration institutions and/or (d) through the court within the civil court.

However, in its August 2013 decision, the Constitutional Court decided that the options provided in section 55(2) are constitutionally invalid as they created uncertainty and inconsistency. Conflict of jurisdiction also appeared when the civil court was conferred the same authority as the religious court in the resolution of Islamic banking disputes.[10] The experiment to have plurality within legal pluralism has failed.

It is also essential to note that the contributions of Islamic political parties in Indonesia to the process and the outcome of the Constitutional Amendments (1999–2002) — by adopting a substantive sharia approach — should be seen as their *ijtihad*. It reflects the ability to deal with a modern constitution without abandoning the principles and objectives of sharia. As I argued elsewhere, in the Muslim world this model is important since the Indonesian experience has demonstrated that a progressive interpretation of sharia does provide a basis for constitutionalism.[11]

For instance, all Islamic political parties take the position that human rights are compatible with the substantive sharia approach. Such acceptance is opposed by other Muslim groups who openly reject the concept of human rights as based on alien Western notions or as a conspiracy against Islam, and by those who take pains to establish a specifically Islamic human rights scheme, as can be seen in the constitutions of Iran, Egypt, the Basic Laws of Saudi Arabia, the Universal Islamic Declaration of Human Rights (UIDHR) and the Cairo Declaration. It seems to me that all Islamic political parties in Indonesia are mindful of the situation during the Soeharto era when many Muslim activists were sent to prison without the protection of human rights. Therefore, it is in the interests of Islamic political parties to ensure that such abuses do not occur in the post-Soeharto era. This explains why they have given their full support to the inclusion of a provision on human rights in the amendment to the 1945 Constitution.[12]

The outcome of general elections and constitutional reform in Indonesia has shown how the call for the inclusion of sharia in article 29 of the Constitution was rejected through democracy.[13] According to the 1998–2002 amendments, Indonesia remains a republic, with a presidential system and three branches of government (Hosen 2011). While democracy opens the opportunity for the establishment of Islamic political parties, in the last four elections (1999, 2004, 2009 and 2014), Islamic political parties failed to win a majority of seats. The Indonesian experience demonstrates that Islamic political parties assign religious meanings to national institutions and tend to more readily endorse the state's policies and practices, and, interestingly, "secular" political parties adopt Islamic issues in their political strategy. For instance, bylaws inspired by sharia have been adopted in some districts by "secular" parties in order to bolster their political machines (Buehler 2008).

The Role of Pressure Groups

Despite the rejection of a formal sharia approach in the constitutional amendments, some Muslim groups and organizations continue to propose sharia as a basis for a state law. In recent years, Majelis Ulama Indonesia (MUI; the Indonesian Council of Ulama) has attempted to pressure the government to use its fatwas as a basis of issuing regulation. For example, the Central Bank of the Republic of Indonesia has used MUI's fatwas to regulate the operation of Islamic banks.[14] The Law on Pornography was also based on one of MUI's fatwas. Moch Nur Ichwan observes that "[i]t would be correct to say that the Draft Law that was debated in Parliament was a product of the MUI, although it was formally submitted by the Ministry of Religious Affairs."[15]

It seems that the MUI acts as a "pressure group", but the question is whether MUI enhances democracy by promoting political participation or whether it endangers democracy by undermining public interests and using its Islamic authority to intimidate. KH. Ma'ruf Amin, Chair of Majelis Ulama Indonesia elaborates on this position:

> Since the idea of changing article 29 on religion has been rejected during constitutional amendment, we will not establish an Islamic state. But at the same time, Indonesia is not a secular state. For instance, Indonesia recognises Religious Courts as one of four components in the court system. This suggests that Indonesia still provide some room for religion to play its role in public life. What we propose is to fulfil such role by ensuring that any law should not contradict Islamic teachings and also by transferring Islamic moral values into state legislation.[16]

Statutes are processed and enforced through state mechanisms and therefore belong to the state and cannot be claimed as belonging to divine law, despite the fact that statutes could consider values (including Islamic ones) in society. Muslims (88 per cent) in Indonesia do not speak with one voice. They do not all have the same understanding of what sharia requires and of which sharia interpretation is convincing. In this sense it should be highlighted that what the MUI meant by "not contradict Islamic teachings" is open for public debate, inside and outside the parliament building. As can be seen from the controversy surrounding the anti-pornography law, the supporters of a "formal Syariah approach" have gone beyond ensuring the bill does not "contradict Islamic teachings" by actively proposing the accommodation of some aspects of sharia in the form of the law at both the national and local levels.

If the Indonesian "middle position" allows for law and religion to overlap, then there is scope for legal religion and religious law. This brings difficulties, as the legal expectation is not always in line with religious commands. Religious arguments will be used in the court and parliament to disempower their competitors in the free marketplace of ideas that, ironically, is guaranteed by the Constitution in the first place.

For instance, the government has been involved in determining which schools of teachings of a particular religion can be accepted in Indonesia. The Constitution does not provide any criteria for deciding whether a certain religion is based on Belief in One God, or which authority would make such a decision.[17] Quite often the government acts as a "judge" by having the right to decide which faiths and beliefs are classified as legitimate sects. In order to secure this role, the government established the Bureau for the Supervision of Religious Movements (Pakem) under the Ministry of Religious Affairs, which comprises people from the attorney general's office. While the Constitutional Court acknowledges that the government should not have the authority to decide on religious issues, the court recognizes that the government could have such authority on the basis of representing the voices or aspirations of mainstream religious interpretations from major religious organizations or groups that are deeply rooted in Indonesian history.[18]

In the case of the Ahmadiyah (a group that claims that Mirza Ghulam Ahmad was a prophet, and consequently that Muhammad was not the last prophet), Indonesia's then minister of religious affairs, Suryadharma Ali, called for the Ahmadiyah to be banned.[19] Several provinces across Indonesia have also brought in local regulations restricting the group's activities. The decrees include prohibiting the Ahmadiyah from distributing pamphlets, putting signs in front of their offices and places of worship, as well as forbidding them from wearing anything to indicate that they are Ahmadiyah members. Three members of the Ahmadiyah community were beaten to death in February 2011 when a thousand-strong mob wielding rocks, machetes, swords and spears stormed the house of an Ahmadiyah leader in Cikeusik, Banten. The government's solution was that the Ahmadiyah should declare themselves as a new religion; no longer part of Islam. The problem is, will Law No. 1 of 1965 allow for the establishment of Ahmadiyah as the seventh religion in Indonesia? If not, then what is the legal justification for the minister to suggest that Ahmadiyah be established as a new religion?

In 2005 MUI issued eleven controversial fatwas (Islamic legal opinion) that led observers to ask whether the world's most populous Muslim nation could spiral into sectarian strife. Those fatwas, among other things, criticized liberal Islamic thought, pluralism, secularism, inter-faith marriage, inter-faith prayers led by non-Muslims, and women leading prayers attended by men, and declared the Ahmadiyah movement heretical. One fatwa stated that "Religious teachings influenced by pluralism, liberalism and secularism are against Islam."[20] This fatwa has been criticized, since secularism, liberalism and pluralism are seen as the elements of democracy. Does it mean that MUI is against democracy?

Azyumardi Azra of the State Islamic University Syarif Hidayatullah in Jakarta argued thus: "The MUI cannot ban Muslims from thinking, because pluralism, liberalism and secularism are not ideologies but ways of thinking. MUI's fatwas are against freedom of expression and human rights in general."[21] According to KH. Ma'ruf Amin, the critics misunderstood the fatwa. The fatwa has nothing to do with liberal democracy or economics. It is only about the Islamic teachings influenced by the ideas of secularism, liberalism and pluralism promoted by the Liberal Islam Network (Jaringan Islam Liberal; JIL). He also claimed these teachings were part of a U.S. government attempt to liberate the Muslim world, following "the war on terror".

It seems that MUI encounters semantic problems when it tries to form its own definitions of pluralism. According to MUI, the definition of religious pluralism involves accepting that beliefs taught by other religions are valid. Using this definition, MUI states clearly that pluralism is forbidden. This does not mean that MUI does not recognize plurality and diversity amongst the Indonesian people. According to its critics, the MUI fatwa has perhaps mistaken pluralism for parallelism or relativism. These critics argue strongly that pluralism is not an attempt to make all religions the same but rather to establish respect and tolerance amongst religions. The critics use other definitions: pluralism is not only simple recognition of the fact that there are many different faith groups active in the country but it also relates to individuals of different religions engaging in dialogues with and learning from each other. For example, Diana Eck of Harvard University explains that:

> [P]luralism is not the sheer fact of this plurality alone, but is active engagement with plurality. Pluralism and plurality are sometimes used as if they were synonymous. But plurality is just diversity, plain and simple — splendid, colorful, maybe even threatening. Such diversity

> does not, however, have to affect me. I can observe diversity. I can even celebrate diversity, as the cliché goes. But I have to participate in pluralism.... Pluralism requires the cultivation of public space where we all encounter one another.[22]

Dr Maulana Hasanudin, Deputy Chair of the Fatwa Committee, then rhetorically asks me: If there are many definitions on pluralism, why then can the MUI not use its own definition, or why do the critics blame MUI for using its own definition?[23] He has a point. This suggests that MUI actually only prohibits its own version of religious pluralism. If others have their own version of what religious pluralism is, then it is possible that such a version has not been covered by the MUI's fatwas. In other words, MUI does not prohibit other versions of pluralism.

Apart from semantic problems, the question remains: why does MUI reject pluralism? A possible answer is the fear of "Christianization", real or imaginary, affecting Indonesian Muslims, which has haunted Muslim leaders and society since the colonial period. Tireless efforts by the relatively well-organized Dutch missionary institutions were successful in Christianizing segments of the Indonesian population, especially in the heathen hinterland and among the outer island tribes. Provided with facilities and privileges, these Christian converts have generally speaking had better opportunities than their Muslim neighbours, who mostly resented Western education and development as collaboration with the despised colonizers,[24] or were excluded from such benefits. By accepting the idea of religious pluralism, perhaps MUI thought that Muslims at the grass-root level would be easily converted to Christianity on the grounds that Christianity and Islam are the same.

The question is, does MUI's proposal of a "formal Syariah approach" in state law as described above, undermine or interrupt Indonesia's struggle to uphold the rule of law in the post-Soeharto era? I propose to observe the situation from the perspectives of legal pluralism.

Legal Pluralism: Accommodation and Limitation

Legal pluralism may be described as the situation resulting from the existence of distinct laws or legal systems within a particular country, especially when this results from the transfer or introduction of another legal system as part of a newly introduced political structure and culture. Legal pluralism can exist in fact without formal recognition by the "dominant" legal system or it can exist in a formally recognized way as part of state law. According to Hooker, "pluralism has shown an amazing vitality as a working system".[25] One may note that one of Hooker's legacies is his optimism about the future of legal pluralism.

Legal pluralism clearly challenges a centralized legal institution. In this context the model of legal pluralism can be seen as against the idea of legal centralism in which law is and should be that of the state, uniform for all persons, exclusive of all other law, and administered by a single set of state institutions. In this sense legal pluralism is seen as promoting discrimination that could lead to further social division because different people will be judged according to different norms and standards. In other words, multiculturalism is recognized, but legal pluralism is avoided. There should be only one law for all.

The question is, "why should multiculturalism extend to languages and exotic dances but in principle not to law?" In answering this question, Gary Bell argues that "multiculturalism applied to the law should lead to an acceptance and celebration of legal pluralism – Islamic law is part of a Muslim's culture and completely denying any recognition of this law goes directly against any profession of multiculturalism".[26]

Many Muslims living in the Western world also propose such an argument. In Ontario, since 1992 Jewish and Catholic groups have adopted arbitration mechanisms based on their own religious framework. The Jewish Court in Toronto, called the Beith Din, has been operating for many years on behalf of the Jewish community. There was little fuss raised over these communities' use of religious principles, until Muslim leaders demanded the same rights. Officials had to decide whether to exclude one religion or whether to scrap the religious family courts altogether. The premier, Dalton McGuinty, decided that "[t]here will be no Shariah law in Ontario. There will be no religious arbitration in Ontario. There will be one law for all Ontarians."[27]

Another controversy arose in the Western world when the Archbishop of Canterbury said the adoption of certain aspects of sharia law in the UK "seems unavoidable". Dr Williams argued that adopting parts of Islamic sharia law would help maintain social cohesion. Dr Williams noted that Orthodox Jewish courts already operated, and that the law accommodated the anti-abortion views of some Christians.[28] The question is, could Muslims choose to have marital disputes or financial matters dealt with in a sharia court or tribunal?

Ihsan Yilmaz's important work examines how Muslims living in modern states (in which they may be either a majority or a minority of the population) resist assimilation into the official legal culture of these modern states; instead, they "skillfully navigate" between meeting the requirements of official law and preserving their own unofficial, customary and Islamic legal traditions. In Yilmaz's work this is demonstrated by three case studies — England, Turkey and Pakistan — and is evident most clearly in the area of family law. These three states have adjusted with varying degrees of success to the legal pluralism that is an inescapable consequence of the post-modern conditions that prevail within them.[29]

This leads me now to examine Masaji Chiba's model of legal pluralism, aimed at guaranteeing citizens' rights but at the same time accommodating pluralism within society.[30] In Chiba's model, at the first level there is official law; namely, the legal system sanctioned by the legitimate state authority, which also includes all the rules that originated in society but have been co-opted, as it were, by the state. The state claims them as its own rules, keeping quiet about the fact that these elements of law were not created by the state in the first place. Many of these rules are now administered as state law or part of the official legal system. The second level is unofficial law; it is the law not approved by any legitimate authority of the state but which is endorsed by a certain group in society, either within or beyond the bounds of the state. In Chiba's view the term unofficial law does not apply to all laws not approved by the state, but is limited to the ones having an influence on the effectiveness of state law, either in the form of opposing, supplementing, modifying or undermining it.

There is another level of law that transcends the legal and yet which needs to be counted in the equation because it influences the operation of legal systems in more substantial ways than most lawyers are prepared to recognize. According to Chiba, a legal postulate is "a value principle or system ... specifically connected with and worked to justify particular official or unofficial law".[31] It may consist of established legal ideas, such as natural law, justice, equity, social and cultural postulates, political ideologies and so on. Instead of simply opposing state law and people's law, Chiba identifies many legal levels. The three levels of law consist of official law, unofficial law, and legal postulates.

I would argue that "Indonesian Syariah" — to borrow Hooker's terminology — is moving gradually from legal postulates (*maqashid al-Syariah*)[32] and unofficial law (ritual practices) into official law (a state law). In Chiba's scheme, religious values could sit properly in legal postulates. For instance, article 28J(2) of the Indonesian Constitution recognizes the importance of religious values in implementing human rights:

In the enjoyment of their rights and freedoms, each person is obliged to submit to the limits determined by law, with the sole purpose of guaranteeing recognition and respect for the rights of others and to fulfil the requirements of justice, and taking into consideration morality, religious values, security, and public order, in a democratic community.

The phrase "religious values" is placed along with justice, morality, security, public order, and the concept of a democratic country. This shows that the practice of human rights may well take into account these elements, and the only limitation is the law itself. This also indicates a pluralistic and inclusive approach, since "religious values" can also be interpreted according to the other religions which exist in Indonesia.

Examples of unofficial law include the government's decision on the beginning and ending of Ramadan and the issuing of MUI's halal certificates. These are largely based on the fatwas issued by Islamic organizations, as I explained elsewhere.[33]

The topic of sharia and legal pluralism in Indonesia is a complex arrangement of legal and public reasoning, moral practice and political authority. In Indonesia the concept of *Bhineka Tunggal Ika* (unity in diversity) has been expanded and implemented in the legal arena. Therefore, accommodating sharia into Indonesian law in the post-Soeharto era is not an issue. The real issue is what is the limit in accommodating sharia? Should sharia be accommodated in every aspect, including *hudud* or criminal law?

In the context of enforcing Islamic law, according to Daniel Price (1999) sharia can be split into five levels:

1. personal status (marriage, divorce);
2. economic matters (banking);
3. proscribing practices seen as un-Islamic (haram consumption, gambling, inappropriate dress);
4. criminal law; and
5. as a guide for government matters.

In the Indonesian context, sharia is moving from the first level, personal status (with the establishment of Law No. 1 of 1974, Law No. 7 of 1989 on the religious court, and the compilation of Islamic law in 1991), to the second level, economic matters (Law No. 3 of 2006 on the religious court, which stated that the court has jurisdiction on economic sharia matters, and Law No. 21 of 2008 on Islamic banking). Sharia bylaws could also be seen as examples of official laws in the third level above.[34] The fourth level can be seen in a limited fashion in the practice of the *hudud* law in Nanggroe Aceh Darussalam (NAD).[35] The fifth level has been rejected through the democratic process of constitutional amendments.[36]

Concluding Remarks

Having discussed the main issues above, a number of observations can be made here.

Firstly, if religious law is an integral part of culture, then the practice of religious law should be celebrated and protected in exactly the same fashion as traditional language, food and dance. This should result in the operation of a state-endorsed pluralistic legal system that accommodates cultural and legal differences amongst differing cultural groups. If Muslims through their Islamic political parties want to propose a bill which is inspired by Islamic teaching, they can do so as long as the proposal meets the rule of law. And at the end of the day the debate will be based on public reason,[37] not the holy texts. Khaled Abou El-Fadl argues that a law which is inspired by the sharia should not be claimed as being part of sharia.[38] According to Smith, religion does enter the public legal sphere and its discourse through a process known as "smuggling".[39] A law on pilgrimage is illustrative. The law does not touch the ritual aspect of hajj (as the obligation to conduct hajj comes not from the law but from God), but only the "technical aspect" of how to regulate sixteen thousand people every year who go to Saudi Arabia for the pilgrimage. This means that there is also a "secular" reason the government needs to get involved in pilgrimage, as the government has to represent a large number of people in dealing with the Saudi Arabia authorities for travel, accommodation and catering arrangements.

Secondly, the establishment of a special court (and special autonomy in the case of NAD) in dealing with sharia should be seen as an example of legal pluralism. It might be asked whether such pluralism could be expanded in the case of non-Muslim laws. The idea of "Perda Injil" (local regulation based on the Bible) in Manokwari is illustrative. This legislation was designed to inculcate Christian values in local society, and was therefore seen as discriminatory towards the Muslim community. The Perda Injil was, however, never implemented by the government of Manokwari due to strong criticism from Muslim as well some Christian authorities. Can another religion also become another legal source? Or should we consider the notion of "one law for all" in which diversity or plurality of religion will not be taken into account in state law? For instance, instead of having special laws on zakat and the hajj, could parliament propose a bill on charity and pilgrimage to cover every aspect of charity and spiritual journeys in all religions? There is also another important question: If a particular statute was inspired by religious doctrine, how far are the government and parliament prepared to accommodate different interpretations of religious doctrine into state law?

Thirdly, participation in religious organizations leads the community to be more open towards the complexities of social life. In this sense it requires a reinterpretation of religious ideas that are conducive to embracing democratic values. By engaging in this reinterpretation, religious groups can play a central role in the development and consolidation of democracy. However, the rejection of pluralism by MUI's fatwa in 2005 is ironic in the sense that MUI's efforts to pressure parliament to accommodate sharia into a state law is seen as another form of pluralism — legal pluralism. It would be problematic if pluralism was regarded as the inclusion of sharia whilst rejecting others. Just how pluralistically inclined are they?

Fourthly, the recognition of sharia into official law at the fourth and fifth levels has the potential to undermine the nature of the Indonesian state, which is "neither [a] secular nor Islamic state".[40] An Islam-inspired agenda is welcome to the extent that it corresponds with, and does not contradict, the Pancasila (the five pillars that eventually became the foundation of the state: Belief in one God, Humanitarianism, National Unity, Representative Democracy, and Social Justice). I would argue that the Pancasila should act as limiting the accommodation of sharia in Indonesia.

Above all, what we see is the emergence of a *qanunisasi* (*"qanunization"*) paradigm, which is characterized by the interaction of official law, unofficial law and legal postulates. Indonesia should be seen as a laboratory for legal pluralism. It is important to acknowledge that the process of *qanunisasi* has followed the democratic procedure and mechanism. In other words, it is a product of democracy in the post-Soeharto era.

Notes

1. M.B. Hooker, *Indonesian Islam: Social Change Through Contemporary Fatawa* (University of Hawai'i Press, 2003), p. 20.
2. Matthias Mahlmann, "Freedom and Faith: Foundations of Freedom of Religion", *Cardozo Law Review* 30 (2009): 2473.
3. András Sajó, "Preliminaries to a Concept of Constitutional Secularism", *International Journal of Constitutional Law* 6 (2008): 605; see also Michael Rosenfield, "Can Constitutionalism, Secularism and Religion be Reconciled in an Era of Globalisation and Religious Revival?", *Cardozo Law Review* 30 (2009): 2333.
4. Abdullahi Ahmed An-Na'im, *Islam and the Secular State: Negotiating the Future of Shari'a* (Cambridge: Harvard University Press, 2008).
5. See Nadirsyah Hosen, *Human Rights, Politics and Corruption in Indonesia: A Critical Reflection on the Post Soeharto Era* (Dordrecht: Republic of Letters, 2010).
6. See Nadirsyah Hosen, "Religious Pluralism, Inclusive Secularism and Democratic Constitutionalism: The Indonesian Experience", in *Muslim Secular Democracy: Voices from Within*, edited by Lily Zubaidah Rahim (New York: Palgrave Macmillan, 2013), pp. 211–32.

7. Peter Alford, "Indonesia 'a Model for Arab Uprisings'", *The Australian*, 27 August 2011 <http://www.theaustralian.com.au/news/world/indonesia-a-model-for-arab-uprisings/story-e6frg6so-1226123161330>.

8. See Melissa Crouch, "Regulating Places of Worship in Indonesia: Upholding Freedom of Religion for Religious Minorities", *Singapore Journal of Legal Studies* (2007): 96–116.

9. Steven Smith, *The Disenchantment of Secular Discourse* (Cambridge: Harvard University Press, 2010).

10. Indonesian Constitutional Court Decision No. 93/PUU-X/2012 <http://www.mahkamahkonstitusi.go.id/putusan/putusan_sidang_93%20PUU%202012-perbankan%20syariah-telah%20ucap%2029%20Agustus%202013.pdf>.

11. Nadirsyah Hosen, *Shari'a and Constitutional Reform in Indonesia* (Singapore: Institute of Southeast Asian Studies, 2007).

12. Nadirsyah Hosen, "Promoting Democracy and Finding the Right Direction: A Review of Major Constitutional Developments in Indonesia", in *Constitutionalism in Asia in the Early Twenty-first Century*, edited by Albert H.Y. Chen (Cambridge: Cambridge University Press, 2014), p. 335.

13. Tim Lindsey, "Legal Infrastructure and Governance Reform in Post-Crisis Asia: The Case of Indonesia", *Asian Pacific Economic Literature* 18, no. 1 (2004): 36; See also Simon Butt and Tim Lindsey, *The Constitution of Indonesia: A Contextual Analysis* (Hart: Oxford, 2012).

14. See Cholil Nafis, *Teori Hukum Ekonomi Syariah* (Jakarta: Universitas Indonesia Press, 2011).

15. Moch Nur Ichwan, "Towards a Puritanical Moderate Islam: The Majelis Ulama Indonesia and the Politics of Religious Orthodoxy", in *Contemporary Developments in Indonesian Islam: Explaining the 'Conservative Turn'*, edited by Martin van Bruinessen (Singapore: Institute of Southeast Asian Studies, 2013), p. 75.

16. KH. Ma'ruf Amin, personal interview, Jakarta, 27 June 2012.

17. Hyung-Jun Kim, "The Changing Interpretation of Religious Freedom in Indonesia", *Journal of Southeast Asian Studies* 29, no. 2 (1998): 357.

18. Indonesian Constitutional Court Decision No 140/PUU-VII/2009 <http://www.mahkamahkonstitusi.go.id/putusan/putusan_sidang_Putusan%20PUU%20140_Senin%2019%20April%202010.pdf>.

19. See Bernhard Platzdasc, "Religious Freedom in Indonesia: The Case of the Ahmadiya", ISEAS Working Paper: Politics & Security Series No. 2 (2011); and Alfitri, "Religious Liberty in Indonesia and the Rights of 'Deviant' Sects", *Asian Journal of Comparative Law* 3, no. 1 (2008).

20. Keputusan Fatwa Majelis Ulama Indonesia (MUI) Nomor: 7/Munas VII/MUI/11/2005 Tentang Pluralisme, Liberalisme, dan Sekulerisme Agama.

The text is available at <http://www.eramuslim.com/berita/tahukah-anda/
fatwa-mui-tentang-pluralisme-liberalisme-dan-sekulerisme-agama.htm>.

21. Quoted from "MUI's Fatwa Encourage Use of Violence", *Jakarta Post*,
     1 August 2005 <http://www.thejakartapost.com/news/2005/08/01/
     mui039s-fatwa-encourage-use-violence.html>.

22. See Diana L. Eck, "The Challenge of Pluralism", The Pluralism Project,
     Harvard University, 1993 <http://www.pluralism.org/articles/eck_1993_
     challenge_of_pluralism>.

23. Dr Maulana Hasanudin, personal interview, 15 June 2012.

24. On this matter, see Karel Steenbrink, *Dutch Colonialism and Islam in
     Indonesia: Conflict and Contact 1596–1950* (Amsterdam: Rodopi, 1993).

25. See M.B. Hooker, *Legal Pluralism: An Introduction to Colonial and Neo-colonial
     Laws* (Oxford: Clarendon Press, 1975), pp. 6–54, for an introduction to the
     concept of legal pluralism.

26. Gary F. Bell, "Multiculturalism in Law is Legal Pluralism – Lessons from
     Indonesia, Singapore and Canada", *Singapore Journal of Legal Studies* (2006):
     315–330.

27. Anna C. Korteweg, "The Syariah Debate in Ontario: Gender, Islam, and
     Representations of Muslim Women's Agency", *Gender & Society* 22, no. 4
     (2008): 434–54.

28. Rowan Williams, "Syariah Law in UK is 'Unavoidable'", 2008 <http://
     news.bbc.co.uk/1/hi/uk/7232661.stm>.

29. Ihsan Yilmaz, *Muslim Laws, Politics and Society in Modern Nation States:
     Dynamic Legal Pluralisms in England, Turkey and Pakistan* (Burlington, VT:
     Ashgate, 2005).

30. Masaji Chiba, *Legal Culture in Human Society: A Collection of Articles and
     Essays* (Tokyo: Shinzansha International, 2002).

31. Ibid., p. 69.

32. In terms of Shariah, there are five *maqasid* (foundational goals). These
     are the preservation of religion, life, lineage, intellect and property. More
     information can be found in M. Sa'd b. Ahmad b. Mas'ud al- Alyubi,
     Maqasid al-Shari`a al-Islamiya wa `Alaqatuha bi Adillah al-Shar`iyyah (Riyad,
     Dar al-hijrah li al-Nasyr wa al-Tawzi`, 1998).

33. Nadirsyah Hosen, "Hilal and Halal: How to Manage Islamic Pluralism in
     Indonesia?", *Asian Journal of Comparative Law* 7, no. 1 (2012).

34. Robin Bush records around 78 regional regulations (*perda*) in 52 districts/
     municipalities (*kabupaten/walikota*) out of a total of 470 districts/ municipalities
     that are considered to be "Syari'ah influenced". Robin Bush, "Regional
     Sharia Regulations in Indonesia: Anomaly or Sympton?", in *Expressing
     Islam: Religious Life and Politics in Indonesia*, edited by Greg Fealy and
     Sally White (Singapore: Institute of Southeast Asian Studies, 2008), p. 176.

Arskal Salim proposes three categories for these regional regulations: (1) those relating to "public order and social problems" — prostitution, gambling, alcohol consumption, etc.; (2) religious skills and obligations — reading the Qur'an, paying zakat (alms or religious tax); and (3) religious symbolism, – primarily the wearing of Muslim clothing. See Arskal Salim, "'Muslim Politics' in Indonesia's Democratization: Religious Majority and the Rights of Minorities in the Post New Order Era", in *Democracy and the Promise of Good Governance*, edited by Andrew MacIntyre and Ross McLeod (Singapore: Institute of Southeast Asian Studies, 2007), p. 126.

35. On the issue of *hudud* law in Aceh, see Arskal Salim, "Politics, Criminal Justice and Islamisation in Aceh", Australian Research Council Federation Fellowship Islam Syariah and Governance Background Paper, No. 3 (2009).

36. See Hosen, *Shari'a and Constitutional Reform in Indonesia*.

37. John Rawls, *Political liberalism* (Columbia University Press, 1993).

38. Khaled Abou El Fadl, "Islam and the Challenge of Democracy: Can individual Rights and Popular Sovereignty Take Root in Faith?", *Boston Review*, April/May 2003 <http://bostonreview.net/forum/khaled-abou-el-fadl-islam-and-challenge-democracy>.

39. Smith, *The Disenchantment of Secular Discourse*.

40. It is a common belief that Indonesia is neither a secular nor an Islamic state. Both terms have negative images in Indonesian society, and therefore the use of the terms "secular" and "Islamic state" have been avoided in legal and political arenas. The design of the 1945 Constitution was to put Indonesia in the middle position. This ambiguity has led some scholars to create new categories of "quasi-secular democracy", "religious secularity" or eclectic *wasatiyyah*. See Lily Zubaidah Rahim, "Introduction: The Spirit of Wasatiyyah Democracy", in *Muslim Secular Democracy: Voices from Within*, edited by Lily Zubaidah Rahim (New York: Palgrave Macmillan, 2013), p. 1–27.

References

Court Judgements

Indonesian Constitutional Court Decision No 140/PUU-VII/2009, available at <http://www.mahkamahkonstitusi.go.id/putusan/putusan_sidang_Putusan%20PUU%20140_Senin%2019%20April%202010.pdf>.

Indonesian Constitutional Court Decision No. 93/PUU-X/2012, available at <http://www.mahkamahkonstitusi.go.id/putusan/putusan_sidang_93%20PUU%202012-perbankan%20syariah-telah%20ucap%2029%20Agustus%202013.pdf>.

Books

An-Na'im, Abdullahi Ahmed. *Islam and the Secular State: Negotiating the Future of Shari'a*. Cambridge: Harvard University Press, 2008.

Butt, Simon, and Tim Lindsey. *The Constitution of Indonesia: A Contextual Analysis*. Oxford: Hart, 2012.

Chiba, Masaji. *Legal Culture in Human Society: A Collection of Articles and Essays*. Tokyo: Shinzansha International, 2002.

Hooker, M.B. *Legal Pluralism: An Introduction to Colonial and Neo-colonial Laws*. Clarendon Press, Oxford, 1975.

————. *Indonesian Islam: Social Change through Contemporary Fatawa*. University of Hawai'i Press, 2003.

Hosen, Nadirsyah. *Shari'a and Constitutional Reform in Indonesia*. Singapore: Institute of Southeast Asian Studies, 2007.

————. *Human Rights, Politics and Corruption in Indonesia: A Critical Reflection on the Post Soeharto Era*. Dordrecht: Republic of Letters, 2010.

M. Sa'd b. Ahmad b. Mas'ud al- Alyubi. *Maqasid al-Shari`a al-Islamiya wa `Alaqatuha bi Adillah al-Shar`iyyah*. Riyad: Dar al-hijrah li al-Nasyr wa al-Tawzi`, 1998.

Nafis, Cholil. *Teori Hukum Ekonomi Syariah*. Jakarta: UI Press, 2011.

Rawls, John. *Political liberalism*. New York: Columbia University Press, 1993.

Smith, Steven. *The Disenchantment of Secular Discourse*. Cambridge: Harvard University Press, 2010.

Steenbrink, Karel. *Dutch Colonialism and Islam in Indonesia: Conflict and Contact 1596–1950*. Amsterdam: Rodopi B.V., 1993.

Yilmaz, Ihsan. *Muslim Laws, Politics and Society in Modern Nation States: Dynamic Legal Pluralisms in England, Turkey and Pakistan*. Burlington, VT: Ashgate, 2005.

Chapters

Bush, Robin. "Regional Sharia Regulations in Indonesia: Anomaly or Sympton?" In *Expressing Islam: Religious Life and Politics in Indonesia*, edited in Greg Fealy and Sally White, pp. 174–91. Singapore: Institute of Southeast Asian Studies, 2008.

Hosen, Nadirsyah. "Religious Pluralism, Inclusive Secularism and Democratic Constitutionalism: The Indonesian Experience". In *Muslim Secular Democracy: Voices from Within*, edited by Lily Zubaidah Rahim, pp. 211–32. New York: Palgrave Macmillan, 2013.

————. "Promoting Democracy and Finding the Right Direction: A Review of Major Constitutional Developments in Indonesia". In *Constitutionalism in Asia in the Early Twenty-First Century*, edited by Albert H.Y. Chen, pp 322–42. Cambridge: Cambridge University Press, 2014.

Ichwan, Moch Nur. "Towards a Puritanical Moderate Islam: The Majelis Ulama Indonesia and the Politics of Religious Orthodoxy". In *Contemporary*

Developments in Indonesian Islam: Explaining the "Conservative Turn", edited by Martin van Bruinessen, pp. 60–104. Singapore: Institute of Southeast Asian Studies, 2013.

Rahim, Lily Zubaidah. "Introduction: The Spirit of Wasatiyyah Democracy". In *Muslim Secular Democracy: Voices from Within*, edited by Lily Zubaidah Rahim, pp. 1–27. New York: Palgrave Macmillan, 2013.

Salim, Arskal. "'Muslim Politics' in Indonesia's Democratization: Religious Majority and the Rights of Minorities in the Post New Order Era". In *Democracy and the Promise of Good Governance*, edited by Andrew MacIntyre and Ross McLeod, pp. 115–37. Singapore: Institute of Southeast Asian Studies, 2007.

Law Review Articles and Working Papers

Alfitri. "Religious Liberty in Indonesia and the Rights of 'Deviant' Sects". *Asian Journal of Comparative Law* 3 (2008): 1–27.

Bell, Gary F. "Multiculturalism in Law is Legal Pluralism – Lessons from Indonesia, Singapore and Canada". *Singapore Journal of Legal Studies* (2006): 315–30.

Crouch, Melissa. "Regulating Places of Worship in Indonesia: Upholding Freedom of Religion for Religious Minorities". *Singapore Journal of Legal Studies* (2007): 96–116.

Hosen, Nadirsyah: "Hilal and Halal: How to Manage Islamic Pluralism in Indonesia?" *Asian Journal of Comparative Law* 7 (2012): 1–18.

Kim, Hyung-Jun. "The Changing Interpretation of Religious Freedom in Indonesia". *Journal of Southeast Asian Studies* 29, no. 2 (1998): 357–70.

Korteweg, Anna C. "The Syariah Debate in Ontario: Gender, Islam, and Representations of Muslim Women's Agency". *Gender & Society* 22 (2008): 434–54.

Lindsey, Tim. "Legal Infrastructure and Governance Reform in Post-Crisis Asia: The Case of Indonesia". *Asian Pacific Economic Literature* 18, no.1 (2004): 12–40.

Mahlmann, Matthias. "Freedom and Faith: Foundations of Freedom of Religion". *Cardozo Law Review* 30 (2009). 2473–93.

Platzdasch, Bernhard. "Religious Freedom in Indonesia: The Case of the Ahmadiyah". *ISEAS Working Paper: Politics & Security Series* no. 2 (2011).

Rosenfield, Michael. "Can Constitutionalism, Secularism and Religion be Reconciled in an Era of Globalisation and Religious Revival?" *Cardozo Law Review* 30 (2009): 2333–368.

Sajó, András. "Preliminaries to a Concept of Constitutional Secularism". *International Journal of Constitutional Law* 6 (2008): 605–29.

Salim, Arskal. "Politics, Criminal Justice and Islamisation in Aceh". *Australian Research Council Federation Fellowship Islam Syariah and Governance Background Paper* no. 3 (2009).

Newspapers

Alford, Peter. "Indonesia 'A Model for Arab Uprisings'". *The Australian*, 27 August 2011 <http://www.theaustralian.com.au/news/world/indonesia-a-model-for-arab-uprisings/story-e6frg6so-1226123161330>.

Khaled Abou El Fadl. "Islam and the Challenge of Democracy: Can Individual Rights and Popular Sovereignty Take Root in Faith?" *Boston Review*, April/May 2003 <http://bostonreview.net/forum/khaled-abou-el-fadl-islam-and-challenge-democracy>.

"MUI's Fatwa Encourage Use of Violence". *Jakarta Post*, 1 August 2005 <http://www.thejakartapost.com/news/2005/08/01/mui039s-fatwa-encourage-use-violence.html>.

Other

Amin, KH. Ma'ruf. Personal interview, Jakarta, 27 June 2012.

Diana L. Eck. "The Challenge of Pluralism". The Pluralism Project, Harvard University, 1993 <http://www.pluralism.org/articles/eck_1993_challenge_of_pluralism>.

Keputusan Fatwa Majelis Ulama Indonesia (MUI) Nomor : 7/Munas VII/MUI/11/2005 Tentang Pluralisme, Liberalisme, dan Sekulerisme Agama. The text is available at <http://www.eramuslim.com/berita/tahukah-anda/fatwa-mui-tentang-pluralisme-liberalisme-dan-sekulerisme-agama.htm>.

Maulana Hasanudin. Personal interview, 15 June 2012.

Williams, Rowan. "Syariah Law in UK is 'Unavoidable'". 2008. Available at <http://news.bbc.co.uk/1/hi/uk/7232661.stm>.

10

Negotiating Legal Pluralism in Court: Fatwa and the Crime of Blasphemy in Indonesia

Melissa Crouch

Understanding the legal traditions of Southeast Asia through the lens of legal pluralism continues to present both promise and challenge. The significant work of M.B. Hooker has, among many other things, made a foundational contribution to our understanding of legal pluralism in Southeast Asia,[1] and in particular to our knowledge of the development of fatwas, the opinion of Islamic legal scholars, in contexts such as Indonesia.[2] In post-authoritarian Indonesia, fatwas remain an unofficial source of law in the eyes of the state. This chapter examines the role and authority of fatwas issued against so-called "deviant" religious believers convicted on charges of blasphemy under article 156a of the Criminal Code.[3] This has been an issue of growing concern in Indonesia since the introduction of democracy and the process of decentralization in 1998, where an increasing number of individuals have been convicted for the offence of blasphemy against Islam.

The process of democratic law reform in Indonesia has focused attention on the development and reform of state law. This chapter seeks to promote a broader perspective that includes other legal orders by addressing the relationship between fatwa and state law and its institutions. In exploring this question, this chapter assumes that the state and religious authorities are not mutually exclusive centres of power. Religious authority cannot simply be understood as an alternative to the authority of the state. Instead, religious authority forms one of a number of normative orders that coexist as part of a broader legal sphere. In this wider context, the chapter contributes to our understanding of how non-state sources invoke the authority of the state, as well as how non-state sources of law are legitimized by state law enforcement agencies and the judiciary, influencing the interpretation and enforcement of state laws in court.

Fatwas issued by local religious leaders on issues of deviancy acknowledge the legal authority of the state and call on the state to implement its decision. In criminal cases of blasphemy, a local fatwa that declares a group to be "deviant" may be used as the primary evidence in the legal process. In criminal trials and court proceedings in Indonesia, various actors often refer to the fatwas of the Indonesian Ulama Council (Majelis Ulama Indonesia; MUI). This raises questions about whether the MUI represents the "Muslim community", as it claims, or whether its fatwas embody a state sanctioned version of Islam.

In terms of criminal proceedings, this chapter demonstrates that a fatwa may be used as the basis or justification for allegations of blasphemy to be lodged with, and investigated by, the police. A fatwa may also be used by the public prosecutor to support its case that the accused should be found guilty of "insulting a religion" in a district court (*Pengadilan Negeri*). Islamic religious leaders may also appear as experts at the trial to testify against the accused and refer to a fatwa as part of his evidence given in court. This is all despite the fact that a fatwa is not recognized as an official or legally binding source of law by the district courts in Indonesia. This raises the issue of how the district courts, as independent judicial institutions sanctioned by the state, reconcile and integrate state criminal law with Islamic fatwa in post-Soeharto Indonesia.

Drawing on illustrations from several cases of blasphemy, this chapter argues that a practice of "religious deference"[4] has emerged in Indonesia. The police, the public prosecutor and the courts may defer to the opinion of Islamic religious leaders, namely a fatwa of the state-sanctioned Indonesia Ulama Council, on issues of religious sensitivity and in situations where the application of the law requires religious interpretation. This principle of religious deference is one means by which law enforcement agencies and the general courts negotiate and reconcile the demands of legal pluralism in Indonesia.

Legal Pluralism, the State and Religion

The field of legal pluralism is one that raises many questions about the nature of law and legal systems. Legal pluralism cautions us from excluding acknowledgment of a source as law simply because it is not the law of the state. That is, we cannot assume that state law is dominant or central, nor that other legal orders are necessarily on an equal level with state law. Embracing a concept of law that is not monolithic but rather plural opens up the possibility of considering legal interactions in all their complexity. These dynamics raise questions about how legal pluralism is defined, what it looks like in particular contexts, how contests between legal orders are played out, and who benefits from legal pluralism.[5]

Many definitions and a large body of literature has evolved on the elusive term "legal pluralism". In essence, legal pluralism has been defined as "the presence in a social field of more than one legal order".[6] Similarly, Moore emphasizes that legal pluralism recognizes law regardless of its origins; that is, the "whole aggregate of governmental and non-governmental norms of social control without any distinctions drawn as to their source".[7] These multiple legal norms present a challenge to the legitimacy of the modern and globalized state.

In his seminal work on legal pluralism in Southeast Asia, Hooker[8] identifies three assumptions that are challenged by legal pluralism. First, legal pluralism questions the superiority of state law to override or abolish traditional legal systems. Second, legal pluralism exposes the claims to superiority made by state law if there are inconsistencies between state law and traditional legal systems, and how state law defines the basis on which traditional legal systems are permitted to exist. Third, legal pluralism makes visible the use of state categories and labels to identify and analyse traditional legal systems. Hooker explores these concepts of legal pluralism through numerous case studies of countries from Asia to Africa.[9] As part of this project, Hooker analysed the experience of legal pluralism in Indonesia, particularly the Dutch colonial legal system as a complex plural legal order where the choice of law to be applied in a circumstance depended on which category of citizen the case concerned.

Other scholars have attributed different meanings to legal pluralism. As Moore has identified, these definitions may include issues of internal pluralism within the administration of the state, the fact that state law may exist alongside regional or international legal orders, and the way that the state may depend on non-state actors to enable the implementation of the law.[10] There are therefore multiple dimensions to legal pluralism in modern contexts.

Regardless of how it is defined, legal pluralism calls us to reconsider the connection between law and power. Benda-Beckmann demonstrates that law "defines and validates positions and relations of power of persons or organisations over other persons, organisations and resources".[11] The law may support or contradict the extent of the authority of those who exercise power. At the same time, these legal constructions of power are not necessarily an accurate reflection or representation of actual power relations.[12] Legal pluralism therefore disrupts and upsets traditional concepts of the relation between law and power, as power must be seen as "relational, relative and embedded in social relationships".[13]

This chapter seeks to approach legal pluralism as both a social reality and a core challenge to our understanding of contemporary legal ordering that requires attention. It acknowledges the complex questions raised by legal pluralism, such as what is the nature of law, which law applies in a specific situation, and who has the power to determine this. While scholarship on legal pluralism emerged from the study of post-colonial societies that had inherited foreign legal systems from their colonial masters, this chapter considers legal pluralism in the context of post-authoritarian Indonesia as a society that has undergone significant democratic reform. In the transition to democracy, the fixation on state law as part of the agenda for the reform of the rule of law raises new questions about the forms of legal pluralism and its accommodation and interaction today.

I seek to examine the relationship between religious authority and the authority of the state, while recognizing that they are not mutually exclusive. I question whether non-state religious fatwas can be said to constitute and inform state law in Indonesia. Given the position of the MUI as a quasi-government body recognized and consulted by the Ministry of Religion, this chapter focuses on how a fatwa shapes, and is shaped by, state authorities and law. In particular, it looks at how the state appropriates religious authority to serve its own ends.

In criminal cases against "deviants" or against those accused of violence against deviants, there remains an ongoing issue of where ultimate authority lies. From one perspective, final authority may be identified with state law, while from another view, ultimate authority rests with religious leaders. I examine when religious law or state law is invoked and why; such as whether religion is employed to extend state control, or how the Blasphemy Law is attributed meaning by non-state law.

This chapter focuses on the interaction between the legal norms of the state and religious authorities. Benda-Beckmann has identified that "religion is often depicted in opposition to the state, as a means for critiquing state power or abuse, or as an alternative moral order that may be called on to undermine state authority".[14] Rather than characterizing the sources of state law and religious authority as in opposition, this chapter examines how these legal orders coexist in Indonesia and the extent to which they rely upon, and defer to, the other.

Fatwa and the Kaleidoscope of Indonesian Legal Pluralism

The dynamics of legal pluralism in Indonesia are complex, and fatwas are just one aspect of the plural legal order. The court system in Indonesia is not based on Islamic sharia, with the exception of the religious courts (Pengadilan Agama). Given that its limited jurisdiction does not include criminal law,[15] and the fact that the religious courts are explicitly recognized by the state, I will not discuss cases in these courts in this chapter. Rather, this section highlights the unique position and dynamic authority of the fatwas of the MUI as a religious body sanctioned by the state. I outline the nature of its fatwas as a source of religious authority, with specific reference to those that declare certain groups and their teachings as "deviant".

The procedure for issuing a fatwa in Indonesia and the sources on which it is based has been the topic of extended discussion in the work of Hooker.[16] He has examined the creation and production of fatwas and the extent to which fatwas are regulated by the Indonesian state. Hooker defines a fatwa as "formal legal advice given by qualified legal scholars".[17] A fatwa is non-binding, usually issued in response to a particular question, practice or belief, and the decision is made in light of past interpretations.[18] There are primarily two reasons that fatwas are not legally binding in Indonesia, as Hooker has emphasized.[19] The first is that the classical understanding of fatwas is that they do not have the status of law. The second is the historical reality that fatwas have never been recognized as a source of official law by the Indonesian state. Nevertheless, any analysis of fatwas and sources of legal power in Indonesia must go beyond the fact that they are not recognized as an official source of state law, to examine the ways these religious pronouncements interact with, and are affirmed by, the state.

There are four main bodies that are sources of fatwas in Indonesia: Muhammadiyah, Persatuan Islam, Nadhatul Ulama and the MUI. This chapter focuses on the fatwas of the MUI because its fatwas have been mentioned in the district courts in criminal cases concerning so-called "deviancy".

The MUI occupies a unique position in relation to the state. The MUI was created as a national, quasi-government institution linked to the Ministry of Religion. On 26 July 1976, it was officially established by ulama representing the then twenty-six provinces.[20] Chaired by Haji Abdul Malik Karim Amrullah (known as "Buya Hamka"), a prominent Islamic religious leader, writer, politician and activist within Muhammadiyah, the MUI gradually established branches at the regional level across Indonesia.

This institution was originally part of Soeharto's plan to control the ulama and the public expression of Islam in Indonesia.[21] The MUI was formed relatively late in comparison to other national religious councils[22] because Islamic religious leaders feared that it might be manipulated by the government to further subordinate Islam.[23] In part this is what occurred, as the New Order government used the MUI as a means to disseminate its policies to the Muslim community, primarily through fatwas.[24]

The interaction between the fatwas of the MUI and state policy occurs at two levels. First, a fatwa may be used to endorse government policies and decisions. A study by Mudzhar[25] found that most fatwas issued from 1975 to 1988 were supportive of government policy. For example, the issue of family planning arose in the 1970s, when the government's approach to family planning failed because it had not convinced religious leaders of its policy and many ulama still taught that it was haram to use the pill or other family-planning methods.[26] In contrast, when the MUI issued a fatwa in the 1980s, it lent greater credibility and acceptance to the government's family-planning programme.[27] In this way, fatwas were a convenient means for the government to legitimate its policies in religious terms in the eyes of the Muslim community.

Second, the fatwas of the MUI have informed and shaped government policy. Fatwas have been influential in the drafting and passage of legislation based on the aspirations of the Muslim community and Islamic law.[28] Adams cites over ten laws that were influenced by the role of the MUI in issuing fatwas, by advice it provided to the government, by the submission of recommendations to the legislature and by its participation as a member of legal drafting teams.[29] Adams also demonstrates how the MUI was instrumental in opposing policies that were perceived to contravene Islamic law. For example, the MUI successfully lobbied the director general of education and culture to overturn the ban on wearing the *jilbab* or *kerudung* (headscarf) in schools in Indonesia.[30] Although it may be a state-sanctioned religious body, the MUI has therefore made some progress in overturning policies that could be seen as inconsistent with Islamic law.

Since 1998 and the downfall of the authoritarian regime, all religious groups, including the MUI, have experienced greater freedom of expression and association as a result of the transition to democracy. Fundamental questions about the nature of the MUI and its relations with the state need to be reconsidered. For example, the impartiality and independence of the MUI is questionable given that there is little distance between it and the state. It is given a seat at the table of consultations on issues relevant to the Muslim community, and now plays a "key regulatory function" in regards to halal certification, Islamic banking and the hajj.[31] This raises issues such as whether the MUI represents the Muslim community or state interests, and who initiates the request for a fatwa.

The process and guidelines for issuing a fatwa are set out in a 1997 decision of the MUI.[32] According to this guideline, the MUI represents a "consensus" among Islamic scholars and is the central umbrella organization for all Indonesian Muslims that is best placed to respond to religious and social issues confronting the community (art. 6). It then outlines the procedure for issuing a fatwa, and in particular stresses that these guidelines are to ensure that any differences between the national and regional branches can be resolved. It defines a fatwa as "a response or explanation from the ulama concerning a religious issue, which is made public". It requires a fatwa to be based on the Qur'an and Sunnah (art. 2[1]) and for a comprehensive study to be conducted before a fatwa is issued (art. 4). The MUI can receive a request for a fatwa from an individual, a community organization or the government, or it can decide to issue an "own motion" fatwa. While the national MUI has general authority to issue a fatwa, the regional branches are required to consult with the national branch first (art. 7). Any difference in opinion between the national and regional branches requires a meeting to be held in order to resolve the matter (art. 8[2]). In practice, however, regional branches often go in their own direction,[33] even though the guideline requires them to be under the supervision of the national branch. This is a cause of concern in blasphemy cases, because it is often the regional branches that issue a fatwa against "deviants".

The MUI at both the national and local level has often issued fatwas against minority groups in an attempt to suppress deviant teachings that present a challenge to orthodox Islamic doctrine and to its members' authority as religious leaders. Such fatwas have been referred to by courts in cases concerning blasphemy. I focus on cases post-1998 because there is no evidence that fatwas were issued in any of the ten blasphemy cases prior to 1998.

The Relationship between Criminal Prosecutions for Blasphemy and Fatwas

No comprehensive statistics are available on convictions for blasphemy in Indonesia, although there were over fifty court cases, or at least 130 individuals convicted, under article 156a of the Criminal Code between 1998 and 2012.[34] Of these, in at least ten cases (which involved the conviction of fourteen people) a fatwa was issued against a group that was considered to be deviant, either by the national or regional branches of the MUI, and the fatwa was then relied upon by the prosecution in court. In most of the other forty court cases, although no fatwa was issued prior to these court cases, religious leaders, particularly from the MUI, often played a key role in the cases by reporting the accused to the police and by giving evidence as witnesses or experts at the trial.

There are several ways in which court trials for blasphemy have relied on fatwas to convict the accused. The police have relied on a fatwa to accept a complaint and conduct investigations. The public prosecutor has relied on a fatwa as a form of evidence against allegedly "deviant" individuals. Religious leaders have been called as experts or witnesses in court trials and referred to fatwas as the basis for their evidence. Judges have also had to consider the merits of fatwas as evidence in court, although the court decisions provide little insight into how judges weigh the validity of a fatwa.

It is necessary to examine how the district courts reconcile the intersection between a fatwa and state law. If the teachings of a religious minority group are declared to be deviant in a fatwa, then, even if the group is not officially banned by the state under the Blasphemy Law, the court may convict an individual for blasphemy on this basis. In doing so, the courts seem to display an attitude of deference towards Islamic religious authority through reliance on fatwas. In examining the attitude of religious deference the courts demonstrate to religious authorities, the question then becomes which religious authorities and sources are deferred to? The MUI is the primary Islamic religious organization recognized by the Ministry of Religion, and in part because of this connection to the state the courts will defer to it.

I illustrate the function of fatwas in court trials by reference to three cases of individuals convicted for blaspheming Islam. The first set of trials involved Lia Eden and two members of her community, primarily because Lia Eden issued her own controversial fatwas, containing teachings that were considered to be "deviant", and then sent a copy to the MUI. The second set of trials involved members of Al-Qiyadah Al-Islamiyah, where a number of local MUI branches issued fatwas and then pursued prosecutions against the leaders of this group. The third case is the trial of Oben Sarbeni, in which conflicting fatwas were issued by two regional branches of the MUI on the grounds of "deviancy".

I analyse each of these cases in turn, looking in particular at the content of fatwas and whether they recognise the authority of the state; the role of members of the MUI; the reliance by the prosecution or expert witnesses on fatwas as evidence; whether the fatwas were issued at the regional or national level; and how the fatwas were dealt with by the judiciary. The consideration given to fatwas appears to be at the discretion of the public prosecutor or the judge. I suggest that this is because of the combined power of religious authority and its connection to the state. As a result, an attitude of "religious deference" has emerged where the public prosecutor and the courts rely on fatwas to validate criminal convictions for blasphemy.

Alternative Sources of Fatwa: The Lia Eden Case

The two separate trials of Lia Eden, and of two members of her community, can be seen as the catalyst for the increasing number of convictions for blasphemy. Lia Eden was the first high profile case of blasphemy in the final years of the unravelling of the New Order and the early years of the transition to democracy. The Eden community began in 1995 under the leadership of Lia Eden (formerly known as Lia Aminuddin) who claimed to have had an encounter with the archangel Gabriel. In 2005 the movement had about fifty members. As early as 1997 a fatwa had been issued by the national MUI against Lia Eden and her teachings.[35] The content suggests that although instructions were directed to Lia Eden and to the Muslim community, the fatwa did not go as far as to call on the state to ban the organization.

The fatwa is only one of a handful of fatwas issued by the national MUI against a specific group at that time.[36] The fatwa noted that in November 1997 Lia Eden was called before the Fatwa Committee several times to explain her actions and teachings, and it described how she claimed to have received a vision that she was the archangel Gabriel. The fatwa explained that the archangel Gabriel appeared to the Prophet Muhammad to announce that he was the final prophet, and that angels no longer reveal themselves to humans. The fatwa quotes several verses from the Qur'an that affirm the belief in the existence of angels as supernatural beings and that highlight their characteristics,[37] as further noted in the Hadith (HR Muslim). It emphasizes that angels are directed by Allah, that angels only appear to the prophets, and that the Prophet Muhammad was the final prophet.[38] It notes that it is the task of the ulama to explain the Qur'an (16:43) and that therefore a person who claims to be an angel cannot undertake this role. It concludes that any person who claims to be the archangel Gabriel is deviant. It specifically instructs Lia Eden and her followers to "return" to the teachings of Islam, and it warns the Muslim community against following her teachings. It does not, however, go as far as to call on the authority of the state to ban the group, as fatwas have done in later cases.

Several years passed after the fatwa was issued, although there were ongoing disagreements between the MUI and Lia Eden, particularly in the early 2000s. Then, in 2005, Lia Eden issued her own fatwa, which included the claim that she was the archangel Gabriel and that one of her followers Muhammad Abdul Rahman was the reincarnation of the Prophet Muhammad. She sent a copy to the MUI and the Ministry of Religion.[39] She also published a brochure titled "The Fatwa of Gabriel v the Fatwa of MUI", setting herself up in direct contrast to the authority of the MUI. In short, her fatwa directly contradicted and challenged that of the MUI.

At the trial, numerous references were made to the fatwa issued in 1997, including by witnesses and experts such as Muhammad Isa Anshary, a member of the MUI. One expert witness was M. Amin Djamaluddin, the president of LPPI, an Islamist organization that conducts research on deviant teachings in order to determine whether they are opposed to the teachings of Islam. From his research, Djamaluddin concluded that Lia Eden's teachings contradicted the teachings of Islam because she taught that pork is not haram (forbidden); that Abdul Rahman is the reincarnation of the Prophet Muhammad; that she is the archangel Gabriel; that prayers can be conducted in two languages; and that her pamphlets contradict some verses of the Qur'an. An expert from the Ministry of Religion also gave evidence that Lia Eden's teachings were contrary to the teachings of Islam.

The public prosecutor submitted a copy of the 1997 MUI fatwa as evidence against Lia Eden in court.[40] Lia Eden's fatwa and brochures were considered by the court to be a direct insult to the MUI.[41] The court described the MUI as a "representative of all the various Islamic organisations in Indonesia that has the responsibility to guard inter-religious harmony and resolve any differences of opinion between religions, particularly Islam". Lia Eden was found guilty of blasphemy and sentenced to two years jail. In the same trial, Muhammad Abdul Rahman was also convicted under article 156a for claiming to be the Prophet Muhammad.[42]

In 2009, in the second case, Lia Eden was convicted for revelations she claimed to receive that were then sent in the form of a letter to all major government departments and Islamic organizations in Indonesia, including the president. In these letters she contended that Islam as a religion should be dissolved, that all religions should unite and that they should all pray in one direction.[43] One of her followers, Wahyu Andito Putro Wibisono, was also convicted under article 156a of the Criminal Code because of his role in distributing the letters (District Court 2009). Again, a central part of the public prosecutor's evidence was the fatwa issued by the MUI in 1997.[44]

These cases are particularly interesting because Lia Eden issued her own fatwa and teachings, directly challenging the authority of the national MUI. In both cases the 1997 MUI fatwa was referred to extensively by the public prosecutor and witnesses and also featured in the court decisions. In sum, the fatwa was treated as core evidence that contributed to the conviction of Lia Eden and some of her followers.

Proliferation of Local Fatwas: The Al-Qiyadah Al-Islamiyah Case

While the case of Lia Eden involved a fatwa issued by the national MUI, there have been many cases of its regional branches issuing fatwas to declare a group deviant, either on their own initiative or in addition to a fatwa issued at the national level. There has been an increasing tendency for fatwas to not only include instructions to the deviant group to repent and to the Muslim community to avoid its teachings but also to call on the state to ban the group. One example is the case of Al-Qiyadah Al-Islamiyah, which is an Indonesian-based religious organization that claims to be based on the teachings of Islam.

Al-Qiyadah Al-Islamiyah was officially formed in 2001 and claimed to have 45,000 followers across Indonesia. The national MUI fatwa against the group and its teachings was preceded by fatwas issued by regional branches of the MUI in several areas. The first was in West Sumatera on 24 September and the second in Yogyakarta on 28 September.[45] Not long after, in October 2007, the national MUI then issued a fatwa declaring the group "deviant" because it used another creed; believed in a prophet after Muhammad; and did not pray, fast or pay zakat.[46] It legitimized its position with reference to several verses from the Qur'an that emphasized the final prophethood of Muhammad and the five pillars of Islam.[47] It urged the group to "repent" and "return to Islam" and it called on the government to ban the group. This to some extent suggests that the national MUI recognized the authority and primacy of state law.

The fatwa of Yogyakarta went further than the national fatwa and claimed that the group recognized the book *Ruhul Qudus yang turun kepada Al-Masih Al-Maw'ud* as its holy book, that the group taught that Muhammad is the same as Jesus, and that only "stupid people" pray facing Mecca. It called on the government to close its places of worship, ban the book, and convict followers under the Blasphemy Law.

Several leaders of the group across Indonesia were taken to court on charges of blaspheming Islam under article 156a of the Criminal Code, including six members in Makassar, South Sulawesi; two members in Padang, West Sumatra; and its national leader, Ahmad Mushaddeq, in Jakarta.[48] The convictions in these cases rested in part on the fatwa and the bans mentioned above, which were submitted to the court as evidence of the "deviancy" of the group. For example, the leader, Ahmad Mushaddeq, was charged in court with blasphemy.[49] The main offence identified was that in July 2006, after spending forty days and nights on a mountain in Bogor, Mushaddeq claimed he had received a revelation from God and proclaimed himself "the Promised Saviour". As the prophet of the Al-Qiyadah Al-Islamiyah group, he was accused of spreading the teachings mentioned above. The court at first instance referred to similar sources as set out in the fatwa to find the accused guilty of blasphemy. On appeal the defendant challenged this reliance on fatwa and argued that the difference between the teachings of MUI and Al-Qiyadah Al-Islamiyah was one of interpretation, not blasphemy. The court on appeal instead relied on the evidence given by three Islamic religious leaders that Muhammad is the final prophet, according to Al-Azhab 40 and the Hadith of Buhari, and that there are no other prophets after Muhammad, according to the Hadith of Attarmizi. The court then went through all the pillars of Islam to demonstrate how the teachings of Mushaddeq differ from the pillars according to the Qur'an and the Hadith, as set out by experts and witnesses at the trial. While the fatwa of the MUI was only mentioned by witnesses, not by the court in its decision, the evidence led by many of the experts in support of the prosecution was clearly built upon the basis established by the fatwa of the national MUI.

The court was not required to address the differences between national and local fatwas in the case of Ahmad Mushaddeq because he was prosecuted in Jakarta and neither of the regional fatwas were from Jakarta. In the next case, the Oben Sarbeni case, the court did have to deal with conflicting fatwas at the regional level.

Conflicting Fatwas: The Oben Sarbeni Case

The case of Oben Sarbeni must be situated within the history of blasphemy cases since the 1990s that originated from Tasikmalaya, a town known as a city of a thousand *pesantren* (Islamic boarding schools) in the province of West Java. In 1996, Saleh, a young Muslim student from Situbondo (East Java), was convicted for declaring that

Muhammad was not the final prophet and for promoting beliefs that "deviated" from Islam.[50] In 1997, Buki Sahidin, an Islamic religious leader, was accused of supporting a Jewish agenda because a star found on the ceiling of his mosque was similar to the Star of David, a symbol of Jewish identity. Buki had also pronounced himself the *Imam Mahdi* (Messiah) and it was suspected that he had links with an international network of Jews. He was sentenced to five years for blasphemy against Islam under article 156a of the Criminal Code.[51]

Then, in 2006, Abraham Bentar Rohadi, a convert from Islam to Christianity, was convicted for insulting Islam by the Tasikmalaya District Court.[52] Further, in 2008, the Tasikmalaya District Court convicted Ishak Suhendra, the Muslim leader of a martial arts institute (*perguruan pencak silat*), Pancadaya Tasikmalaya, for insulting Islam through the teachings in his book *The Reality of Religion*. According to the MUI, his teachings are false because, for example, he promotes what is perceived to be a wrong interpretation of the word *"basmalah"* (bismillah); he claims that all religions are true, that there are only three rather than five pillars of Islam, and he proscribes fifty *rakaat*[53] in one day, rather than the orthodox position of seventeen. The local MUI issued a fatwa against his teachings, and he was later sentenced to four years jail under article 156a of the Criminal Code.[54]

The case of Oben Sarbeni follows in the wake of this history of blasphemy prosecutions in Tasikmalaya. This case involved conflicting fatwas issued against the accused at the local level. Oben Sarbeni was a forty-two-year-old *mubalig* who was the leader of Pondok Pesantren Anwarul Huda from January 2009 to July 2010.[55] He was taken to court on charges of blaspheming against Islam for promoting teachings that were considered to be "deviant". This included instructing his students (*santri*) that his teacher, Ahmad Sulaeman, was the saviour of the Muslim community and that the students must confess that Ahmad is the Imam Mahdi. As part of this teaching he invited students to enter a special room to look at a photo of Ahmad Sulaeman and claimed that the spirit of the Prophet Muhammad had entered the physical body of Ahmad Sulaeman. He was accused of teaching that when students pray they should first address Ahmad, and then the Prophet Muhammad. Although Oben initially spoke about "Ahmad Sulaeman" in the third person, the prosecution argued that Oben later referred to himself as the saviour. He was also accused of changing the words of the creed and the *Asmaul Husna* (ninety-nine names of Allah), among other teachings that were considered to be "deviant" and insulting to Islam.

One of the key issues in the court case was the conflicting fatwas issued by two local MUI branches. In September 2009 the MUI of Garut issued a fatwa against KH. Ahmad Sulaeman, the teacher of Oben Sarbeni, although it concluded that there was not enough evidence that his teachings deviated from the teachings of Islam.[56] Less than a year later, in June 2010, the MUI of Tasikmalaya issued a fatwa against Oben Sarbeni, a former follower of KH. Ahmad Sulaeman.[57] The fatwa made three key statements. It found that the teachings developed by Oben Sarbeni were "deviant" (*dhallun*) and "deviate" (*mudhillun*) because they departed from the principles of the true teachings of Islam. It ordered and invited Oben Sarbeni and his followers to immediately return to the teachings of Islam according to the Qur'an and the Hadith. Finally, it called on the government to ban the spread of these teachings and prevent the group's activities.

In February 2011 the case was heard at first instance in the District Court of Tasikmalaya. The fatwa of the MUI of Tasikmalaya was a central piece of evidence in the case, and the head of the Fatwa Commission of the MUI of Tasikmalaya, KH. Udin Sa'dudin Bin KH. Soleh Yusuf, gave evidence as a witness on behalf of the prosecution. The prosecutor demanded the maximum sentence of five years, and the judge found Oben guilty and handed down this penalty. In March 2011 the accused took his case on appeal to the Appellate Court of Bandung. The accused based his case on a number of procedural irregularities during the trial and the failure by the prosecution to comply with the Code of Criminal Procedure. Ironically, further breaches occurred when, on 15 March 2011, the court reduced the sentence to four years, although no reason for its finding that the accused had committed blasphemy were provided in the judgment.

The accused appealed to the Supreme Court based on claims that further breaches of procedure and legal errors had occurred in the Appellate Court of Bandung. The accused's lawyers, from the Indonesian Legal Aid Institute, tore the prosecution's case apart systematically and in great detail, similar to the style of the late Yap Thiam Hien, a human rights lawyer.[58]

The lawyers for the accused set out a long list of reasons why the trial was illegal, why the evidence of many of the witnesses was inadmissible, and how the Code of Criminal Procedure had been breached in other ways. For example, the decision of the Appellate High Court of Bandung was issued in a sitting without the attendance of the public prosecutor or the defendant, who had not been informed of the hearing (contrary to art. 195 of the Code of Criminal Procedure). In addition, the parties only received the decision of the Appellate Court on 26 April 2011, more than a month after the decision was allegedly handed down. This was in breach of article 243(1) of the Code of Criminal Procedure, which requires the court to send the decision to the parties within seven days (in this case, by 24 March 2011).

The lawyers for the accused also argued that the judges had "panicked" due to pressure and threats from radical Islamic groups who wanted the accused to be convicted. The lawyers claimed that the judges had "closed his/her eyes to the legal facts" of the case.[59] They highlighted the atmosphere of "terror" and "intimidation" at the court trial, with court proceedings being interrupted by shouts from radical Islamic groups present. In this way the lawyers painted a picture of a trial conducted incompetently and lacking in independence.

A large part of the accused's case on appeal focused on the role and authority of the fatwa of the MUI. The lawyers for the prosecution highlighted the discrepancy between the fatwa issued by the Garut branch and that issued by the Tasikmalaya branch. They argued that the Tasikmalaya fatwa was used as the main basis for the prosecution to file a case against the accused. They argued that this was illegal because the fatwa was not issued in accordance with the MUI's own procedure documented in its 1997 guidelines (as explained above).[60] That is, the MUI had failed to gather information and verify the complaints against Oben.

The lawyers for the accused argued that the criminal investigation conducted by the police was also illegal because it was solely based on the fatwa of the MUI and no prior warning had been given to the accused.[61] This argument was based on their novel interpretation of the Blasphemy Law, in which they tried to argue that the Blasphemy Law required a person to be given a warning by the government first before they could be charged with the criminal offence of blasphemy. They referred to a 2007 media report of Hukumonline (the major online portal on Indonesian law) that quoted the former attorney general of Indonesia, Hendarman Supanji, who stated that article 156a of the Criminal Code can only be relied on after the Coordinating Board[62] has conducted an investigation into whether the group is "deviant" or not. Only if they decide the teachings are deviant, Supanji noted, might a person then be convicted under article 156a.

Therefore, because the accused had not been given a warning by the government, they argued that the police had no basis to conduct an investigation for blasphemy. They also argued that the fatwa of the MUI should not be used by the public prosecutor as the basis for the indictment of the accused.[63] The lawyers for the accused further argued that legal certainty would be undermined if the courts allowed the MUI to effectively coordinate prosecutions for blasphemy, which they claimed had occurred in this case.[64] This, of course, is not the interpretation that the courts have adopted in the past. If the court had adopted this interpretation, most individuals accused of blasphemy would never have been prosecuted, given that the Coordinating Board is rarely active in investigating these cases prior to the case going to court.

In addition to questioning the validity of law enforcement agencies who had based their actions and cases on the fatwa, the lawyers for the accused also questioned the authority of the local MUI branches to issue fatwas.[65] They pointed out that according to the 1997 MUI guidelines concerning fatwa mentioned above, the city or regency level branches do not have authority to issue their own fatwas without the approval of the national MUI. Given that the Tasikmalaya branch is at the city level, they therefore argued that the fatwa had not been issued according to MUI's own guidelines. They emphasized the primacy of following the procedure under the Blasphemy Law, which prioritized the role of the Coordinating Board and fails to mention the MUI. This case is interesting because it appears to be the first in which the fatwa guidelines issued by the national MUI in 1997 were used to demonstrate that a regional fatwa was invalid without the authority of the national MUI.

Criminal Justice and Deference to Religious Authority

The introduction of democracy in Indonesia displaced the former centre of power, the authoritarian state. This has allowed for sources of authority outside the state legal structure to vie for state recognition and sanction. This chapter has reflected on the development of legal pluralism in post-authoritarian Indonesia through a case study of the application and interpretation of the offence of blasphemy contained in the Criminal Code. Religious fatwas of the MUI are one manifestation of legal pluralism. Although fatwas are not "law" as recognized by the Indonesian state, fatwas are clearly given legitimacy by both religious leaders and the state. In turn, fatwas on issues such as deviancy seek state approval and reinforcement by calling on the state to ban so-called deviant groups.

The processing of criminal trials for blasphemy suggests that there is a pattern of deference shown by the public prosecutor and the courts to religious authority in the form of written fatwas. This limited form of religious deference arises from the unique position of the MUI as a state-sanctioned, quasi-government body. It is partly out of necessity, because the offence of blasphemy requires the court to decide whether a group is "deviant". A fatwa in this regard gives meaning to the application of the Blasphemy Law. The reference to a fatwa is also partly pragmatic because, by relying on a fatwa, the blame for any potential disagreement with the law or its application lies "outside" the state, and on the shoulders of religious leaders. This may be convenient for the state in an era of globalization, where it is under pressure due to its international obligations on religious freedom.

The acknowledgment of fatwas suggests that legitimacy not only resides with the state or the courts, as an institutionalized form of power, but also with religious authorities. Therefore, it is only if we consider fatwas as a source of law in Indonesia that we can go deeper in our understanding of the dynamics of state responses to deviancy and judicial interpretations of the offence of blasphemy. In considering how the state relates to fatwas, I have argued that there is an attitude of religious deference between religious authorities and state officials such as public prosecutors and the judiciary. The district courts legitimate and justify decisions in cases of blasphemy by either silence in the face of fatwas produced as evidence and therefore implicit acceptance, or by explicit mention in the reasons for their decisions. In Indonesia the fatwas of the MUI in practice operate as one of a number of legal orders that have influence over, and are shaped by, state law. This process of integrating fatwas into the interpretation of state criminal law is crucial to understand the reasoning of the courts in convictions for blasphemy. The attitude of religious deference between the courts and religious authorities is illustrative of the dynamics of legal pluralism, which forces us to look beyond state law in order to understand criminal trials in contemporary Indonesia.

Notes

1. M.B. Hooker, *Legal Pluralism: An Introduction to Colonial and Neo-colonial Laws* (Oxford: Clarendon Press, 1975).
2. M.B. Hooker, *Indonesian Islam: Social Change through Contemporary Fatwa* (Hawaii: University of Hawai'i Press, 2003).
3. This provision was inserted by Presidential Instruction No 1/PNPS/1965 on the Prevention of Mistreatment of Religion and/or Blasphemy, which was upgraded to the status of a law in 1969. It is commonly referred to as the Blasphemy Law, and that is how I will refer to it in this chapter.
4. I use the term "religious deference" in a different though perhaps analogous way to the concept of "judicial deference", which is a term used to explain the approach taken by courts in the United States in cases for review of administrative action. According to the principle of judicial deference, the courts acknowledge that they do not have the expertise to decide such a matter but rather defer to the technical knowledge of the administrative body. This approach, however, limits the scope of matters of fact that can be reviewed by the courts. Further, according to the Chevron doctrine, the courts defer to the opinion of administrative agencies if the interpretation of statutes is unclear, which has severely limited the scope of judicial review. In this chapter I use the term "religious deference" to refer to the attitude and approach of both law enforcement agencies and the courts to the fatwas of religious leaders on matters of religious sensitivity.
5. F. von Benda-Beckmann, "Who's Afraid of Legal Pluralism?", *Journal of Legal Pluralism and Unofficial Law* 47 (2002): 37–82.

6. J. Griffiths, "What is Legal Pluralism?", *Journal of Legal Pluralism and Unofficial Law* 24 (1986): 1.

7. S.F. Moore, "Certainties Undone: Fifty Turbulent Years of Legal Anthropology 1949–1999", *Journal of the Royal Anthropological Institute* 7, no. 1 (March 2001): 106.

8. Hooker, *Legal Pluralism*, p. 4.

9. Ibid.

10. Moore, "Certainties Undone", p. 107.

11. F. von Benda-Beckmann, K. von Benda-Beckmann and A Griffiths, *The Power of Law in a Transnational World: Anthropological Enquiries* (Oxford: Berghahn Books, 2009), p. 1.

12. Ibid., p. 5.

13. Ibid., p. 4.

14. Ibid., p. 17.

15. The jurisdiction of the Religious Courts is restricted to matters of marriage and divorce, wills, inheritance, *wakaf* (charitable trusts) and, more recently, sharia economics. Law 3/2006 amending Law 7/1989 on the Religious Judiciary, art. 49. "*Syariah* economics" is defined in the Elucidation to include sharia banking, insurance, obligations, security, costs, institutional pension funds, business, Islamic pawning and micro-finance institutions (art. 49). This has been further explained in the Compilation of Laws on Syariah Economics, available at the website for the Directorate General of the Religious Courts <www.badilag.net>.

16. Hooker, *Indonesian Islam*.

17. M.B. Hooker, *Indonesian Syariah: Defining a National School of Islamic Law* (Singapore: Institute of Southeast Asian Studies, 2008), p. 26.

18. H. Federspiel, *A Dictionary of Indonesian Islam* (Centre for International Studies, Ohio University, 1995), p. 59.

19. Hooker, *Indonesian Syariah*, p. 26.

20. Fatwa of the Indonesian Ulama Council of the Regency of Garut No. 111/MUI-GRt/ IX/1430-2009 dated 12 September 2009.

21. Hooker, *Legal Pluralism*, p. 60.

22. There is also a national council for Protestants, Catholics, Hindus, Buddhists and Confucians.

23. Mohamad Atho Mudzhar, "The Council of Indonesian Ulama on Muslims' Attendance at Christmas Celebrations", in *Islamic Legal Interpretations: Mufti's and their Fatwa*, edited by Muhammad Khalid Masud, Brinkley Messick, and David S. Powers (Cambridge: Harvard University Press, 1996), p. 236.

24. Mohamad Atho Mudzhar, "The Ulama, the Government and Society in Modern Indonesia: The Indonesian Council of Ulama Revisited", in *Islam*

in an Era of Globalisation: Muslim Attitudes towards Modernity and Identity, edited by Johan Meulemman (New York: RoutledgeCurzon, 2002), p. 317.

25. Mudzhar, "The Council of Indonesian Ulama on Muslims' Attendance at Christmas Celebrations", p. 236.

26. Tarmizi Taher, *Aspiring for the Middle Path: Religious Harmony in Indonesia* (Jakarta: PPIM/Censis, 1997), pp. 27–28, 57.

27. For an analysis of the fatwa, see Hooker, *Indonesian Islam*, pp. 166–75. For a copy of the fatwa, see Ministry of Religion, *Himpunan Fatwa Majelis Ulama Indonesia* (Jakarta, 2003) pp. 188–94.

28. H.W. Adams, *Pola Penyerapan Fatwa Majelis Ulama Indonesia Dalam Peraturan Perundang-undangan 1975–1997* (Jakarta: Ministry of Religion, 2004) pp. 1–2.

29. MUI was involved in the drafting of Law 1/1974 on Marriage; the Education Law; Law 7/1989 on the Religious Courts; Law 7/1992 on Shariah Banking (revised by Law 9/1998); Law 7/1996 on Halal Labelling and Handling; Law 17/1999 on the Organisation of the Hajj; Law 38/1999 on Zakat Administration; Regulation of the Minister of Religion 4/1968 on the Creation of Badan Amil Zakat; Government Regulation 28/1977 on Property as a Charitable Trust (*wakaf*); Presidential Instruction 1/1992 on the Compilation of Islamic Laws; Law 44/1999 on the Special Province of Aceh; Law 9/1976 on Narcotics; Law 4/1979 on Child Safety; and Law 23/1990 on Health. See generally Adams, *Pola Penyerapan Fatwa Majelis Ulama Indonesia*.

30. Decision of the Director General of Primary and Secondary Education No. 052/C/Kep/D.82 dated 17 March 1982 on School Uniforms. Adams, *Pola Penyerapan Fatwa Majelis Ulama Indonesia*, pp. 162–66.

31. T. Lindsey, "Monopolising Islam? The Indonesian Ulama Council and State Regulation of the Islamic Economy", *Bulletin of Indonesian Economic Studies* 48, no. 2 (2012): 253, 272.

32. Decision of the MUI Leadership Council No. U-596/MUI/X/1997 on Guidance on Determining MUI Fatwa, dated 2 October 1997.

33. Hooker, *Indonesian Islam*, p. 230.

34. A list of these cases is on file with the author. These cases are discussed further in M. Crouch, *Law and Religion in Indonesia: Conflict and the Courts in West Java* (Routledge, 2013).

35. Ministry of Religion, *Himpunan Fatwa Majelis Ulama Indonesia*, pp. 114–27.

36. Other examples include a fatwa against the following groups: Ahmadiyah (1980), Shiites (1984), Darul Arqam (1994), and a general fatwa against groups that believe in a prophet after the Prophet Muhammad (1983). See Ministry of Religion, *Himpunan Fatwa Majelis Ulama Indonesia*, pp. 95–109.

37. See Qur'an 2:177; 4:136; 72:26-27; and 21:20; 16:50; 21:26-28, respectively.

38. Q 33:40; 5:3.

39. District Court Central Jakarta, Decision No. 677/PID.b2006/PN.JKT.PST concerning the accused Lia Eden, dated 29 June 2006.

40. Ibid., p. 43.

41. Ibid., p. 64.

42. District Court Central Jakarta, Decision No. 1110/PID.B/2006/PN.JKT.PST concerning the accused Muhammad Abdul Rachman, dated 6 December 2006.

43. District Court Central Jakarta, Decision No. PDM-577/JKT.PST/03/2009 concerning the accused Lia Eden and Wahyu Andito Putrowibison, dated 30 March 2009.

44. Ibid.

45. Fatwa of the MUI of Yogayakarta No. B-149/MUI-DIY/FATWA/IX/2007 on Al Qiyadah Al Islamiyah, dated 28 September 2007; Fatwa of the MUI of West Sumatra No. 1/Kpt.F/MUI/SB/IX/2007 on Al Qiyadah Al Islamiyah dated 24 September 2007.

46. Fatwa of the National Indonesian Ulama Council No. 4/2007 on Al Qiyadah Al Islamiyah, dated 3 October 2007.

47. This included Qur'an 33:40; 6:153; 2:217; 2:115; 3:32.

48. District Court South Jakarta, Decision No. 227/Pid/B/2008/PN.JKT.SEL concerning the accused Ahmad Musaddeq, dated 23 April 2008; High District Court Central Jakarta, Decision No. 135/PiD/2008/PT.DKT concerning the case of Ahmad Musaddeq, dated 29 May 2008.

49. Ibid.

50. Rumadi, *Delik Penodaan Agama Dan Kehidupan Beragama Dalam RUU KUHP*, (Jakarta: Wahid Institute, 2007), pp. 25–37.

51. James T. Siegel, "Kiblat and the Mediatic Jew", *Indonesia* 69 (April 2000): 37–38.

52. District Court Tasikmalaya, Decision No. 117/PID.B/2006/PN.TSM concerning the accused Abraham Bentar (Tasikmalaya Apostasy Case), dated 17 May 2006.

53. *Rakaat* refers to the movements and words followed by Muslims in performing their daily prayers.

54. Tasikmalaya District Court, Decision No. 281/Pid.B/2008/PN.TSM concerning the accused H. Ishak Suhendra, dated 28 October 2008.

55. Supreme Court, Decision No. 1151 K/Pid/2011 in the case of Oben Sarbeni Bin H. Hodin, dated 7 September 2011.

56. Fatwa of the Indonesian Ulama Council of the Regency of Garut No. 111/MUI-GRt/ IX/1430-2009, dated 12 September 2009.

57. Decision of the MUI Fatwa Commission of the City of Tasikmalaya No. 181/A.01/MUI-Kota Tsm/VII/2010 concerning the teachings developed by Oben Sarbeni, dated 25 June 2010.
58. See, generally, Dan S. Lev, *No Concessions: The Life of Yap Thiam Hien, Indonesian Human Rights Lawyer* (Seattle: University of Washington Press, 2000).
59. Supreme Court, Decision No. 1151 K/Pid/2011 in the case of Oben Sarbeni Bin H. Hodin, dated 7 September 2011.
60. Ibid., p. 10.
61. Ibid., p. 24.
62. The Coordinating Board was a body established by law in 1984 that was given wide powers to investigate religions or beliefs that were considered to be "deviant". Its members consist of representatives from several government offices, chaired by a representative of the Attorney General's office.
63. Supreme Court Decision 2011, p. 10.
64. Ibid., p. 29.
65. Ibid., p. 30.

References

Books

Adams, H.W. *Pola Penyerapan Fatwa Majelis Ulama Indonesia Dalam Peraturan Perundang-undangan 1975–1997*. Jakarta: Ministry of Religion. 2004.

Benda-Beckmann, F. von, K. von Benda-Beckmann, and A Griffiths. *The Power of Law in a Transnational World: Anthropological Enquiries*. Oxford: Berghahn Books, 2009.

Feener, M. *Muslim Legal Thought in Modern Indonesia*. Cambridge: Cambridge University Press, 2007.

Hooker, M.B. *Legal Pluralism: An Introduction to Colonial and Neo-colonial Laws*. Oxford: Clarendon Press, 1975.

———. *Islamic Law in Southeast Asia*. Oxford: Oxford University Press, 1984.

———. *Indonesian Islam: Social Change through Contemporary Fatwa*. Honolulu: University of Hawai'i Press, 2003.

———. *Indonesian Syariah: Defining a National School of Islamic Law*. Singapore: Institute of Southeast Asian Studies, 2008.

Lev, Dan S. *No Concessions: The Life of Yap Thiam Hien, Indonesian Human Rights Lawyer*. Seattle: University of Washington Press, 2011.

Ministry of Religion. *Himpunan Fatwa Majelis Ulama Indonesia*. Jakarta, 2003.

Rumadi. *Delik Penodaan Agama Dan Kehidupan Beragama Dalam RUU KUHP.* Jakarta: Wahid Institute, 2007.

Periodicals and Working Papers

Benda-Beckmann, F von. "Who's Afraid of Legal Pluralism?" *Journal of Legal Pluralism and Unofficial Law* 47 (2002): 37–82.

Crouch, M. "Judicial Review and Religious Freedom: The Case of Indonesian Ahmadis". *Sydney Law Review* 34, no. 3 (2012): 545–72.

———. "Law and Religion in Indonesia: The Constitutional Court and the Blasphemy Law". *Asian Journal of Comparative Law* 7, no. 1 (2012): 1–46.

Griffiths, J. "What is Legal Pluralism?" *Journal of Legal Pluralism and Unofficial Law* 24 (1986): 1.

Hasyim, S. "The Council of Indonesian Ulama (Majelis Ulama Indonesia, MUI) and Religious Freedom". Discussion Paper 12, Institut de Recherche sur l'Asie du Sud-Est Contemporaine (Research Institute on Contemporary Southeast Asia, Irasec), 2011 <http://www.irasec.com>.

Hosen, N. "Behind the Scenes: Fatwas of Majelis Ulama Indonesia (1975–1998)". *Journal of Islamic Studies* 15, no. 2 (2004): 147–79.

Lindsey, T. "Monopolising Islam? The Indonesian Ulama Council and State Regulation of the Islamic Economy". *Bulletin of Indonesian Economic Studies* 48, no. 2 (2012): 253.

Merry, S.E. "Legal Pluralism". *Law and Society Review* 22 (1988): 869.

Moore, S.F. "Certainties Undone: Fifty Turbulent Years of Legal Anthropology 1949–1999". *Journal of the Royal Anthropological Institute* 7, no. 1 (March 2001): 95–116.

Siegel, James T. "Kiblat and the Mediatic Jew". *Indonesia* 69 (2000): 9–40.

Tamanaha, Brian. "Understanding Legal Pluralism: Past to Present, Local to Global". *Sydney Law Review* 30 (2008): 375–411.

Fatwas

Decision of MUI Fatwa Commission No Kep-768/MUI/XII/1997 on the Angel Gabriel (Lia Eden), dated 22 December 1997.

Decision of the MUI Fatwa Commission of the City of Tasikmalaya No 181/A.01/MUI-Kota Tsm/VII/2010 concerning the teachings developed by Oben Sarbeni, dated 25 June 2010.

Decision of the MUI Leadership Council No. U-596/MUI/X/1997 on Guidance on Determining MUI Fatwa, dated 2 October 1997.

Fatwa of the Indonesian Ulama Council No 4/2007 on Al Qiyadah Al Islamiyah, dated 3 October 2007.

Fatwa of the Indonesian Ulama Council of the Regency of Garut No 111/
MUI-GRt/ IX/1430-2009, dated 12 September 2009.

Fatwa of the MUI of West Sumatra No 1/Kpt.F/MUI/SB/IX/2007 on Al
Qiyadah Al Islamiyah, dated 24 September 2007.

Fatwa of the MUI of Yogayakarta No B-149/MUI-DIY/FATWA/IX/2007 on Al
Qiyadah Al Islamiyah, dated 28 September 2007.

Court Decisions

Constitutional Court, Decision No 140/PUU-VII/2009 concerning the Request
for Judicial Review of the Blasphemy Law, dated 19 April 2010.

Defence in Criminal Case No 64/Pid/B/2008/PN.PDG of Dedi Priadi and
Gerry Lutfhy Yudistira, dated 29 April 2008.

District Court, Central Jakarta, Decision No 1110/PID.B/2006/PN.JKT.PST
concerning the accused Muhammad Abdul Rachman, dated 6 December 2006.

District Court, Central Jakarta, Decision No 677/PID.b2006/PN.JKT.PST concerning
the accused Lia Eden, dated 29 June 2006.

District Court, Central Jakarta, Decision No PDM-577/JKT.PST.03/2009 in the
accused Lia Eden and Wahyu Andito Putrowibison, dated 1 June 2009.

District Court, South Jakarta, Decision No 227/Pid/B/2008/PN.JKT.SEL
concerning the accused Ahmad Musaddeq, dated 23 April 2008.

District Court, Tasikmalaya (West Java), Decision No 281/Pid.B/2008/PN.TSM
concerning the accused H Ishak Suhendra, 28 October 2008

High District Court, Central Jakarta, Decision No 135/PiD/2008/PT.DKT
concerning the case of Ahmad Musaddeq, dated 29 May 2008.

Indictment, Central Jakarta District Court Case No PDM-577/JKT.PST/03/2009
concerning the accused Lia Eden and Wahyu Andito Putrowibison, dated
30 March 2009.

Supreme Court, Decision No 1151 K/Pid/2011 in the case of Oben Sarbeni Bin
H. Hodin, dated 7 September 2011.

11

Islamic Law in Israel: A Case Study in Legal Pluralism

Aharon Layish

In his article "Legal Pluralism and the Study of *Sharī'a* Courts", Ido Shahar presents several historical instances of legal pluralism and concludes by saying that "the time has come for a systematic assessment of the relevancy of a legal pluralistic perspective for the study of the *sharī'a* courts". He, moreover, comes forward with specific suggestions for future research.[1] Shahar is concerned with legal pluralism as a theme in the sociology and anthropology of law in addition to considering it as an issue for legal theory.[2] The purpose of the present study is to provide the reader with a general outline of the status of the *sharī'a* within the Israeli legal system and its application in *shar'ī*, civil and tribal judiciaries. Some of the issues discussed here have already been dealt with within the context of legal history. In what follows, an attempt is made to present them in the context of legal pluralism.[3]

Israel is a unique case of legal pluralism due to its unique legal history. With the collapse of the Ottoman Empire at the end of World War I and the occupation of Palestine by Britain, the country ceased to be part of a Muslim state, with all the legal consequences that involved, though the *millet* system as part of the Ottoman Muslim legal heritage — consisting of communal organization and autonomous religious courts — has survived, while adapting itself to the new political circumstances.[4] With the emergence of the State of Israel, the Muslim community became a religious minority in a Jewish democratic state. The Muslim Supreme Council, established by the British Mandate in 1921 with a view to compensating the Muslim community for the lack of Islamic sovereignty, ceased to exist, and with it collapsed the entire Muslim establishment, including *sharī'a* courts and the *waqf* administration. The religious elite left the country during the events that preceded the emergence of the state.

The new *shar'ī* judiciary in Israel has been integrated into the general judicial system. In 2002 it was subordinated to the Ministry of Justice instead of the Ministry for Religious Affairs. The law applicable in the *sharī'a* courts is an integral part of the Israeli legal system. The *sharī'a* courts, like all other religious courts, are subject to judicial review by the High Court of Justice (HCJ);[5] the *qāḍīs*, who are nominated by the president of the state, deliver an oath of allegiance to the state and broadly speaking are bound by its laws.[6] From an Islamic dogmatic-legalistic standpoint, this is apparently a problematic situation: under *sharī'a* a non-Muslim cannot testify against a Muslim,[7] and prevalent *shar'ī* opinion is that a non-Muslim cannot appoint a Muslim *qāḍī*.[8]

Until recently the Ottoman *millet* system in domains pertaining to communal organization and the judiciary remained almost intact. The heritage of this system is the main key to understanding the substance of the legal pluralism in Israel.[9] Thus the Muslims, unlike the Jews and the Christians, were not recognized in the Palestine Order-in-Council as a "religious community". The *sharī'a* courts were left with exclusive jurisdiction in virtually all matters of personal status and *waqf*, while the rabbinical and Christian courts enjoyed exclusive jurisdiction only in matters of marriage and divorce. In 1951 the exclusive jurisdiction of the *sharī'a* courts in matters of succession was replaced with concurrent jurisdiction — that is, with the consent of all the legal heirs. In 2001 the jurisdiction of the civil Family Courts was equalized with that of the *sharī'a* courts except for marriage and divorce, which were left within the latter's exclusive jurisdiction.[10]

Characteristic in the context of legal pluralism is a dispute between different religious courts over jurisdiction in a matter of custody. The *sharī'a* court ruled that the children of a mixed marriage be transferred to the custody (*ḥaḍāna*) of the Muslim father. The Christian mother resorted to a civil Family Court, which ruled that the mother was entitled to the custody of the children and to their maintenance from the father. The Sharī'a Court of Appeal ruled that the issue of jurisdiction should be decided in accordance with the minor's religion, which follows that of the minor's father (his mother's religion being irrelevant). The Supreme Court overruled the Sharī'a Court of Appeal's decision and decided that under section 55 of the Palestine Order-in-Council 1922, it was up to the president of the Supreme Court to decide the identity of the court before which the case should be brought.[11]

The Eclectic Expedient within the *Shar'ī* Legal System

The four Sunni schools of Islamic law share, with differences of emphasis, the same legal methodology (*uṣūl al-fiqh*) — the textual sources of the Qur'an and the Sunna, the systematic analogy (*qiyās*) from the textual sources and the consensus (*ijmā'*) of the *fuqahā'*, specialists of *fiqh* (Islamic jurisprudence).[12] However, as far as the positive law (*furū'*) is concerned, it may rightly be argued that in some specific subjects they represent distinctive legal systems.[13] Juristic disagreements (*ikhtalāf*) — or, to express this positively, a multiplicity of opinions within each of the schools and among the schools — is perhaps the most salient feature of legal pluralism in the Islamic legal system. In modern times this multiplicity has been — and is being — used on an enormous scale within the framework of legislation to adapt various domains of Islamic law to the conditions of a modern state. The legal term for this eclectic expedient is *takhayyur* (lit. selection), which means combining different legal doctrines from the dominant school or other schools, or from early independent jurists, in an attempt to support reformist norms that have been predetermined.[14]

This expedient originated already in the Ottoman trend of codifying sections of the *sharī'a* in the nineteenth century. Thus the Mejelle, the

Civil Code of 1876, is based on a selection of doctrines culled from the Ḥanafī school. The Mejelle was designed for the civil (*niẓāmī*) courts established alongside the *sharīʿa* courts; certain sections thereof were applied also in the *sharīʿa* courts. In 1984 the Mejelle was abolished in Israel, with the proviso that its validity remain intact in the *sharīʿa* courts.[15]

The Ottoman Family Rights Law of 1917 was the first official codification of matters of personal status introduced in an attempt to improve the status of women. The eclectic expedient was the main method for introducing the reforms.[16] Thus the Ḥanbalī doctrine, which admits the insertion into the marriage contract of conditions curtailing the spouse's matrimonial rights, has been adopted in order to enable the wife to stipulate that her husband is prohibited from marrying another wife, and that if he violates the condition, either she or her co-wife will be divorced. Under the Ḥanafī school, which was the dominant school in the Ottoman Empire, conditions in the marriage contract are allowed only to the extent that they do not infringe upon the spouses' matrimonial rights. Similarly, the Mālikī doctrine admitting judicial dissolution on the wife's initiative was adopted, thereby enabling the wife to obtain a divorce on the basis of such legal grounds as the husband's absence (art. 126) or disputes between the spouses (art. 130).

Already in the early years of the State of Israel, *qāḍī*s, in the absence of *muftī*s, used their legal authority, beyond their judicial role, in an attempt to adjust the law of personal status to changes in the family structure and in the status of women. In conferences convened in 1963, 1966 and 1974, the *qāḍī*s resorted to the pragmatic eclectic method in order to support liberal reforms inspired by reforms promulgated in Arab countries. These pertain to such matters as the insertion of stipulations in the marriage contract, the prohibition of conditional divorce (which is permitted under Ḥanafī law), family arbitration as a mechanism to transform unilateral divorce into judicial dissolution, and provision of alimony to divorced women beyond the waiting period (*ʿiddat al-ṭalāq*).

Qāḍī Aḥmad Nāṭūr, while acting as president of the Sharʿīa Court of Appeal, strove consciously to apply the eclectic method in the judicial practice of the Sharīʿa Court of Appeal. He views the legal literature of the schools as one large reservoir out of which it is possible to derive doctrines compatible with the requirements of modern times. The multiplicity of the schools and the differences of opinion among the *fuqahā'* can provide appropriate remedies for legal problems under any circumstances. The "*'ulamā'*'s *ijtihādāt*" (to use Nātūr's phrase) seems to refer to the process of selecting doctrines out of the reservoir of *fiqh* literature.[17] Phrased another way, the *fiqh* as a whole is the basic norm for moulding the legal norm or judicial practice (*qā'ida li'l-ḥukm*).[18] The *fiqh* rules of personal status are so abundant that there is no need to seek remedies from other sources — by implication, the Knesset's (Israeli parliament) legislation and the case law of the Supreme Court. Until the early 1970s the eclectic expedient was rejected by some *qāḍīs*, graduates of al-Azhar who strictly adhered to the Ḥanafī school — to the point that they were not ready to apply provisions in the Ottoman Family Rights Law based on the Mālikī school, such as article 130 (family arbitration).[19]

The judicial decree (*marsūm qaḍā'ī*) is thus an important mechanism for introducing reforms in matters of personal status, in the spirit of the reforms introduced in Arab countries, and outside the framework of the Knesset's legislation. In the mid-1990s, Aḥmad al-Nātūr initiated this mechanism, based on inspiration drawn from the Sudanese legal circular (*manshūr qaḍā'ī*). Britain introduced the legal circular in Sudan as an instrument for adapting the *sharī'a* to the changing conditions of the time, under the control of a British "legal officer". The Grand Qāḍī (*qāḍī al-quḍāt*) from time to time issued legal circulars that dealt with a variety of subjects by means of the eclectic expedient, deviating occasionally from the authoritative view of the Ḥanafī school. Until the country attained its independence in 1956, many of the grand *qāḍīs* in Sudan were recruited from among senior *ulamā* in Egypt, graduates of al-Azhar, with a reformist orientation. The legal circular fulfilled a vital role also in reinstating the *sharī'a* in Sudan under Numayrī.[20]

However, unlike the Sudanese legal circular, the Israeli *marsūm* is not anchored in law. Actually, the members of the Sharī'a Court of Appeal, as well as the *qāḍīs* of the regional *sharī'a* courts of first instance, voluntarily commit themselves to apply the decree in their decisions. It is argued that the *marsūm* is based on the doctrine of *siyāsa shar'iyya*, "governance in accordance with the *sharī'a*" — that is, a ruler's regulation that takes into account practical considerations of the government and the public interest.[21] It is further argued that in the absence of a Muslim sovereign in Israel, the *qāḍī*s are in charge of dispensing justice (*ʿadl*).[22] Alternatively, it is argued that in the absence of a statutory basis, the marsūm should be perceived as an interpretation of the *sharīʿa*, something that is within the legitimate authority of the *qāḍī*s. It is interesting to note in this connection that there is a growing tendency among the *qāḍī*s to replace the traditional personal *ijtihād* with a collective *ijtihād*.[23] In any case, the validity of the decrees has not so far been contested in the HCJ on the ground of excess of jurisdiction.

Some of the *marsūm*s make extensive use of the eclectic expedient within the schools of law and reformist legislation of some Arab countries. The second *marsūm*[24] transferred the function of fixing the rate of the wife's maintenance (*nafaqa*) from the *mukhbirūn*, local informants, to the *qāḍī*s, in an attempt to facilitate the adaptation of the standard of maintenance to the wife's real needs in a modern society. This reform is allegedly based on the doctrine of *maṣlaḥa* (public interest), creative interpretation of the legal literature and the eclectic expedient. For the purpose of fixing criteria for the rates of maintenance, President Nāṭūr distinguished between two fundamental approaches in the *fiqh* of the schools. According to the first approach, the rate should be fixed in accordance with the economic situation of the two spouses; according to the second approach, the husband's economic situation. The Egyptian Law No. 25 of 1929 adopted the second approach (art. 16), and it seems that this approach was also adopted by the *marsūm*.

The *marsūm* likewise introduced an important innovation in the domain of evidential rules in the wake of modern legislation in Arab countries. A *qāḍī* may fix maintenance on the basis of written evidence — that is, official written documents (*wathāʾiq*) — in cases where no witnesses are available to prove the husband's wealth. Broadly speaking, written documents are not acknowledged as evidence in Islamic law. In order to acknowledge as legal evidence such official documents as those relating to salary payments, income tax, national insurance and employment service, President Nāṭūr prefered enlisting an irregular (*shādhdh*) opinion in the *fiqh* literature rather than acknowledging hearsay evidence (*shahāda samāʿiyya*).[25]

Another *marsūm* adopts the device of "compulsory bequest", within the limits of one-third of the estate, in favour of an orphaned grandchild.[26] This is a far-reaching, substantive reform. The orphaned grandchild, that is, one whose father predeceased his grandfather, is totally deprived of the estate by his uncles, the grandfather's sons, by virtue of the rule of degree: among relatives of the same class (*parentela*),[27] the nearer in degree to the *praepositus* excludes from the estate the more remote. *Sharī'a* does not recognize the doctrine of representation (*tanzīl, tamthīl, niyāba*) in succession: the orphaned grandchild does not take the portion his father would have taken had he died *after* the *praepositus*; neither does *sharī'a* recognize absolute freedom of testamentary disposition. The division of the estate in accordance with the *shar'ī* inheritance and testamentary rules were settled once and for all in the textual sources of the Qur'an and the Sunna, and the individual has almost no control over his estate after his death. By virtue of *ultra vires* rules in the Sunni law, in the absence of the heirs' consent, a will in excess of one-third of the estate or in favour of a legal heir is not valid. The Shī'ī law admits a bequest in favour of a legal heir.[28]

This *marsūm* was inspired by the Egyptian Law of Testamentary Disposition of 1946, and the Jordanian and Syrian Laws of Personal Status of 1976 and 1953, respectively. The *marsūm* deviates from the Jordanian and Syrian laws in that cognate grandchildren too, though only within the first degree with regard to the testator (i.e., excluding great-grandchildren and their issue), benefit from the "compulsory bequest".[29] The concept of compulsory bequest is a distinctly unsophisticated device. Since the orphaned grandchild is not a legal heir, there is no *shar'ī* prohibition on making a will in his favour within the aforementioned limitations. The main *shar'ī* justification for the compulsory bequest is "public interest" (*maṣlaḥa*). There is, however, an attempt to derive support from the Mālikī jurist Ibn Rushd (d. 595/1198), who defines a will in terms of a gift (*hiba*) that becomes effective only after the testator's death, regardless of whether he used an explicit expression (*lafẓ*) indicating the gift. The Explanatory Note to the Syrian Law of 1953 claims that the "compulsory bequest" is based on Ibn Ḥazm (d. 456/1065), who commends making a testamentary disposition in favour of relatives other than legal heirs; this seems to refer to Q. 2:180, which ordains making a will in favour of parents and close relatives, something conceived of as an obligation upon the pious. The reference is to *ẓāhirī* (i.e., literal) interpretation of the aforementioned verse. All schools agree that this verse was later abrogated by the Qur'anic rules of inheritance.[30]

Statutory Legislation, Islamic Law and *Qaḍī*s

In what follows I attempt to assess the tolerance of the state legislature towards *shar'ī* legal norms and principles, on the one hand, and the willingness of the *shar'ī* judiciary to absorb secular statutes in its decisions, on the other.

The British Mandate in Palestine preserved the Ottoman heritage of legal pluralism in terms of communal organization and autonomous religious courts,[31] gave effect to the recent Ottoman reforms and scrupulously maintained the status quo in the legal system subject to indispensable changes arising from the new political situation.[32] A case in point is the Ottoman Family Rights Law of 1917 — a statute based materially on *sharī'a* — that originally was intended to be applicable as a unified family law for all the Ottoman subjects, Muslims, Christians and Jews. In 1919 the British rule adopted this family law but restricted its applicability to Muslims alone. Similarly, when introducing reforms in matters of marriage and divorce under the inspiration of Western norms, the British legislator did this by means of penal legislation that does not abrogate the validity of the religious law. Thus "customary marriage" (*'aqd 'urfī*), i.e., marriage without registration, entails a criminal sanction but the *shar'ī* marriage contract remains intact. This applies also to the ban on the marriage of minor girls and on polygamy; moreover, the legislator even provided a "good defence" against a charge of violating the ban on polygamy to Muslims qua Muslims and exempted them from the criminal sanction.[33]

The Knesset aims to replace both the Ottoman-Muslim and the English legal heritage with genuine Israeli law, which derives its inspiration from universal, liberal, humanistic and democratic values and Jewish law.[34] Thus, section 1 of the Foundations of Law Act of 1980 provides that in the event of a lacuna in a statute, case law or where reasoning from analogy of a similar rule fails, the normative lacuna is to be filled "in the light of the principles of freedom, justice, rectitude and conciliation found in Jewish tradition".[35] The Knesset introduced many reforms in the domains of family law, inheritance and *waqf*, some of which are quite daring. The keynote of these reforms is section 1 of the Women's Equal Rights Law 1951, which provides: "A man and a woman shall have equal status with regard to any legal act; any provision of law which discriminates, with regard to any legal act, against women as women, shall be of no effect." The Knesset recognized the mother as the natural guardian of her children along with their father (*sharī'a* recognizes only the father as the natural guardian, and after him the minor's male agnates in a specified order), introduced equality with respect to inheritance between the sexes and between agnates and cognates (according to the *shar'ī* rules of inheritance, males and the agnates, respectively, have priority), and equalized the resources between the spouses (*sharī'a* recognizes complete separation between the spouses' properties). Out of regard for the legal systems of the various religious communities, the Knesset subjected its legislation in matters pertaining to personal status to three restrictions:

(i)   Abstention from interfering with any religious prohibition or permission to marriage or divorce, while adopting instead procedural provisions and penal sanctions as deterrents in preference to substantive provisions which would have invalidated the relevant religious law;

(ii) In matters for which provisions superseding religious law were enacted, the parties were in some cases given an option to litigate in accordance with religious law. Thus in matters pertaining to inheritance, the realization of this option is contingent on the consent of all legal heirs to the jurisdiction of the *sharī'a* court;

(iii) The *sharī'a* courts must apply the Knesset statutes only if the latter are *explicitly* addressed to religious courts.[36]

In 1950, in the wake of the circumstances preceding the emergence of the State of Israel, most of the Muslim *waqf* was declared absentees' property. In 1965, far-reaching reforms were introduced in this institution: the full ownership of the *waqf* property, which according to the dominant view in the Ḥanafī school belongs to God, was vested, retroactively from 1950, in the Custodian on Absentees' Property. This implies that Muslim-endowed property, to the extent that it is within the category of absentees' property, ceased legally to be *waqf*. The 1965 law instructs the custodian to release the full ownership of family (*dhurrī, ahlī*) *waqf* to the beneficiaries in accordance with their shares in the entitlement (*istiḥqāq*) to the proceeds of the *waqf*, and the full ownership of *waqf khayrī* (for public welfare) to the boards of trustees established in several towns. The boards may use the proceeds from the property and the consideration received for property sold to educational, social welfare, health, religious worship and like purposes for the benefit of the Muslim community without being bound by the *shar'ī* rules pertaining to *waqf* (the boards, however, may not sell mosques).[37]

Broadly speaking, until the early 1970s the Israeli *qāḍīs* were not concerned about the legitimacy of their subordination to the Knesset's legislation. Though some of the *qāḍīs* were not fully aware of the reforms intended to improve the status of women or to use to this end the wide discretion granted them by the Knesset, others had no inhibitions in applying the Knesset's legislation; they would rely on it explicitly in their decisions, adopting its legal norms even when these could not be reconciled with *shar'ī* norms.[38] Occasionally, the Sharī'a Court of Appeal would urge the regional *qāḍī* to adhere to the Women's Equal Rights Law 1951, or to the Capacity and Guardianship Law 1962. In one case, the Sharī'a Court of Appeal ruled:

> We cannot ignore the statutory laws (*lā yumkinunā ihmāl al-qawānīn al-waḍ'iyya*), which view any person below 18 as a minor and equalize between the two parents for the matter of guardianship of minors in accordance with Articles 3 and 14 of the Capacity and Guardianship Law 1962, respectively.[39]

Some of the *qāḍīs* would display a keen awareness of the ban on divorce against the wife's will or the ban on polygamy and would warn the husband against committing a criminal offense or, when committed, would call the wife's attention to her right to bring a criminal charge against her husband. Some would welcome the Knesset's legislation of a penal nature in matters of marriage and divorce, believing the penal sanctions to reinforce *shar'ī* norms anchored in ethical sanctions. Moreover, some *qāḍīs* would not shrink from calling for secular legislation of a substantial nature to ensure the subsistence of a divorced woman, on the basis of the doctrine of *siyāsa shar ʿiyya*.[40] This approach is in line with the so-called "jurisprudence of minorities" (*fiqh al-aqalliyyāt*), an ideology intended to facilitate integration of Muslims in non-Muslim states, which may find support in the Qur'an and the Hadith, and in such legal doctrines as *maṣlaḥa*, *darūra* (necessity), *siyāsa shar ʿiyya*, *maqāṣid al-sharī ʿa* (the goals of Islamic law[41]) and *taysīr al-fiqh* (facilitation of fiqh doctrines).[42]

The *qāḍīs* also assisted in bringing to trial violators of criminal legislation pertaining to marriage and divorce in such cases as divorcing one's wife against her will while approving the *shar ʿī* validity of the divorce.[43] Moreover, the *qāḍīs* did not hesitate to invite the Knesset's intervention in issues where it was impossible to apply the *sharī ʿa* without committing a criminal offense. Thus, for instance, since the wife's barrenness is not a ground for legal dissolution of the marriage under the Ottoman Family Rights Law, they implicitly requested that the Knesset promulgate that barrenness should be deemed a "good defence" against a charge of divorcing one's wife against her will, or a ground for taking a co-wife with the *sharī ʿa* court's permission. The Sharī ʿa Court of Appeal requested the Knesset "to find a solution that will ensure the Muslims' right to progeny (*ḥaqquhum fī ʾl-dhurriyya*)", in the same manner that the issue was handled in article 179 of the Criminal Law 1977, which provides immunity to Jewish husbands against the sanction applicable on polygamy in the event that permission for marriage has been granted by a rabbinical court and endorsed by the two chief rabbis. It was claimed that the absence of such permission with respect to Muslims represented discrimination against Muslims in relation to Jews and that the "common-law wife" was not a practical solution with respect to Muslims.[44]

Since the early 1990s the question of Muslims' subordination to a non-Muslim legislature has become acute; there is an increasing tendency in the Sharī ʿa Court of Appeal to regard the *sharī ʿa* courts as the last stronghold of *sharī ʿa* in a non-Muslim state; hence it attempts to avoid applying Israeli statutes and instead bases judicial decisions on the authoritative textual sources and *fiqh* doctrines. President Aḥmad Nāṭūr, who led this new trend since the constitution of a permanent Sharī ʿa Court of Appeal in 1994, is of the opinion that the Israeli law should be binding on the religious court only when it is explicitly addressed to it.[45] Otherwise, the *sharī'a* courts must apply *sharī'a* alone, since this is, in his view, the rationale of the judicial autonomy granted to the religious communities.[46] He opposes the application of the Property Relations between Spouses Law 1973[47] and the Basic Law: Human Dignity and Liberty 1992, although he regards the latter as a "revolutionary law" of tremendous importance in a social sense.[48] Qāḍī Nāṭūr and Qāḍī Zakī Mudlij are of the opinion that the Capacity and Guardianship Law 1962 is not addressed to religious courts, although the HCJ has ruled otherwise.[49] Qāḍī Fārūq Zuʿbī maintains that the basic norm in legislation should be God's commandments in the Qur'an, Prophetic Sunna, and *ijtihād* of the Prophet's Companions, the righteous *khulafā'* and the founders of the schools of law.[50] Qāḍī Nāṭūr maintains that the *qāḍī*s are requested to adjudicate in accordance with the Qur'an in all matters pertaining to substantive law as well as to the law of evidence and procedure.[51] Thus the Sharī'a Court of Appeal totally ignores the principle of equality between the sexes, which is the core of the Women's Equal Rights Law 1951; it instructs the *qāḍī*s of the courts of first instance to treat the testimony of two women as equal to the testimony of one man.[52] These pronouncements by the members of the Sharī'a Court of Appeal are of special interest, given the fact that these *qāḍī*s attained their legal education in Israeli universities and that they lack formal *shar'ī* education. Moreover, in recent years the Sharī'a Court of Appeal has decided in several cases — contrary to judicial practice in past years —to ignore violations of the Knesset's legislation.[53]

The polarization in the attitudes of the *shar'ī* judiciary towards the Israeli legal system (represented by the Knesset's legislation and case law[54]) is due to increasing religious tensions. Qāḍī Iyād Zaḥālka maintains that the image of Israel as a Jewish democratic state has caused the *sharī'a* courts to lose their Muslim religious identity. These tensions have been intensified by the Israeli–Palestinian conflict. Thus Shaykh Rā'id Ṣalāḥ, the head of the northern branch of the Islamic movement in Israel, which is ideologically close to the Muslim Brotherhood, suggests constituting an independent *shar'ī* judiciary, separate from the state judiciary.[55] Within this context, Qāḍī Nāṭūr's call to Muslims to apply the *sharī'a* in civil matters (which are not within the jurisdiction of the *sharī'a* courts), by resorting to arbitrators who will be appointed by the *qāḍīs*,[56] should be assessed as an attempt to circumvent the exclusive jurisdiction of the state's civil courts by using voluntary arbitration.

The Status of the *Sharī'a* in Civil Courts

Legal pluralism manifests itself also in the precincts of the civil courts, especially the Supreme Court sitting as a court of appeal or as the HCJ when dealing with matters pertaining to the personal status and *waqf* of Muslims. Needless to say, the civil judiciary is subject to Israeli principles of law and rules of evidence and procedure.[57] The vast majority of civil judges have no legal education or training in Islamic law; they have no free access to *fiqh* literature. When the need to identify a *shar'ī* legal norm arises, the judges resort to secondary sources and reference books, mainly on Anglo-Muhammadan law.[58] Naturally, the civil judge is less attentive than the *shar'ī qāḍī* to the sensitivities of the Muslim public. He deems himself committed first and foremost to constitutional norms such as those embodied in the Women's Equal Rights Law 1951, or the Basic Law: Human Dignity and Liberty 1992, or legal norms created by the Supreme Court. Thus the Supreme Court ruled, on the basis of article 63 of the Civil Wrongs Ordinance (New Version), that a woman who has been divorced against her will (an arbitrary act that is conceived of as unreasonable behaviour even though the wife's consent to divorce is irrelevant under Islamic law), in contravention of a criminal prohibition, is entitled to claim damages on grounds of breach of statutory obligation.[59]

In 1954 it was pleaded in the HCJ that the Knesset's ban on polygamy constituted an infringement of Muslims' freedom of religion and was in contradiction to section 5 of the Women's Equal Rights Law, which provides that "this Law shall not effect any religious-legal prohibition or permission relating to marriage or divorce". The HCJ rejected the plea on the grounds that freedom of religion is the freedom to do what religion commands, and not what it permits, and since Islam does not command but merely permits polygamy, its prohibition does not infringe upon the freedom of religion.[60] In a letter to the president of the Supreme Court, Qāḍī Ṭāhir

Ḥammād requested the HCJ to treat freedom of religion in terms of the five *shar'ī* legal-ethical qualifications (*al-aḥkām al-khamsa*) under which any aspect of Muslim behaviour is categorized. These are: (i) obligatory (*wājib*, as a preventive measure against a husband committing adultery), (ii) recommended (*mandūb*), (iii) indifferent (*mubāḥ*, leaving the option to the individual), (iv) reprehensible (*makrūh*), and (v) forbidden (*ḥarām*). According to these categories, freedom of religion means also the freedom to do what religion permits (which belongs to the category of "indifferent").[61]

Occasionally, Muslims seek relief in civil courts when this is not available in the *sharī'a* court.[62] In such circumstances the Supreme Court does not hesitate to interfere by creating a civil legal norm complementary to the *sharī'a*. Thus in one case an unmarried woman gave birth to a child fathered by a married Muslim who denied paternity. The woman requested the *sharī'a* court to oblige the man to undergo a DNA test and, once paternity was established, pay her daughter maintenance. The *sharī'a* court rejected the woman's plea, ruling that in the absence of a valid *shar'ī* marriage contract between the parties, there was no legal ground for claiming filiation (*ilḥāq nasab*) to, or maintenance for, the child, nor was it possible to oblige the defendant to undergo a DNA test.[63] According to the Ḥanafī doctrine, a child born out of wedlock is deemed illegitimate even if the biological father acknowledges paternity; the child has a right neither to maintenance nor to inheritance from his biological father. The Shāfi'ī doctrine maintains that an illegitimate daughter is deemed totally alien to her biological father, to the extent that he may marry her.[64] Both the Sharī'a Court of Appeal[65] and the District Court denied relief to the woman, the latter *in limine* on the grounds of lack of competence.

The Supreme Court sitting as a court of appeal on civil matters, however, ruled in 1995 that having regard to the minor's civil rights and on the basis of the Basic Law: Human Dignity and Liberty 1992, since the minor was debarred from legal paternity under Islamic law, she was entitled to benefit from "civil paternity", that is, biological, natural paternity by virtue of which minors are entitled to know their filiation in order to ensure their property, family and human rights, and that this legal relief could be obtained in the civil (rather than the religious) court. Once civil paternity is established, a minor is entitled to maintenance and to his or her share in the father's estate.

The Supreme Court's decision introduced a new civil constitutional legal norm alongside the *shar ʿī* norm and totally separated from it. The Supreme Court's decision is based on a multiplicity of legal sources: Israeli legislation and case law, norms of the state of Israel as a Jewish democratic state,[66] Jewish law, and American and English case law. The Supreme Court clarified the position of Islamic law on the relevant issues relying on the Anglo-Muhammadan law.[67]

Needless to say, the entire process that culminated in the Supreme Court's decision is the embodiment of legal pluralism in its full range and complexity. It is therefore no surprise that Qāḍī Nāṭūr deems the legal norm of civil paternity a "religious disaster" from the point of view of Islam and a dangerous revolutionary intervention in the *shar ʿī* rules pertaining to permission and prohibition.[68]

Absorption and Islamization of Israeli-Inspired Legal Concepts

Another manifestation of legal pluralism is the *shar ʿī qāḍīs'* tendency to absorb, by way of Islamization, Israeli-inspired legal concepts and doctrines. In this section we observe how this has occurred in the *qāḍīs'* tacit or overt embrace of concepts such as "the best interest of the child", natural justice, standing and precedent.

Best Interest of the Child

Sharīʿa places the child's mother first among the women entitled to custody (*ḥaḍāna*). The mother's legally institutionalized right to custody exists so long as she is not disqualified on such grounds as her marriage to a stranger or to a relative within the prohibited degrees for marriage (*maḥram*) with respect to the child. After the mother, in order of priority to custody come female relatives in a fixed order of entitlement according to the rule of the class (*parentela, ṭabaqa*) and degrees of heirs, anchored in *sharīʿa* with a clear preference of cognatic over agnatic relationship.[69] Although the *qāḍīs* attempt to justify the order of entitlement to custody on the strength of the principle of the child's best interest, it is obvious that this principle is secondary to the entitlement right of female relatives. In fact, the child's best interest is not recognized in *sharī'a* as a general principle;[70] rather, it is used as rationalization for the special position of the mother and female cognates.

Qāḍī Nāṭūr, in contrast, strongly insists that the best interest of the child is an independent fundamental principle anchored in *sharī'a*. In his view, the two parents have an equal right to custody. The principle of the welfare of the child should guide in each case according to its specific circumstances. He further maintains that the welfare of the child in *sharī'a* is in harmony with article 25 of the Capacity and Guardianship Law 1962.[71] This is a clear attempt to absorb and Islamize the principle of the best interest of the child as conceived of in Israeli law. The welfare of the child that emerges from the judicial practice of the Sharī'a Court of Appeal is based on the theory of presumptions (*farḍiyya*), e.g., children of tender age are presumed to be in the custody of their mother unless it is established that there are good reasons to rule otherwise.[72]

Natural Justice

Another example of absorption by way of Islamization is the concept of natural justice. Usually, the Sharī'a Court of Appeal uses the term "justice" within its Islamic meaning: "justice of God",[73] which is anchored in the Qur'an, the Hadith and exegesis. *'Adl* in the sense of God's justice, in connection with the requital of human acts, constitutes one of the five fundamental dogmas (*uṣūl*) in the Mu'tazilī doctrine. The *qāḍī* must adjudicate in the light of God's justice. The idea of material justice does not constitute a vital element in the theory of *sharī'a*.[74]

However, alongside the references to God's justice in the judicial practice of the Sharī'a Court of Appeal, there are occasionally explicit or implicit references to "natural justice" within the meaning common in the Israeli Supreme Court[75] — in such cases as the necessity to link the nuptial gift (*mahr, ṣadāq*) to the cost of living; the *qāḍī's* duty to provide reasoning (*ta'līl*) for his sentences; and the right to appeal to a higher forum (which is, broadly speaking, alien to Islamic law).[76]

Qāḍī Zaḥālka nevertheless claims that justice in the judicial practice of the Sharī'a Court of Appeal is based on Islamic legal principles and the faith of God as manifested in the Qur'an and the Sunna, rather than natural justice as defined in universal law.[77]

The Right of Standing

According to sharī'a, a legal action requires a claimant. There is no public prosecutor whose function it is to take action in criminal offences (homicide and bodily harm, for example, are within the domain of private law). However, a qāḍī may take action in matters concerning public welfare. The "Inspector of the Market" (muḥtasib) is the public representative in charge of the duty "to command right and forbid wrong" (al-amr bi'l-ma'rūf wa'l-nahy 'an al-munkar); in actual fact, he fulfils the functions of the public prosecutor.[78] In civil claims between two parties, a third party has no right of standing; the Law of Procedure of the Sharī'a Courts of 1917 has no provision regarding a third party's right of standing.

There is, however, some evidence in the judicial practice of the sharī'a courts that the concept of a third party's right of standing (khuṣūma) has been adopted in matters of personal status. Qāḍī Nāṭūr justifies this practice by stretching towards public law (ḥuqūq allāh) matters within private law (ḥuqūq al-'ibād), with respect to which there is no right of standing to a third party. He claims that any individual can step into the muḥtasib's shoes and become a private prosecutor.[79] He and the Sharī'a Court of Appeal seem to have been inspired by the HCJ's inclination to broaden the scope of the right of standing.[80] This right is granted not only to individuals claiming their personal interest to have been prejudiced but also to pleaders claiming to present an issue of a constitutional or public nature that touches directly upon the rule of law.[81]

Precedent

The Sharī'a Court of Appeal has decided that decisions by it that have introduced new rules, by reinterpreting fiqh doctrines or by selecting doctrines from schools other than the Ḥanafī school, are binding on the regional *sharīʿa* courts of first instance, but the Sharīʿa Court of Appeal is not bound by its own decisions.[82] Binding precedent, in the Western sense of the term, is alien to Islamic law, since, broadly speaking, there was no hierarchy of courts in pre-modern times. Neither is the *muftī*'s legal opinion binding. There is good reason to believe that the immediate source of inspiration for the concept of legal precedent in the *sharʿī* judiciary is the Israeli Supreme Court, whose decisions are binding on all kinds of courts, secular and religious alike.[83] The introduction of precedent in the *sharʿī* judiciary is justified by the need to create legal certainty regarding the legal norm in the *sharīʿa* courts; this certainty is expected to contribute to the stability of judicial practice in the *sharʿī* judiciary, which is intensively exposed to the Knesset's legislation and to the case law of the Supreme Court. Qāḍī Nāṭūr finds support for the absorption of the binding precedent in the doctrine of *siyāsa sharʿiyya*,[84] the application of which, as already noted, is traditionally reserved to the Muslim sovereign.[85]

The terms "judicial legislation" (*tashrīʿ qaḍāʾī*) and "legislative adjudication" (*qaḍāʾ tashrīʿī*) in Qāḍī Zuʿbī's legal methodology seem also to be inspired by the Israeli Supreme Court.[86] The *qāḍīs* reject the contention that either Israeli legal principles or universal principles are being absorbed or Islamized by the Sharīʿa Court of Appeal, or that *sharīʿa* is undergoing a process of "Israelization"; rather, they claim, *sharīʿa* is undergoing a process of renovation and adapting itself to the changes of place and time under the inspiration of Yūsuf al-Qaraḍāwī.[87] What appears to be the Islamization of certain Israeli legal concepts and principles may arguably demonstrate the *qāḍīs*' important role in creating and sustaining legal pluralism.[88]

Tribal Law, Islamic Law and State Law

The interaction between *sharīʿa* and tribal customary law (*ʿāda, ʿurf*) is another important manifestation of legal pluralism in Israel, especially among the sedentary Bedouin of the Negev, the Galilee and the Judean Desert in the West Bank. *Sharīʿa* and tribal customary law are two profoundly different legal systems. Whereas *sharīʿa* is perceived as a divinely revealed law as interpreted by its authoritative exponents and imposed by the state authority, customary law reflects the praxis and collective experience of ordinary people shaped into legally binding norms over a long period of time.[89]

Arab custom made a vital contribution to the development of Islamic law, both as a historical source providing legal norms for Islamic positive law (furū‘) and as an independent material source for creating legal norms (aṣl). However, custom was never formally fully recognized as a source of law within Islamic legal methodology in pre-modern times, although it had a status very close to this in the Ḥanafī school.[90] The Ḥanafī jurist Ibn ‘Ābidīn (d. 1836) elevated custom by means of the doctrine of necessity (ḍarūra) and inspired its recognition as a source of law in the Mejelle, which, though based on the Ḥanafī school, is a product of statutory codification.[91]

The interaction between the sharī‘a and custom in the family law takes place first and foremost in the sharī‘a courts. Most of the qāḍīs in Israel make concessions to tribal law at the expense of sharī‘a, in an attempt to bring the Bedouin within the orbit of orthodox Islam. Thus they acknowledge as shar‘ī marriage a customary, "gift" (‘aṭā’) marriage, which does not meet all shar‘ī requirements, and they confirm affiliation (ilḥāq nasab) of the children born to the parties of such a union. Other qāḍīs, particularly those with a conservative shar‘ī background, are determined to impose Islamic law on the Bedouin, without compromise.[92]

At the same time, tribal customary law is yielding ground to Islamic law on *its own territory*, i.e., in the precinct of the tribal qāḍī (ḥakam, muḥakkam). The process of Islamization is most pronounced in the domains of private property and marriage and family, but also in succession, contracts and obligations, and blood offences. The main agents of Islamization are the shar‘ī qāḍī, the shar‘ī marriage solemnizer (ma’dhūn), the muftī and the civil court applying the Mejelle (or civil law based on the Mejelle) in the Judean Desert.

Broadly speaking, since the promulgation of the Foundations of Law Act 1980, custom has ceased to be of any practical significance in the Israeli legal system; unless custom is explicitly recognized in a statute or in a case law, it does not exceed the bounds of an historical-academic event.[93] Some civil judges when dealing with such cases as homicide on the grounds of so-called "protection of family honour" or "women's chastity" take the tribal procedure of ṣulḥa, a traditional institution for settling bloody disputes, into account at the stage of detention or on imposing punishment. In 2004 the Supreme Court (Criminal Appeal 7564/04) ruled that *ṣulḥa* agreement should be taken into account in considerations of imposing punishment with a view to stopping a chain of endless violence. The decision was inspired by the Basic Law: Human Dignity and Liberty 1992. In the wake of that decision there is an increasing tendency in the civil courts to integrate *ṣulḥa* in the procedure of the criminal law as a bridging mechanism between the offender and his victim.[94]

Conclusion

We have seen above that the use of the eclectic expedient in Israel through the judicial practice of the Sharīʿa Court of Appeal (which in turn is related to earlier codification of Islamic law based on the eclectic expedient) has undermined the independent nature of the Islamic legal schools by blurring the boundaries between them, thus converting them into one large reservoir of legal material. For example, the reforms introduced in the law of inheritance by means of this expedient have created effects that would have been — to use Hallaq's wording — "inconceivable under the *fiqh* system".[95] This is in stark historical contrast to the way in which the Mamluks and the Ottomans succeeded in enlarging the reservoir of legal doctrines without destroying the framework of the four Sunni schools. Chief *qāḍī*s, one from each of the schools, were appointed in large cities such as Cairo and Damascus, thus leaving to the individual the option of choosing the appropriate court according to the specific doctrine of the school applying to the subject matter under review without adhering to any particular school. The quadruple structure of the judiciary made it possible to maintain a uniform but flexible legal system offering solutions to a variety of legal problems that could not be solved within one particular school. To achieve stability and certainty in judicial practice, the *qāḍī*s were instructed to adhere to the *taqlīd*, the established positive law, of each of the relevant schools.[96]

Moreover, the eclectic expedient by means of codification of specified domains of Islamic law has caused irrevocable damage to the schools because state codification in itself brings about the transformation of *sharīʿa* from jurists' law to statutory law[97] — unless there is, as in the case of Egypt, a proviso to the effect that in the event of a lacuna in statutory provisions the court may resort to the Ḥanafī school.[98] In the Israeli context it has been contended that the application of the eclectic expedient in the judicial practice of the Sharīʿa Court of Appeal "causes legal anarchy or even a state of *non droit*".[99] The result has been largely destructive in nature: the eclectic expedient has made no positive contribution to the elaboration of a new comprehensive, systematic integrative legal methodology.[100]

The application of the *sharīʿa* by the civil Family Court in Israel will, in the long run, inevitably bring about the emergence of a new entity of Islamic law, an Israeli version of Islamic law that is likely to resemble in some respects the Anglo-Muhammadan Law of British India. This is especially so because in recent years its jurisdiction has been equalized with that of the *sharīʿa* court (excluding matters of marriage and divorce). In matters of personal status, the Family Court is expected to apply substantive Islamic law subject to the amendments that have been introduced by the Knesset, in the light of Israeli principles of law as shaped by the statutory legislation and case law and in accordance with the civil rules of evidence and procedure. Moreover, even within the precincts of the *sharīʿa* courts, in spite of the current tendency in the Sharīʿa Court of Appeal to maintain its traditional *sharʿī* identity, we can see the further absorption of legal concepts and doctrines by way of their Islamization and adaptation to traditional *sharīʿa*. This is in part due to the exposure of *qāḍīs*, most of whom are graduates of Israeli universities, to Israeli law.

Immanuel Naveh estimates that the precedent set by the Supreme Court with respect to civil paternity may have far-reaching repercussions on matters of the personal status of Muslims in Israel. In his opinion, the possibility cannot be ruled out that basic rights in these matters will be reshaped once the civil court (i.e., the Supreme Court) is requested to constitute for them a civil normative pattern.[101] For the long run it is possible to anticipate the emergence of a dual legal system in matters of personal status according to the division of the judiciary: (i) The *sharīʿa* courts will apply the Ottoman Family Rights Law and — in cases of a lacuna in that law — uncodified *sharīʿa* within the space reserved for the *sharʿī* judiciary by the

Knesset's legislation and the Supreme Court and (ii) the civil Family Courts dealing with matters of personal status of Muslims in accordance with Islamic law applicable to these matters will be strongly inspired by Israeli legal norms as shaped by Israeli legislation and case law.

Unlike medieval times, the Islamization of tribal customary law in modern times has left an imprint on neither Islamic legal methodology nor Islamic positive law; its only result has been the emergence, in the voluntary tribal judiciary, of a hybrid version of a realistic, pragmatic Islamic customary law, outside the supervision of the *ulamā*.[102]

Notes

1. Ido Shahar, "Legal Pluralism and the Study of *Sharīʿa* Courts", *Islamic Law and Society* 15, no. 1 (2008): 112, 140–41. I am grateful to my colleague Ido Shahar for his valuable remarks and suggestions on an earlier draft of this article. All remaining shortcomings are my own responsibility. Thanks are also due to Veronica Taylor for the stylistic editing of the article and to Gary F. Bell for taking care of the bibliography. This article is up to date as of July 2016.

2. For a theoretical introduction to the concept of legal pluralism, see Ido Shahar, "Practicing Islamic Law in a Legal Pluralistic Environment: The Changing Face in Muslim Court in Present-Day Jerusalem" (PhD dissertation, Ben Gurion University of the Negev, Beʾer Sheva, 2006), pp. 11–30. On legal pluralism in the Arab world from a sociological and anthropological perspective, see Baudouin Dupret, Maurits Berger, and Laila al-Zwaini, eds., *Legal Pluralism in the Arab World* (The Hague: Kluwer Law International, 1999); Subhi Abu-Ghosh, "The *Shariʿa* Courts from the Perspective of Israeli Pluralism", in *Perspectives on Israeli Pluralism: Proceedings of a Conference on Pluralism in Israel*, edited by K.O. Cohen and J.S. Gerber (New York: Israel Colloquium, 1991), pp. 45–52.

3. Unless otherwise indicated, this study is based materially on Aharon Layish, "Adaptation of a Jurists' Law to Modern Times in an Alien Environment: The *Sharīʿa* in Israel", *Die Welt des Islams* 46, no. 2 (2006): 168–222; Aharon Layish, "The Heritage of the Ottoman Rule in Israeli Legal System: The Concept of *Umma* and Millet System", in *The Law Applied: Contextualizing the Islamic Shariʿa: A Volume in Honor of Frank E. Vogel*, edited by Peri Bearman, Wolfhart Heinrichs, and Bernard G. Weiss (London: Tauris, 2008), pp. 128–48; Aharon Layish, "*Qāḍīs* and *Sharīʿa* in Israel", *Asian and African Studies* 7 (1971): 237–72; Aharon Layish,

Women and Islamic Law in a Non-Muslim State: A Study Based on the Decisions of the Sharīʿa *Courts in Israel* (New York: Wiley; Jerusalem: Israel Universities Press, 1975).

4. Cf. Shahar, "Practicing Islamic Law", pp. 37–46. On legal pluralism in Palestine during the British Mandate, see Edoardo Vitta, *The Conflict of Laws in Matters of Personal Status in Palestine* (Tel Aviv: S. Bursi, 1947).

5. See Izhak England, *Religious Law in the Israeli Legal System* (Jerusalem: Faculty of Law, Hebrew University, 1975), pp. 148, 162–64.

6. For further details, see Layish, "*Qāḍīs and Sharīʿa*", pp. 237–38; Layish, *Women and Islamic Law*, pp. 1–4; Shahar, "Practicing Islamic Law", pp. 53–58.

7. Yohanan Friedmann, *Tolerance and Coercion in Islam: Interfaith Relations in the Muslim Tradition* (Cambridge: Cambridge University Press, 2003), p. 35.

8. See below.

9. Some observers tend to relate this legal pluralism to the so-called "colonial situation". See Yüksel Sezgin, "A Political Account for Legal Confrontation between State and Society: The Case of Israeli Legal Pluralism", *Studies in Law, Politics, and Society* 32 (2004). Cf. Adam S. Hofri-Winogradow, "A Plurality of Discontent: Legal Pluralism, Religious Adjudication and the State", *Journal of Law and Religion* 26, no. 1 (2010): 83–84, and the sources mentioned in fns. 82, 86.

10. Cf. Ido Shahar, "Legal Reform, Interpretive Communities and the Quest for Legitimacy: A Contextual Analysis of a Legal Circular". In *Law, Custom, and Statute in the Muslim World: Studies in Honor of Aharon Layish*, edited by Ron Shaham (Leiden: Brill, 2007), pp. 205, 207, 211.

11. Cf. Moussa Abou Ramadan, "Judicial Activism of the *Shariʿah* Appeals Court in Israel (1994–2001): Rise and Crisis", *Fordham International Journal* 27 (2003): 267. On forum shopping in Jerusalem, see Shahar, "Practicing Islamic Law", 136ff.; Shahar, "Legal Pluralism", pp. 136–37.

12. Wael B. Hallaq, *Sharīʿa, Theory, Practice, Transformations* (Cambridge: Cambridge Universirty Press, 2009), pp. 72ff.

13. Thus the Mālikī school is the only school that recognizes judicial dissolutions on such legal grounds as the husband's absence, non-provision of maintenance, cruelty, sexual impotence, and incurable disease, while the Ḥanafī school recognizes judicial annulment on the ground of a defect in the marriage. The Mālikī school, unlike other schools, does not recognize the doctrine of *radd*, the residue of the estate after the Qur'anic heirs have taken their prescribed portions; in the absence of male agnates, the Public Treasury becomes a residuary heir. For the same reason, the

Mālikī school, contrary to other schools, does not allow testamentary disposition of the entire estate even in the absence of surviving relatives. The Ḥanbalī school has a unique approach regarding the insertion of stipulations in the marriage contract that curtail the spouse's matrimonial rights. See Noel J. Coulson, *A History of Islamic Law* (Edinburgh: Edinburgh University Press, 1964), pp. 86ff., 97ff., 189–90.

14. A sophisticated version of *takhayyur* is *talfīq* (lit.: "patching"), which means bringing together legal doctrines culled from different sources contradicting each other in a set of statutory provisions dealing with one specific topic. See Wael B. Hallaq, *A History of Islamic Legal Theories: An Introduction to Sunnī uṣūl al-fiqh* (Cambridge: Cambridge University Press, 1997), p. 210; Hallaq, *Sharīʿa*, pp. 448–49.

15. See Englard, *Religious Law*, p. 55; Immanuel Nave, *"Yesum ha-shariʿa be-ʿarkaʾot ezraḥiyot ba-meʾa ha-ʿesrim: Meḥqar hashwaʾati lefi pesiqa be-ʿinyenei maʿamad ʾishi u-waqf shel muslemim be-medina muslemit (mitzrayim) uve-medina lo muslemit (yisraʾel)"* [Application of the sharīʿa in civil courts in the twentieth century: A comparative study based on decisions of civil courts in matters of personal status and waqf of Muslims in a Muslim state (Egypt) and in a non-Muslim state (Israel)] (PhD dissertation, Hebrew University of Jerusalem, 1997), pp. 379–80.

16. Cf. Shahar, "Legal Pluralism", pp. 114ff.

17. Iyāḍ Zaḥālka, Qāḍī of the Sharīʿa Court of Jerusalem (West) and one-time director of the sharīʿa courts, refers to the eclectic expedient as *ijtihād naqlī*; that is, the intellectual effort of devising a new rule by "transferring" a doctrine from any given school or juristic view. He claims that Qāḍī Naṭūr deems this expedient a legitimate mechanism for renovating sharīʿa. See Iyāḍ Zakhālka, *"Zehut batei ha-din ha-sharʿiyim be-yisraʾel"* [The identity of the sharīʿa courts in Israel], in *Le-nochaḥ beit ha-din ha-sharʿi. Tahalichei shinuy be-maʿamadan shel nashim muslemiyot be-yisraʾel uva-mizraḥ ha-tichon* [Facing the Shariʿa Court: Transformation in the status of Muslim women in Israel and the Middle East], edited by Liat Kozma (Tel Aviv: Resling, 2011), pp. 76, 83; Iyāḍ Zakhālka, *"Maʿmad batei ha-din ha-sharʿiyim be-qerev ha-tzibur ha-ʿaravi"* [The Arab public view on the status of the sharīʿa courts], in *Miʿuṭim muslemiyim be-mdinot rov lo-muslemi: Ha-Tenuʿa ha-islamit be-yisraʾel ke-miqre mivḥan* [Muslim minorities in non-Muslim majority countries: The Islamic movement in Israel as a test case], edited by Elie Rekhess and Arik Rudnitzky (Tel Aviv: Moshe Dayan Center, Tel Aviv University, 2011), p. 93.

18. *Al-Kashshāf ʿan qarārāt al-istiʾnāf al-ṣādira ʿan maḥkamat al-istiʾnāf al-sharʿiyya al-ʿulyā fī ʾl-quds al-sharīf, 1992–1997* [The explorer of the decisions of the

Supreme Sharīʿa Court of Appeal in noble Jerusalem, 1992–1997], 6 vols. (Herzliya: The Interdisciplinary Center, 1999), 1995, p. 2. On another occasion Qāḍī Nāṭūr ruled that "the sharīʿa courts rely on the sharīʿa as a foundation for judicial decision (taʿtamid al-sharīʿa asāsan liʾl-ḥukm)", al-Kashshāf, 1997, part 1, file 39/97, p. 135.

19. Ṣubḥī Abū Ghūsh, ed. Qarārāt sharʿiyya min al-maḥkama al-istiʾnāfiyya [Sharʿī decisions of the Court of Appeal] (Jerusalem: Ministry for Religious Affairs, 1992), file 12/80, pp. 92–94; Layish, Women and Islamic Law, p. 333.

20. Aharon Layish and Gabriel R. Warburg, The Reinstatement of Islamic Law in Sudan under Numayrī: An Evaluation of a Legal Experiment in the Light of Its Historical Context, Methodology, and Repercussions (Leiden: Brill, 2002), pp. 72–75, 98–101.

21. Frank E. Vogel, "Siyāsa, 3. In the Sense of Siyāsa Sharʿiyya", The Encyclopaedia of Islam, 2nd ed., IX: 694–96.

22. Cf. Abou Ramadan, Judicial Activism, p. 286.

23. Zaḥālka, "The Identity of the Sharīʿa Courts", p. 84.

24. Al-Kashshāf, 1995, pp. 9–19.

25. Ibid., 1995, pp. 17–18.

26. Ibid., 1995, pp. 20–30.

27. Parentela is a class (ṭabaqa) of male agnates who share the same parent, and their issue. For the order of parentelas in Islamic rules of inheritance, see Noel J. Coulson, Succession in the Muslim Family (Cambridge: Cambridge University Press, 1971), p. 33.

28. Ibid, pp. 213–14, 235.

29. Ibid., pp. 255–58.

30. David S. Powers, Studies in Qur'an and Ḥadīth: The Formation of the Islamic Law of Inheritance (Berkeley: University of California Press, 1986), pp. 143ff. For the use of the talfīq device in Arab legislation pertaining to "compulsory bequest", see Coulson, Succession, 221.

31. Cf. Bernard Botiveau, "Palestinian Law: Social Segmentation Versus Centralization", in Legal Pluralism in the Arab World, edited by Dupret, Berger, and al-Zuwaini, pp. 77–83; Ido Shahar, "Falasṭinim be-veit din yisraʾeli: Tarbut, sheliṭa ve-hitnagdut be-veit ha-din ha-shariʿ be-maʿarav yerushalayim" [Palestinians in an Israeli court: Culture, domination and resistance in the Sharīʿa Court in West Jerusalem] (MA thesis, Faculty of Social Sciences, Hebrew University of Jerusalem, 2000), p. 45; Kilian Bälz, "The Secular Reconstruction of Islamic Law: The Islamic Supreme Constitutional Court and the 'Battle over the Veil' in State-Run Schools", in Legal Pluralism in the Arab World, edited by Dupret, Berger,

and al-Zuwain, pp. 231–33 (models of legal pluralism); Shimon Shetreet, *'Al ha-shefiṭa: Ma'arechet ha-tzedeq ba-mishpaṭ* [On adjudication: Justice on trial] (Tel Aviv: Yedi'ot Aḥaronot & Sifrei Ḥemed, 2004), p. 59.

32. Cf. England, *Religious Law*, p. 13; Shetreet, *On Adjudication*, p. 65; Lynn Welchman, *Beyond the Code: Muslim Family Law and the Shari'a Judiciary in the Palestinian West Bank* (The Hague: Kluwer Law International, 2000), pp. 39–40.

33. Layish, *Women and Islamic Law*, pp. 3–4.

34. Layish, "*Umma* and Millet", pp. 129ff., 144–45.

35. Aharon Barak, *Shofet be-ḥevra democraṭit* [The judge in a democracy] (Haifa and Jerusalem: Haifa University Press, Keter & Nevo, 2004), p. 218.

36. Cf. Shahar, "Practicing Islamic Law", pp. 58–62.

37. Aharon Layish, "The Muslim *Waqf* in Israel", *Asian and African Studies* 2 (1966): 61–67. Cf. Michael Damper, *Islam and Israel: Muslim Religious Endowments and the Jewish State* (Washington, DC: Institute for Palestine Studies, 1994), Ch. 3.

38. Layish, *Women and Islamic Law*, pp. 334–35.

39. Abū Ghūsh, *Shari'a Court of Appeal*, file 42/86, p. 157. Cf. Layish, *Women and Islamic Law*, p. 264.

40. Layish, *Women and Islamic Law*, pp. 335–37

41. These goals serve the public interest, the most important of which are protection of life, religion, private property, mind and offspring. See Hallaq, *Shari'a*, p. 104.

42. Andrew F. March. "Sources of Moral Obligation to non-Muslims in the 'Jurisprudence of Muslim Minorities' (*fiqh al-aqalliyyāt*)", *Islamic Law and Society* 16, no. 1 (2009): 34–94; Khaled Abou El Fadl, *The Great Theft: Wrestling Islam from the Extremists* (New York: HarperCollins, 2005), chaps. 10–11.

43. Abū Ghūsh, *Shari'a Court of Appeal*, file 2/88, pp. 77–81; Layish, *Women and Islamic Law*, 335; Layish, *Qāḍīs and Shari'a*, 266ff.

44. Abū Ghūsh, *Shari'a Court of Appeal*, file 23/88, pp. 103–7. Cf. ibid., file 25/76, p. 197; Layish, *Women and Islamic Law*, p. 86n10.

45. Cf. England, *Religious Law*, pp. 153–54.

46. Zaḥālka, "The Identity of the *Shari'a* Courts", pp. 83–84. Qāḍī Zaḥālka justifies submission to Israeli statutes explicitly addressed to religious courts on the grounds that they are based on democratic and universal values and serve the interest of the individual and the public order. See ibid., pp. 84–85.

47. Yitzhak Reiter, "*Qāḍīs* and the Implementation of Islamic Law in Present Israel", in *Islamic Law: Theory and Practice*, edited by Robert Gleave and E. Kermeli (London: Tauris, 1997), pp. 215–17. On property relations between the spouses, see Ya'akov Meron, "Yaḥasei mamon bein benei zug muslemin" [Property relations between Muslim spouses], *'Iyunei Mishpaṭ* 3 (1973): 279–98; Meron, "Women's Equal Rights (A Muslim Solution)", *Israel Law Review* 7 (1972): 315–18.

48. Zaḥālka, "The Identity of the *Sharī'a* Courts", pp. 85–86. In another case, Qāḍī Nātūr ruled that protection of human dignity and liberty should be based on the sharī'a rather than on Israeli law. See *Sharī'a Court of Appeal*, file 1944/99. Cf. Abou Ramadan, "Judicial Activism", pp. 278–79.

49. *Al-Kashshāf*, 1995, file 92/95, pp. 358–59; Ibid., 1997, part 1, file 135/96, p. 297. Cf. Pinhas Shifman, "*Mishmoret u-mezonot yeladim*" [Custody and maintenance for children], in *Ma'mad ha-'isha ba-ḥevra uva-mishpaṭ* [Women's status in Israeli law and society], edited by Frances Raday, Carmel Shalev, and Michal Liban-Kooby (Tel Aviv: Schoken, 1995), p. 536.

50. *Al-Kashshāf*, 1997, part 2, file 60/97, pp. 43–44. Cf. Abu-Gosh, "*Sharī'a* Courts & Pluralism", p. 45.

51. Abou Ramadan, *Judicial Activism*, p. 278.

52. Zaḥālka, "The Identity of the *Sharī'a* Courts", p. 88.

53. Shahar, "Practicing Islamic Law", pp. 182ff.

54. Hofri-Winogradow, "A Plurality of Discontent", pp. 84–85.

55. Zaḥālka, "The Identity of the *Sharī'a* Courts", pp. 75–76; Zaḥālka, "The Arab Public View", 95–96; Abou Ramadan, *Judiciary Activism*, 292–96.

56. Zaḥālka, "The Arab Public View", p. 94.

57. In matters pertaining to evidence, the sharī'a courts apply the Mejelle, and in procedure, the Ottoman shar'ī procedure law, 1917; Moussa Abū Ramaḍān, "Ma'amado shel ḥoq ha-mishpaḥa ha-'othmani" [The status of the Ottoman family law], in *Facing the Shari'a court*, edited by Kozma, p. 51.

58. Naveh, "Application of the *Sharī'a* in Civil Courts", pp. 374, 389–92; Ya'akov Meron, *Ha-Din ha-muslemi be-re'iya hashwa'atit* [Muslim law in comparative perspective] (Jerusalem: Magnes, 2001), pp. 57–59.

59. Aharon Layish, "Ma'amad ha-'isha ha-muslemit be-veit ha-din ha-shar'i be-yisra'el" [The status of Muslim woman in the sharī'a court in Israel]. In *Women's Status in Israeli Law and Society*, edited by Raday, Shalev, and Liban-Kooby, p. 373. On statutory obligation, see Haim H. Cohen, *Ha-Mishpaṭ* [The law] (Jerusalem: Bialik Institute, 1999), pp. 733ff.

60. HCJ, file 49/54 Milḥim Na'if Milḥim v. the *shar'ī* judge of Acre and the District; *Pisqei Din* 8, pp. 910, 913. For further details, see Naveh,

"Application of the *Sharīʿa* in Civil Courts", pp. 126–31, 384; Moussa Abou Ramadan, "The Transition from Tradition to Reform: The *Shariʿa* Appeals Court Rulings on Child Custody (1992–2001)", *Fordham International Journal* 26 (2003): 618.

61. Layish, *Qāḍīs and Sharīʿa*, p. 268; Layish, *Women and Islamic Law*, pp. 81ff.; Abu-Gosh, "*Sharīʿa* Courts & Pluralism", 50–51; Yaʿakov Meron, "Ribuy nashim la-muslemim ve-ḥuqatiyut isuro" [Polygamy for the Muslims and the constitutionality of its prohibition], *Mishpatim* 3 (1973): 515–19. Cf. Mordechai Kremnitzer, "BG"TS veha-tefisa ha-reḥava shel tafkido: Ketav hagana" [High Court of Justice and the broad conception of its role: Pleading in defence], in *Activism shipuṭi: Beʿad ve-neged. Meqomo shel BG"TS ba-ḥevra ha-yisraʾelit* [Judicial activism: For and against. The role of the High Court of Justice in Israeli society], edited by Ruth Gavison, Mordechai Kremnitzer, and Yoav Dotan (Tel Aviv: Yediʾot Aḥaronot, Sifrei Ḥemed & Jerusalem: Magnes, 2000), pp. 235ff.

62. Naveh, "Application of the *Sharīʿa* in Civil Courts", p. 387.

63. The Sharīʿa Court of Haifa, file 34/87 (*ilḥāq nasab*), 3 May 1987.

64. Muḥammad Muṣṭafā Shalabī, *Aḥkām al-usra fī ʾl-islām. Dirāsa muqārina bayna fiqh al-madhāhib al-sunniyya waʾl-madhhab al-jaʿfarī waʾl-qānūn* [Family law in Islam: Comparative study between the doctrines of the Sunnī schools of law, the Jaʿfarī school, and the statute] (Beirut: Dār al-Nahḍa al-ʿArabiyya, 1973), pp. 683–94. Cf. Muḥammad Abū Zahra, *al-Aḥwāl al-shakhṣiyya* [Personal status law] (Cairo: Dār al-Fikr al-ʿArabī, n.d. [after 1957], p. 454; Muḥammad Muḥyī al-Dīn ʿAbd al-Ḥamīd, *al-Aḥwāl al-shakhṣiyya fī ʾl-sharīʿa al-islāmiyya maʿa al-ishāra ilā mā yuqābiluhā fī ʾl-sharāʾiʿ al-ukhrā* [Personal status law in Islamic sharīʿa in comparison with other religious laws] (Cairo: Maṭbaʿat al-Istiqāma, 1361/1942), pp. 470ff.

65. The Sharīʿa Court of Appeal, file 41/87, 20 October 1987.

66. Cf. Barak, *The Judge*, pp. 80ff.

67. Civil Appeal, file 3077/90, *Pisqei Din* 49, part 2 (1995), pp. 578–629. Cf. Naveh, "Application of the *Sharīʿa* in Civil Courts", pp. 223ff.; Yaʿakov Meron, "Din shtuqi ba-mishpaṭ ha-muslemi" [The law of the illegitimate child in Islamic law], *Hapraklit* 43 (1997): 407–15; Abou Ramadan, "Custody", p. 610.

68. Zaḥālka, "The Identity of the *Sharīʿa* Courts", pp. 86–87.

69. See Shalabī, *Aḥkām al-usra*, pp. 737–38.

70. Cf. Harald Motzki, "Child Marriage in Seventeenth-Century Palestine". In *Islamic Legal Interpretation: Muftis and Their Fatwas*, edited by Muhammad Kh. Masud, Brinkley Messick, and David S. Powers (Cambridge, MA: Harvard University Press, 1996), p. 135.

71. *Al-Kashshāf*, 1995, file 92/95, pp. 358–59. Cf. Abū Ghūsh, *Sharī'a Court of Appeal*, file 13/83, p. 140; Abu-Ghosh, "*Sharī'a* Courts & Pluralism", p. 47.

72. Cf. Shifman, "Custody", p. 537.

73. See, e.g., *al-Kashshāf*, 1997, part 2, file 153/97, p. 219, files 75/98, 198/98.

74. Emile Tyan, "'Adl", *The Encyclopaedia of Islam*, 2nd ed., I: 209i; W. Montgomery Watt, "'Akīda", *The Encyclopaedia of Islam*, 2nd ed., I: 334ii; L. Gardet, "Allāh", *The Encyclopaedia of Islam*, 2nd ed. I: 410i; Gardet, "'Ilm al-Kalām", *The Encyclopaedia of Islam*, 2nd ed. III: 1143ii.

75. On the principles of Israeli natural justice, see England, *Religious Law*, pp. 161ff.

76. On the religious courts' duty to observe the principles of natural justice, see England, *Religious Law*, p. 112.

77. Zaḥālka, "The Identity of the *Sharī'a* Courts", p. 77.

78. Joseph Schacht, *An Introduction to Islamic Law* (Oxford: Clarendon University Press, 1964), pp. 189–90. Cf. *Mejelle-i aḥkām-i 'adliyye (Qovetz dinei ha-mishpaṭ)* [Collection of the legal rules of the Ottoman Civil Code, 1869-76], translated and annotated by Gad Frumkin (Jerusalem: 'Azri'el, 1952), sec. 1634; Michael Cook, *Forbidding Wrong in Islam: An Introduction* (Cambridge: Cambridge University Press, 2003), pp. 65ff.

79. Schacht, *Introduction*, p. 52; Layish & Warburg, *Sudan*, Glossary, s.v. *ḥisba, muḥtasib*. Cf. Abū Ghūsh, *Sharī'a Court of Appeal*, file 3/76, p. 185; *al-Kashshāf*, 1997, pt. 2, file 113/97, pp. 129–30.

80. Abū Ghūsh, *Sharī'a Court of Appeal*, file 39/89, pp. 125–31. For further details, see Layish, "Adaptation", pp. 204–6 and the references there to the decisions of the Sharī'a Court of Appeal.

81. Kremnitzer, "Pleading in Defence", p. 185; Yoav Dotan, "Activism shipuṭi be-BG"TS" [Judicial activism in the High Court of Justice], in *Judicial Activism: For and Against*, edited by Kremnitzer Gavison and Dotan, pp. 11–13. Cf. Barak, *The Judge*, p. 69.

82. Zaḥālka, "The Identity of the *Sharī'a* Courts", pp. 76, 81.

83. Aharon Barak, *Shiqul da'at shipuṭi* [Judicial discretion] (Tel Aviv: Papirus, Tel Aviv University Press, 1987), pp. 150–51; Barak, *The Judge*, p. 67. England (*Religious Law*, p. 134), by contrast, is of the opinion that the decisions of the Supreme Court are not binding on the religious courts.

84. Qāḍī Zaḥālka uses the expression *siyāsa qaḍā'iyya*, "judicial policy", which seems to have the same connotation. See Zaḥālka, "The Identity of the *Sharī'a* Courts", pp. 80–81.

85. On the penetration of Western legal terminology into modern legal theory (*uṣūlī*) textbooks, see Monique C. Cardinal, "Islamic Legal Theory Curriculum: Are the Classics Taught Today?", *Islamic Law and Society* 12,

no. 2 (2005): 246–53. Thus Shalabī considers the doctrine of precedent akin to consensus (*ijmāʿ*), and Abū Zahra classifies it as a form of inferential analogy (*qiyās*); Ibid., p. 252.

86. On judicial legislation, see Barak, *Judicial Discretion*, pp. 147ff.; Barak, *The Judge*, pp. 25–26. Cf. Englard, *Religious Law*, p. 115 (the religious court as a legislative organ).

87. Zaḥālka, "The Identity of the Sharīʿa Courts", p. 90.

88. Cf. Shahar, *Palestinians*, p. 67. Cf. Sezgin, "Israeli Legal Pluralism", pp. 213–16; Abou Ramadan, "Custody", p. 618. On different kinds of relationship between the two normative systems, see Englard, *Religious Law*, p. 37.

89. Aharon Layish, *Legal Documents from the Judean Desert: The Impact of the Sharīʿa on Bedouin Customary Law*, with the assistance of Mūsā Shawārbah and including his linguistic essay (Leiden: Brill, 2011), p. 6.

90. Gideon Libson, "ʿUrf 1. The Status of Custom in Islamic law", *Encyclopaedia of Islam*, 2nd ed. X: 887ii.

91. Wael B. Hallaq, "A Prelude to Ottoman Reform: Ibn ʿĀbidīn on Custom and Legal Change", in *Histories of the Modern Middle East. New Directions*, edited by Israel Gershoni, Hakan Erdem, and Ursula Wokoeck (Boulder, CO: Rienner, 2002), pp. 53, 55, 61

92. Aharon Layish, "Shariʿa u-minhag ba-mishpaḥa ha-muslemit be-yisraʾel" [Sharīʿa and custom in the Muslim family in Israel], *Hamirah Hehadash* 13, no. 4 (1974): pp. 339–408; Layish, *Women and Islamic Law*, p. 334.

93. Cohen, *The Law*, p. 257.

94. Nurit Tsafrir, "Arab Customary Law in Israel: Ṣulḥa Agreements and Israeli Courts", *Islamic Law and Society* 13, no. 1 (2006): 76ff.; Ron Shapiro, "Higiʿa ha-ʿet le-sulḥa" [The time is ripe for ṣulḥa], *Hapraklit* 48 (2006): 433ff.

95. Hallaq, *Sharīʿa*, p. 469.

96. Yossef Rapoport, "Legal Diversity in the Age of *Taqlīd*: The Four Chief *Qāḍīs* under the Mamluks", *Islamic law and Society* 10, no. 2 (2003): 210ff.; Shahar, "Legal Pluralism", pp. 131ff.

97. Abū Ramaḍān claims that codification of the sharʿī family law intensifies the process of its secularization because it makes it easier for the Supreme Court to apply statutory provisions independently from the sharʿī literature; Abū Ramaḍān, "Ottoman Family Law", p. 50.

98. Aharon Layish, "The Transformation of the *Sharīʿa* from Jurists' Law to Statutory Law in the Contemporary Muslim World", *Die Welt des Islams* 44, no. 1 (2004): 102.

99. Abou Ramadan, "Custody", p. 627. Qāḍī Zaḥālka, on the other hand, maintains that "adopting views from other schools is widely acknowledged and does not deviate from Islamic legal methodology"; see Zaḥālka, "The Identity of the Sharīʿa Courts", p. 84.

100. Cf. Hallaq, *Legal Theories*, p. 211.

101. Naveh,x "Application of the *Sharīʿa* in Civil Courts", p. 226.

102. Aharon Layish and Avshalom Shmueli, "Custom and *Sharīʿa* in the Bedouin Family according to Legal Documents from the Judaean Desert", *Bulletin of the School of Oriental and African Studies* 42, no. 1 (1979): 29–45; Aharon Layish, "Islamization of Custom as Reflected in Awards of Tribal Arbitrators in the Judaean Desert", *Jerusalem Studies in Arabic and Islam* 35 (2008): 285–334; Layish, *Judean Desert Documents*, pp. 3–15.

References

Laws

Mejelle-i aḥkām-i ʿadliyye. (Qovetz dinei ha-mishpaṭ) [Collection of the legal rules of the Ottoman Civil Code, 1869-76], translated and annotated by Gad Frumkin. Jerusalem: ʿAzriʾel, 1952.

Court Cases

Abū Ghūsh, Ṣubḥī, ed. *Qarārāt sharʿiyya min al-maḥkama al-istiʾnāfiyya* [Sharʿī decisions of the Court of Appeal]. Jerusalem: Ministry for Religious Affairs, 1992.

Al-Kashshāf ʿan qarārāt al-istiʾnāf al-ṣādira ʿan maḥkamat al-istiʾnāf al-sharʿiyya al-ʿulyā fī ʾl-quds al-sharīf, 1992–1997 [The explorer of the decisions of the Supreme Sharīʿa Court of Appeal in noble Jerusalem, 1992–1997], 6 vols. Herzliya: The Interdisciplinary Center, 1999.

Civil Appeal file 3077/90, *Pisqei Din* 49, part 2 (1995).

Sharīʿa Court of Appeal, file 41/87, 20 October 1987.

Sharīʿa Court of Appeal, file 3/76

Sharīʿa Court of Haifa, file 34/87 (*ilḥāq nasab*), 3 May 1987.

Books

ʿAbd al-Ḥamīd, Muḥammad Muḥyī al-Dīn. *al-Aḥwāl al-shakhṣiyya fī ʾl-sharīʿa al-islāmiyya maʿa al-ishāra ilā mā yuqābiluhā fī ʾl-sharāʾiʿ al-ukhrā* [Personal status law in Islamic sharīʿa in comparison with other religious laws]. Cairo: Maṭbaʿat al-Istiqāma, 1361/1942.

Abou El Fadl, Khaled. *The Great Theft: Wrestling Islam from the Extremists.* New York: HarperCollins, 2005.

Abū Zahra, Muḥammad. *al-Aḥwāl al-shakhṣiyya* [Personal status law]. Cairo: Dār al-Fikr al-ʿArabī, n.d. [after 1957].

Barak, Aharon. *Shiqul daʿat shipuṭi* [Judicial discretion]. Tel Aviv: Papirus, Tel Aviv University Press, 1987.

————. *Shofet be-ḥevra democraṭit* [The judge in a democracy]. Haifa and Jerusalem: Haifa University Press; Keter & Nevo, 2004.

Cohen, Haim H. *Ha-Mishpaṭ* [The law]. Jerusalem: Bialik Institute, 1999.

Cook, Michael. *Forbidding Wrong in Islam: An Introduction*. Cambridge: Cambridge University Press, 2003.

Coulson, Noel J. *A History of Islamic Law*. Edinburgh: Edinburgh University Press, 1964.

————. *Succession in the Muslim Family*. Cambridge: Cambridge University Press, 1971.

Damper, Michael. *Islam and Israel: Muslim Religious Endowments and the Jewish State*. Washington, DC: Institute for Palestine Studies, 1994.

Dupret, Baudouin, Maurits Berger, and Laila al-Zwaini, eds., *Legal Pluralism in the Arab World*. The Hague: Kluwer Law International, 1999.

Englard, Izhak. *Religious Law in the Israeli Legal System*. Jerusalem: Faculty of Law, Hebrew University, 1975.

Friedmann, Yohanan. *Tolerance and Coercion in Islam: Interfaith Relations in the Muslim Tradition*. Cambridge: Cambridge University Press, 2003.

Hallaq, Wael B. *A History of Islamic Legal Theories: An Introduction to Sunnī uṣūl al-fiqh*. Cambridge: Cambridge University Press, 1997.

————. *Sharīʿa, Theory, Practice, Transformations*. Cambridge: Cambridge University Press, 2009.

Layish, Aharon. *Women and Islamic Law in a Non-Muslim State: A Study Based on the Decisions of the Sharīʿa Courts in Israel*. New York: Wiley; Jerusalem: Israel Universities Press, 1975.

————. *Legal Documents from the Judean Desert: The Impact of the Sharīʿa on Bedouin Customary Law*. With the assistance of Mūsā Shawārbah and including his linguistic essay. Leiden: Brill, 2011.

Layish, Aharon, and Gabriel R. Warburg. *The Reinstatement of Islamic Law in Sudan under Numayrī: An Evaluation of a Legal Experiment in the Light of Its Historical Context, Methodology, and Repercussions*. Leiden: Brill, 2002.

Meron, Yaʾakov. *Ha-Din ha-muslemi be-reʾiya hashwaʾatit* [Muslim law in comparative perspective]. Jerusalem: Magnes, 2001.

Powers, David S. *Studies in Qurʾan and Ḥadīth: The Formation of the Islamic Law of Inheritance*. Berkeley: University of California Press, 1986.

Schacht, Joseph. *An Introduction to Islamic Law*. Oxford: Clarendon University Press, 1964.

Shalabī, Muḥammad Muṣṭafā. *Aḥkām al-usra fī ʾl-islām. Dirāsa muqārina bayna fiqh al-madhāhib al-sunniyya waʾl-madhhab al-jaʿfarī waʾl-qānūn* [Family law in Islam: Comparative study between the doctrines of the Sunni schools of law, the Jaʿfarī school, and the statute]. Beirut: Dār al-Nahḍa al-ʿArabiyya, 1973.

Shetreet, Shimon. ʿAl ha-shefiṭa: Maʿarechet ha-tzedeq ba-mishpaṭ [On adjudication: Justice on trial]. Tel Aviv: Yediʿot Aharonot & Sifrei Ḥemed, 2004.

Vitta, Edoardo. *The Conflict of Laws in Matters of Personal Status in Palestine*. Tel Aviv: S. Bursi Ltd., 1947.

Welchman, Lynn. *Beyond the Code: Muslim Family Law and the Shariʿa Judiciary in the Palestinian West Bank*. The Hague: Kluwer Law International, 2000.

Chapters

Abu-Ghosh, Subhi. "The *Shariʿa* Courts from the Perspective of Israeli Pluralism". In *Perspectives on Israeli Pluralism: Proceedings of a Conference on Pluralism in Israel*, edited by K.O. Cohen and J.S. Gerber, pp. 45–52. New York: Israel Colloquium, 1991.

Abū Ramaḍān, Moussa. "*Maʿamado shel ḥoq ha-mishpaḥa ha-ʿothmani*" [The status of the Ottoman family law]. In *Le-nochaḥ beit ha-din ha-sharʿi. Tahalichei shinuy be-maʿamadan shel nashim muslemiyot be-yisraʾel uva-mizraḥ ha-tichon* [Facing the Shariʿa Court: Transformation in the status of Muslim women in Israel and the Middle East], edited by Liat Kozma, pp. 49–73. Tel Aviv: Resling, 2011.

Bälz, Kilian. "The Secular Reconstruction of Islamic Law: The Islamic Supreme Constitutional Court and the 'Battle over the Veil' in State-Run Schools". In *Legal Pluralism in the Arab World*, edited by Baudouin Dupret, Maurits Berger, and Laila al-Zwaini, pp. 229–43. The Hague: Kluwer Law International, 1999.

Botiveau, Bernard. "Palestinian Law: Social Segmentation versus Centralization". In *Legal Pluralism in the Arab World*, edited by Baudouin Dupret, Maurits Berger, and Laila al-Zwaini, pp. 73–87. The Hague: Kluwer Law International, 1999.

Dotan, Yoav. "Activism shipuṭi be-BG"TS" [Judicial activism in the High Court of Justice]. In *Activism shipuṭi: Beʿad ve-neged. Meqomo shel BG"TS ba-ḥevra ha-yisraʾelit* [Judicial activism: For and against. The role of the High Court of Justice in Israeli society], edited by Ruth Gavison, Mordechai Kremnitzer, and Yoav Dotan, pp. 5–68. Tel Aviv: Yediʾot Aharonot, Sifrei Ḥemed; Jerusalem: Magnes, 2000.

Hallaq, Wael B. "A Prelude to Ottoman Reform: Ibn ʿĀbidīn on Custom and Legal Change". In *Histories of the Modern Middle East. New Directions*, edited by Israel Gershoni, Hakan Erdem, and Ursula Wokoeck, pp. 37–61. Boulder, CO: Rienner, 2002.

Kremnitzer, Mordechai. "BG"TS veha-tefisa ha-reḥava shel tafkido: Ketav hagana" [High Court of Justice and the broad conception of its role: Pleading in defence]. In *Activism shipuṭi: Beʿad ve-neged. Meqomo shel*

BG"TS ba-ḥevra ha-yisra'elit [Judicial activism: For and against. The role of the High Court of Justice in Israeli society], edited by Ruth Gavison, Mordechai Kremnitzer, and Yoav Dotan, pp. 185–252. Tel Aviv: Yedi'ot Aḥaronot, Sifrei Ḥemed; Jerusalem: Magnes, 2000.

Layish, Aharon. "Maʿamad ha-'isha ha-muslemit be-veit ha-din ha-sharʿi be-yisra'el" [The status of Muslim woman in the sharīʿa court in Israel]. In *Maʿmad ha-'isha ba-ḥevra uva-mishpaṭ* [Women's status in Israeli law and society], edited by Frances Raday, Carmel Shalev, and Michal Liban-Kooby, pp. 364–79. Tel Aviv: Schoken, 1995.

———. "The Heritage of the Ottoman Rule in Israeli Legal System: The Concept of *Umma* and Millet System". In *The Law Applied: Contextualizing the Islamic Shariʿa: A Volume in Honor of Frank E. Vogel*, edited by Peri Bearman, Wolfhart Heinrichs, and Bernard G. Weiss, pp. 128–48. London: Tauris, 2008.

Motzki, Harald. "Child Marriage in Seventeenth-Century Palestine". In *Islamic Legal Interpretation: Muftis and Their Fatwas*, edited by Muhammad KH. Masud, Brinkley Messick, and David S. Powers, pp. 129–40. Cambridge, MA: Harvard University Press, 1996.

Reiter, Yitzhak. "*Qāḍīs* and the Implementation of Islamic Law in Present Day Israel". In *Islamic Law: Theory and Practice*, edited by Robert Gleave and E. Kermeli, pp. 205–31. London: Tauris, 1997.

Shahar, Ido. "Legal Reform, Interpretive Communities and the Quest for Legitimacy: A Contextual Analysis of a Legal Circular". In *Law, Custom, and Statute in the Muslim World: Studies in Honor of Aharon Layish*, edited by Ron Shaham, pp. 199–227. Leiden: Brill, 2007.

Shifman, Pinhas. "*Mishmoret u-mezonot yeladim*" [Custody and maintenance for children]. In *Maʿmad ha-'isha ba-ḥevra uva-mishpaṭ* [Women's status in Israeli law and society], edited by Frances Raday, Carmel Shalev, and Michal Liban-Kooby, pp. 534–45. Tel Aviv: Schoken, 1995.

Zakhālka, Iyād. "*Maʿmad batei ha-din ha-sharʿiyim be-qerev ha-tzibur ha-ʿaravi*" [The Arab public view on the status of the sharīʿa courts]. In *Miʿuṭim muslemiyim be-mdinot rov lo-muslemi: Ha-Tenuʿa ha-islamit be-yisra'el ke-miqre mivḥan* [Muslim minorities in non-Muslim majority countries: The Islamic movement in Israel as a test case], edited by Elie Rekhess and Arik Rudnitzky, pp. 85–98. Tel Aviv: Moshe Dayan Center, Tel Aviv University, 2011

Zakhālka, Iyād. "*Zehut batei ha-din ha-sharʿiyim be-yisra'el*" [The identity of the sharīʿa courts in Israel]. In *Le-nochaḥ beit ha-din ha-sharʿi. Tahalichei shinuy be-maʿamadan shel nashim muslemiyot be-yisra'el uva-mizraḥ ha-tichon* [Facing the Sharīʿa Court: Transformation in the Status of Muslim Women in Israel and the Middle East], edited by Liat Kozma, pp. 75–96. Tel Aviv: Resling, 2011.

Periodicals

Abou Ramadan, Moussa. "Judicial Activism of the *Shariʿah* Appeals Court in Israel (1994–2001): Rise and Crisis". *Fordham International Journal* 27 (2003): 254–98.

———. "The Transition from Tradition to Reform: The *Shariʿa* Appeals Court Rulings on Child Custody (1992–2001)". *Fordham International Journal* 26 (2003): 594–655.

Cardinal, Monique C. "Islamic Legal Theory Curriculum: Are the Classics Taught Today?" *Islamic Law and Society* 12, no. 2 (2005): 224–72.

Gardet, L., "Allāh". *The Encyclopaedia of Islam*, 2nd ed. I: 406–17.

———. "ʿIlm al-Kalām". *The Encyclopaedia of Islam*, 2nd ed. III: 1141–50.

Hofri-Winogradow, Adam S. "A Plurality of Discontent: Legal Pluralism, Religious Adjudication and the State". *Journal of Law and Religion* 26, no. 1 (2010): 57–89.

Layish, Aharon. "The Muslim *Waqf* in Israel". *Asian and African Studies* 2 (1966): 41–76.

———. "*Qāḍīs* and *Shariʿa* in Israel". *Asian and African Studies* 7 (1971): 237–72.

———. "Shariʿa u-minhag ba-mishpaḥa ha-muslemit be-yisraʾel" [Shariʿa and custom in the Muslim family in Israel]. *Hamirah Hehadash* 13, no. 4 (1974): 337–409.

———. "The Transformation of the Shariʿa from Jurists' Law to Statutory Law in the Contemporary Muslim World". *Die Welt des Islams* 44, no. 1 (2004): 85–112.

———. "Adaptation of a Jurists' Law to Modern Times in an Alien Environment: The *Shariʿa* in Israel". *Die Welt des Islams* 46, no. 2 (2006): 168–222.

———. "Islamization of Custom as Reflected in Awards of Tribal Arbitrators in the Judaean Desert". *Jerusalem Studies in Arabic and Islam* 35 (2008): 285–334.

Layish, Aharon, and Avshalom Shmueli. "Custom and *Shariʿa* in the Bedouin Family according to Legal Documents from the Judaean Desert". *Bulletin of the School of Oriental and African Studies* 42, no. 1 (1979): 29–45.

Libson, Gideon. "ʿUrf 1. The Status of Custom in Islamic law". *Encyclopaedia of Islam*, 2nd ed. X: 887–88.

March, Andrew F. "Sources of Moral Obligation to non-Muslims in the 'Jurisprudence of Muslim Minorities' (*fiqh al-aqalliyyāt*)". *Islamic Law and Society* 16, no. 1 (2009): 34–94.

Meron, Yaʾakov. "Women's Equal Rights (A Muslim Solution)". *Israel Law Review* 7 (1972): 315–18.

———. "Ribuy nashim la-muslemim ve-ḥuqatiyut isuro" [Polygamy for the Muslims and the constitutionality of its prohibition]. *Mishpatim* 3 (1973): 515–19.

———. "*Yaḥasei mamon bein benei zug muslemin*" [Property relations between Muslim spouses]. ʿIyunei Mishpaṭ 3 (1973): 279–301.

———. "Din shtuqi ba-mishpaṭ ha-muslemi" [The law of the illegitimate child in Islamic law]. *Hapraklit* 43 (1997): 407–15

Rapoport, Yossef. "Legal Diversity in the Age of *Taqlīd*: The Four Chief *Qāḍīs* under the Mamluks". *Islamic law and Society* 10, no. 2 (2003): 210–28.

Sezgin, Yüksel. "A Political Account for Legal Confrontation between State and Society: The Case of Israeli Legal Pluralism". *Studies in Law, Politics, and Society* 32 (2004): 199–235.

Shahar, Ido. "Legal Pluralism and the Study of *Sharīʿa* Courts". *Islamic Law and Society* 15, no. 1 (2008): 112–41.

Shapiro, Ron. "Higiʿa ha-ʿet le-sulḥa" [The time is ripe for ṣulḥa]. *Hapraklit* 48 (2006): 433–58.

Tsafrir, Nurit. "Arab Customary Law in Israel: Ṣulḥa Agreements and Israeli Courts". *Islamic Law and Society* 13, no. 1 (2006): 76–98.

Tyan, Emile. "ʿAdl". *The Encyclopaedia of Islam*, 2nd ed., I: 209–10.

Vogel, Frank E. "Siyāsa, 3. In the Sense of Siyāsa Sharʿiyya", *The Encyclopaedia of Islam*, 2nd ed., IX: 694–96.

Watt, W. Montgomery. "ʿAḳīda". *The Encyclopaedia of Islam*, 2nd ed., I: 333–36.

Dissertations

Nave, Immanuel. "*Yesum ha-shariʿa be-ʿarkaʾot ezraḥiyot ba-meʾa ha-ʿesrim: Meḥqar hashwaʾati lefi pesiqa be-ʿinyenei maʿamad ʾishi u-waqf shel muslemim be-medina muslemit (mitzrayim) uve-medina lo muslemit (yisraʾel)*" [Application of the sharīʿa in civil courts in the twentieth century: A comparative study based on decisions of civil courts in matters of personal status and waqf of Muslims in a Muslim state (Egypt) and in a non-Muslim state (Israel)]. PhD dissertation, The Hebrew University of Jerusalem, 1997.

Shahar, Ido. "Falasṭinim be-veit din yisraʾeli: Tarbut, sheliṭa ve-hitnagdut be-veit ha-din ha-shariʿ be-maʿarav yerushalayim" [Palestinians in an Israeli court: Culture, domination and resistance in the Sharīʿa Court in West Jerusalem]. MA thesis, Faculty of Social Sciences, The Hebrew University of Jerusalem, 2000.

———. "Practicing Islamic Law in a Legal Pluralistic Environment: The Changing Face in Muslim Court in Present-Day Jerusalem". PhD dissertation, Ben Gurion University of the Negev, Beʿer Sheva, 2006.

12

The Road to Democracy Goes through Religious Pluralism: The Indonesian Case and Thoughts on Post-Mubarak Egypt

Giora Eliraz

A significant key for understanding the successful transition to democracy in Indonesia, home to the largest Muslim community in the world, is a long-standing tradition of pluralism, to use modern terms. This tradition is well-anchored in the highly diverse society of Indonesia, that has roots in local Hindu-Buddhist cultures that contain pluralistic motifs.[1] Remarkably, pluralistic motifs have not left Islam untouched in Indonesia. According to Robert W. Hefner, the people of the Indonesian archipelago have long grappled with what social theorists today often regard as a uniquely modern issue — cultural pluralism. Thus, for centuries intellectual and organizational pluralism have been a distinctive feature of Indonesian Islam and there were diverse ideas and religious views about the way to be a good Muslim in the Malay-Indonesian world.[2] The distinctive narrative of Islam's introduction to the Indonesian archipelago also provides insights for understanding the nature of Islam there. Formative earlier periods of this narrative, starting around the fourteenth century, are intimately connected with mystical, spiritual Sufi traditions, known for religious tolerance and an inclusive pluralistic approach. In addition, whereas the historical breakthrough of Islam was largely marked by a use of force, the process of Islamization in Indonesia and the neighbouring region was carried out largely in a peaceful way;[3] maritime traders, Sufi teachers and Sufi orders (*tarikats*), as well as marriage of foreign Muslims to native women and conversion of court circles, played an essential role in this process. Hence, the spread of Islam in Southeast Asia, according to A.H. Johns, was "hesitant, modest and discreet" and "what was achieved in one century in the Middle East took virtually a millennium in Southeast Asia".[4] Indeed, not rarely, pluralistic values were seriously ignored and violated throughout the history of Indonesia. Notwithstanding this, a considerable resistibility of these values has enabled numerous cultures, ethnic groups, religions, social communities and language groupings to tighten together and become one nation that has survived the storms of history. Pluralistic values have also navigated Indonesia to democracy.*

Religious Pluralism: Terminology and Concepts

The concept of religious pluralism per se has been in use for less than a century, but its seeds go back to the European and American contexts of the early eighteenth century. Growing awareness of religious diversity pushed communities on to a long path of development, gradually moving from limited improvements in the rights of religious minorities towards religious pluralism based on equal rights. Varied concepts have been drawn into this process. Consequently, religious pluralism has become an ambiguous concept that is often used incorrectly as a synonym for other concepts such as religious tolerance and religious diversity.[5] Ronald Massanari argues that understanding of the term *religious pluralism* depends in part on what is meant by *religious*, and its ambiguity is also caused by various interpretations of the term *pluralism*.[6] According to Diana L. Eck, pluralism is but one of several responses to diversity and modernity. She seeks to define pluralism by first explaining what pluralism is not. First, pluralism is not the sheer fact of plurality, since it requires active engagement with it. Similarly, it is not the mere recognition of different religious traditions and ensuring their legitimate rights, since it requires positive engagement with claims of religious diversity and efforts to understand difference through dialogue. Second, pluralism is not simply tolerance that does nothing to remove ignorance of one another. Tolerance enables coexistence, but in contrast to pluralism it neither requires new knowledge nor invites understanding or any new creation. Tolerance is even another expression of privilege, since if one is in a position to allow someone to do something he also has the prerogative to keep them from doing it. Third, pluralism is not simply relativism, though there are similarities, since relativism assumes a stance of openness, whereas pluralism assumes both openness and commitment; however, there are relativists who deny the very heart of any religious truth. Fourth, pluralism is not syncretism. Whereas syncretism is the creation of a new religion by fusing elements of different traditions, pluralism is based on respect for differences.[7]

Chad Meister points to an interchangeable use of religious diversity and religious pluralism in discussions about the variety and multiplicity of religions, while in other times they have had very different meanings. For example, religious diversity is often used to refer to significant differences of belief among religious adherents with respect to doctrinal, social, or political matters and religious practice. As to religious pluralism, it is often used to denote an acceptance and encouragement of diversity or a view that salvation or liberation can be found in all of the great world religions.[8] Martin E. Martin, who also notes that religious diversity has acquired religious pluralism as a kin, suggests to separate diversity and pluralism for the sake of clearness and efficiency.[9] He illustrates the difference between the two by saying, among other things, "To be told that there is much diversity within a nation or region need inspire no more than a reaction such as 'Wow! That's a lot of variety,' or 'So what?'". But to "speak of 'pluralism' and you venture to a terrain in which people have thought about what to do about diversity."[10] According to Mark Silk, religious pluralism is understood as a social norm and cultural construct rather than a mere synonym for religious diversity that puts all religions on an equal footing vis-a-vis the state.[11]

Religious Pluralism and the Indonesian Polity:
The Sukarno and Soeharto Eras

Indonesia's declaration of independence in August 1945 was preceded by intense debate, the roots of which go back to the 1930s, between secular nationalists who wanted to establish the new state on a secular foundation and Islamic activists who wanted to establish it as an Islamic state based on sharia, the Islamic law. The secular nationalists won; the new Indonesian state, populated mainly by Muslims, has adopted a secular oriented ideology, the Pancasila ("The Five Principles"), that is often described as a religiously neutral one. Its first principle, "Belief in the One and Only God", treats equally all five recognized religions: Islam, Catholicism, Protestantism, Hinduism and Buddhism. About six decades later, Confucianism, known locally as *Agama Khonghucu*, also received recognition as an official religion. Accordingly, the Constitution of 1945 avoided setting Islam as a state religion, and its article 29 affirms "the state is based upon the belief in the One and Only God". This article provides to all "the right to worship according to his or her own religion or belief". Even seven words that required Muslims to observe the Islamic law, *dengan kewajiban menjalankan syariat Islam bagi pemeluk- pemeluknya* ("with the obligation for adherents of Islam to follow sharia") were removed at the last moment from the preamble to the Constitution, known as the Jakarta Charter (*Piagam Jakarta*).[12] As a response to the reality of a highly diverse society, the forefathers of the Indonesian state sought a philosophical and legal formula that would enable peaceful coexistence and secure national unity and territorial integrity. For this purpose they also adopted *Bhinneka Tunggal Ika* ("unity in diversity") as the national motto.[13] The concept of tolerance seems to largely dominate the early state discourse on religious and cultural diversity; the modern egalitarian concept of religious pluralism per se was then rather new. Nevertheless, aspects of religious pluralism can be found in the foundations of the Indonesian state, or, as Nadirsyah Hosen says, by not referring to any particular belief, article 29 in the Constitution of 1945 "deals with religious pluralism, autonomy and freedom of religion".[14]

From the outset the foundations of the new state faced strong opposition from Islamists who did not want to give up the vision of an

Islamic state based on sharia. The central government even encountered in the period 1948–62 a serious armed struggle by Islamist militias. This bloody chapter entered into the national narrative as the Darul Islam rebellions. The omission of the "seven words" from the preamble of the Constitution also served as a bone of contention with Islamist groups.[15] Islamist opposition, both violent and non-violent, and political manifestations of Islam were opposed by the government

Seeking to strengthen its legitimacy and to advance the progress of modernization, Soeharto's New Order government (1966–98) campaigned strongly for the Pancasila. The government declared Pancasila as the source for all legal principles[16] and made efforts to further enforce it, including by demanding the main Muslim organizations recognize it as their "sole foundation" (asastunggal). The two largest and most significant Muslim organizations, Nahdlatul Ulama (NU) and Muhammadiya, made such recognition during the 1980s.

A considerable tailwind to Pancasila was provided by Islamic neo-modernism, a liberal Islamic movement that emerged in Indonesia in the late 1960s and early 1970s. The neo-modernists, who came from a younger generation of Muslim intellectuals, asked to connect Islamic doctrine and thought with basic liberal themes. They hoped in this way to find an outlet from the unresolved conflict between the secular-oriented worldview of the ruling elites and the Islamist worldview. Believing that reconciliation between the state and Islam could be found by reforming the theological approach, they suggested *ijtihad*, independent theological reasoning, as an alternative to the traditional blind imitation, *taqlid*. They hoped it would enable the contextualization of a theological interpretation appropriate to the contemporary circumstances and particularities of Indonesia. The neo-modernists were not the first to promote *ijtihad* in Indonesia; they were preceded by the Islamic modernist movement whose conceptual roots come mainly from the Egyptian Muhammad 'Abduh (1849–1905). Inspired also by 'Abduh, the neo-modernists justified applying human judgment and reason to theological interpretations by saying that *ijtihad* would not affect the transcendent teachings of Islam but only its mundane realm. According to them the holistic nature of Islam neither requires the mixing of divine values and profane state matters nor the regulation of every aspect of life by religion. Rather, Islam should provide moral values that serve as guidelines for human life, and its implementation should be done culturally, not politically. Hence, the concept of "cultural Islam" should replace "political Islam". Nurcholish Madjid (1939–2005), who was among the prominent forefathers of neo-modernism in Indonesia, also called for the secularization of worldly issues instead of viewing them as transcendental. His statement, "Islam Yes Partai Islam No" ("Islam yes, Islamic party no") has become a significant motto. The neo-modernist movement accepted Pancasila as the basis of the Indonesian polity and denied demands to establish Indonesia as an Islamic state. The Pancasila was presented as the best political formula for Indonesia since it also supplies an ideal blueprint for the non-sectarian identity of the state by assuring harmonious relations among all faiths. The neo-modernists granted a religious-historical legitimacy to the Pancasila by saying that it ought to be considered in a similar light to the Medina Charter, the contract that was signed by the Prophet Muhammad, Jews, Christians and polytheists. The Medina Charter, which granted Muslims the right to rule in Medina, is said to consider all inhabitants of Medina as members of a single *umma* (in a sense of political community) and to guarantee rights for non-Muslims. It was therefore argued by the neo-modernists that the Medina Charter was a relevant model for Indonesia, with its suggestion of a genuine spirit of religious pluralism and freedom of religion within an Islamic context. The neo-modernists also played a pioneering role in promoting the concept of religious pluralism in the Islamic and national discourse; it was an important idea for them, connected as it was with their democratic values. Interestingly, their commitment to the notion of religious pluralism served the interests of the Soeharto regime to shape a pluralistic society founded on religious cooperation and harmony. Indeed, the meeting of interests between them and the regime facilitated the propagation of their progressive ideas and enabled them, though being an elitist intellectual circle, to have significant impact. Ironically, the neo-modernists contributed to developments that eventually led Indonesia to democracy and the end of Soeharto's regime. For example, they were instrumental in constructing a massive and robust civil society, a process that was largely sustained by the considerable growth of a new middle class and an increase in the size of the private sector due to rapid economic growth, including an accelerated process of urbanization. Wider circles in the Muslim mainstream, salient among them leaders and activists of the NU and Muhammadiyah, shared efforts to strengthen civil society, including by establishing non-governmental organizations (NGOs), inspired by pluralistic, democratic ideals. The fact that Abdurrahman Wahid, the charismatic leader of the NU and one of the forefathers of the neo-modernist movement, became in 1999 the first democratically elected president, illustrates the straight line that leads from this elitist intellectual movement to the transition to democracy. [17]

Growing openness from the Muslim mainstream since the 1980s to progressive ideas, including pluralism, also manifested in the case of Islamic resurgence. The Islamic resurgence in the Middle East and elsewhere in the Islamic world that began in the late 1960s was closely connected with growing pietism and the strengthening of Islamic conservatism, as well as with the increasing power of political Islam, fundamentalism, Islamic radicalism and militancy. The Islamic resurgence in Indonesia began in the late 1970s and caused more Muslims to turn to devout observations of religious duties and to an orthodox way of life. It was followed, however, by only limited manifestations, relatively speaking, of political Islam and Islamic extremism. It was even marked by a high degree of tolerance, and exposed Muslims, mainly from within the urban middle class, to ideals of Islamic liberalism, including religious pluralism.[18] As Robert W. Hefner put it, "Unlike some of its Middle Eastern counterparts, however, a key feature of this revival [in Indonesia] has been the emergence of an intellectually vital and politically influential community of liberal, or, ... 'civil pluralist' Muslims".[19] The Islamic resurgence in Indonesia also caused an increasing popularity of Sufism, known for its inclusive and pluralistic approach. It has even expanded beyond its traditional popular and rural space to include educated urban sectors, whereas the Islamic resurgence in the Middle East was largely scripturalist in its nature, and as such tended to reject Sufi traditions as idolatrous innovations.[20]

Programmes of mass education, which began to be implemented in late 1960s, supported Soeharto's government in promoting the state ideology. The official curriculum of religious studies, incorporated from elementary school to university, was instrumental in this purpose. A significant role in promoting religious pluralistic values has been played for years by the prestigious and influential network of Islamic institutions for higher education, known as Institut Agama Islam Negeri

(IAIN; "State Institutes of Islamic Religion").[21] These institutes were reformed during the 1970s. The reformed curriculum exposed students to various Islamic schools of law and theology, to other religions and to the modern sciences. The students have also been encouraged to synthesize classical Islamic studies with modern critical approaches, and to support *ijtihad* for finding solutions to modern questions. [22]

This accumulation of developments since the 1970s caused religious pluralist values to go hand-in-hand with the formation of a strong Muslim civil society inspired by progressive ideas, including pluralism, human rights, democracy and gender equality. In the final years of the New Order these ideas became central themes for Muslim activists, the driving force of the democratic shift. It is rather distinctive that reform-minded Muslims, not secular nationalists as is usually the case elsewhere, have proved to be the largest audience for democratic and pluralistic ideals in Indonesia.[23]

The Reformasi Era and the Issue of Religious Pluralism

The early years of Indonesia's transition to democracy were marked by deep political uncertainty and turmoil. The disappearance of the authoritarian regime unleashed long-suppressed radical Islamist trends, sectarian passions and separatist aspirations. Serious doubts prevailed then about the survival of the secular-oriented polity and the future of democracy. Nevertheless, in the first democratic elections of 1999 the majority voted for political parties of secular, national-oriented ideology. The parliamentary elections of 2004, 2009 and 2014 proved that it was not an ephemeral voting pattern.

The democratic era has offered other indicators for the support given within the Muslim mainstream to the basic axioms of the Indonesian polity, including religious pluralism. It was significantly manifested in the intensive debate on sharia between 1999 and 2002. Soon after the fall of Soeharto, Islamist groups sought to revive their long-suppressed ambition to make Islam the basis of the state (*dasar negara*) by calling for an amendment to the preamble to the 1945 Constitution. But the majority of political parties opposed this. Consequently the debate shifted to the status of sharia in the body of the Constitution. Sharia groups saw the inclusion of the "seven words" in article 29 as the proper way to give Islamic law a significant role. But the parliament, the People's Consultative Assembly (Majelis Permusyawaratan Rakyat; MPR), rejected this in 2002.[24] This decision was backed by both the NU (with an estimated membership of over 40 million) and Muhammadiyah (with an estimated membership of over 30 million). However, within the ranks of Muhammadiyah (and even of the NU, considered to be less conservative and more inclusive) there seem to be many who wish to see sharia as the foundational law of the state.[25] Due to the little support they received at the national level, the pro-sharia groups turned their efforts to applying Islamic law at provincial and district levels. This move, known as PERDA Syar'ah (*Peraturan Daerah syari'ah*; sharia bylaws), has been facilitated by a decentralization policy initiated by the government mainly aimed at responding to long-standing anti–central government sentiments, especially in the Outer Islands.[26] Thus, Islamists have used the decentralization policy for promoting sharia-inspired regulations or laws at the local level. They include, for example, ordering an Islamic dress code and banning alcohol and practices that are considered to deviate from Islam. Advocates of this move also support it in the name of democratic freedom and even implicitly in the name of legal pluralism. Its opponents see the sharia-inspired regulations or bylaws that have been enacted as a threat to state neutrality on religious matters, the unitary state, democracy, pluralism, rights of non-Muslim and to the entire spirit of the Pancasila. [27]

In Reformasi Indonesia, both government and civil society organizations try to advance, to a certain degree, a concept of pluralism, including religious pluralism. This has been triggered by a growing understanding that pluralism is essential for Indonesia in order to facilitate negotiations between various parties, for building democracy and for countering the doctrines of emerging Islamic political parties and the growing manifestations of intolerance caused by extremist groups.[28] In a speech he gave in April 2010, then president Susilo Bambang Yudhoyono said, "Regardless of how one defines that elusive term 'democracy', and no matter what political model you embrace, I have no doubt that, in our time, the future belongs to those who are willing to responsibly embrace pluralism, openness, and freedom."[29] It should be noted that the incumbent president, Joko Widodo, known as Jokowi, who took office in October 2014, reached his presidential position with the credentials of a champion of true religious diversity and plurality. The fact that he is the first Indonesian president not to have emerged from the traditional leading elites has also sustained hopes for improving the process of democratization and strengthening pluralism.

The growing understanding in post-Soeharto Indonesia — by both the central government and the mainstream Muslim organizations — about the importance of protecting religious plurality and the strong link between it and the process of democratization, has been partly followed by action. Thus, for example, the government has shown increasing determination and effectiveness in fighting terror, carried out by fanatics motivated by hatred of the "other". The government and mainstream Muslim organizations also cooperate in encouraging interfaith dialogue and understanding and in waging a war of ideas against extreme religious doctrines. Significant attention is given to the *pesantren* (Islamic boarding schools), which have often been reported by the world media as being infiltrated by fanatic doctrines. Experts argue that only a very tiny minority of *pesantren* have been affected by extremist teachings and interpretations.[30] And it seems that the light cast on the *pesantren* has led to growing understanding in Indonesia of the need to reform and modernize their curricula and to contain the diffusion of radical perspectives. This has had the benefit of making students more resistant to such perspectives and has trained them as emissaries of a moderate brand of Islam, with a strengthened loyalty to the Pancasila and to values of tolerance and pluralism. Perhaps the increasing shockwaves from Salafi jihadism in the Middle East has sharpened understanding even further of both government and civil society of the need to struggle against ideologies that promote hatred of the "other".

A particularly determined call for religious pluralism is coming from the circles of liberal Islam that emerged in the democratic era in response to the growing assertiveness of Islamic radicalism. But though its activists have absorbed many ideas of neo-modernism, their circumstances are less favourable, paradoxically, to those in which the neo-modernists functioned during the Soeharto era. This is largely due to the growing presence of extreme Islamist groups in the public sphere and to the controversial image that liberal Islamic circles have within the Muslim mainstream; they are accused for example of being too sympathetic to the Western agenda, of harbouring the misapprehension that everything is open to interpretation, and for not being in keeping with mainstream Islamic thought.[31] Liberal Islamic circles have even met opposition from the Indonesian Ulama Council (Majelis Ulama Indonesia; MUI), considered to be the country's highest Islamic authority. In July 2005 the MUI issued a fatwa declaring that pluralism, secularism and religious liberalism contradict the teachings of Islam and that the Islamic community of believers (*umat Islam*) is forbidden to follow these doctrines.[32] Significant figures from within the Muslim mainstream criticized the fatwa, arguing among other things that religious pluralism is needed to maintain diversity and plurality within society. Yet, support for this fatwa was also expressed within mainstream Muslim circles. The MUI explained its move by saying that the fatwa was not aimed at eliminating tolerance, mutual understanding and cooperation among the followers of different religions but rather a ban on the concept that pluralism indicates all religions are the same and that the ultimate truth is available in all religions. Such a perception, according to the MUI, is not compatible with Islamic teachings, which assert that Islam is the true religion that completes and revises previous religions.[33]

Indeed, though there has been increasing understanding of the significance of religious tolerance and pluralism, plurality in the Reformasi era faces severe challenges. There have even been doubts expressed, both within and outside Indonesia, as to whether the country represents a successful model of democracy in an Islamic context. Thus, though the authorities have proved in recent years to be effective in preventing major terrorist attacks by militant Muslim groups, such groups, strongly inspired by a hatred of the "other", are still active. The permission given to Aceh in the early days of the post-Soeharto era to establish a system of sharia as an adjunct to the national civil and criminal law as part of the special autonomy the province was granted, has led to it enacting a number of Islamic bylaws. These bylaws are often harshly enforced by hardliner "morals police" and they have been criticized for discriminating against women and for increasing religious intolerance. Similarly, the advances of local sharia-inspired bylaws in other parts of the archipelago have often been criticized for going against pluralism, democratic freedom and the rights of women and minorities. Also salient are the manifestations of intolerance by hard-line Islamists, mainly against Christians, the Ahmadi community, whose beliefs are considered heretical by many Indonesian Muslims, and Shiites, considered by many hardliners to be followers of a deviant sect. The government, that fights decisively against terrorists who are also inspired by a hatred towards the "other", faces criticism for not being similarly decisive in suppression of religious intolerance. Also, Indonesia's huge middle class, whose great majority is believed to support religious tolerance, is argued to avoid taking sufficient concrete actions against religious intolerance.

Indeed, Indonesia's democracy is not yet fully fledged and still has significant shortcomings. Nevertheless, no one can deny the considerable distance Indonesia has covered in its democratic journey since 1998. A useful comparison is the case of Egypt, the most suitable from among the Arab Spring countries methodologically. Such a comparison affords a balanced perspective for understanding what has been achieved in the Reformasi era in Indonesia. It also offers significant insight on the future for democracy in post-Mubarak Egypt.

Egypt and the Democratic Path: Vagueness and Difficult Questions

Egypt has played a significant role in the narrative of Islam in Indonesia, in particular since the late nineteenth century, mainly by transmitting ideas and knowledge, in an Islamic context, through varied channels. For example, generations of young seekers of knowledge from the Indonesian archipelago moved to Egypt to study, most of them at Al-Azhar University in Cairo. Studying in Egypt also offered the unique opportunity of experiencing the complex political developments and of exposure to varied streams of thoughts and fervent ideological conflicts and debates.

When the revolution of 25 January 2011 erupted, the few thousand Indonesian students in Egypt could witness with their own eyes the first formative and decisive days of the dramatic shift.

The author of this chapter raised then the possibility that some of them might feel a sort of national pride while being caught amid protests, violence and anarchy; their country, that is often described as a remote periphery of the Islamic world, had already succeeded in developing many attributes of a consolidated democracy. At the same time I also noted that perhaps the events in Egypt and the manifestations of religious intolerance at home would further strengthen their belief in the need for Indonesia to move further towards the goal of becoming a fully fledged democracy.[34]

Indeed, a comparison of the experiences of Indonesia and Egypt offer much food for thought. Like Indonesia, Egypt is a large country, a significant regional actor, and home to a dominant Sunni majority. Similarly, but more than a decade later than Indonesia, Egypt experienced a popular uprising, triggered mainly by middle-class circles against an authoritarian regime, headed also by an ex-general who had ruled for about three decades. Interestingly, Indonesia's experience with democracy had been considered to a certain degree a worthy case for study in the earlier period of post-Mubarak Egypt, of particular relevance due to the significant hurdles the country had to surmount in order to achieve it. Thus, a dialogue has developed between political activists, NGOs, academics and media professionals of the two countries, who seek to examine the applicability of lessons derived from Indonesia's transition to democracy for the Egyptian context.[35]

Attempts to predict the future of democracy for Egypt entails peering through thickening mist at a great number of variables. Religious pluralism is just one of these variables, but the Indonesian case indicates its distinctive added value to the democratic equation. Taking a panoramic view of Indonesia from the 1970s onwards provides a perspective on the nation's successful transition to democracy; the issue of religious pluralism is salient in this context. Taking a parallel comparative view of Egypt for the same period, focusing on the axes of Islam, politics and society, provides significant insights into the future of democracy for the post-Mubarak era; the issue of religious pluralism is also involved in such thinking.

Among the incentives that led to the Islamic resurgence in Egypt from the late 1960s were economic distress, chronic poverty, a high rate of unemployment, widespread corruption, the luxurious lifestyles of the elite, a malfunctioning of the central authorities in regard to economics and social welfare, and disillusion with the ideological myth of secular Arab nationalism. These circumstances, along with the growing pietism triggered by the Islamic resurgence, facilitated efforts by Islamist groups to recruit members and gain popular sympathy. Young educated people in particular were receptive to the message of these groups, which provided clearly defined answers and goals, feelings of solidarity, a sense of belonging, and charismatic leaders. The Muslim Brotherhood (MB), a deeply rooted and well-organized mass movement, greatly benefited from this state of affairs. Whereas extremist groups were motivated to wage jihad against the "infidel" (*kafir*) regime, from the 1970s the MB adopted a pragmatic approach to advance their formative goal of establishing what it perceives as true Islamic society based on sharia. It also gradually showed ideological moderation, including by expressing support for democracy. Though banned from establishing its own party, it successfully used the limited channels for political participation and representation that existed under the then multi-party system, including making alliances with other opposition parties and having its members run for parliament independently. Eventually it positioned itself as the leading opposition force. But it never abandoned the significant Islamist idea that the sharia, rather than any man-made law, is the supreme law that establishes the entire codes of behaviour for the *umma*, the community of believers. Its long-standing slogan, *Al-Islam huwa al-hal* ("Islam is the solution"), epitomizes this perception, which also denies the separation of state from religion. Obviously, the ambivalent rhetoric of the MB, including the contradictions between its declared commitment to democracy and its strong loyalty to Islamist perceptions, caused secular liberals in Mubarak's Egypt to be highly suspicious of it.[36]

Largely unobserved, another Islamist actor has been growing gradually since the 1970s: the Salafis. With their focus on strict personal piety, they turned away from politics, negated opposition to the ruler and even criticized the MB for its engagement in politics. At the same time they actively preached strict puritan perceptions among the lower and middle classes, on university campuses and the city streets, and developed strong grass-roots networks among numerous mosques and organizations across the country. In this way they hoped to establish the lives of Muslims along strict Islamic laws.[37] The group kept a very low political profile during the early dramatic stages of the revolution;

it was not until the ouster of Mubarak that they made the shift to become a declared political actor.

At the opposite side of the ideological spectrum are the secular liberal circles. The ideas of the European Enlightenment and liberal philosophy have inspired generations of educated Egyptians. This process is strongly connected with Western cultural influences on Muslim lands and societies. Liberal thought increasingly diffused into Egyptian intellectual discourses in the first decades of the twentieth century, enriching them with ideas and concepts such as democracy, gender equality and rationalism. These ideas challenged traditional concepts, perceptions and institutions. Thus, modern Western perceptions of politics, including the separation of the state from religion, challenged basic Islamic axioms related to politics and modes of governance.[38] In the first half of the twentieth century, Egypt even experienced a sort of political pluralism; in 1923 a multi-party constitutional monarchy was established. Liberal ideas on politics and society continued to be expressed in the years preceding World War II, though the power of the parliament was noticeably undermined from the early 1930s and the power of the king increased.[39] Eventually, with the military coup of 1952, the multi-party constitutional monarchy ceased to exist. Nevertheless, liberal voices did not disappear during the almost sixty years of the authoritarian regime. The increasing power of the Islamists did not deter certain intellectuals from calling for Egypt to be established with a secular identity and a Western-style democracy and from bitterly debating with the Islamists over whether the legal system should be derived from sharia or from secular legal tradition.[40] But the secular liberals were a secondary actor compared to the growing presence of the Islamists, with their increasingly vociferous oppositional role, despite the regime's efforts to oppress them.

Into the polarized discourse of this period of Egypt's history another voice began to emerge — a call to reconciliation between a commitment to Islamic principles and progressive democratic values. It was the emerging voice of Hizb al-Wasat, commonly known as the Al-Wasat Party (Center Party). The party was founded in 1996 by a group of activists who broke away from the Muslim Brotherhood. This group embraced progressive democratic values such as political pluralism, the alternation of power, equal citizenship, equality between men and women, human rights and political pluralism. Theologically, the group, a sort of political association, believes that sharia should be considered a living entity that interacts with all aspects of life; therefore, a compatibility between modern values and Islam can be achieved through dynamic re-interpretation of sharia. The Al-Wasat Party has even opened its door to secular Muslims and non-Muslims. Its impact on the Islamic discourse during the Mubarak era, however, cannot be compared to that of the significant historical role played by such liberal Islamic thought as neo-modernism in Suharto-era Indonesia. The Al-Wasat Party was marginalized by the authoritarian regime and its application for legal status was denied. Significantly, the neo-modernist movement in Indonesia fully accepted the secular-oriented Pancasila as the basis of the Indonesian polity and rejected demands to establish Indonesia as an Islamic state. In this way the movement largely encouraged the ideological acceptance of Pancasila by the Muslim mainstream. Its heritage even encouraged the idea of the separation of state from religion during the post-Soeharto era. In sharp contrast, the political perception of the Al-Wasat Party is firmly anchored in an Islamist framework based on sharia.[41]

The accumulation of differences between the Egyptian and Indonesian political contexts during their respective authoritarian regimes is also illustrated through the narrative of the Egyptian Constitution. Whilst in Indonesia the Islamists' aspirations to see the "seven words" reinstated to the preamble of the Constitution were blocked, constitutional Islamization can be observed in Egypt since the early 1970s. It is the controversial article 2 that clearly highlights this process and attests to the growing power of the Islamists. Egyptian constitutions since 1923, with the exception of the Constitution of 1958, have affirmed Islam as the state religion. In 1971, while suffering a crisis of legitimacy and facing a growing challenge from the Islamists, the Egyptian regime under President Sadat enacted a new constitution. Through an amendment of article 2 the regime hoped to legitimize its law in Islamic terms and thereby appease the Islamists. Thus, in comparison to previous constitutions, article 2 of 1971 goes further in indicating the Islamic nature of the state by stating that "The principles of the Islamic shari'a are a principal source of the legislation." Hoping, presumably, to further appease the Islamists and gain broader support within their ranks, in 1981 Sadat's regime made another concession to them with an additional amendment to article 2: instead of stating that the principles of sharia are merely *a* principal source of the legislation, this time article 2 provides that "the principles of the Islamic *shari'a* are the principal source of the legislation."[42] Further amendments to the 1971 Constitution were made in 2005 and 2007. The revised article 2 — which was strongly defended by the MB — remained unchanged during the Mubarak era.[43] Following the 25 January revolution the 1971 Constitution was suspended by the Supreme Council of the Armed Forces, which ruled soon after Mubarak's ouster. An abbreviated version of this constitution, with some amendments, was ratified by referendum in March 2011. Article 2 was left untouched.[44] This was considered an achievement for the MB and a blow to liberal-oriented circles, the original driving force of the revolution, who hoped the new political era would enhance the idea of the separation of state and religion.

Less than a year later, significant evidence emerged that the Islamists, the MB in particular, were the greatest benefactors of the political upheaval. In the first democratic elections to the People's Assembly (Majlis Al-Sha'ab), the lower house of parliament, held between November 2011 and January 2012, the Islamists gained altogether more than 70 per cent of the votes. The alliance led by the MB party, Hizb al-Hurriyah wal-'Adalah ("Freedom and Justice Party"; FJP), won about 47 per cent and the ultra-conservative Salafi party, Hizb al-Nūr ("The Light Part"), came second with 24 per cent.[45] In Indonesia, parties in support of the national secular agenda together received the majority of votes in all the democratic elections. The sharp contrast in the political landscapes between Indonesia and Egypt is further evidenced by the electoral achievements of the Salafis, that came as a surprise to many — which could not be said about the achievements of the MB in the first democratic elections. Whilst the MB's perceptions of democracy and related concepts may leave space for varied interpretations, the Salafist worldview does not. The Salafis accept democracy as a mechanism only, but strictly deny the basic democratic concept of rule by the people, separation of state and religion, and the idea of human sovereignty and man-made laws.

Shortly after the elections, in mid-June 2012, the newly elected parliament was dissolved based on a ruling of the Supreme

Constitutional Court (SCC) saying that parts of the electoral law were unconstitutional.[46] This ruling, however, did not prevent the MB from again manifesting its power just a few days later; the MB candidate, then the leader of the FJP, Mohammad Mursi, won the presidential elections. In other words, an Islamist was democratically elected as the first civilian president of Egypt. In Indonesia, in sharp contrast, all presidents of the Reformasi era have been explicitly committed to significant liberal perceptions of politics and society, including the separation of the state and religion, religious pluralism and gender equality. Shortly before his nomination as president, Muhammad Mursi said, "My party believes that a woman should not assume the post of president, but I do not mind appointing a woman as my vice-president.... A woman can become prime minister."[47] The democratic political system in Indonesia, in contrast, already enabled a woman, Megawati Sukarnoputri, to be nominated as president in July 2001. This happened despite Islamist circles, from both within and outside the established political arena, publicly rejecting the idea of having a woman president when Megawati led her party, Partai Demokrasi Indonesia-Perjuangan ("Indonesian Democratic Party of Struggle"), to the first parliamentary elections in 1999.

Clear signs of the problematic nature of MB rule over Egypt and of Mursi's presidency soon appeared. Significant indicators started to show up in the second half of 2012, shortly after Mursi took office. Egypt then experienced the controversial process of writing and ratifying, through referendum, a new constitution for the post-Mubarak era. This process epitomized the fragile and polarized nature of the Egyptian political scene. It was also partly interwoven with another controversial event: President Muhammad Mursi's constitutional declaration of November 2012 that granted him near-absolute powers and protected the controversial Islamist-dominated assembly that was drafting the Constitution from dissolution by court, actually making it immune to judicial oversight.[48] These developments met strong opposition and brought back thousands to Tahrir Square in Cairo in protest. The protests were motivated by the fear of a return to a dictatorship, of a full monopoly of power by the MB, and of an Islamist constitution that would seriously oppress civil liberties, women and the rights of non-Muslims.

But the protests did not prevent the approval of the new constitution in December 2012 through a national referendum. Actually, this constitution, which was suspended in July 2013 with the removal of Mursi from power by the military following protests against him and the MB by millions of Egyptians, can be described as more Islamically conservative than any of the previous constitutions of Egypt. Yet it was not much more Islamic than the constitution it replaced, and it was still far from establishing a constitutional foundation for a theocracy. Thus, for example, the controversial article 2, which is considered to be the main article that defines the legal status of Islam in the state, remained unchanged: "Islam is the religion of the state and Arabic its official language. Principles of Islamic *shari'a* are the principal source of legislation."[49] Indeed, the newly added article 219 played in some sense into the hands of ultraorthodox circles by making less vague the phrase "principles of Islamic *shari'a*" in article 2. It was done by the addition of: "[The expression] 'principles of Islamic shari'a' refers to the general methods of juridical argumentation, to fundamental juridical rules and principles, and to the [written] sources recognized by the Sunni juridical schools."[50] It was argued that the purpose of this article was to avoid narrow interpretations of article 2; for example, liberal interpretation, according to which the principles of sharia are synonymous with universal principles such as freedom and equality, or the interpretation given to it by the SCC in 1996, according to which future but not existing legislation must conform only to the parts of sharia whose validity is absolute and that are not disputed by different schools of Islam.[51] At the same time other articles that might be seen as having a certain democratic and liberal colour can also be found. Article 3, for example, expresses tolerance towards members of the monotheistic faiths by saying: "The canon principles of Egyptian Christians and Jews are the main source of legislation for their personal status laws, religious affairs, and the selection of their spiritual leaders."[52] The inclusion of this article was rejected by most Salafi streams but was supported by the MB and Al-Azhar. Article 5 of this constitution states, identically to article 3 in the previous constitution, "Sovereignty is for the people alone and they are the source of authority. The people shall exercise and protect this sovereignty, and safeguard national unity in the manner specified in the Constitution." This statement strongly opposes the fundamental

Islamist perception that sovereignty belongs to God alone. Similarly, article 6 includes the basic democratic principle of equal citizenship by saying that the political system is based also on the principle of "citizenship under which all citizens are equal in rights and duties". Article 33 states: "All citizens are equal before the law. They have equal public rights and duties without discrimination."[53] Nevertheless, even articles and clauses that have outwardly liberal content were criticized, among other things, on the ground that the language used is too vague.[54] The above-mentioned article 3 on religious minorities, for example, was said to meet an objection within the Christian Coptic community, whose members had been increasingly targeted by acts of sectarian violence, though the Coptic Church accepted it. The objection was based mainly on an assumption that the aim of article 3 was to get Copts to agree to article 2 and to enable Muslims to boast of their tolerance towards the Copts, while article 2 actually prevents equality among citizens by stating that Islam is the state religion and the sharia is the principal source of legislation.[55]

The problematic nature of this constitution with respect to the relationship between the state and religion, including the issue of religious pluralism, is not embedded in the text itself but rather in the political context of the time. Amid the controversial process of drafting the constitution, Nathan J. Brown wrote:

> The 2012 constitution will be operating in a very different political context, so that even the step of adopting past language is likely to produce very different results.... Egypt's new constitution will not so much resolve all controversies as it will set up a period of prolonged trench warfare.... Islamist forces are likely to move forward gradually rather than by suddenly capturing the state. This struggle will likely take place over many years, and the outcome will determine what the vague language of the constitution actually means in the lives of ordinary Egyptians.[56]

Thus, for example, though Egypt under Sadat and Mubarak was required to incorporate sharia provisions into the Constitution due mainly to increasing bottom-up pressure from Islamists and the understanding that power legitimacy should also be defined in Islamic terms, the state ideology itself was essentially secular. The SCC then gradually developed an approach for the interpretation of article 2 by establishing Islamic norms to which the state's law must confirm. But at the same time the SCC implicitly gave preference to a rationalist and utilitarian approach in its interpretation of the sharia. Consequently, the court's interpretation is said to preserve and even reinforce liberal constitutional doctrines that it had already developed.[57] Hence, there was enough ground for concern among many Egyptians, until the removal of Mursi from power, that the Islamists, led by the MB, would ask to use both article 2 and article 219 to advance a far-reaching process of Islamization. In other words, the MB, that seemed to be deterred by the strong protests from liberal and secular-oriented circles from going too far with implementation of its Islamist vision by drafting a strictly Islamist constitution, was largely suspected of trying to facilitate an Islamist agenda through the interpretation of the new constitution.

Indeed, MB statements and arguments during the earlier period of the revolution, not to mention during the year in which it ruled the country, sustained such suspicion. In fact, the political wins garnered by the MB urged it, as both an Islamist mass movement and as a party, to placate concerns about its aims and plans. This was done by stressing its commitment to civil democratic ideas, including those of women's rights and rights of minorities, in particular those of Christian Copts, the major religious minority. MB scholars and others, who are not necessarily identified as MB officials and members, have also asked since the early stage of the revolution to ward off fears of theocracy. But the MB tended then to place concepts such as democracy and a civil state in an Islamic framework, including by sustaining and justifying them also by arguing that the ideological and institutional roots lead to formative Islamic perceptions and history. Such an approach seems to be largely anchored in polemical apologetics that have been employed by Muslim thinkers in the Arab world for decades. Painting modern Western-oriented ideas and modes of government in an Islamic colour has enabled Muslim thinkers in the modern era to justify their acceptance by Muslims, to refute an alleged Western ideological "attack" and to deny a superiority of Western civilization by saying that Islam first taught what the West now seeks to teach the Muslims.[58]

Hence, through the ambivalence and ambiguity of MB's rhetoric, it is evident that the movement places democracy in an Islamic framework rather than in a liberal one. Senior MB officials even made it clear after drafting the Constitution of 2012 that they still consider full implementation of sharia to be their end goal, but one to be achieved later once the people's hearts and minds have been gradually attuned to it.[59] In an earlier stage of the revolution, Mursi himself expressed hope that "the Islamic framework can to a great extent control the government and the behaviour of the state in the future".[60] And during the presidential election campaign he promised to implement sharia.[61] Such a view was also evident after he was elected president. According to him, "all agree that the Islamic *sharia* is the constitution that rules all aspects of life. Only what was conveyed in the honourable Koran will be read and only it will be heeded.... [The Koran] will be the basis for all matters pertaining to the general populace — not only Muslims — and to their activities in politics, agriculture, economy and all other fields."[62]

Though certain references to religious tolerance are evident in the Constitution of 2012, there is also ground to question whether the MB, whose ideology exists in an Islamic framework, can respond to the reality of religious diversity, not through a mere patronage perception of religious tolerance but through the paradigm of the modern concept of religious pluralism. The concept of "tolerance" (Arabic, *tasamuh* and *samaha*) in Islamic thinking is mainly related to the treatment and status of non-Muslims in an Islamic state, in a sense of forbearance and in treating the People of the Book (Jews, Christians, and Zoroastrians) in a kindly and forgiving manner. The Arabic word for the modern concept of "pluralism", *ta'adudiyya*, was constructed in the late twentieth century. Since the beginning of its involvement in Egypt's political arena in the 1980s, the MB has given priority to practical politics. Hence, issues related to the interpretation of Islamic law, such as the status of non-Muslims, had for years limited presence in MB discourse and discussions.[63] The secular liberal circles of Egypt, in contrast, discussed both religious and cultural pluralism, considering them necessary for plurality and building democracy. They are therefore involved in discussions in various forums that aim to strengthen pluralistic values as an essential fruit of the new political era.

A couple of years ago a Lebanese political thinker, Radwan al-Sayyid, complained about the decrease in the perception of a bond between democracy and pluralism (ta'dudiyyah) in the Arab world. He noted that the Islamists understand democracy as the rule of the majority; since Muslims are the majority in the entire Arab world, the Islamists support democracy and pursue it, but only as long as the majority of voters are with them. As to pluralism, a foundation of democratic societies, the Islamists only consider it in terms of the "rights of minorities" (huquq al-'aqaliyat) or, as they call it, "particular rights" (imtiyazat). He added that he heard such arguments in Algeria, Morocco and Egypt from people who explained that they have no problem with democracy itself but rather with the concept of pluralism, in particular cultural pluralism (ta'dudiyyah thaqafiyya), "since it means fragmentation of the society as a preparation for creating small countries".[64] Obviously, an Islamist-oriented understanding of religious diversity through a patronage perception of religious tolerance, rather than through the liberal notion of religious pluralism, is prone to be influenced by changing interests and attitudes. It seems that the MB in Egypt shares such an Islamist stance. Rachel M. Scott noted before the Egyptian Arab Spring that some Islamists who accept democracy understand it in terms of majority rule as defined by the Muslim majority, which the Copts must respect. She adds that, for the MB, advocating democracy is an effective political strategy. However, she says, "the problem is that there are doubts about whether this goes beyond the people's right to elect an Islamic system".[65] Her words are certainly more current now than ever.

The end of MB rule in Egypt in July 2013 led to calls for a comprehensive rethinking of the future trajectory for the country. Again, relations between the state and religion and the idea of religious pluralism figure among the complex and significant questions that need to be considered. So far, the Egyptian reality in the post–Mursi era offers only insufficient, vague indicators. Thus, for example, the post–Mursi era Constitution — drafted through a process dominated by non-Islamist figures and approved by referendum in January 2014 — reversed the direction of Islamization that marked the Constitution of 2012. Nevertheless, the Constitution of 2014 reaffirms Islam as the state religion and even leaves unchanged article 2, including the statement that the principles of sharia are the principle source for legislation. However, the Constitution specifies the sole right of the SCC in interpreting the principles of sharia. In addition, the controversial article 219, a clear political achievement for the Islamists in the previous constitution, was omitted, notwithstanding the participation in the drafting process of the ultraconservative Salafist Nour Party that supported the ouster of Mursi.[66]

Moreover, it seems that from the perspective of the Christians in Egypt — the largest religious minority in the country, accounting for an estimated ten per cent of the population — the Constitution of 2014 improves their standing. A black cloud of concern was lifted from the Christians (most of them Copts) with the removal of the MB from power. Prior to July 2013 deep concern prevailed among Christians that the Constitution of 2012 was just the first step in the MB's goal of creating an Islamic state under strict sharia law. It should also be said that the Christians, whose delegates participated in drafting the Constitution of 2014, also expressed satisfaction with article 235 that instructs parliament to issue a law regulating the building and restoration of churches. It is considered the first time that the right to build churches has been guaranteed by the Constitution. At the same time, however, attacks against Christians and their properties, apparently initiated by zealous Islamists, have not entirely ceased.

Certainly, many other variables need to be taken into account when considering the future of democracy in Egypt. Significant among them still is the political role played by the army; in other words, civil–military relations. Indeed, the post-Mursi regime declared from the outset a commitment to lead the country to democracy, laid down a plan for the transition to democracy, and the new Constitution of 2014 defines the state as a democratic republic. At the same time, this constitution strengthened the political power of the armed forces. In the same year, the former army chief, Abdel Fatah al-Sisi, who had led the military intervention of 2013, resigned from the army and won the presidential election. But whilst the Indonesian model of democracy saw a substantial reduction in the involvement of the army in politics, Egypt's current political reality sees the army still playing a pivotal role.

Conclusion

The political landscape of post-Mubarak Egypt is still heavily veiled, and whether the country will complete a transition to democracy remains uncertain. In the current complicated political and economic situation, with wide segments of society facing economic hardship and with feelings of insecurity among religious minorities not fully dissipated, significant segments of society may not place a high priority on democratic values. People in such a situation may place a greater emphasis on a strong, effective, centralized government, hoping to escape poverty and gain feelings of security.

The Indonesian experience clearly indicates that the road to democracy needs a strength of commitment from the leading social forces to survive the crisis of the transitional period and be able to implement progressive democratic values, significant among which is religious pluralism based on a solid egalitarian foundation. Thus, the degree of commitment to religious pluralism by leading civil political actors and by the wider sectors of Egyptian society might be used as a sort of litmus test for learning about democratic advancement in the country. Such observable criteria are necessary due to the vague political reality of Egypt.

Whilst there is still a way to go for Indonesia to become a fully fledged democracy, the comparative view we have discussed here points to the root of the success the country has had in achieving some significant attributes of a consolidated democracy, including a relatively wider consenusus on the importance of religious pluralism. At the same time, this comparative view also provides significant insight into the future of democracy for Egypt. Considering the broader historical perspective, two elements have been salient in facilitating the transition to democracy in Indonesia. The first is the essential role played by what Robert W. Hefner coined "civil pluralist" Muslims, a key distinctive feature of the Islamic resurgence in Indonesia. According to Hefner, "civil pluralist" Muslims "deny the necessity of a formally established Islamic state, emphasize that it is the spirit and not the letter of Islamic law (shari'ah) to which Muslims must attend, stresses the need for programmes to elevate the status of women, and insist that the Muslim world's most urgent task is to develop moral tools to respond to the challenge of modern pluralism."[67] This vital element in Indonesian society, inspired by pluralistic values, was a driving force in the protests against the authoritarian regime and played a significant role in building democracy. The second element is the formative liberal Islamic thought, namely the neo-modernist movement, that during the Soeharto era encouraged the acceptance of progressive, pluralistic concepts by the Muslim mainstream. The advocates of this influential stream of thought also enabled the bridging of the gap between the secular-oriented worldview of the ruling elites — including the national agenda of modernization and development — and an Islamic worldview.

But such vital influential elements are missing in the Egyptian context. Neither massive, organized pluralistic Muslim civil society nor an influential liberal Islamic stream of thought have emerged in Egypt in recent decades. Whilst the earlier stage of the Egyptian Arab Spring of January 2011 and the massive protests of June–July 2013 against MB rule represented an impressive demonstration of the will of the Egyptian people, this does not necessarily point to the existence of a wider civil society inspired by deep pluralistic values with a democratic vision and agenda. In the Indonesia of 1998, the salient slogan of the protestors against the authoritarian regime was *"reformasi"* (reform). This slogan generally indicated, and it still does, the desire for substantial political change; or, more precisely, a democratic direction. But such political sentiments are still missing in Egypt; a significant battle cry chanted by the demonstrators against both Mubarak and Mursi, including his MB movement, was *"irhal"* ("leave", or "go away"). There is ground to think that the battle cry that bound millions of Egyptians together was based first of all on shared rage, frustration and fear, much less on a shared democratic vision.

Hence, perhaps a significant missing link in the narrative of post-Mubarak Egypt is a substantial Muslim pluralistic civil society that can lead the transition to a real democracy. Egypt is still thus largely torn by conflicting political visions and agendas and a basic conceptual polarization between a secularism that is not completely adequate for democracy and Islamism to which many democratic, pluralistic values are extrinsic.

Notes

* This paper takes into account developments until late 2014.

1. For Hindu and Buddhist perspectives on religious diversity, see Arvind Sharma, "A Hindu Perspective", in *The Oxford Handbook of Religious Diversity*, edited by Chad V. Meister (Oxford: Oxford University Press), pp. 309–29; David Burton, "A Buddhist Perspective", in *The Oxford Handbook of Religious Diversity*, edited by Meister, pp. 321–36; Joseph Runzo, "Pluralism and Relativism", in *The Oxford Handbook of Religious Diversity*, edited by Meister, p. 63.

2. Robert W. Hefner, *Civil Islam: Muslims and Democratization in Indonesia* (Princeton: Princeton University Press, 2000), p. 14; Robert W. Hefner, "Modernity and the Challenge of Pluralism: Some Indonesian Lessons", *Studia Islamika* 2, no. 4 (1995): 41; Robert W. Hefner, "Islam in an Era of Nation-States: Politics and Religious Renewal in Muslim Southeast Asia", in *Islam in an Era of Nations-States: Politics and Religious Renewal in Muslim Southeast Asia*, edited by Robert W. Hefner and Patricia Horvatich (Honolulu: University of Hawai'i Press, 1997), p. 29.

3. See Azyumardi Azra, "The Transmission of Islamic Reformism to Indonesia: Networks of Middle Eastern and Malay-Indonesian 'Ulama' in the Seventeenth and Eighteenth Centuries" (PhD dissertation, Columbia University, 1992), p. 18; W.J. Drewes, "New Light on the Coming of Islam to Indonesia?", in *The Propagation of Islam in the Indonesian-Malay Archipelago*, edited by Alijah Gordon (Kuala Lumpur: Malaysian Sociological Research Institute, 2001), pp. 133–34; M.C. Ricklefs, *A History of Modern Indonesia: Since c.1200*, 3rd ed. (Stanford: Stanford University Press, 2001), pp. 17, 36–58.

4. A.H. Johns, "Islam in Southeast Asia", in *The Encyclopedia of Religion*, vol. 7, edited by Mircea Eliade (New York: Macmillan, 1987), p. 406.

5. On religious pluralism, see Chris Beneke, *Beyond Toleration: The Religious Origins of American Pluralism* (Oxford: Oxford University Press, 2006); Martin E. Marty, "Religious Pluralism and Civil Society", *Annals of the American Academy of Political and Social Science* 612 (July 2007): 14–25; Mark Silk, "Defining Religious Pluralism in America: A Regional Analysis", *Annals of the American Academy of Political and Social Science* 612 (July 2007): 64–81; John Bowden, "Religious Pluralism and the Heritage of the Enlightenment", in *Islam and Global Dialogue: Religious Pluralism and the Pursuit of Peace*, edited by Roger Boase (Aldershot, Hants: Ashgate, 2005), pp. 13–20; Diana L. Eck, "Is Our God Listening? Exclusivism, Inclusivism, and Pluralism", in *Islam and Global Dialogue*, Boase, pp. 21–50.

6. Ronald Massanari, "The Pluralism of American 'Religious Pluralism'", *Journal of Church and State* 40, no. 3 (Summer 1998): 589.

7. Eck, *Is Our God Listening? Exclusivism, Inclusivism, and Pluralism*, pp. 41–45. On the difference between religious pluralism and religious relativism, see also Joseph Runzo 2010, pp. 61–76.

8. Chad V. Meister, "Introduction", in *The Oxford Handbook of Religious Diversity*, edited by Chad V. Meister (Oxford: Oxford University Press), pp. 3–4.

9. Martin E. Marty, "Historical Reflections on Religious Diversity", in *The Oxford Handbook of Religious Diversity*, edited by Chad V. Meister (Oxford: Oxford University Press), p. 9.

10. Marty, *Historical Reflections on Religious Diversity*, p. 16.

11. Silk, *Defining Religious Pluralism in America: A Regional Analysis*, pp. 64–65.

12. On the Pancasila and the constitution in the pre-Reformasi era, see Nadirsyah Hosen, *Shariʿa and Constitutional Reform in Indonesia* (Singapore: Institute of Southeast Asian Studies, 2007), pp. 59–80, 194–97; Nadirsyah Hosen, "Religion and Indonesian Constitution: A Recent Debate", *Journal of Southeast Asian Studies* 36, no. 3 (2005): 419–20; Bahatiar Effendy, *Islam and the State in Indonesia* (Singapore: Institute of Southeast Asian Studies, 2003), pp. 13–64; M.B. Hooker, *Indonesian Syariah: Defining a National School of Islamic Law* (Singapore: Institute of Southeast Asian Studies), pp. 5–9; M.B. Hooker, "The State and Shari'a in Indonesia", in *Shariʿa and Politics in Modern Indonesia*, edited by Arskal Salim and Azyumardi Azra (Singapore: Institute of Southeast Asian Studies, 2003), pp. 33–47; Duglas E. Ramage, *Politics in Indonesia: Democracy, Islam and the Ideology of Tolerance* (London: Routledge, 1997), pp. 14–22; Hyung-Jun Kim, "The Changing Interpretation of Religious Freedom in Indonesia", *Journal of Southeast Asian Studies* 29, no. 2 (September 1998): 357–60: Abubakar Eby Hara, "Pancasila and the Perda Syariʿah Debates in the Post-Suharto Era: Toward a New Political Consensus", in *Islam in Contention: Rethinking of State and Islam in Indonesia*, edited by Okamoto Masaaki, Ota Atsushi, and Ahmad Suaedy (Jakarta: Wahid Institute; Kyoto: Center for Southeast Asian Studies; Taipei: Center for Asia-Pacific Area Studies, 2010), pp. 38-40.

13. For the perception of diversity in the Indonesian archipelago through a broader historical perspective, see Anthony Reid, *To Nation by Revolution: Indonesia in the 20th Century* (Singapore: NUS Press, 2010), pp. 198–204.

14. Hosen, *Shariʿa and Constitutional Reform in Indonesia*, p. 194. See also Anis Malik Thoha, "Discourse of Religious Pluralism in Indonesia", *Islam in Asia* 2, no. 2 (December 2005).

15. Hosen, *Religion and Indonesian Constitution: A Recent Debate*, pp. 419–40.

16. See Hooker, *Indonesian Syariah: Defining a National School of Islamic Law*, p. 7.

17. On neo-modernism, see Effendy, *Islam and the State in Indonesia*, pp. 65–123; Bahtiar Effendy, "Islam and the State in Indonesia: Munawir Sjadzali and the Development of a New Theological Underpinning of Political Islam", *Studia Islamika* 2, no. 2 (1995): 97–121; M. Din Syamsuddin, "Islamic Political Thought and Cultural Revival in Modern Indonesia", *Studia Islamika* 2, no. 4 (1995): 47–68; Greg Barton, "Islamic Liberalism and the Prospects for Democracy in Indonesia", in *Democracy in Asia*, edited by Michèle Schmiegelow (New York: St. Martin's Press, 1997), pp. 427–51; Greg Barton, "Neo-Modernism: A Vital Synthesis of Traditionalist and Modernist Islamic Thought in Indonesia", *Studia Islamika* 2, no. 3 (1995): 1–75; Greg Barton, "Indonesia's Nurcholish Madjid and Abdurrahman Wahid as Intellectual 'Ulama': The Meeting of Islamic Traditionalism and Modernism in neo-Modernist Thought", *Studia Islamika* no. 1 (1997): 29–81; Hendro Prasetyo, "Interview with Munawir Sjadazli", *Studia Islamika* 1, no. 1 (April–June 1994): 185–205; Nurcholish Madjid, "In Search of Islamic Roots for Modern Pluralism: The Indonesian Experiences", in *Toward a New Pardigm: Recent Developments in Indonesian Islamic Thought*, edited by Mark R. Woodward (Arizona State University, Program for Southeast Asian Studies, 1996), pp. 96–97; Luthfi Assyaukanie, *Islam and the Secular State in Indonesia* (Singapore: Institute of Southeast Asian Studies, 2009), pp. 97–139, 205; Ali Bulac, "The Medina Document", in *Liberal Islam: A Sourcebook*, edited by Charles Kurzman (New York: Oxford University Press, 1988), pp. 169–78; Robert W. Hefner, "Secularization and Citizenship in Muslim Indonesia", in *Religion, Modernity, and Postmodernity*, edited by David Martin, Paul Heelas, and Paul Morris (Oxford: Blackwell, 1998), pp. 147–68; Remy El-Dardiry, "Islam Encountering Enlightenment: Clash or Symbiosis? A Comparative Analysis of the Dutch and Indonesian Discourse on Liberal Islam", *Liberal Islam Network* (online), 4 December 2005, pp. 16–19; Ahmad Bunyan Wahib, *Liberal Islam in Indonesia: The Attitude of Jaringan Islam Liberal Towards Religious Freedom and Pluralism* (MA thesis, Universiteit Leiden, 2004), pp. 29–36, 80, 87; Howard M. Federspiel, *Indonesia in Transition: Muslim Intellectuals and National Development* (Commack, NY: Nova Science, 1998), pp. 104–5; Giora Eliraz, "Distinctive Contemporary Voice: Liberal Islam Thought in Indonesia", *Studia Islamika* 15, no. 3 (2008): 1–38; Anis Malik Thoha, *Discourse of Religious Pluralism in Indonesia*, paper submitted to a seminar on Al-Qur'an dan Cabaran Pluralisme Agama: Pengajaran Masa Lalu, Keperihalan Semasa dan Hala Tuju Masa Depan (Institut Kefahaman Islam Malaysia, IKIM, 19–20 July 2011); M. Hilaly Basya, "The Concept of Religious Pluralism in Indonesia: A Study of the MUI's Fatwa and

the Debate among Muslim Scholars", *Indonesian Journal of Islam and Muslim Societies* 1, no. 1 (June 2011): 69–93; Ali Munhanif, "Islam and the Struggle for Religious Pluralism in Indonesia: A Political Reading of the Religious Thought of Mukti Ali", *Studia Islamika*, pp. 79–126; Bakti Andi Faisal, "Islam and Modernity: Nurcholish Madjid's Interpretation of Civil Society, Pluralism, Secularization, and Democracy", *Asian Journal of Social Science* 33, no. 3 (2005): 486–505; Martin Van Bruinessen, *What Happened to the Smiling Face of Indonesian Islam? Muslim Intellectualism*, RSIS, Nanyang Technological University, Singapore, Working Paper Series, no. 222 (January 2011), p. 20.

18. See Giora Eliraz, *Islam in Indonesia: Modernism, Radicalism and the Middle East Dimension* (Brighton: Sussex Academic Press, 2004), pp. 87–88.

19. Hefner, "Secularization and Citizenship in Muslim Indonesia", p. 148.

20. Julia Day Howell, "Sufism and the Indonesian Islamic Revival", *Journal of Asian Studies* 60, no. 3 (August 2001): 701–29.

21. IAIN Jakarta has been changed to UIN Jakarta (UIN, Universitas Islam Negeri, "State Islamic University") and IAIN Yogyakarta has been changed to UIN Yogyakarta.

22. On the IAIN, see Abdullah Saeed, "Towards Religious Tolerance through Reform in Islamic Education: The Case of the State Institute of Islamic Studies of Indonesia", *Indonesia and the Malay World* 27, no. 79 (1999): 177–91; Robert W. Hefner, *Civil Islam: Muslims and Democratization in Indonesia*, p. 120; Malcolm Cone, "Neo-Modern Islam in Suharto's Indonesia", *New Zealand Journal of Asian Studies* 4, no. 2 (December 2002): 52–67; Greg Barton, "Islam and Politics in the New Indonesia", in *Islam in Asia*, edited by Jason F. Isaacson and Colin Rubenstein (New Brunswick: Transaction, 2002), pp. 18–20; Greg Barton, "The Prospects for Islam", in *Indonesia Today: Challenges of History*, edited by Grayson Lloyd and Shannon Smith (Singapore: Institute of Southeast Asian Studies, 2001), p. 252.

23. Hefner, *Civil Islam*; Robert W. Hefner, "Islam and Nation in the Post-Suharto Era", in *The Politics of Post-Suharto Indonesia*, edited by Adam Schwarz and Johnathan Pairs (Singapore: Raffles, 1999), pp. 49, 64. See also Adam Schwarz, *A Nation in Waiting: Indonesia's Search for Stability*, 2nd ed. (Boulder, CO: Westview, 2000), pp. 328–29; Michael Vatikiotis, "Mixing Religion, Politics", *Jakarta Post* (online), 21 September 2007; Tony Hotland, "Media Should Promote Islam and Democracy: Discussion", *Jakarta Post* (online), 5 March 2008.

24. See Hosen, *Shari'a and Constitutional Reform in Indonesia*, pp. 81–96, 188–223; Hosen, "Religion and Indonesian Constitution", pp. 419–20.

25. See Giora Eliraz, *Islam and Polity in Indonesia: An Intriguing Case Study* (Washington: Hudson Institute, February 2007), p. 7.

26. On the decentralization policy, see Rachael Diprose, *Passing on the Challenges or Prescribing Better Management of Diversity? Decentralisation, Power Sharing and Conflict Dynamics in Central Sulawesi, Indonesia*, Centre for Research on Inequality, Human Security and Ethnicity (CRISE), Working Paper no. 38 (University of Oxford, 2007), pp. 3–9.

27. See Hara, "Pancasila and the Perda Syariʿah Debates in the Post-Suharto Era", pp. 35–75. See also Ulma Haryanto, "Indonesia's Religious Tolerance Wanes While Dogmatic Bylaws Gain Ground: Institute", *Jakarta Post* (online), 30 December 2011; Hakimul Ikhwan, "Are Shariatization and Democracy Compatible?", *Jakarta Post* (online), 22 June 2012.

28. See Assyaukanie, *Islam and the Secular State in Indonesia*, p. 205; Abdullahi Ahmed An-Naʾim, *Islam and the Secular State: Negotiating the Future of Shariʿa* (Cambridge, MA: Harvard University Press, 2008), pp. 224–25.

29. "Keynote Speech: Dr. Susilo Bambang Yudhoyono", 12 April 2010, World Movement for Democracy. See also Sondang Grace Sirait, "Chinese and Proud of Nation's Cultural Diversity", *Jakarta Post* (online), 31 May 2011. See also Rendi Akhmad Witular, "SBY Urges End to Debate on Pancasila's Merits", *Jakarta Post* (online), 2 June 2006; "Group Says Pancasila Way to Halt Assault on Pluralism", *Jakarta Post* (online), 1 June 2006.

30. See Angel Rabasa, "Islamic Education in Southeast Asia", *Current Trends in Islamist Ideology*, vol. 2 (12 September 2005), pp 97–108; Greg Barton, "Gentle, Friendly Face of Indonesia and Islam", *The Age* (online), 2 January 2010; University of Melbourne, "Indonesia's Islamic Schools: Modern Institutions, Not Radicalism Breeding Grounds", media release, 12 August 2005; Suparto, "While Reform of Islamic Education is Necessary, Secularisation is Not", *Inside Indonesia*, no. 77 (January–March 2005), pp. 22–23; Lyn Parker, "Teaching Religious Tolerance", *Inside Indonesia*, no. 102 (October–December 2010).

31. On the liberal Islamic discourse of the post-Suharto era, see Eliraz, "Distinctive Contemporary Voice"; Ahmad Ali Nurdin, "Islam and State: A Study of the Liberal Islamic Network in Indonesia, 1999–2004", *New Zealand Journal of Asian Studies* 7, no. 2 (December 2005): 20–39; Ahmad Bunyan Wahib, *Liberal Islam in Indonesia: The Attitude of Jaringan Islam Liberal towards Religious Freedom and Pluralism*; El-Dardiry, "Islam Encountering Enlightenment"; Mohamad Ihsan Alief, "Political Islam and Democracy: A Closer Look at the Liberal Muslims", in *Piety and Pragmatism: Trends in Indonesian Islamic Politics*, Asia Program Special Report, no. 110, edited by Amy McCreedy (Woodrow Wilson Center, Asia Program, April 2003),

pp. 14–19; Greg Fealy, "A Conservative Turn: Liberal Islamic Groups Have Prompted a Backlash", *Inside Indonesia*, no. 87 (July–September 2006), pp. 23–24.

32. Keputusan Fatwa Majelis Ulama Indonesia, Nomor: 7/Munas VII/MUI/II/2005, Tentang Pluralisme, Liberalisme dan Sekularisme Agama.

33. See Basya, "The Concept of Religious Pluralism in Indonesia", pp. 69, 93.

34. Giora Eliraz, "Egypt Uprising a Live Course on Politics for Indonesia and Malaysian Students", *Jakarta Post* (online), 17 February 2011.

35. See Dukung Mesir Jalani Masa Transisi Menuju Demkrasi, official website of the Indonesian Embassy, 29 July 2011; Mohamed Kassem,"Egypt-Indonesia Democratisation Explored", *Egyptian Gazette* (online), 23 May 2011; "IPD Workshop: Egypt–Indonesia Dialogue on Democratic Transition – Jakarta, 25–26 May *2011*", Centre for Democratic Institutions, The Australian National University (online); "Speech of President B.J. Habibie at the Forum on 'Pathways of Democratic Transition,' Cairo, 5 June 2011", official website of the Indonesian Embassy, 8 June 2012; "Indonesia Supports Egypt's Transition Process to Democracy", website of Ministry of Foreign Affairs, Republic of Indonesia, 29 July 2011; "Egypt Asks for Indonesia's Help in Implementing Democracy", *Jakarta Globe* (online), 29 March 2011; "IPD Workshop: Indonesia–Egypt Dialogue on Democratic Transition Continues – Jakarta, 11–12 April *2012*", Centre for Democratic Institutions, The Australian National University (online); "Egypt–Indonesia Hold Dialogue on Path to Democracy", Institute for Peace and Democracy (IPD), 6 November 2012; Giora Eliraz, "The Path from Dictatorship to Democracy", *Jerusalem Post*, 11 July 2011; Giora Eliraz, "Indonesian Democracy Comes to Tunisia", *Australia/Israel Review* 39 (April 2014).

36. On the MB in Egypt during the Sadat and Mubarak eras, see Alison Pargeter, *The Muslim Brotherhood: The Burden of Tradition* (London and Beirut: Saqi Books, 2010), pp. 15–60; Carrie Rosefsky Wickham, *Mobilizing Islam: Religion, Activism and Political Change in Egypt* (New York: Columbia University Press, 2002), pp. 103–49, 214–26; Israel Elad-Altman, "Democracy, Elections and the Egyptian Muslim Brotherhood", *Current Trends in Islamist Ideology*, vol. 3 (Hudson Institute, 2006), pp. 24–37; Israel Elad-Altman, "Illusions about Islamism", *Jerusalem Report*, 8 August 2005; Amr Hamzawy and Nathan J. Brown, *The Egyptian Muslim Brotherhood: Islamist Participation in a Closing Political Environment*, Carnegie Papers, no. 19 (March 2010); Robert S. Leiken and Steven Brooke, "The Moderate Muslim Brotherhood, Friend or Foe?", *Foreign Affairs* 86, no. 2 (March–April 2007): 107–21; Mona El-Ghobashy, "The Metamorphosis of the Egyptian Muslim Brothers", *International Journal of Middle East Studies*, no. 37

(2005), pp. 373–95; *Egypt's Muslim Brothers: Confrontation or Integration?*, International Crisis Group, Middle East/North Africa Report no. 76, 18 June 2008; Sana Abed-Kotob, "The Accommodationists Speak: Goals and Strategies of the Muslim Brotherhood of Egypt", *International journal of Middle East Studies* 27, no. 3 (1995): 321–39.

37. On the Salafis in Egypt, see Jonathan Brown, *Salafis and Sufis in Egypt*, the Carnegie Papers (Washington, DC: Carnegie Endowment for International Peace, December 2011); Eric Trager, "Thought the Muslim Brotherhood Was Bad? Meet Egypt's Other Islamist Party", *New Republic* (online), 2 December 2011; David D. Kirkpatrick, "In Egypt, a Conservative Appeal Transcends Religion, *New York Times* (online), 10 December 2011; Alastair Beach, "The Salafi Spring: In post-Mubarak Egypt, Salafism is on the Rise", *The Majalah* (online), 11 July 2011.

38. See Albert Hourani, *Arabic Thought in the Liberal Age: 1798–1939* (London: Oxford University Press, 1970), pp. 161–92; Nadav Safran, *Egypt in Search of Political Community: An Analysis of the Intellectual and Political Evolution of Egypt, 1904–1952* (Cambridge, MA: Harvard University Press, 1961), pp. 85–164; Israel Gershoni and James P. Jankowski, *Egypt, Islam, and the Arabs: The Search for Egyptian Nationhood, 1900–1930* (Oxford: Oxford University Press, 1986), pp. 60–63, 77–95; James Whidden, "The Generation of 1919", in *Re-envisioning Egypt 1919–1952*, edited by Arthur Goldschmidt, Amy J. Johnson, and Barak A. Salmoni (Cairo and New York: American University in Cairo Press, 2005), pp. 19–45; Meir Hatina, "On the Margins of Consensus: The Call to Separate Religion and State in Modern Egypt", *Middle Eastern Studies* 36, no. 1 (January 2000), pp. 35–54; Giora Eliraz, "The Social and Cultural Conception of Mustafa Sadiq al-Rafi'i, *Asian and African Studies* 13 (1979): 101–29; Mansoor Moaddel, "Discursive Pluralism and Islamic Modernism in Egypt", *Arab Studies Quarterly* 24 (2002): 1–29.

39. See Israel Gershoni and James P. Jankowski, *Confronting Fascism in Egypt: Dictatorship versus Democracy in the 1930s* (Stanford University Press, 2009); Meir Hatina, *Identity Politics in the Middle East* (London: Tauris, 2007), pp. 13–29.

40. See Hatina, *Identity Politics in the Middle East*, pp. 113–37; Giora Eliraz, "Democracy in Indonesia and Middle East countries", *Jakarta Post* (online), 30 November 2007; Nancy E. Gallagher, "Islam v. Secularism in Cairo: An Account of the Dar al-Hikma Debate", *Middle Eastern Studies* 25, no. 2 (April 1989): 208–15.

41. On the Al-Wasat Party, see Carrie Rosefsky Wickham, "The Path to Moderation: Strategy and Learning in the Formation of Egypt's Wasat

Party", *Comparative Politics* 36, no. 2 (January 2004): 205–28; Wickham, *Mobilizing Islam*, pp. 217–21; Augustus Richard Norton, "Thwarted Politics: The Case of Egypt's Hizb al-Wasat", in *Remaking Muslim Politics: Pluralism, Contestation*, edited by Robert Hefner (Princeton, NJ: Princeton University Press, 2005), pp. 130–60; Rachel M. Scott, *The Challenge of Political Islam: Non-Muslims and the Egyptian State* (Stanford: Stanford University Press, 2010), pp. 122–65; *Mapping Islamic Actors in Egypt* (Netherlands-Flemish Institute in Cairo and Al-Ahram Center for Political and Strategic Studies, 2012), pp. 108–9 <http://media.leidenuniv. nl/legacy/mapping-islamic-actors---version-2.2.pdf>.

42. See Clark Lombardi, *State Law as Islamic Law in Modern Egypt: The Incorporation of the Shari'a into Egyptian Constitutional Law* (Leiden: Brill, 2006), pp. 123–40; L. Lavi, "An Examination of Egypt's Draft Constitution Part I: Religion and State – The Most Islamic Constitution in Egypt's History", *MEMRI* (online), Inquiry and Analysis no. 904, 3 December 2012.

43. See Kriten Stilt, "'Islam is the Solution': Constitutional Visions of the Egyptian Muslim Brotherhood", *Texas International Law Journal* 46, no. 1 (Fall 2010): 87–89; *Egypt's Muslim Brothers: Confrontation or Integration?* International Crisis Group, pp. 16–17.

44. See Michele Dunne and Mara Revkin, "Overview of Egypt's Constitutional Referendum", Carnegie Endowment for International Peace (online), 16 March 2011.

45. The moderate Islamist Al-Wasat Party, that was officially approved as a party in the post-Mubarak era, gained 3.7 per cent of the vote in the first democratic elections.

46. A year later, in June 2013, shortly before Mursi was removed from power, the SCC ruled that the Shura Council, the upper house, was also illegally elected.

47. The citation appears in "Where They Stand – Egyptian Candidates Shafiq and Mursi", BBC, 6 June 2012 <http://www.bbc.co.uk/news/world-africa-18296326>. It is based on the Egyptian private CBC TV, 10 May 2012. See also Munir Adib, Mohamed Talaat Dawod, and Hany ElWaziry, "Muslim Brotherhood Member: Copts and Women 'Unsuitable for Presidency'", *Egypt Independent* (online), 20 February 2011.

48. For the text of the declaration, see "English text of Morsi's Constitutional Declaration", *ahramonline*, 22 November 2012. In June 2013 the SCC ruled as illegal the law governing the selection of the members of the controversial constitution-drafting assembly.

49. Nariman Youssef, "Egypt's Draft Constitution Translated", *Egypt Independent* (online), 2 December 2012.

50. L. Lavi, "An Examination of Egypt's Draft Constitution Part II: The Egyptian Public Debate over Religion and State", *MEMRI* (online), Inquiry & Analysis Series Report No. 906, 5 December 2012.

51. Ibid.

52. Youssef, "Egypt's Draft Constitution Translated".

53. Ibid.

54. On the constitution of 2012, and in particular on the religious aspect of it, see Lavi, "An Examination of Egypt's Draft Constitution Part I"; Lavi, "An Examination of Egypt's Draft Constitution Part II"; L. Lavi, "An Examination of Egypt's Draft Constitution Part III: Presidential Powers, Status of Military and Judiciary, Civil Freedoms", *MEMRI* (online), Inquiry & Analysis Series Report No. 908, 13 December 2012; Eric Trager, "Egypt's Looming Competitive Theocracy", *Current Trends in Islamist Ideology* 13, 27 December 2012, pp. 27–37; "Have We Lost Egypt?", an interview with Eric Trager and Nathan Brown, *The Washington Institute* (online), 14 December 2012; Holger Albrecht, "Egypt's 2012 Constitution; Devil in the Details, Not in Religion", United States Institute of Peace (online), 25 January 2013; Mirette F. Mabrouk, "The View from a Distance: Egypt's Contentious New Constitution", Saban Center at Brookings (online), Middle East memo, no. 28, January 2013 (online): Chibli Mallat, "Reading the Draft Constitution of Egypt: Setbacks in Substance, Process, and Legitimacy", *ahramonline*, 2 December 2012; "Comparison of Egypt's Suspended and Draft Constitutions", BBC (online), 30 November 2012.

55. Lavi, "An Examination of Egypt's Draft Constitution Part II".

56. Nathan J. Brown, "Egypt's Constitution: Islamists Prepare for a Long Political Battle", Carnegie Endowment for International Peace (online), 23 October 2012.

57. Lombardi, *State Law as Islamic Law in Modern Egypt*, pp. 270–74. See also pp. 123–269.

58. See Wilfred Cantwell Smith, *Islam in Modern History* (Princeton, NJ: Princeton University Press, 1957), p. 149; Rachel M. Scott, *The Challenge of Political Islam: Non-Muslims and the Egyptian State*, p. 107.

59. Lavi, "An Examination of Egypt's Draft Constitution Part I".

60. "An interview with the MB's Mohamed Morsy" (conducted by Dalia Malek), *Arabist.net*, 18 May 2011 <http://www.arabist.net/blog/2011/5/18/an-interview-with-the-mbs-mohamed-morsy.html>. See also David D. Kirkpatrick, "Power Struggle Begins as Egypt's President is Formally Sworn In", *New York Times* (online), 30 June 2012.

61. Tom Perry, "Brotherhood Man Promises Islamic Law in Egypt", Reuters (online), 25 May 2012; Katie Kiraly, "In Their Own Words: Egyptian Presidential Candidates Morsi and Shafiq", *The Washington Institute for Near East Policy*, 15 June 2012.

62. L. Lavi, "An Examination of Egypt's Draft Constitution Part II".
63. Scott, *The Challenge of Political Islam*, pp. 92–121. On attitudes in Islam towards other religions and religious diversity, see Yohanan Friedmann, *Tolerance and Coercion in Islam: Interfaith Relations in the Muslim Tradition* (Cambridge: Cambridge University Press, 2003).
64. Radwan al-Sayyid, "Al-Dimuqratiya wal-Ta'dudiyyah", *Al-Mustaqbal*, no. 2266, 16 May 2006.
65. Scott, *The Challenge of Political Islam*, p. 107.
66. For the Arabic text and the English translation of the constitution of 2014, see "English Translation of Egypt's 2013 Draft Constitution", *Atlantic Council*, 6 December 2013 <http://www.atlanticcouncil.org/en/blogs/egyptsource/english-translation-of-egypt-s-2013-draft-constitution>. On the constitution, see also Nathan Brown and Michelle Dunne, "Egypt's Draft Constitution Rewards the Military and Judiciary", Carnegie Endowment for International Peace (online), 4 December 2013; Eric Trager, "Egypt's New Constitution: Bleak Prospects", *The Washington Institute* (online), Policy Watch 2183, 16 December 2013; L. Lavi, "Egypt's Draft Constitution 2014: Focus on De-Islamization, Expansion of Military Power", *Right Side News* (online), 12 January 2014; Nada Hussein Rashwan, "Inside Egypt's draft constitution: Role of Sharia Redefined", *ahramonline*, 12 December 2013; Mariam Rizk and Osman El Sharnoubi, "Egypt's Constitution 2013 vs. 2012: A Comparison", *ahramonline*, 12 December 2013; Ayat Al-Tawy, "Inside Egypt's Draft Constitution: Progress on Key Freedoms", *ahramonline*, 12 December 2013; Marta Latek, *Egypt's New Constitution and Religious Minorities' Rights: Prospects of Improvement?* European Parliamentary Research Service (online), briefing, 23 January 2014.
67. Hefner, "Secularization and Citizenship in Muslim Indonesia", p. 148.

References

Laws

Keputusan Fatwa Majelis Ulama Indonesia, Nomor: 7/Munas VII/MUI/II/2005, Tentang Pluralisme, Liberalisme dan Sekularisme Agama [Fatwa decision of the Assembly of Indonesian Ulamas, Number 7/Munas VII/MUI/II/2005, on Religious Pluralism, Liberalism and Secularism].

Books

An-Na'im, Abdullahi Ahmed. *Islam and the Secular State: Negotiating the Future of Shari'a*. Cambridge, MA: Harvard University Press, 2008.
Assyaukanie, Luthfi. *Islam and the Secular State in Indonesia*. Singapore: Institute of Southeast Asian Studies, 2009.

Beneke, Chris. *Beyond Toleration: The Religious Origins of American Pluralism.* Oxford: Oxford University Press, 2006.

Effendy, Bahatiar. *Islam and the State in Indonesia.* Singapore: Institute of Southeast Asian Studies, 2003.

Eliraz, Giora. *Islam in Indonesia: Modernism, Radicalism and the Middle East Dimension.* Brighton: Sussex Academic Press, 2004.

——. *Islam and Polity in Indonesia: An Intriguing Case Study.* Washington: Hudson Institute, February 2007.

Federspiel, Howard M. *Indonesia in Transition: Muslim Intellectuals and National Development.* Commack, NY: Nova Science, 1998.

Friedmann, Yohanan. *Tolerance and Coercion in Islam: Interfaith Relations in the Muslim Tradition.* Cambridge: Cambridge University Press, 2003.

Gershoni, Israel, and James P. Jankowski. *Egypt, Islam, and the Arabs: The Search for Egyptian Nationhood, 1900–1930.* Oxford: Oxford University Press, 1986.

——. *Confronting Fascism in Egypt: Dictatorship versus Democracy in the 1930s.* Stanford University Press, 2009.

Hatina, Meir. *Identity Politics in the Middle East.* London: Tauris, 2007.

Hourani, Albert. *Arabic Thought in the Liberal Age: 1798–1939.* London: Oxford University Press, 1970.

Hefner, Robert W. *Civil Islam: Muslims and Democratization in Indonesia.* Princeton, NJ: Princeton University Press, 2000.

Hooker, M.B. *Indonesian Syariah: Defining a National School of Islamic Law.* Singapore: Institute of Southeast Asian Studies, 2008.

Hosen, Nadirsyah. *Shari'a and Constitutional Reform in Indonesia.* Singapore: Institute of Southeast Asian Studies, 2007.

Lombardi, Clark. *State Law as Islamic Law in Modern Egypt: The Incorporation of the Shari'a into Egyptian Constitutional Law.* Leiden: Brill, 2006.

Pargeter, Alison. *The Muslim Brotherhood: The Burden of Tradition.* London and Beirut: Saqi Books, 2010.

Ramage, Duglas E. *Politics in Indonesia: Democracy, Islam and the Ideology of Tolerance.* London: Routledge, 1997.

Reid, Anthony. *To Nation by Revolution: Indonesia in the 20th Century.* Singapore: NUS Press, 2010.

Ricklefs, M.C. *A History of Modern Indonesia: Since c.1200*, 3rd ed. Stanford: Stanford University Press, 2001.

Rosefsky Wickham, Carrie. *Mobilizing Islam: Religion, Activism and Political Change in Egypt.* New York: Columbia University Press, 2002.

Safran, Nadav. *Egypt in Search of Political Community: An Analysis of the Intellectual and Political Evolution of Egypt, 1904–1952.* Cambridge, MA: Harvard University Press, 1961.

Schwarz, Adam. *A Nation in Waiting: Indonesia's Search for Stability*, 2nd ed. Boulder, CO: Westview, 2000.

Scott, Rachel M. *The Challenge of Political Islam: Non-Muslims and the Egyptian State*. Stanford: Stanford University Press, 2010.

Smith, Wilfred Cantwell. *Islam in Modern History*. Princeton: Princeton University Press, 1957.

Chapters

Alief, Mohamad Ihsan. "Political Islam and Democracy: A Closer Look at the Liberal Muslims". In *Piety and Pragmatism: Trends in Indonesian Islamic Politics*, Asia Program Special Report, no. 110, edited by Amy McCreedy. Woodrow Wilson Center, Asia Program, 2003.

Barton, Greg. "Islamic Liberalism and the Prospects for Democracy in Indonesia". In *Democracy in Asia*, edited by Michèle Schmiegelow. New York: St. Martin's, 1997.

———. "The Prospects for Islam". In *Indonesia Today: Challenges of History*, edited by Grayson Lloyd and Shannon Smith. Singapore: Institute of Southeast Asian Studies, 2001.

———. "Islam and Politics in the New Indonesia". In *Islam in Asia*, edited by Jason F. Isaacson and Colin Rubenstein. New Brunswick: Transaction, 2002.

Bowden, John. "Religious Pluralism and the Heritage of the Enlightenment". In *Islam and Global Dialogue: Religious Pluralism and the Pursuit of Peace*, edited by Roger Boase. Aldershot: Ashgate, 2005.

Bulac, Ali. "The Medina Document". In *Liberal Islam: A Sourcebook*, edited by Charles Kurzman. New York: Oxford University Press, 1988.

Burton, David. "A Buddhist Perspective". In *The Oxford Handbook of Religious Diversity*, edited by Chad V. Meister, pp. 321–36. Oxford: Oxford University Press, 2011.

Drewes, W.J. "New Light on the Coming of Islam to Indonesia?" In *The Propagation of Islam in the Indonesian-Malay Archipelago*, edited by Alijah Gordon. Kuala Lumpur: Malaysian Sociological Research Institute, 2001.

Eck, Diana L. "Is Our God Listening? Exclusivism, Inclusivism, and Pluralism". In *Islam and Global Dialogue: Religious Pluralism and the Pursuit of Peace*, edited by Roger Boase. Aldershot: Ashgate, 2005.

Hara, Abubakar Eby. "Pancasila and the Perda Syari'ah Debates in the Post-Suharto Era: Toward a New Political Consensus". In *Islam in Contention: Rethinking of State and Islam in Indonesia*, edited by Okamoto Masaaki, Ota Atsushi, and Ahmad Suaedy. Jakarta: Wahid Institute; Kyoto: Center for Southeast Asian Studies; Taipei: Center for Asia-Pacific Area Studies – CAPAS, 2010.

Hefner, Robert W. "Islam in an Era of Nation-States: Politics and Religious Renewal in Muslim Southeast Asia". In *Islam in an Era of Nations-States: Politics and Religious Renewal in Muslim Southeast Asia*, edited by Robert W. Hefner and Patricia Horvatich. Honolulu: University of Hawai'i Press, 1997.

————. "Secularization and Citizenship in Muslim Indonesia". In *Religion, Modernity, and Postmodernity*, edited by David Martin, Paul Heelas, and Paul Morris. Oxford: Blackwell, 1998.

————. "Islam and Nation in the Post-Suharto Era". In *The Politics of Post-Suharto Indonesia*, edited by Adam Schwarz and Johnathan Pairs. Singapore: Raffles, 1999.

Hooker, M.B. "The State and Shari'a in Indonesia". In *Shari'a and Politics in Modern Indonesia*, edited by Arskal Salim and Azyumardi Azra. Singapore: Institute of Southeast Asian Studies, 2003.

Johns, A.H. "Islam in Southeast Asia". In *The Encyclopedia of Religion*, edited by Mircea Eliade, vol. 7. New York: Macmillan, 1987.

Madjid, Nurcholish. "In Search of Islamic Roots for Modern Pluralism: The Indonesian Experiences". In *Toward a New Paradigm: Recent Developments in Indonesian Islamic Thought*, edited by Mark R. Woodward. Arizona State University: Program for Southeast Asian Studies, 1996.

Marty, Martin E. "Historical Reflections on Religious Diversity". In *The Oxford Handbook of Religious Diversity*, edited by Chad V. Meister. Oxford: Oxford University Press, 2010.

Meister, Chad V. "Introduction". In *The Oxford Handbook of Religious Diversity*, edited by Chad V. Meister. Oxford: Oxford University Press, 2010.

Norton, Augustus Richard. "Thwarted Politics: The Case of Egypt's Hizb al-Wasat". In *Remaking Muslim Politics: Pluralism, Contestation*, edited by Robert Hefner. Princeton, NJ: Princeton University Press, 2005.

Runzo, Joseph. "Pluralism and Relativism". In *The Oxford Handbook of Religious Diversity*, edited by Chad V. Meister. Oxford: Oxford University Press, 2010.

Sharma, Arvind. "A Hindu Perspective". In *The Oxford Handbook of Religious Diversity*, edited by Chad V. Meister, pp. 309–29. Oxford: Oxford University Press, 2011.

Whidden, James. "The Generation of 1919". In *Re-envisioning Egypt 1919–1952*, edited by Arthur Goldschmidt, Amy J. Johnson, and Barak A. Salmoni. Cairo; New York: American University in Cairo Press, 2005.

Periodicals

Abed-Kotob, Sana. "The Accommodationists Speak: Goals and Strategies of the Muslim Brotherhood of Egypt". *International Journal of Middle East Studies* 27, no. 3 (1995): 321–39.

Barton, Greg. "Neo-Modernism: A Vital Synthesis of Traditionalist and Modernist Islamic Thought in Indonesia". *Studia Islamika* 2, no. 3 (1995): 1–75.

———. "Indonesia's Nurcholish Madjid and Abdurrahman Wahid as Intellectual 'Ulama': The Meeting of Islamic Traditionalism and Modernism in Neo-modernist Thought". *Studia Islamika* 4, no. 1 (1997): 29–81.

Basya, M. Hilaly. "The Concept of Religious Pluralism in Indonesia: A Study of the MUI's Fatwa and the Debate among Muslim Scholars". *Indonesian Journal of Islam and Muslim Societies* 1, no. 1 (June 2011): 69–93.

Brown, Jonathan. "Salafis and Sufis in Egypt". *Carnegie Papers*. Washington, DC: Carnegie Endowment for International Peace, December 2011.

Cone, Malcolm. "Neo-Modern Islam in Suharto's Indonesia". *New Zealand Journal of Asian Studies* 4, no. 2 (December 2002): 52–67.

Elad-Altman, Israel. "Democracy, Elections and the Egyptian Muslim Brotherhood". *Current Trends in Islamist Ideology* 3 (February 2006): 24–37.

Effendy, Bahtiar. "Islam and the State in Indonesia: Munawir Sjadzali and the Development of a New Theological Underpinning of Political Islam". *Studia Islamika* 2, no. 2 (1995): 97–121.

Egypt's Muslim Brothers: Confrontation or Integration? International Crisis Group, Middle East/North Africa Report no. 76, 18 June 2008.

El-Ghobashy, Mona. "The Metamorphosis of the Egyptian Muslim Brothers". *International Journal of Middle East Studies*, no. 37 (2005): 373–95

Eliraz, Giora. "The Social and Cultural Conception of Mustafa Sadiq al-Rafi'i". *Asian and African Studies* 13 (1979): 101–29.

———. "Distinctive Contemporary Voice: Liberal Islam Thought in Indonesia". *Studia Islamika* 15, no. 3 (2008): 1–38.

———. "Indonesian Democracy Comes to Tunisia". *Australia/Israel Review* 39 (April 2014): 25–26.

Faisal, Bakti Andi. "Islam and Modernity: Nurcholish Madjid's Interpretation of Civil Society, Pluralism, Secularization, and Democracy". *Asian Journal of Social Science* 33, no. 3 (2005): 486–505.

Fealy, Greg. "A Conservative Turn: Liberal Islamic Groups Have Prompted a Backlash". *Inside Indonesia*, no. 87 (July–September 2006): 23–24.

Gallagher, Nancy E. "Islam v. Secularism in Cairo: An Account of the Dar al-Hikma Debate". *Middle Eastern Studies* 25, no. 2 (April 1989): 208–15.

Hamzawy, Amr, and Nathan J. Brown. "The Egyptian Muslim Brotherhood: Islamist Participation in a Closing Political Environment". *Carnegie Papers*, no. 19 (March 2010).

Hatina, Meir. "On the Margins of Consensus: The Call to Separate Religion and State in Modern Egypt". *Middle Eastern Studies* 36, no. 1 (January 2000): 35–54.

Hefner, Robert W. "Modernity and the Challenge of Pluralism: Some Indonesian Lessons". *Studia Islamika* 2, no. 4 (1995): 21–45.

Hosen, Nadirsyah. "Religion and Indonesian Constitution: A Recent Debate". *Journal of Southeast Asian Studies* 36, no. 3 (2005): 419–40.

Howell, Julia Day. "Sufism and the Indonesian Islamic Revival". *Journal of Asian Studies* 60, no. 3 (August 2001): 701–29.

Hyung-Jun Kim. "The Changing Interpretation of Religious Freedom in Indonesia". *Journal of Southeast Asian Studies* 29, no. 2 (September 1998): 357–73.

Leiken, Robert S., and Steven Brooke. "The Moderate Muslim Brotherhood, Friend or Foe?" *Foreign Affairs* 86, no. 2 (March/April 2007): 107–21.

Marty, Martin E. "Religious Pluralism and Civil Society". *Annals of the American Academy of Political and Social Science* 612 (July 2007): 14–25.

Massanari, Ronald. "The Pluralism of American 'Religious Pluralism'". *Journal of Church and State* 40, no. 3 (Summer 1998): 589–601.

Moaddel, Mansoor. "Discursive Pluralism and Islamic Modernism in Egypt". *Arab Studies Quarterly* 24 (2002): 1–29.

Munhanif, Ali. "Islam and the Struggle for Religious Pluralism in Indonesia: A Political Reading of the Religious Thought of Mukti Ali". *Studia Islamika* 3, no. 1 (1996): 79–126.

Nurdin, Ahmad Ali. "Islam and State: A Study of the Liberal Islamic Network in Indonesia, 1999–2004". *New Zealand Journal of Asian Studies* 7, no. 2 (December 2005): 20–39.

Parker, Lyn. "Teaching Religious Tolerance". *Inside Indonesia*, no. 102 (October–December 2010).

Prasetyo, Hendro. "Interview with Munawir Sjadazli". *Studia Islamika* 1, no. 1 (April–June 1994): 185–205.

Rabasa, Angel. "Islamic Education in Southeast Asia". *Current Trends in Islamist Ideology* 2 (September 2005): 97–108.

Rosefsky Wickham, Carrie. "The Path to Moderation: Strategy and Learning in the Formation of Egypt's Wasat Party". *Comparative Politics* 36, no. 2 (January 2004): 205–28.

Saeed, Abdullah. "Towards Religious Tolerance through Reform in Islamic Education: The Case of the State Institute of Islamic Studies of Indonesia". *Indonesia and the Malay World* 27, no. 79 (1999): 177–91.

Silk, Mark. "Defining Religious Pluralism in America: A Regional Analysis". *Annals of the American Academy of Political and Social Science* 612 (July 2007): 64–81.

Stilt, Kriten. "'Islam is the Solution': Constitutional Visions of the Egyptian Muslim Brotherhood". *Texas International Law Journal* 46, no. 1 (Fall 2010): 87–89.

Suparto. "While Reform of Islamic Education is Necessary, Secularisation is Not". *Inside Indonesia*, no. 77 (January–March 2005): 22–23.

Syamsuddin, M. Din. "Islamic Political Thought and Cultural Revival in Modern Indonesia". *Studia Islamika* 2, no. 4 (1995): 51–68.

Thoha, Anis Malik. "Discourse of Religious Pluralism in Indonesia". *Islam in Asia* 2, no. 2 (December 2005): 111–30.

Trager, Eric. "Egypt's Looming Competitive Theocracy". *Current Trends in Islamist Ideology* 13 (December 2012): 27–37.

———. "Think Again: The Muslim Brotherhood". *Foreign Policy*, 28 January 2013.

Van Bruinessen, Martin. "What Happened to the Smiling Face of Indonesian Islam? Muslim intellectualism". *RSIS, Nanyang Technological University, Singapore, Working Paper Series*, no. 222 (January 2011).

Verra and Fitriani. "Indonesia's Rising Middle Class: Tweeting to Be Heard". *RSIS Commentaries*, no. 104/2012, 19 June 2012.

Dissertations

Azra, Azyumardi. "The Transmission of Islamic Reformism to Indonesia: Networks of Middle Eastern and Malay-Indonesian 'Ulama' in the Seventeenth and Eighteenth Centuries". PhD dissertation, Columbia University, 1992.

Wahib, Ahmad Bunyan. "Liberal Islam in Indonesia: The Attitude of Jaringan Islam Liberal Towards Religious Freedom and Pluralism". MA thesis, Universiteit Leiden, 2004.

Newspapers

Adib, Munir, Mohamed Talaat Dawod, and Hany ElWaziry. "Muslim Brotherhood Member: Copts and Women 'Unsuitable for Presidency'". *Egypt Independent* (online), 20 February 2011.

Al-Sayyid, Radwan. "Al-Dimuqratiya wal-Ta'dudiyyah". *Al-Mustaqbal*, 16 May 2006.

Barton, Greg. "Gentle, Friendly Face of Indonesia and Islam". *The Age* (online), 2 January, 2010.

Beach, Alastair. "The Salafi Spring: In Post-Mubarak Egypt, Salafism is on the Rise". *The Majalah* (online), 11 July 2011.

"Egypt Asks for Indonesia's Help in Implementing Democracy". *Jakarta Globe* (online), 29 March 2011.

Elad-Altman, Israel. "Illusions about Islamism". *Jerusalem Report*, 8 August 2005.

Eliraz, Giora. "Democracy in Indonesia and Middle East countries". *Jakarta Post* (online), 30 November 2007.

———. "Egypt Uprising a Live Course on Politics for Indonesia and Malaysian Students". *Jakarta Post* (online), 17 February 2011.

———. "The Path from Dictatorship to Democracy". *Jerusalem Post*, 11 July 2011.

"Group Says Pancasila Way to Halt Assault on Pluralism". *Jakarta Post* (online), 1 June 2006.

Haryanto, Ulma. "Indonesia's Religious Tolerance Wanes While Dogmatic Bylaws Gain Ground: Institute". *Jakarta Post* (online), 30 December 2011.

Hotland, Tony. "Media Should Promote Islam and Democracy: Discussion". *Jakarta Post* (online), 5 March 2008.

Ikhwan, Hakimul. "Are Shariatization and Democracy Compatible?" *Jakarta Post* (online), 22 June 2012.

Kassem, Mohamed. "Egypt–Indonesia Democratisation Explored". *Egyptian Gazette* (online), 23 May 2011.

Kirkpatrick, David D. "In Egypt, a Conservative Appeal Transcends Religion. *New York Times* (online), 10 December 2011.

———. "Power Struggle Begins as Egypt's President is Formally Sworn In". *New York Times* (online), 30 June 2012.

Lavi, L. "Egypt's Draft Constitution 2014: Focus on De-Islamization, Expansion of Military Power". *Right Side News* (online), 12 January 2014.

"Pluralism — Beyond Unity in Diversity". *Jakarta Post* (online), 16 August 2005.

Sirait, Sondang Grace. "Chinese and Proud of Nation's Cultural Diversity". *Jakarta Post* (online), 31 May 2011.

Trager, Eric. "Thought the Muslim Brotherhood Was Bad? Meet Egypt's Other Islamist Party". *New Republic* (online), 2 December 2011.

Vatikiotis, Michael. "Mixing Religion, Politics" *Jakarta Post* (online), 21 September 2007.

Witular, Rendi Akhmad. "SBY Urges End to Debate on Pancasila's Merits". *Jakarta Post* (online), 2 June 2006.

Youssef, Nariman. "Egypt's Draft Constitution translated", *Egypt Independent* (online), 2 December 2012.

Online Citations

Al-Tawy, Ayat. "Inside Egypt's Draft Constitution: Progress on Key Freedoms". *ahramonline*, 12 December 2013.

Albrecht, Holger. "Egypt's 2012 Constitution: Devil in the Details, Not in Religion". *United States Institute of Peace* (online), 25 January 2013.

"An Interview with the MB's Mohamed Morsy" (conducted by Dalia Malek). *Arabist.net*, 18 May 2011 <http://www.arabist.net/blog/2011/5/18/an-interview-with-the-mbs-mohamed-morsy.html>.

Brown, Nathan J. "Egypt's Constitution: Islamists Prepare for a Long Political Battle". Carnegie Endowment for International Peace, 23 October 2012.

Brown, Nathan and Michelle Dunne. "Egypt's Draft Constitution Rewards the Military and Judiciary". *Carnegie Endowment for International Peace*, 4 December 2013.

"Comparison of Egypt's Suspended and Draft Constitutions". BBC, 30 November 2012.

Dukung Mesir Jalani Masa Transisi Menuju Demkrasi. Official Website of Indonesian Embassy, 29 July 2011.

Diprose, Rachael. *Passing on the Challenges or Prescribing Better Management of Diversity? Decentralisation, Power Sharing and Conflict Dynamics in Central Sulawesi, Indonesia*. Centre for Research on Inequality, Human Security and Ethnicity (CRISE), Working Paper no. 38.

Dunne, Michele, and Mara Revkin. "Overview of Egypt's Constitutional Referendum". Carnegie Endowment for International Peace (online), 16 March 2011.

El-Dardiry, Remy. "Islam Encountering Enlightenment: Clash or Symbiosis? A Comparative Analysis of the Dutch and Indonesian Discourse on Liberal Islam". *Liberal Islam Network*, 4 December 2005.

"English Text of Morsi's Constitutional Declaration". *ahramonline*, 22 November 2012.

"English Translation of Egypt's 2013 Draft Constitution". *Atlantic Council*, 6 December 2013 <http://www.atlanticcouncil.org/en/blogs/egyptsource/english-translation-of-egypt-s-2013-draft-constitution>.

"Have We Lost Egypt?", an interview with Eric Trager and Nathan Brown. *The Washington Institute*, 14 December 2012.

"Indonesia's Islamic Schools: Modern Institutions, Not Radicalism Breeding Grounds" (Media Release). The University of Melbourne, 12 August 2005.

"Indonesia Supports Egypt's Transition Process to Democracy". Website of Ministry of Foreign Affairs, Republic of Indonesia, 29 July 2011.

"IPD Workshop: Egypt–Indonesia Dialogue on Democratic Transition – Jakarta, 25–26 May 2011". Centre for Democratic Institutions, The Australian National University.

"IPD Workshop: Indonesia–Egypt Dialogue on Democratic Transition Continues – Jakarta, 11–12 April 2012". Centre for Democratic Institutions, The Australian National University.

Latek, Marta. *Egypt's New Constitution and Religious Minorities' Rights: Prospects of Improvement?* European Parliamentary Research Service, Briefing, 23 January 2014.

Lavi, L. "An Examination of Egypt's Draft Constitution Part I: Religion and State – The Most Islamic Constitution In Egypt's History". MEMRI, Inquiry and Analysis Series no. 904, 3 December 2012.

———. "An Examination of Egypt's Draft Constitution Part II: The Egyptian Public Debate over Religion and State", MEMRI, Inquiry and Analysis Series no. 906, 5 December 2012.

———. "An Examination of Egypt's Draft Constitution Part III: Presidential Powers, Status of Military and Judiciary, Civil Freedoms", MEMRI, Inquiry and Analysis Series no. 908, 13 December 2012

Mabrouk, Mirette F. "The View from a Distance: Egypt's Contentious New Constitution". Saban Center at Brookings, Middle East memo no. 28, January 2013.

Mallat, Chibli. "Reading the Draft Constitution of Egypt: Setbacks in Substance, Process, and Legitimacy". *ahramonline*, 2 December 2012.

"Muslim Scholar: Prophet Mohamed Established First Civil State". *Youm7*, 27 November 2011.

Netherlands-Flemish Institute in Cairo and Al-Ahram Center for Political and Strategic Studies. "Mapping Islamic Actors in Egypt". March 2012 <http://media.leidenuniv.nl/legacy/mapping-islamic-actors---version-2.2.pdf>.

Perry, Tom. "Brotherhood Man Promises Islamic Law in Egypt". Reuters, 25 May 2012.

Rashwan, Nada Hussein. "Inside Egypt's Draft Constitution: Role of Sharia Redefined". *ahramonline*, 12 December 2013.

Rizk, Mariam, and Osman El Sharnoubi. "Egypt's Constitution 2013 vs. 2012: A Comparison". *ahramonline*, 12 December 2013.

"Speech of President B.J. Habibie at the Forum on 'Pathways of Democratic Transition', Cairo, 5 June 2011". Official website of the Indonesian Embassy, 8 June 2012.

Trager, Eric. "Egypt's New Constitution: Bleak Prospects". The Washington Institute, Policy Watch 2183, 16 December 2013.

"Where They Stand – Egyptian Candidates Shafiq and Mursi". BBC, 6 June 2012 <http://www.bbc.co.uk/news/world-africa-18296326>.

Yudhoyono, Susilo Bambang. "Keynote Speech: Dr. Susilo Bambang Yudhoyono". World Movement for Democracy, 12 April 2010.

Other

"Egypt–Indonesia Hold Dialogue on Path to Democracy". Institute for Peace and Democracy (IPD), 6 November 2012.

Kiraly, Katie. "In Their Own Words: Egyptian Presidential Candidates Morsi and Shafiq". Washington Institute for Near East Policy, 15 June 2012.

Thoha, Anis Malik. "Discourse of Religious Pluralism in Indonesia". Paper submitted to a seminar on Al-Qur'an dan Cabaran Pluralisme Agama: Pengajaran Masa Lalu, Keperihalan Semasa dan Hala Tuju Masa Depan. Institut Kefahaman Islam Malaysia (IKIM), 19–20 July 2011.